ADDIE on Steroids

The Ultimate AI-Powered Instructional Design Guide

David Barras-Baker

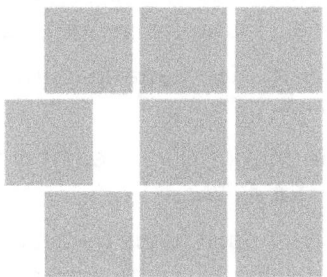

ADDIE.FixMySkills.com

2025

© **2025 David Barras-Baker**

All rights reserved.

No part of this publication may be reproduced, stored in a retrieval system, or transmitted in any form or by any means, electronic, mechanical, photocopying, recording, or otherwise, without the prior written permission of the publisher, except in the case of brief quotations for review purposes.

ISBN (eBook): 978-1-7641805-0-4

Published by **Creating Value**

Perth, Western Australia

This book is a work of non-fiction. Every reasonable effort has been made to ensure the accuracy of the information.

The publisher and author disclaim liability for any errors, omissions, or outcomes arising from the use of this material.

National Library of Australia Cataloguing-in-Publication data is available upon request. Legal deposit copies submitted.

Foreword

By Barry Vorster, Digital Workplace Strategist

When I first met David Barras-Baker back in 1997, while completing my Master of Education in eLearning at the University of Pretoria, I was a young instructional designer and a keen learning technology enthusiast.

From my earliest interactions with David and Barras-Baker & Associates, I was struck by their professionalism, their forward thinking, and their ability to translate emerging technology into meaningful learning.

Every time I worked with them, I came away impressed.

Nearly three decades later, nothing has changed, except that David is still at the forefront, pushing boundaries. ADDIE on Steroids reflects the same clarity of thought and practical wisdom he showed back then but now sharpened by decades of experience. This isn't a gentle update to a classic framework.

It's a reimagining of how instructional design, human-centred learning, and digital transformation can and should intersect in 2025.

In my own career in digital workplace transformation, I've seen how quickly the ground shifts, hybrid work, AI, cloud platforms, and the relentless demand for agility.

ADDIE on Steroids doesn't simply keep up; it leads. It fuses tried-and-true instructional design with AI-driven speed, lean delivery methods, and a relentless focus on the learner experience.

Equally important is the shift from learning as an isolated activity to learning that is embedded in the flow of work and augmented by intelligent systems. This book recognises that impact is created not just by designing courses, but by designing work environments where skills are developed and applied in real time.

Here, David's thinking dovetails with the emergence of Talent Intelligence, using data, analytics, and AI to understand capability, predict needs, and connect learning directly to organisational outcomes.

What sets David apart is that he doesn't write from the ivory tower of theory. He offers tools, practical guidance, and cautionary lessons that help you avoid costly mistakes while creating learning experiences that truly engage.

If you're serious about building learning that is smarter, faster, and has measurable impact in the modern workplace, you're holding the right book.

Preface

When I first encountered the ADDIE model, I didn't fall in love with it. It wasn't sexy. It wasn't fast. It wasn't even particularly modern. But it worked. And that alone was worth a closer look.

My fascination with learning design started long before digital transformation became a buzzword. In 1984, I attended the ADCIS Conference in Washington DC, an event that shaped my thinking forever. It was there I heard Donald Bitzer, one of the great pioneers of computer-based learning and co-creator of PLATO, speak about how people truly learn. His insights, simple yet profound, still resonate with me to this day.

For those unfamiliar, PLATO (Programmed Logic for Automated Teaching Operations) was a groundbreaking system developed by Control Data Corporation and the University of Illinois, long before the internet as we know it existed. It delivered networked, interactive learning at a time when most people were still using paper manuals and overhead projectors. PLATO proved something radical for its time: that technology, when thoughtfully applied, could fundamentally change how people acquire and retain knowledge.

That experience influenced how I approached learning throughout my career – from aviation training to corporate training, consulting, and digital design. And every time I experimented with new ideas, new technologies, or new delivery models, I kept coming back to ADDIE. Not as a religion, but as a framework.

A thinking scaffold. A way to bring order to chaos, strategy to action, and clarity to conversations that otherwise felt like noise.

ADDIE on Steroids was born out of equal parts frustration and respect. Frustration that too many learning professionals were still building "tick-the-box" training. Frustration that stakeholders often undervalued planning. And frustration that so many learning teams were still flying blind in an age of intelligent tools and data-rich insights.

This book is the upgrade I wish I had when I started. It's for instructional designers who are tired of reinventing the wheel. For L&D leaders who want their teams to think and act like performance consultants.

For professionals who understand that AI won't replace us, but it will replace the ones who don't adapt.

What you'll find in these pages is not just a model, but a method. Not just theory, but traps, techniques, examples, and AI considerations drawn from decades of hands-on experience and constant exploration.

And one final note: I didn't write this for applause. I wrote it because I care deeply about learning that works.

I hope it helps you create more of it.

David Barras-Baker
Perth, Australia
2025

The History Of The ADDIE Model

Overview	The ADDIE model, an acronym for Analyse, Design, Develop, Implement, Evaluate, was developed in the 1970s as a structured framework for instructional systems design (ISD).
	Originally created for the U.S. military, it has evolved into the most widely recognised methodology for designing learning solutions.
Origin Story	ADDIE was born out of the U.S. Army's need for a systematic approach to training during the Cold War. The Center for Educational Technology at Florida State University was commissioned in 1975 to develop an approach that could standardise instructional design across military branches.
Why it was developed	The goal was to ensure that training programs were effective, efficient, and consistent. The Army needed a model that could guide the design and development of instructional materials that matched specific job roles and performance outcomes, ensuring operational readiness.
Original Structure	The initial version of ADDIE was linear and rigid, with clearly defined phases that had to be followed in strict sequence. It was designed as a waterfall model, where each phase had to be completed before moving on to the next.
The Evolution	Over time, practitioners found that a more iterative approach was needed.
	ADDIE evolved into a flexible, cyclical model where feedback loops between phases allowed for continuous improvement.
	The modern interpretation is dynamic, adaptable, and scalable for both traditional and digital learning environments.
Wider Adoption	The success of ADDIE in military and government training led to its adoption by corporations, universities, and nonprofits. Its clear structure made it ideal for project teams, instructional designers, and educators who needed a repeatable and scalable process.
Universality Today	Today, ADDIE is considered the default global framework for instructional design. It underpins most eLearning authoring tools, LMS implementations, corporate L&D workflows, and even AI-based design systems. Its simplicity, flexibility, and logic continue to make it the go-to model across industries.
Common Misconceptions	Many view ADDIE as outdated or overly linear, but this stems from misunderstanding.
	Modern ADDIE is not about rigid steps, it's a framework, not a prescription. Its real strength lies in its adaptability and emphasis on continuous evaluation and learner-centered design.
Why This Matters	Understanding ADDIE's roots helps designers appreciate its core purpose: to ensure learning solutions are intentional, measurable, and aligned with real-world outcomes. The evolution of ADDIE reflects the evolution of learning itself, from instructor-led to tech-enabled to AI-enhanced.
Key Takeaways	The ADDIE model remains relevant because it adapts with the times. Its principles endure because they are grounded in logic, learner needs, and performance outcomes.
	The model's longevity is a testament to its clarity, utility, and foundational role in modern instructional design.

About the Author

David Barras-Baker has been at the forefront of digital learning for over four decades, not just following the trends, but making history.

In 1984, while serving as an instructor at South African Airways, David helped pioneer one of the first commercial uses of computer-based training (CBT) anywhere in the world.

Working with the PLATO system developed by Control Data Corporation, he introduced a radical new way to deliver technical and safety training, long before personal computers became mainstream and well before the internet shaped modern education. In the pre-digital era, this was not just innovative, it was revolutionary.

David's career has spanned continents, technologies, and learning paradigms. From those early days of cathode-ray terminals and hardwired content to today's AI-enhanced microlearning, he has consistently anticipated where learning was headed and guided others along the way.

His work has touched industries as varied as aviation, mining, government, and corporate enterprise, always with the same focus: making learning relevant, actionable, and deeply human.

Now based in Western Australia, David continues to push boundaries as a learning strategist, instructional designer, and AI prompt engineer.

ADDIE on Steroids is both a culmination and a manifesto, a guide forged from experience yet designed for what comes next. It preserves the solid structure of the traditional ADDIE model while supercharging it with agile thinking, automation, and artificial intelligence.

But more than a model, David's mission is transformation. He believes that learning is not just about knowledge transfer, but performance improvement, human empowerment, and systemic change.

That belief has never wavered, whether he was designing for PLATO in 1984 or scripting AI-driven learning ecosystems in 2025.

When he's not writing, designing, or consulting, David enjoys deep philosophical inquiry, crafting exceptional Gin in his home distillery, and dreaming up ways to make technology serve human potential, not the other way around.

Your Exclusive ADDIE on Steroids Resource Hub

Thank you for purchasing *ADDIE on Steroids*!

You've made a smart move toward supercharging your instructional design with AI and modern best practices.

As a bona fide owner of this book, you now have access to a collection of **exclusive resources** designed to save you time, spark creativity, and help you apply what you've learned faster.

Simply scan the QR code below (or visit the link if you're reading digitally) to unlock:

- **Templates** to kickstart your projects
- **AI prompt libraries** tailored to instructional designers
- **Checklists, tips, and bonus guides** not available anywhere else
- **Updates and new tools** as we keep evolving ADDIE on Steroids

Access Instructions

1. Scan the QR code below with your phone or tablet camera.
2. Follow the link to our secure resource hub.
3. Use the **proof of purchase key** you received with your book (or follow the simple verification process).

Enjoy lifetime access as we continue to add new materials, bonus content, and time-saving innovations.

Scan for Your Resources
or visit: **addie.fixmyskills.com**

You're not just reading a book; you're joining a community of forward-thinking learning professionals.

These resources are a way of saying thanks and ensuring your journey with ADDIE on Steroids delivers maximum value.

How to Use this Book

Why this is Important

Establishes the **strategic relevance** of the step. Sets context and clarifies the consequences of skipping or misusing it.

Tips

Offers **quick wins** and field-tested advice to help you fast-track success and avoid unnecessary friction.

Traps

Flags **common mistakes** that derail projects. Knowing these helps you sidestep failure before it happens.

Techniques

Practical **methods and approaches** you can apply immediately, drawn from best practice and real-world examples.

Examples

Brings theory to life through **relatable scenarios** that show how others have applied this step-in context.

How it's done

Provides a **step-by-step walkthrough** of the process, what to do, when, and how. Ideal for execution and onboarding.

Core Elements

Outlines the **essential ingredients** required for success at this stage, what must not be overlooked.

Checklist

Gives you a **concise verification tool** to confirm you've covered all bases before moving forward.

AI Considerations

Shows how to **amplify results with AI**, save time, enhance quality, or manage scale using current and emerging tools.

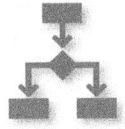
Key Takeaways

Synthesizes the **most critical points** into a short list you can reference quickly, reinforcing retention and reuse.

Table of Contents

Part 1: The **ANALYSIS** phase 3
- Project Initiation 4
- Initial Planning 16
- Risk and Assumption Analysis 33
- Resource and Task Review 44
- Data and Evidence Audit 51
- Success Metrics Definition 62
- Instructional Goal Definition 73
- Learner and Needs Analysis 94
- Feasibility and Cost Analysis 103

Part 2: The **DESIGN** phase 111
- Learning Experience Design 112
- Gamification and Interactivity Planning 130
- Assessment Design 147
- Media and Content Strategy 155
- Accessibility and Inclusion Strategy 173
- AI Integration Planning 184
- Pilot Testing Preparation 198
- Pre-Production Logistics 208

Part 3: The **DEVELOPMENT** phase 217
- Content Development 218
- Translation and Localisation Prep 228
- Media Production 241
- Courseware Assembly 253
- Pilot Preparation and Readiness 263
- Personalisation Tag Planning 273

Part 4: The **IMPLEMENTATION** phase 288
- Pilot Test Execution 289

Pilot Feedback Evaluation 296
Facilitator and Manager Briefing 306
Change Management Enablement 323
Course Deployment 340

Part 5: The **EVALUATION** phase 348

Measure Learning Impact 349
ROI and Business Impact Reporting 368
Compliance and Audit Readiness 385
AI-Enhanced Evaluation Practices 402
Continuous Improvement Cycle 416

Part 1: The **ANALYSIS** phase

The **Analysis Phase** is the diagnostic engine room of the ADDIE model, a space where assumptions are unpacked, facts are surfaced, and clarity is engineered before any design takes shape. It is the most critical thinking-intensive stage, where strategic alignment meets instructional intent.

This phase is not just about identifying what learners don't know; it's about establishing why a solution is needed at all, what form that solution should take, and how feasible it will be to deliver. It maps the terrain ahead by systematically examining business needs, performance gaps, organisational constraints, learner attributes, available resources, and technological capabilities.

In ADDIE on Steroids, Analysis goes deeper than surface-level needs assessments.

It begins with **Project Initiation,** clarifying scope, stakeholders, and purpose. Then moves into **Initial Planning, Task and Resource Audits**, and **Stakeholder Alignment**.

Here, instructional designers operate as strategic consultants, not just content developers. The goal is to anchor learning to real-world performance, not theoretical ideals.

A robust **Learner and Needs Analysis** ensures the learning design speaks to the right audience, in the right tone, with the right level of difficulty, and through the most accessible means.

This is followed by **Feasibility and Cost Analysis**, where data-driven scrutiny is applied to budgets, timelines, and platform limitations to test what's possible before moving to the Design phase.

The Analysis phase also leverages AI-enhanced insights for both **resource auditing** and **learning needs diagnostics**, allowing teams to spot trends, prioritise interventions, and future-proof their learning ecosystems.

By the end of this phase, the following should be crystal clear:

- The what, why, and who of the learning initiative.
- The constraints that must be managed.
- The learner persona and environmental context.
- The business value of proceeding, or not proceeding, with a learning solution.

Done well, this phase ensures that instructional design is not only creative but relevant, accountable, and feasible.

It lays the intellectual and operational scaffolding that every downstream phase that Design, Development, Implementation, and Evaluation will depend on.

In short, this is where clarity begins and wasted effort ends.

Project Initiation

Overview

The **Project Initiation** step in the Analysis phase of the ADDIE model is the foundation upon which successful instructional design projects are built.

This crucial step sets the tone and direction for the entire project by defining its scope, objectives, timeline, and resource needs.

It brings together stakeholders and the project team, ensuring alignment on goals and expectations.

A well-executed Project Initiation creates a shared vision that informs all subsequent phases, minimising misunderstandings, and delays.

Key sub-steps are:

- **Identify Project**
  Define the project's scope, objectives, timeline, and success criteria, ensuring these align with organisational priorities.

- **Identify Project Team**
  Assemble the right team members, assigning clear roles and responsibilities to ensure accountability and efficiency.

- **Stakeholder Alignment**
  Ensure all key stakeholders are aligned on project objectives, priorities, and expectations through clear communication and collaborative engagement.

By establishing clarity and cohesion early, this step ensures a structured approach, guiding the project toward achieving its intended outcomes.

Project Initiation

Outcomes

The outcomes of the Project Initiation step are designed to create a solid framework for the project, ensuring alignment with organisational and learning goals.

Key outcomes include:

- **Define and Document Scope**
  Develop a detailed project scope outlining goals, deliverables, boundaries, and success metrics.
  Provide clarity on what the project will and will not address, avoiding scope creep.

- **Set Outcomes and Deliverables**
  Define measurable outcomes that align with the organisation's strategic priorities and learner needs.
  Establish clear deliverables to guide development and evaluation processes.

- **Assemble a Competent Project Team**
  Select individuals with the necessary expertise and availability.
  Assign roles and responsibilities to ensure accountability throughout the project.

- **Establish Communication Protocols**
  Define communication methods (e.g., meetings, updates, project dashboards) to keep stakeholders informed and engaged.
  Ensure clarity in reporting lines and decision-making processes.

- **Identify Potential Risks and Constraints**
  Anticipate challenges, such as resource limitations, time constraints, and scope risks.
  Develop mitigation strategies to address potential obstacles proactively.

Summary

The **Project Initiation** step is a cornerstone of the instructional design process, establishing the framework for a cohesive and goal-oriented project.

By clearly defining the scope, setting outcomes, and assembling a capable project team, this step ensures strategic alignment and minimises potential risks.

Effective communication protocols and risk identification further contribute to a robust foundation, preparing the project for success.

Tools like a **project charter**, **kick-off meetings**, and the **RACI matrix** can facilitate this step, ensuring a smooth start.

A well-defined initiation phase prevents common issues such as role confusion and scope ambiguity, enabling the team to navigate subsequent phases with confidence.

With the groundwork laid during this step, the project is well-positioned to deliver impactful learning outcomes and meet organisational objectives.

Project Initiation
Identify Project

Why this is important

A project's outcome is shaped not just by its plan but by the people who bring it to life.

The project team is the engine room of the course design process, their insight, collaboration, and execution determine the quality and relevance of the final product.

Selecting the right mix of people at the start avoids downstream misalignment, delays, and costly rework.

The goal is not just to fill seats around a table, but to assemble a functional, empowered, and representative team that can operate with clarity, speed, and shared intent.

Tips

- Build a team that reflects the full ecosystem of the course, not just the back office
- Include representation from design, content, delivery, systems, operations, and user groups
- Secure people with decision-making power, not just availability
- Align each member's skills to specific project needs, avoid "symbolic" roles
- Communicate expectations around availability, responsiveness, and feedback cycles early
- Ensure the team has enough diversity of perspective to challenge assumptions productively
- Appoint a project lead with both authority and stakeholder trust
- Make sure the team is empowered to adapt, not locked into fixed lanes

Traps

- Assigning team members based on who's available, not who's qualified
- Overlooking critical contributors like frontline supervisors or systems administrators
- Letting strong personalities dominate before roles are clarified
- Skipping role documentation because "everyone knows what they're doing"
- Assuming SMEs can double as instructional designers or vice versa
- Forgetting to include those responsible for post-launch support or maintenance
- Creating a team that reflects hierarchy, not capability
- Selecting a project lead without the bandwidth or the political capital to drive outcomes

Techniques

- Use a RACI matrix (Responsible, Accountable, Consulted, Informed) to map out project roles and decision paths
- Create a one-page visual team map showing each person's function, contact point, and primary deliverable
- Use stakeholder influence grids to prioritise inclusion and communication pathways
- Schedule a project team kick-off focused on relationships and alignment, not just tasks
- Include an external reviewer or devil's advocate if the project is high-risk or high-profile
- Encourage the team to co-author working norms, particularly around feedback, scope changes, and blockers

Project Initiation
Identify Project

Examples

- A blended learning initiative for remote mine site workers includes a UX designer, a site safety supervisor, an instructional designer, and an Indigenous liaison officer
- A compliance training project brings in a legal SME, a document controller, a delivery lead, and a frontline manager to co-review each module
- A digital upskilling program assigns both a data analyst (to monitor learner progress) and a help desk representative (to flag recurring learner support issues)
- A first-aid program team includes two first responders and a trauma nurse to ensure realism in scenario design and assessment

How it's done

1. Begin with a role map, what functions are needed for this project to succeed?
2. Identify real people who match those functions, and check availability, influence, and fit
3. Brief sponsors and stakeholders, and confirm resourcing
4. Draft a team charter or working agreement, even if informal
5. Document and distribute the RACI matrix or equivalent role guide
6. Conduct a team induction or alignment session, review scope, success criteria, and comms flow
7. Track involvement over time and be ready to adapt the team as the project evolves

Core Elements

- Role-aligned team composition (design, SME, delivery, tech, learner rep)
- A clearly nominated project lead with defined decision authority
- Documented responsibilities and escalation pathways
- Stakeholder inclusion from the start (not just at review checkpoints)
- Systems, operations, or compliance voices integrated where applicable
- A clear working rhythm, with meetings, updates, and review cycles
- Psychological safety and space for challenge within the team
- Embedded accountability for timelines, budget, and learner impact

Checklist

1. Has the full team been assembled with clear role alignment and documentation?
2. Are there representatives from each critical area, content, systems, compliance, frontline, and learner groups?
3. Is a project lead nominated, available, and empowered to make decisions?
4. Has a team induction or kick-off session occurred to align expectations and rhythm?
5. Are team norms and feedback pathways agreed and documented?
6. Is there clarity on communication cadence and format?
7. Are there mechanisms in place to escalate issues or decisions?
8. Are backups identified for critical roles?
9. Has every team member confirmed commitment within project time frames?
10. Are there embedded mechanisms for reviewing team function mid-project?

Project Initiation
Identify Project

AI Considerations

- Use conversational AI to prototype early-stage discussions with stakeholders and simulate project scoping dialogues
- Implement AI-assisted planning tools (e.g. Gantt generators or workload estimators) to visualise task ownership and dependencies
- Use AI-driven skill matching tools to find the best internal talent for each project role
- Generate draft role descriptions, RACI charts, or meeting agendas using generative AI
- Use AI to analyse previous projects to suggest optimal team configurations or highlight past success factors
- Implement AI chatbots to simulate project team kick-off conversations for new leads or PMs
- Use AI tools to monitor team sentiment and communication gaps (especially in distributed teams)
- Automate stakeholder communications, meeting notes, and decision logs for team transparency
- Deploy generative AI to summarise project team decisions and generate visible, versioned logs for audit and alignment

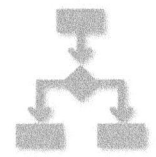

Key Takeaways

Choosing the right team is more than a resourcing task, it's a strategic decision that determines project success.

A high-performing team reflects the diversity of voices, skills, and power structures involved in real-world learning environments.

Role clarity, representation, rhythm, and decision rights aren't optional, they are the foundation of effective collaboration.

Project Initiation
Identify Project Team

Identify Project Team

Why this is important

Identifying the right project team is one of the most strategically important decisions in any learning initiative.

The project's success depends not just on technical skillsets, but on the team's ability to collaborate, adapt, and deliver under pressure.

An effective team blends subject expertise, instructional design, project coordination, and learner insight, supported by clear roles, defined responsibilities, and shared accountability.

Failing to establish the right mix early can lead to inefficiencies, misaligned deliverables, or critical blind spots in content and delivery strategy.

This step ensures that the people who shape the solution are equipped, engaged, and empowered from day one.

Tips

- Identify the full range of competencies required early in the process, including design, development, content expertise, and delivery
- Ensure team members are empowered to make decisions, not just attend meetings
- Consider representation from compliance, operations, or frontline roles, depending on project type
- Include learner representatives when designing for culturally or linguistically diverse audiences
- Clarify expectations for communication frequency, channels, and documentation
- Establish a single point of contact or project lead to manage coordination

Traps

- Choosing team members based solely on availability rather than relevance or capability
- Failing to assign clear decision-making authority, leading to bottlenecks or rework
- Ignoring frontline input, resulting in beautifully built solutions that miss real-world constraints
- Assigning roles informally without written documentation
- Overlooking personality dynamics that can erode team cohesion
- Assuming everyone shares the same understanding of project scope and goals

Project Initiation
Identify Project Team

Techniques

- **Skills Matrix**
  Map required skills against potential team members to identify strengths, gaps, and overlaps. This ensures the team is well-rounded and fit for purpose.
- **Kick-off Meetings**
  Hold an initial session to introduce the project team, clarify scope and goals, define roles, and establish communication protocols. Use this to build early cohesion and set expectations.
- **Project Team Charter**
  Develop a formal document outlining each team member's role, responsibilities, decision-making authority, and availability. Include escalation pathways and communication expectations.
- **Role-Based Communication Protocols**
  Define how and when each role should communicate with others. e.g., project updates, SME reviews, developer handoffs to avoid bottlenecks and siloed work.
- **Regular Check-ins and Retrospectives**
  Schedule weekly or phase-based syncs to track progress, surface blockers, and recalibrate priorities as needed. Include retrospectives to learn and improve collaboration dynamics.
- **Collaboration Tools and Shared Dashboards**
  Use platforms like Trello, Asana, Slack, Teams, or ClickUp to manage tasks, centralise communication, and visualise project timelines. This improves visibility and shared accountability.
- **Backup Resource Planning**
  Identify alternates or deputies for critical roles in advance. This reduces risk if key team members become unavailable during design or development.

Examples

- *Project Manager*
  Leads the project, sets timelines, oversees tasks, and ensures team members have resources needed to succeed.
- *Instructional Designer*
  Responsible for curriculum planning, developing instructional materials, and ensuring alignment with learning objectives.
- *Subject Matter Expert (SME)*
  Provides expertise and guidance on content accuracy, relevance, and detail.
- *Graphic Designer*
  Creates visual elements to enhance the learning experience, ensuring graphics align with the instructional goals.
- *Developer*
  Manages technical aspects, such as creating eLearning modules, interactive features, and managing platform compatibility.

Project Initiation
Identify Project Team

How it's done

- **Define Project Scope and Objectives**
  Clearly define and document the project's scope, deliverables, and timelines. This provides a unified direction for the project team and sets clear expectations.

- **Identify Required Expertise**
  Determine the specific skillsets needed to achieve project objectives. This includes identifying roles such as instructional designers, SMEs, graphic designers, developers, and project managers.

- **Assess Team Availability**
  Confirm the availability of team members and ensure they can commit the necessary time and resources. Contact potential contributors and assess any constraints.

- **Identify Key Stakeholders**
  Compile a list of project stakeholders, including sponsors and end-users. Involve them in planning to align their requirements with the project's goals and objectives.

- **Establish Communication Channels**
  Set up effective communication channels and protocols using tools and platforms, such as project management software. This ensures smooth and clear communication throughout the project.

- **Assign Roles and Responsibilities**
  Define specific roles for each team member based on their expertise. Clearly communicate these responsibilities to ensure accountability and prevent role confusion.

- **Create Team Documentation**
  Document the team structure, roles, and communication guidelines. Distribute a team charter or reference document to all members for clarity and ongoing reference.

Core Elements

- **Project Scope Defined**
  Ensure the project scope, objectives, and key milestones are clearly documented.

- **Team Roles Identified**
  Identify all roles, including instructional designer, SME, graphic designer, developer, and project manager.

- **Team Member Availability Confirmed**
  Verify the availability and commitment levels of potential team members.

- **Stakeholders Identified**
  List and document the roles of all key stakeholders.

- **Communication Channels Established**
  Set up appropriate tools and protocols for clear communication.

- **Roles and Responsibilities Assigned**
  Assign roles based on skills and expertise, ensuring all team members understand their responsibilities.

- **Team Documentation Created**
  Develop and distribute a project team charter or structure document.

- **Initial Meeting Scheduled**
  Schedule a kick-off meeting to align the team on roles, responsibilities, and project goals.

Project Initiation
Identify Project Team

Checklist

1. Has the required project team composition been defined and documented?
2. Are team members selected based on skillsets aligned to project needs?
3. Is there representation from all relevant departments (e.g. L&D, IT, operations, compliance)?
4. Have roles and responsibilities been clearly communicated?
5. Is there a designated project lead with authority and availability?
6. Are backup personnel identified for critical roles in case of absence?
7. Has team diversity (in expertise, background, and learner empathy) been considered?
8. Are expectations for collaboration, reporting, and review cycles aligned?
9. Have all team members confirmed availability within project timelines?
10. Is the team empowered to make necessary decisions during the design process?

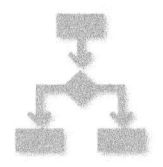
AI Considerations

- **AI-Assisted Skills Mapping**
  Use AI tools to analyse résumés, bios, or past project contributions to match individuals to required skillsets quickly and objectively.
- **AI-Powered Availability Forecasting**
  Leverage AI-enabled resource planning tools to check availability across teams, flag conflicts, and suggest optimal team compositions based on projected workload.
- **Personality and Collaboration Profiling**
  Use AI-driven assessments to evaluate team dynamics, communication styles, or potential collaboration risks, particularly useful for assembling balanced, high-functioning teams.
- **Automated Role Documentation**
  Generate first-draft role descriptions, responsibilities, and reporting lines using generative AI based on project scope and team composition.
- **AI-Driven Stakeholder Mapping**
  Scan org charts, email networks, or historical project data to identify hidden influencers or overlooked roles that should be included on the team.
- **Virtual Assistant for Team Coordination**
  Deploy AI tools like scheduling assistants, intelligent reminders, or Slackbots to support coordination, nudges, and meeting prep among team members.

Key Takeaways

The strength of any instructional design project lies in the team behind it. This sub-step ensures the right people are in the right roles, with clear responsibilities, aligned expectations, and the authority to act.

By assembling a balanced, cross-functional team, and supporting it with clear documentation, defined communication protocols, and shared tools, you set the stage for streamlined execution and resilient collaboration.

It's not just about filling seats; it's about forming a decision-capable, learner-informed, and delivery-ready unit.

This proactive alignment avoids common pitfalls like rework, stakeholder gaps, or delayed approvals, and builds a foundation of trust, agility, and shared ownership that drives the project forward.

Project Initiation
Stakeholder Alignment

Stakeholder Alignment

Why this is important

Stakeholders hold the vision, influence, constraints, and often the budget behind any learning initiative.

Without alignment, courses risk being misdirected, misunderstood, or irrelevant.

True alignment is not about passive sign-off, but active engagement, clarifying roles, expectations, success measures, and constraints early.

When stakeholders are synchronised with the project team, decision-making becomes faster, support becomes stronger, and the course is far more likely to succeed in both content and context.

Tips

- Identify stakeholders across strategic, operational, and learner-facing levels
- Schedule dedicated alignment meetings early in the process, not just ad hoc updates
- Use visual tools to communicate scope, timeline, and learning outcomes
- Clarify their role: are they a sponsor, contributor, gatekeeper, or reviewer?
- Surface unspoken agendas early (e.g. "This training needs to prove ROI fast")
- Secure formal endorsement where possible to accelerate future decisions
- Establish a cadence of interaction: when will they be involved, and how?

Traps

- Engaging stakeholders too late when decisions are already made
- Assuming verbal enthusiasm means commitment
- Involving too many people, leading to design-by-committee paralysis
- Failing to surface tensions between stakeholder expectations and learner realities
- Not checking stakeholder understanding of learning principles (they may push for content that doesn't translate pedagogically)
- Allowing key decisions to remain vague or undocumented

Techniques

- Stakeholder mapping: plot influence vs. interest to define communication strategy
- Conduct alignment workshops with key stakeholders to co-create shared success criteria
- Use an "alignment canvas", a one-page summary of project goals, risks, audiences, and responsibilities
- Document expectations around feedback windows, sign-off points, and escalation routes
- Present multiple design options with pros/cons, help stakeholders make informed trade-offs
- Use storytelling or journey maps to convey the learner's perspective to stakeholders

Examples

- A regional sales director outlines market-specific compliance challenges, influencing both the tone and content of the final course
- An IT stakeholder flags LMS limitations during alignment, leading to a shift in assessment format
- Stakeholder workshops result in re-prioritising course modules to match key business milestones
- A legal stakeholder insists on copy review; their early involvement prevents a costly post-launch rework

Project Initiation
Stakeholder Alignment

How it's done

- **Identify and Engage Stakeholders**
  Compile a comprehensive list of all relevant stakeholders, including sponsors, end-users, and team members. Engage with them early to ensure alignment with the project's goals and scope.
- **Develop and Distribute a Communication Plan**
  Create a detailed communication plan that outlines the methods, frequency, and channels for updates and discussions. Distribute this plan to all stakeholders to set clear expectations.
- **Schedule and Facilitate Alignment Meetings**
  Organise regular stakeholder alignment meetings to review project goals, scope, and progress. Use these meetings to address any concerns and gather feedback.
- **Create a Shared Repository**
  Establish a shared digital repository for storing all project-related documents, agreements, and updates. Ensure all stakeholders have access to this repository to maintain transparency and collaboration.

Core Elements

- List of identified stakeholders with mapped roles
- Clear articulation of stakeholder expectations
- Agreed communication plan (frequency, format, channel)
- Visibility into project scope, learner profile, and constraints
- Sign-off responsibilities and escalation processes
- Confirmation of shared success criteria
- Alignment tools (e.g. stakeholder map, canvas, comms tracker)

Checklist

1. Have all relevant stakeholders been identified and categorised by role and influence?
2. Have their expectations, priorities, and constraints been documented?
3. Have alignment meetings or workshops been conducted to co-define success?
4. Is there an agreed communication and review schedule?
5. Are stakeholder sign-off responsibilities clearly assigned?
6. Have potential points of misalignment been flagged and addressed?
7. Are stakeholders aware of their role in reviewing, contributing, or approving content?
8. Has a single-page alignment summary been circulated and endorsed?
9. Are there mechanisms to monitor ongoing stakeholder engagement or drift?
10. Are expectations for post-launch support or data reporting clearly defined?

Project Initiation
Stakeholder Alignment

AI Considerations

- Use AI to map organisational structure and identify key stakeholders based on project theme
- Generate stakeholder briefs and alignment canvases from meeting transcripts or intake forms
- Use AI-powered meeting tools to summarise alignment sessions, decisions, and action items
- Deploy sentiment analysis to assess tone and engagement in stakeholder feedback
- Use generative AI to create "what if" scenarios to test the impact of stakeholder decisions (e.g. delayed sign-off, reduced scope)
- Automate stakeholder comms, progress updates, milestone summaries, or feedback loops
- Run simulated alignment interviews using chat-based AI to prepare junior IDs for real sessions

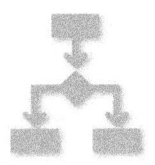

Key Takeaways

Stakeholder alignment is not an item on a checklist, it's a dynamic process that shapes the entire project. The earlier alignment is built, the stronger the foundation for shared ownership, trust, and clarity. Projects that fail often do so not because of poor design, but because the stakeholders were never truly aligned in the first place.

Initial Planning

The Initial Planning step in the Analysis phase of the ADDIE model translates early project insights into an actionable framework.

This step formalises the operational structure, ensures alignment among team members and stakeholders, and sets realistic boundaries for time, scope, and delivery.

By addressing these elements upfront, instructional designers can proactively manage complexity, reduce project ambiguity, and establish a strong rhythm for execution.

This foundational clarity helps prevent miscommunication, delays, and design drift later in the lifecycle.

Key Sub-Steps are:

- **Planning Meeting**
  Bring all key players together to establish alignment on goals, clarify roles, surface constraints, and build shared ownership of the project's direction.

- **Define Project Scope**
  Establish the boundaries of the learning solution, what is included, what's excluded, and what assumptions or constraints must be recognised from the outset.

- **Identify Key Stakeholders**
  Clarify who needs to be consulted, who must approve key deliverables, and who will be involved at each review gate to ensure smooth governance.

- **Confirm Delivery Model**
  Select the high-level delivery method (e.g. eLearning, instructor-led, blended) based on learner needs, platform constraints, and organisational context.

- **Set High-Level Timeline**
  Draft a milestone-driven schedule that includes key review points, delivery deadlines, and dependencies to support pacing and coordination.

- **Outline Governance and Off Pathways**
  Document how decisions will be made, who has authority at various levels, and how escalations or changes in direction will be handled.

- **Establish Communication Protocols**
  Agree on how updates will be shared, which channels will be used, and how feedback loops and collaboration will be managed throughout the project.

Overview

Initial Planning
Stakeholder Alignment

Outcomes

The outcomes of the Initial Planning step are to ensure that the project launches with clear direction, coordinated stakeholders, and realistic parameters for success.

This phase sets the tone for effective execution by aligning purpose, people, process, and planning from the outset.

Key outcomes include:

- **Establish a Shared Understanding of the Project Scope**
  Define the instructional solution's boundaries, expected deliverables, constraints, and strategic goals.
- **Align and Activate Key Stakeholders**
  Identify key influencers, decision-makers, and contributors, and clarify their roles, responsibilities, and involvement across the project lifecycle.
- **Select an Appropriate Delivery Model**
  Confirm the overarching delivery approach, whether digital, face-to-face, or hybrid, to guide subsequent design and development choices.
- **Draft a High-Level Timeline with Milestones**
  Create a realistic project schedule with key milestones, review gates, and interdependencies to guide the pacing and sequencing of work.
- **Define Governance and Escalation Protocols**
  Establish clear mechanisms for decision-making, issue escalation, approvals, and change management to maintain control and agility.
- **Set Up Communication Channels and Cadence**
  Agree on preferred communication methods, update frequencies, and feedback pathways to keep the team aligned and informed throughout.
- **Surface Early Risks and Constraints**
  Identify potential barriers related to resourcing, technology, access, or scope, and develop early mitigation strategies to reduce disruption later.

Summary

Initial Planning is the anchor that holds the project steady before the current picks up. It transforms intention into structure, defining scope, setting direction, and aligning all key players before instructional design begins in earnest.

By clarifying who's involved, what needs to happen, how it will unfold, and where decision-making authority lies, this phase minimises confusion and lays a resilient foundation for agile execution. It ensures that timelines are grounded, communication is seamless, and delivery models are matched to context.

When done well, Initial Planning prevents missteps, rework, and stakeholder drift.

When skipped or rushed, it invites misalignment, unmanaged risks, and inefficiencies that ripple throughout the project.

This is where momentum is created, clarity is codified, and project integrity is protected from the very start.

Initial Planning
Planning Meeting

Planning Meeting

Why this is important

A well-structured planning meeting sets the foundation for project success by bringing clarity to key roles, learner characteristics, course scope, and instructional needs. It ensures that all team members, such as instructional designers, SMEs, and project managers, have clearly defined responsibilities from the outset.

The session also provides an opportunity to begin crafting a learner profile, ensuring the course is tailored to the target audience's needs and contexts.

Aligning early on around the course description helps confirm the intended objectives, structure, and assessment strategy.

Most critically, the planning meeting initiates the learning needs assessment process, which identifies current skill levels and uncovers gaps that the course must address. This collaborative alignment ensures a focused, relevant, and efficient design process moving forward.

Tips

- **Prepare Clear Role Descriptions**
  Specify each team member's contributions and responsibilities to avoid role confusion.
- **Use Data for Learner Profiles**
  Gather comprehensive learner information through reliable sources like surveys or interviews to create an accurate learner profile.
- **Draft a Preliminary Course Outline**
  Start with a flexible course outline that can be refined with team input.
- **Prioritise Needs Assessment**
  Focus on identifying performance gaps and areas for improvement, which will shape the course's core content.

Traps

- **Overlooking Stakeholder Involvement**
  Not involving stakeholders or key project members can lead to misaligned objectives and unmet expectations.
- **Ignoring Team Dynamics**
  Neglecting communication and collaboration can result in a fragmented team approach.
- **Overcomplicating the Course Outline**
  Avoid overly complex structures at the planning stage to maintain flexibility and adaptability.
- **Assuming Learner Needs**
  Relying on assumptions rather than actual data can lead to misaligned content and ineffective instruction.

Techniques

- **Kick-off Meeting Agenda**
  Prepare an agenda that covers all necessary planning elements, including role assignments, course scope, and learner profile discussion.
- **SWOT Analysis for Learner Profile**
  Use a SWOT (Strengths, Weaknesses, Opportunities, Threats) analysis to identify gaps in learner skills and knowledge.
- **Mind Mapping for Course Structure**
  Visualise course modules and topics using mind maps to capture team input and organise ideas.
- **Use of Collaboration Tools**
  Implement tools like Trello, Asana, or Slack to facilitate ongoing communication and task management.

Initial Planning
Planning Meeting

Examples

- ***Instructional Designer***
  Responsible for curriculum planning and instructional materials aligned with learning needs and objectives.
- ***Subject Matter Expert (SME)***
  Provides content expertise, ensuring accuracy and relevance.
- ***Graphic Designer***
  Develops visuals that support learning objectives and enhance engagement.
- ***Project Manager***
  Oversees project timeline, coordinates resources, and ensures the team remains aligned with project goals.

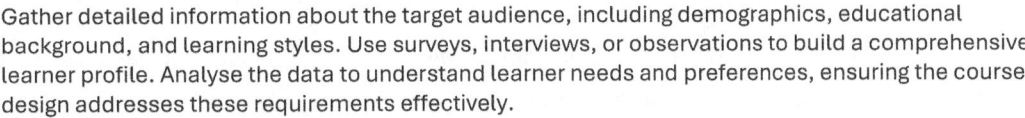

How it's done

- **Identify the Project Team**
  Compile a list of potential team members based on their expertise and availability. Define roles and responsibilities for key positions such as instructional designers, SMEs, project managers, and others. Invite the selected team members to participate in the Planning Meeting to align on goals and objectives.
- **Develop the Learner Profile**
  Gather detailed information about the target audience, including demographics, educational background, and learning styles. Use surveys, interviews, or observations to build a comprehensive learner profile. Analyse the data to understand learner needs and preferences, ensuring the course design addresses these requirements effectively.
- **Outline the Course Description**
  Define the course's scope, objectives, and desired outcomes. Develop an outline that includes topics, modules, and assessment methods. Determine the course format, duration, and delivery platform to ensure alignment with learner needs and organisational goals.
- **Conduct a Learning Needs Assessment**
  Identify knowledge gaps and areas requiring skill development. Share the learning objectives and performance gaps with the team. Prioritise course content.

Core Elements

- **Project Team Identified**
  Clearly defined team roles, including instructional designer, SME, and project manager.
- **Learner Profile Developed**
  Comprehensive profile of learners covering demographics, skill levels, and preferences.
- **Course Description Drafted**
  Preliminary course objectives, outline, and assessment methods are established.
- **Learning Needs Assessment Conducted**
  Knowledge gaps and specific learner needs are documented.
- **Roles and Responsibilities Assigned**
  Each team member has clear and assigned responsibilities.
- **Communication Channels Established**
  Effective communication protocols and platforms are set up.
- **Stakeholders Identified**
  Key stakeholders and their involvement are documented.
- **Kick-off Meeting Scheduled**
  Planning Meeting agenda prepared and distributed to ensure alignment on project goals.

Initial Planning
Planning Meeting

Checklist

1. Conduct a Planning Meeting with all key team members
2. Define project scope, objectives, and initial assumptions
3. Identify and document key project stakeholders
4. Assign roles and responsibilities to each project team member
5. Develop a preliminary learner profile using data-driven methods
6. Outline the course description including modules, objectives, and assessments
7. Conduct a learning needs assessment to identify performance gaps
8. Select and confirm the delivery model and format
9. Draft a high-level timeline with milestones and review gates
10. Establish governance framework and decision-making pathways
11. Define communication protocols and collaboration tools
12. Schedule and document the kick-off meeting with agenda shared in advance

AI Considerations

- Use AI-powered scheduling tools to optimise project timelines and identify potential bottlenecks in resource allocation
- Generate first-draft planning documents, meeting agendas, or stakeholder briefs using generative AI
- Use AI to analyse historical project performance data and flag patterns of scope creep or misalignment
- Employ AI tools to model "what-if" planning scenarios for changes in team capacity, budget, or delivery method
- Use chat-based AI to run simulated planning meetings for training new project managers or instructional designers
- Leverage AI to rapidly compare learner profile inputs with existing content or delivery methods in the LMS
- Apply AI to assess risk exposure based on task dependencies and resourcing gaps

Key Takeaways

The Planning Meeting is where alignment becomes action. It sets the trajectory for the entire instructional design project by anchoring roles, expectations, and early assumptions in a shared framework.

This sub-step transforms scattered insights into a cohesive game plan, shaping the learner profile, surfacing initial content structures, and prioritising performance gaps through collaborative dialogue.

More than a procedural formality, the meeting builds trust, activates accountability, and fosters early buy-in from all team members and stakeholders.

Done right, it reduces ambiguity, pre-empts misunderstandings, and ensures every contributor moves forward with clarity and purpose.

Initial Planning
Define Project Scope

Define Project Scope

 **Why this is important**	Defining the project scope is the cornerstone of successful instructional design planning. It provides a shared understanding of what the learning initiative aims to achieve, what will be included, and what must be deliberately excluded. This boundary-setting activity prevents scope creep, manages stakeholder expectations, and ensures that time and resources are allocated wisely. A clearly defined scope also provides a reference point for all downstream decisions, from content inclusion to resourcing, scheduling, and evaluation. Without it, projects risk ballooning in complexity, losing strategic focus, or failing to deliver measurable value.
 **Tips**	• Begin the scope discussion by anchoring it to the problem the training is solving, not just the content that could be covered. • Be explicit about exclusions, ambiguity invites scope creep. • Include contextual boundaries: geography, roles, systems, time frame, and technologies. • Use visual diagrams or concept maps to validate the scope in stakeholder meetings. • Ensure that the scope directly supports defined business objectives or compliance requirements.
 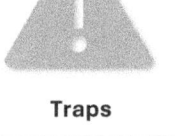 **Traps**	• Assuming that all stakeholder requests must be included, this dilutes impact and clarity. • Treating the scope as static, it must be revisited if there are major shifts in audience, tech, or policy. • Omitting downstream delivery constraints when defining what's "in" (e.g. devices, bandwidth, language). • Allowing SMEs to redefine the scope during content creation phases. This undermines planning discipline.
  **Techniques**	• **MoSCoW Prioritisation**: Classify elements into Must-haves, Should-haves, Could-haves, and Won't-haves. • **Scope Canvas**: Use a one-page visual to summarise purpose, audience, inclusions, exclusions, and success markers. • **Kickoff Workshops**: Run a collaborative scoping session using post-its or digital whiteboards to surface assumptions. • **Reverse Scoping**: Start with desired end-state or evaluation outcome and work backwards to define essential components.
 **Examples**	• *IN SCOPE:* "Create a 3-module onboarding series for new graduate engineers covering safety protocols, organisational values, and equipment handling." • *OUT OF SCOPE:* "Ongoing refresher training, regional policy variations, and manager-specific onboarding processes." • *Delivery Note:* "Training to be delivered asynchronously via mobile-accessible eLearning modules with offline access."

Initial Planning
Define Project Scope

How it's done

1. Review the project brief and business case to understand intent.
2. Meet with sponsors and SMEs to surface expectations and desired outcomes.
3. Facilitate a collaborative session to define what content, audience, delivery modes, and platforms are included.
4. Document all agreed inclusions and exclusions with rationale.
5. Validate against resource constraints and organisational priorities.
6. Obtain formal sign-off and circulate the scope document to all project participants.

Core Elements

- Purpose of the learning intervention
- Intended audience(s) and exclusions
- Geographic, technical, and regulatory boundaries
- List of in-scope topics and modules
- Deliberate exclusions with rationale
- Agreed delivery methods and platforms
- Sign-off protocol with stakeholder names and dates

Checklist

1. Draft initial scope document from project brief.
2. Facilitate stakeholder scoping workshop.
3. Clarify all inclusions, exclusions, and constraints.
4. Map learning scope to business or compliance goals.
5. Align scope with delivery model and available technology.
6. Validate and refine based on SME and sponsor feedback.
7. Obtain formal sign-off on scope document.
8. Distribute scope to project team and reference throughout project.

AI Considerations

- Use generative AI to transform rough scope notes or transcripts into structured documents.
- Apply NLP tools to compare proposed scope against business goals or learner needs assessments.
- Use AI to flag contradictions or redundancies within scoped topics.
- Leverage project management AI to simulate resource demands based on scope elements.
- Employ AI-generated visuals (e.g., diagrams or flowcharts) to simplify complex scoping outcomes for stakeholders.

Key Takeaways

Defining the project scope is not just a formality, it's a strategic safeguard that anchors the entire instructional design process. It ensures that all contributors are aligned on what the project will deliver, what it will not, and why those boundaries exist.

This clarity protects against scope creep, keeps design efforts focused, and supports efficient use of time, people, and technology.

A well-defined scope sets the foundation for effective planning, stakeholder alignment, and downstream development. It allows instructional designers to tie learning content directly to business outcomes, compliance needs, and delivery constraints.

Techniques like MoSCoW prioritisation, scope canvases, and reverse scoping enable teams to visualise, refine, and agree on what matters most.

Without a clear scope, even the best-designed content risks becoming unfocused, overly complex, or irrelevant. With it, instructional design remains purposeful, efficient, and strategically aligned from start to finish.

Initial Planning
Identify Key Stakeholders

Identify Key Stakeholders

 **Why this is important**	Identifying key stakeholders at the outset of a learning project is critical to ensuring that the right voices are heard, the right decisions are made, and the right people are accountable for outcomes. Stakeholders influence content, provide approvals, allocate budgets, enable access to learners, and champion the learning product post-launch. Missing or misidentifying stakeholders can result in rework, resistance, or reputational damage. A clear stakeholder map avoids confusion, defines engagement expectations, and improves project velocity by ensuring that decisions are made by the right people at the right time.
 **Tips**	• Go beyond obvious names, look for system owners, compliance officers, front-line managers, and help desk personnel who will be affected. • Use the RACI model to categorise involvement and avoid stakeholder overload. • Validate stakeholder roles in a live workshop to surface assumptions and gain buy-in. • Include "invisible influencers", people who are not formal approvers but whose opinions can sway adoption. • Keep stakeholder information visible and up to date as the project progresses.
 **Traps**	• Relying solely on the sponsor's view of who matters, this can result in missed perspectives. • Confusing "responsible" with "accountable", the person doing the work is not always the one who must sign off. • Failing to document decision authorities, leading to conflicting feedback loops. • Neglecting to engage downstream stakeholders such as trainers, help desk teams, or line managers who will support the rollout.
 **Techniques**	• **Stakeholder Mapping Workshop:** Facilitate a live session with sticky notes or Miro to map roles, influence, and expectations. • **Power vs. Interest Grid:** Identify which stakeholders need to be managed closely versus kept informed. • **Persona Creation:** Build profiles for key stakeholder types, what they care about, how they prefer to be engaged. • **Engagement Matrix:** Define when and how each stakeholder will be engaged throughout the project.
 **Examples**	• A compliance officer responsible for policy alignment **= Accountable** • A frontline team lead who reviews relevance **= Consulted** • The LMS administrator **= Informed** • The Head of HR who funds the project **= Responsible and Accountable**

Initial Planning
Identify Key Stakeholders

 **How it's done**	1. Identify initial list of stakeholders based on project documentation and sponsor input. 2. Map each stakeholder to a role using RACI or similar framework. 3. Validate the stakeholder list in a kick-off session or 1:1 interviews. 4. Define the level and timing of engagement for each person or role. 5. Maintain a stakeholder register with contact details and communication preferences. 6. Share the map with the project team and refer to it regularly during reviews.
 **Core Elements**	• Stakeholder register (name, role, contact, department) • RACI role assignments (Responsible, Accountable, Consulted, Informed) • Stakeholder influence/interest level • Engagement timing and touchpoints • Communication preferences or blockers • Revision history to track updates
 **Checklist**	1. Draft a preliminary list of stakeholders. 2. Assign RACI roles to each. 3. Validate list with project sponsor. 4. Confirm responsibilities and decision-making levels. 5. Communicate involvement expectations. 6. Share the map with the design team and SMEs. 7. Update the register when team changes occur. 8. Revisit stakeholder engagement strategy at each phase transition.
 **AI Considerations**	• Use AI to extract stakeholder candidates from organisational charts or project emails. • Apply sentiment analysis to stakeholder communications to flag emerging risks. • Use AI to cluster stakeholders by communication preferences or historical project behaviour. • Generate stakeholder engagement plans from templates using role-based prompts. • Summarise stakeholder feedback and translate it into decision-ready themes.
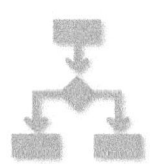 **Key Takeaways**	Identifying key stakeholders early in the project ensures that the right people are informed, consulted, and accountable throughout the instructional design process. A clear and accurate stakeholder map not only aligns responsibilities but also builds project momentum by clarifying decision pathways and reducing approval bottlenecks. Stakeholders influence content, timing, technology use, learner access, and post-launch support. Tools like the RACI model, power-interest grids, and engagement matrices help prioritise who needs to be involved and when. Including both formal approvers and informal influencers avoids blind spots and ensures a more robust, accepted solution. Failing to engage the right people at the right time leads to rework, misalignment, and resistance. Doing it well, on the other hand, builds trust, accelerates delivery, and increases the learning product's long-term impact.

Initial Planning
Confirm Delivery Model

Confirm Delivery Model

 **Why this is important**	The delivery model is the foundation upon which all instructional design decisions are built. It determines how learners will access the training (e.g., online, in-person, blended), when they will engage (self-paced vs. scheduled), and what technologies or human resources will be required. Confirming the delivery model early in the planning phase helps prevent mismatches between instructional intent and practical deployment. It directly impacts content format, media production, learner support strategies, and platform requirements. A well-defined delivery model also influences assessment design, facilitator involvement, and the overall learner experience. Without early clarity, the risk of rework or failure to meet learner needs increases significantly.
 **Tips**	• Anchor your delivery model choice in the **realities of the learner environment**, not just stakeholder preference. • Consider **device access, connectivity, digital literacy**, and daily workflow constraints when choosing a format. • Engage IT, HR, and end-users in validating platform suitability. • Document not just what the delivery model is, but why it was chosen, this helps when defending trade-offs later. • Consider **future scalability**, will the same model work for other regions, departments, or languages?
 **Traps**	• Choosing a delivery model based on budget alone, without considering effectiveness or usability. • Assuming eLearning is always cheaper or faster than instructor-led delivery, this is often false. • Ignoring hybrid possibilities (e.g., live coaching + self-paced content) that might better serve the learning objective. • Forgetting to define the learner support plan tied to the delivery model (e.g., helpdesk, chatbots, facilitators).
 **Techniques**	• **Learner Environment Analysis**: Use surveys, interviews, or field data to understand device access, internet stability, and work routines. • **Delivery Decision Matrix**: Weigh multiple delivery options (e.g., eLearning, vILT, mobile-first) against criteria like reach, budget, interactivity, and assessment depth. • **Pilot Testing**: Trial a small cohort using the proposed model to validate assumptions. • **Persona Mapping**: Model delivery preferences and constraints per audience type or role.
 **Examples**	• A geographically dispersed audience of field workers with mobile phones and low connectivity may require **offline mobile eLearning** with periodic SMS check-ins. • A highly technical program aimed at new engineers may benefit from a **blended model**: theory via asynchronous modules followed by live scenario-based virtual labs. • A leadership program targeting high-potential managers may use **virtual instructor-led training (vILT)** with executive coaches and peer discussion boards.

Initial Planning
Confirm Delivery Model

How it's done

1. Review the learner profile and environmental constraints gathered during the analysis phase.
2. Identify the delivery methods that are feasible and pedagogically appropriate (e.g., eLearning, vILT, F2F, coaching, mobile-first).
3. Compare delivery options using a set of agreed evaluation criteria (cost, scale, engagement, speed).
4. Engage learners, facilitators, and platform owners to validate practical implementation challenges.
5. Decide on a primary delivery model and identify any blended or support components.
6. Document the model clearly, including justification and any dependencies.
7. Communicate the confirmed model to content developers, media teams, and platform admins.

Core Elements

- Defined delivery modality (e.g., eLearning, blended, cohort-based, virtual)
- Rationale for choice, aligned to learner environment and business context
- Platform(s) to be used (e.g., LMS, LXP, Zoom, MS Teams, mobile app)
- Role of facilitators, mentors, coaches, or peer learning
- Support model (e.g., tech helpdesk, discussion forums, automated guidance)
- Scalability and localisation considerations
- Accessibility and compliance implications

Checklist

1. Review learner access, geography, and digital literacy.
2. Evaluate feasible delivery methods based on constraints and objectives.
3. Shortlist top delivery options using a delivery matrix.
4. Conduct validation with sample learners or SME groups.
5. Finalise delivery model and document reasoning.
6. Identify supporting infrastructure and personnel required.
7. Align delivery model with content production and assessment strategy.
8. Share model definition with all downstream stakeholders.

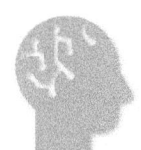
AI Considerations

- Use AI to analyse learner environment data (e.g., bandwidth stats, device logs) to suggest feasible delivery formats.
- Generate delivery model comparison matrices based on input constraints.
- Use AI simulations to test the impact of different delivery models on learner outcomes or logistics.
- Leverage generative AI to automatically create learner journeys or storyboards based on the chosen delivery model.
- Analyse historical project data to recommend delivery models that succeeded with similar audiences or topics.

Key Takeaways

Confirming the delivery model early in the instructional design process is essential for aligning learning strategy with real-world execution.

It determines how, when, and where learners will engage with the content and has downstream implications for media development, platform configuration, learner support, and assessment methods.

A well-matched delivery model bridges instructional intent with learner realities, considering access, environment, interactivity, and scalability.

Techniques such as persona mapping, environment analysis, and delivery decision matrices support data-driven decisions that avoid costly rework or engagement failures.

Choosing the wrong model, or deferring the decision, can result in misaligned content, underutilised platforms, and frustrated learners.

Confirming the right model ensures the solution is not only instructionally sound but operationally viable and learner-centric from day one.

Initial Planning
Set High-Level Timeline

Set High-Level Timeline

Why this is important

A high-level timeline provides the strategic backbone of the entire ADDIE process.

It enables all participants to see key milestones, dependencies, and deadlines at a glance, from project initiation through to evaluation and sustainment.

Without a well-structured timeline, projects drift, resources clash, and sequencing breaks down.

Stakeholders also lose confidence when delivery dates shift without warning.

A clear timeline ensures coordination between design, development, pilot testing, deployment, and evaluation, especially when external vendors, SMEs, and multiple departments are involved.

Tips

- Anchor your timeline to **external deadlines** (e.g., compliance dates, fiscal periods, or launch windows) first.
- Work **backwards from the desired go-live date** to determine critical path activities.
- Include **buffer periods** for review, feedback cycles, and rework, everything always takes longer than planned.
- Use **visual tools** like Gantt charts or swim lanes to communicate progress and dependencies clearly.
- Maintain **version control**, don't overwrite timelines without clearly documenting the change and its impact.

Traps

- Assuming SMEs will be instantly available, their time is often contested and not prioritised.
- Failing to allocate time for quality assurance, stakeholder sign-offs, or technical deployment.
- Overlooking sequencing dependencies, e.g., assessments need to align with objectives, media cannot be built before scripts.
- Treating the high-level timeline as "set in stone", it should be flexible but disciplined.

Techniques

- **Backward Planning**:
  Start with go-live and map each milestone in reverse to identify critical dependencies.
- **Critical Path Analysis**:
  Focus on tasks that directly affect the project end date.
- **Timeboxing**:
  Allocate fixed durations to phases or activities to prevent overrun.
- **Traffic Light Tracking**:
  Use red/amber/green indicators to visually show schedule risks during reviews.

Examples

- **Target Launch:** December 15
- **Timeline Highlights:**
    - Storyboards complete by October 1
    - Pilot test runs November 5–9
    - SME sign-off of final build by November 28
- **Buffers Included:** 5 days for stakeholder feedback per review round, 1 week for technical QA and bug fixes.

Initial Planning
Set High-Level Timeline

How it's done

1. Identify external constraints (e.g. launch dates, compliance deadlines, financial periods).
2. Define key project phases and their dependencies across ADDIE.
3. Estimate durations based on experience, resource availability, and content complexity.
4. Create a visual timeline (e.g. Gantt, roadmap) and validate with core team.
5. Add buffer time and identify milestone review points.
6. Communicate timeline across all functions and update regularly as changes occur.

Core Elements

- Go-live date
- Milestone dates (storyboards, pilot, QA, sign-offs)
- Duration estimates for ADDIE phases
- Dependencies and sequencing notes
- Buffer allocations
- Risk points and decision gates
- Timeline visualisation (Gantt, roadmap, swimlane)

Checklist

1. Confirm target go-live or compliance dates.
2. Identify and sequence all project phases and handoffs.
3. Estimate realistic durations with SMEs and content leads.
4. Build visual timeline and version it.
5. Include review, feedback, and QA loops.
6. Share with all stakeholders and update at key review points.
7. Escalate early if slippage occurs.
8. Track progress with traffic lights or earned value markers.

AI Considerations

- Use AI project tools to generate draft timelines based on scope and content type.
- Predict potential bottlenecks by analysing SME availability patterns.
- Simulate various delivery models (e.g., parallel vs. waterfall) and compare timelines.
- Auto-generate Gantt charts or roadmap visuals from plain-text timelines.
- Use natural language prompts to generate rescheduling scenarios or notify stakeholders when slippage occurs.

Key Takeaways

A high-level timeline is more than a project schedule, it's the strategic framework that orchestrates all ADDIE activities. It brings visibility, accountability, and rhythm to the project, aligning cross-functional efforts and managing stakeholder expectations.

Anchored to critical deadlines, the timeline guides decision making, resource allocation, and sequencing across phases. Visual techniques like Gantt charts and traffic light systems help surface risks early, while built-in buffers protect against inevitable rework.

When timelines are well-structured and transparent, teams stay focused, stakeholders stay confident, and surprises are minimised. When poorly managed, delays multiply, quality suffers, and credibility is eroded.

Getting the timeline right early is a signal that the project is in capable hands.

Initial Planning
Outline Governance and Sign-Off Pathways

Outline Governance and Sign-Off Pathways

 **Why this is important**		Without clear governance and sign-off structures, even the best-designed instructional projects can collapse into chaos. Governance defines how decisions are made, who holds the authority to approve or escalate issues, and what documentation is required to progress through each phase of the project. It prevents bottlenecks, power struggles, and "design by committee," while also establishing accountability and transparency. A well-articulated sign-off pathway ensures that everyone, from SME to sponsor, knows their role in approving deliverables, so progress isn't delayed by confusion or second-guessing.
 **Tips**		• Document the **governance structure at the start**, not once things start going wrong. • **Map decisions to ADDIE phases** so each approval step has a clear trigger and deliverable. • Include **escalation paths** for when decisions can't be made or when stakeholders are unavailable. • Ensure **sign-off authority aligns with organisational hierarchy and project impact**, don't ask SMEs to approve budget decisions or sponsors to sign off on instructional flow. • Visualise the governance process in a simple flowchart or RACI grid.
 **Traps**		• Assuming verbal approvals are sufficient, always record formal sign-offs. • Having too many approvers in a single phase, this leads to delays and conflicting feedback. • Allowing unqualified personnel (e.g., someone unfamiliar with instructional design) to veto pedagogical decisions. • Not defining what constitutes a "signed-off" deliverable, is it an email? A PDF with signatures? A checkbox in a project tool?
 **Techniques**		• **Governance Map**: Create a one-page diagram of key roles, responsibilities, and decision gates. • **Sign-Off Log**: Maintain a record of approvals for each key deliverable with names, dates, and decisions. • **RACI Matrix**: Define who is Responsible, Accountable, Consulted, and Informed for each major phase and deliverable. • **Approval Templates**: Use standardised email templates or digital forms to formalise and track sign-offs efficiently.

 **Examples**		• *Governance Layering:*
		   o Instructional designers propose storyboard
		   o SME validates content accuracy
		   o L&D manager signs off on learning strategy
		   o Sponsor approves deployment and budget
		• *Escalation Path:*
		   o If SME is unresponsive for 5+ days, project manager escalates to business unit head.

Initial Planning
Outline Governance and Sign-Off Pathways

How it's done

1. Identify key governance roles across all ADDIE phases.
2. Define who has the authority to approve each type of deliverable (e.g., learning outcomes, scripts, modules, launch plans).
3. Document decision-making pathways and escalation options.
4. Create sign-off checkpoints and link them to the high-level timeline.
5. Use a central tool or document to track all formal approvals.
6. Review the governance plan with all stakeholders during kickoff to confirm clarity.

Core Elements

- Governance model (centralised, distributed, hybrid)
- Sign-off authority per phase or deliverable
- Escalation protocol for decision delays
- Formal sign-off criteria and formats (e.g., form, email, digital signature)
- Roles matrix (RACI or equivalent)
- Sign-off log with version tracking

Checklist

1. Identify governance roles and approvers.
2. Define approval responsibilities for each ADDIE phase.
3. Document escalation protocols.
4. Create visual map or flowchart of decision points.
5. Establish documentation standards for approvals.
6. Communicate governance structure at project kickoff.
7. Maintain sign-off log with dates, decisions, and rationale.
8. Reconfirm governance plan if project resourcing changes.

AI Considerations

- Use AI to generate governance maps from organisational charts or stakeholder inputs.
- Auto-track approvals using AI-integrated project management tools (e.g., timestamped eSignatures).
- Flag overdue sign-offs or misaligned authority structures based on workflow patterns.
- Generate RACI matrices from structured interviews or onboarding forms.
- Summarise governance protocols into stakeholder-friendly guides using plain language generators.

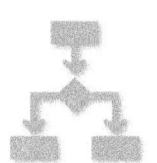
Key Takeaways

Establishing clear governance and sign-off pathways is essential to maintaining project momentum, accountability, and design integrity.

It defines who has the authority to approve what, when decisions are expected, and how escalation is handled if progress stalls.

Well-structured governance prevents bottlenecks, conflicting feedback, and power struggles by clarifying decision rights at each phase of the ADDIE process.

It also ensures that approvals are documented, traceable, and respected, protecting the project from scope creep, last-minute reversals, and unnecessary delays.

Techniques like governance maps, sign-off logs, and RACI matrices create transparency and discipline without adding bureaucracy.

With the right people signing off at the right time, instructional design becomes faster, smoother, and far more defensible.

Initial Planning
Establish Communication Protocols

Establish Communication Protocols

Why this is important

Clear and consistent communication is the glue that holds a project together.

Without defined communication protocols, even well-scoped, well-resourced projects risk falling into confusion, misalignment, or stakeholder disengagement.

Communication protocols outline who needs to be informed, when, about what, and through which channels.

They also specify the rhythm of meetings, the documentation standards for updates, and the escalation process for risks or blockers.

Establishing communication protocols early ensures that everyone stays informed, accountable, and aligned across every phase of the ADDIE process, especially when teams are distributed, cross-functional, or external vendors are involved.

Tips

- Match communication **channel to complexity**, use email for updates, meetings for decisions, and dashboards for progress visibility.
- Include **response time expectations** to avoid frustration (e.g., 48 hours for feedback; immediate for blockers).
- Formalise the **meeting cadence** (weekly stand-ups, milestone reviews, design sprints).
- Use a **shared platform** (e.g., Teams, Slack, Trello) as a **single source of truth**.
- Document communication expectations in the kickoff pack and revisit them at each phase.

Traps

- Relying solely on email for critical discussions, it creates silos and version control issues.
- Assuming everyone interprets "ASAP" the same way, vague language leads to mismatched urgency.
- Overloading stakeholders with unnecessary updates, this causes disengagement.
- Not having a plan for communicating **delays or failures**, these require careful messaging.

Techniques

- **Communication Matrix**: Document who gets what info, when, how, and why.
- **Meeting Maps**: Define recurring meetings by purpose, frequency, owner, and participants.
- **Issue Escalation Ladders**: Establish thresholds for when issues must be escalated, and to whom.
- **Tone Calibration**: Set guidelines for tone, formality, and escalation in written communication.

Examples

- *Weekly Monday Check-ins:*
  for the design team via MS Teams
- *Biweekly Sponsor Updates:*
  via email with dashboard snapshot
- *Feedback Loops:*
  SME feedback expected within 3 business days, else project manager to escalate
- *Urgent Issues:*
  Logged via Slack with "#critical" tag and follow-up within 24 hours

Initial Planning
Establish Communication Protocols

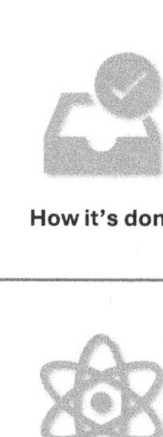 **How it's done**	1. Identify key communication audiences (designers, SMEs, stakeholders, vendors, learners). 2. Determine what information each group needs, how often, and in what format. 3. Choose communication channels based on team size, location, urgency, and preferences. 4. Create a communication plan matrix outlining all flows. 5. Define meeting cadences and ownership of each channel. 6. Share the communication plan with all project participants during kickoff. 7. Regularly review and adjust protocols based on project feedback or bottlenecks.	
 **Core Elements**	• Communication matrix (audience × info × channel × frequency) • List of official tools (Teams, Slack, email, SharePoint, LMS) • Meeting schedules and agendas • Feedback cycles and response expectations • Escalation ladder for issues and delays • Archive or documentation policy (e.g., where meeting notes and decisions are stored)	
 **Checklist**	1. Identify all project communication audiences. 2. Define communication needs and timing per audience. 3. Choose and standardise communication channels. 4. Establish meeting cadence, owners, and agendas. 5. Set clear expectations for response times and decision cycles. 6. Document communication protocols in the project charter or kickoff pack. 7. Share protocols with all participants. 8. Monitor effectiveness and adjust throughout the project lifecycle.	
 **AI Considerations**	• Use AI to summarise meeting transcripts and auto-distribute action items. • Generate stakeholder-specific updates tailored to their role and concerns. • Analyse team communication patterns for gaps or overload using AI dashboards. • Auto-flag overdue responses and suggest escalation triggers. • Create templated communication plans and adjust them using AI based on project complexity or team size	
 **Key Takeaways**	Effective communication is the scaffolding that supports every other element of instructional design. By setting clear communication protocols early, teams ensure that expectations, decisions, risks, and progress are shared with the right people, at the right time, in the right way. Without these protocols, even well-structured projects can unravel due to missed updates, unclear responsibilities, or disengaged stakeholders. Tools like communication matrices, meeting maps, and escalation ladders help create rhythm and reliability, especially in distributed, cross-functional, or vendor-supported teams. When communication is intentional and disciplined, collaboration thrives, issues are resolved faster, and stakeholders stay aligned. In the ADDIE model, this isn't just a support task, it's a strategic enabler of project success.	

Risk and Assumption Analysis
Establish Communication Protocols

Risk and Assumption Analysis

Overview

Risk and Assumption Analysis is the strategic safeguard of the ADDIE process.

The moment the project team steps off the creative runway and scans the horizon for turbulence.

This step anticipates what might derail progress: misaligned expectations, resource shortfalls, technology failures, unproven assumptions, or external disruptions.

It begins with identifying project risks and documenting assumptions, then proceeds to evaluate how severe and likely each risk is, before defining proactive mitigation strategies and responsive contingency plans.

It culminates in the establishment of an ongoing monitoring protocol, because risks evolve and assumptions age.

Far from being a pessimistic exercise, this step instils resilience. It transforms the team's posture from reactive to prepared, enabling smarter decision-making under pressure and ensuring that setbacks, when they occur, don't become project-ending events.

Each of the five sub-steps plays a distinct role in this proactive defence system:

- **Identify Project Risks**: Surface the threats most likely to impact time, cost, quality, or performance.
- **Document Critical Assumptions**: Make invisible assumptions explicit, so they can be validated, adjusted, or retired.
- **Evaluate Risk Impact and Probability**: Prioritise risks through structured scoring to focus efforts on the most consequential threats.
- **Plan Mitigation and Contingency Strategies**: Define concrete actions to prevent risks or reduce their damage if they materialise.
- **Establish Ongoing Risk Monitoring**: Implement tools, routines, and owners to keep risk visibility high throughout the project lifecycle.

Outcomes

Upon completing the Risk and Assumption Analysis step, the project team will have:

- A **comprehensive, prioritised risk register** with impact and probability scores
- A **catalogue of validated, revised, or retired assumptions** documented with rationale
- **Mitigation strategies** and **contingency plans** assigned to major risks
- **Clear ownership** of risks, including monitoring roles and escalation protocols
- A **structured risk and assumption monitoring plan**, integrated into project rituals
- Improved design and delivery resilience based on foresight, not just reaction
- Increased stakeholder confidence in project governance and readiness

Summary

Instructional design is not just about crafting compelling learning, it's also about navigating uncertainty.

The Risk and Assumption Analysis step brings that discipline into focus.

It acknowledges that things can and do go wrong, and that foresight is a competitive advantage.

By proactively identifying risks, validating what's being taken for granted, and putting plans in place to respond to volatility, the project gains flexibility without losing structure.

When learning initiatives fail, it's often not due to poor content but to unmanaged unknowns.

This step turns chaos into clarity. It builds institutional memory, operational maturity, and adaptive capacity.

It doesn't eliminate risk, but it ensures you're never blindsided by it.

Risk and Assumption Analysis
Identify Project Risks

Identify Project Risks

Why this is important

Identifying risks early in a learning project is essential for maintaining momentum, controlling costs, and protecting instructional quality.

Risks are potential events or conditions that, if they occur, will negatively impact one or more aspects of the project, scope, time, cost, quality, or learner outcomes.

By anticipating what could go wrong, you can reduce the likelihood of failure and create safeguards that ensure continuity, even in the face of uncertainty.

This proactive lens distinguishes seasoned instructional designers from reactive content producers.

Tips

- Look across **all dimensions of risk**, technical, instructional, resource, compliance, and learner readiness.
- Include **project team members** and **stakeholders** in a group risk identification session to surface blind spots.
- Use historical data from past projects to guide risk identification.
- Don't just focus on likely risks, sometimes the rare ones are the most damaging.

Traps

- Treating risk identification as a one-time task, it should evolve as the project unfolds.
- Failing to document risks formally, verbal concerns get forgotten or dismissed.
- Ignoring interdependencies (e.g., if content is delayed, so is testing, so is deployment).
- Downplaying cultural or organisational resistance to training, this is a critical risk vector in change-driven initiatives.

Techniques

- **Risk Brainstorming Workshops**:
  Facilitated sessions to surface threats across each ADDIE phase.
- **Risk Category Grids**:
  Use a table to explore risks across categories like content, SME availability, tech access, etc.
- **Root Cause Analysis**:
  For previously failed projects, identify what went wrong and use that to guide new risk spotting.
- **Pre-mortem Analysis**:
  Imagine the project has failed, ask, "What went wrong?" to uncover risks before they happen.

Examples

- *Technical Risk:*
  LMS platform does not support interactive media elements.
- *Human Risk:*
  Key SME may be unavailable during critical review phases due to competing priorities.
- *Instructional Risk:*
  Proposed assessments may be misaligned with learning objectives.
- *Environmental Risk:*
  Target learners may have limited device access or poor internet reliability.

Risk and Assumption Analysis
Identify Project Risks

How it's done

1. Convene a small group of designers, SMEs, and sponsors for a structured risk identification workshop.
2. Explore each project phase and delivery element to surface risks, from planning to rollout.
3. Categorise risks and log them in a structured format (e.g., Excel, project management tool).
4. Assign preliminary ownership or observation responsibilities.
5. Validate the list with external perspectives (e.g., compliance, IT, front-line users).

Core Elements

- Risk description
- Risk category (technical, instructional, organisational, etc.)
- Area of impact (time, cost, quality, learner experience)
- Potential triggers or indicators
- Risk owner (if already known)
- Date identified

Checklist

1. Schedule and facilitate a cross-functional risk identification session.
2. Explore risk categories systematically across ADDIE.
3. Use a risk log template to capture outputs.
4. Assign provisional risk owners or observers.
5. Share risk log with stakeholders for validation.
6. Review log regularly throughout the project lifecycle.

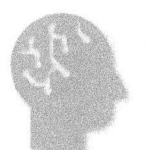
AI Considerations

- Use AI to analyse previous project data to identify common risk patterns.
- Auto-scan project documents (briefs, scopes, schedules) to detect inconsistency or ambiguity.
- Generate risk checklists tailored to delivery model and content type.
- Summarise risk workshop outputs and categorise them using NLP.
- Flag interdependencies between risks (e.g., SME delay → script delay → build delay).

Key Takeaways

Risk identification is not a defensive exercise, it's a mark of strategic maturity in instructional design.

By actively surfacing potential threats early, teams gain the power to prevent disruptions, allocate resources wisely, and adapt confidently when challenges arise.

Structured risk identification helps uncover hidden vulnerabilities across technical systems, human inputs, content integrity, and learner access.

It also sharpens team awareness of dependencies that can quietly derail timelines and quality.

Using tools like risk grids, pre-mortem analysis, and historical reviews empowers teams to turn uncertainty into foresight.

When risk management is embedded into planning, not bolted on later.

learning projects stay on track, even when the unexpected strikes.

Document Critical Assumptions

Why this is important

Assumptions are the invisible scaffolding of every learning project.

They are the beliefs, expectations, or conditions we accept as true, without evidence, to move forward.

While some assumptions are necessary to prevent analysis paralysis, **unexamined assumptions become hidden risks**.

By documenting and regularly reviewing these assumptions, you build transparency, invite validation, and create early-warning systems for issues that could derail delivery.

Treating assumptions as living hypotheses ensures that your project strategy remains grounded, testable, and adaptable.

Tips

- Phrase assumptions using **conditional language**: "We assume that... if this is false, then..."
- Challenge assumptions during stakeholder discussions, silence doesn't mean agreement.
- Separate **fixed assumptions** (e.g., "LMS will be used") from **fluid ones** (e.g., "SMEs will be available weekly").
- Identify **dependencies** tied to each assumption, what could break if the assumption fails?

Traps

- Assuming technology, platforms, or people will function "as usual" without validation.
- Letting assumptions hide in vague phrases like "we'll just," "should be fine," or "it's always like that."
- Failing to revisit assumptions during key milestones or when the context changes.
- Treating assumptions as facts in planning documents, it leads to brittle execution when things go sideways.

Techniques

- **Assumption Mapping Workshop**:
  Facilitate a whiteboard session with the team to surface all underlying assumptions.
- **If–Then Modelling**:
  Use a structured format: If X is true, then we can Y. If not, we will Z.
- **Assumption Audits**:
  Review assumptions at the start of each ADDIE phase to confirm continued validity.
- **Dependency Mapping**:
  Visualise which deliverables or decisions rely on each assumption.

Examples

- **SME Availability:**
  "We assume the SME can review content within 48 hours throughout development."
- **Platform Capability:**
  "We assume the LMS supports SCORM 1.2 and xAPI simultaneously."
- **Learner Access:**
  "We assume all learners have daily access to a connected device and can log in individually."
- **Support Teams:**
  "We assume the helpdesk is trained and available before launch to support queries."

Risk and Assumption Analysis
Document Critical Assumptions

How it's done

1. After defining scope and delivery model, prompt the team with "What are we assuming to be true?"
2. Record all assumptions in a shared document or log.
3. For each assumption, define what would happen if it were false, and whether the impact is high or low.
4. Assign a reviewer or owner for each assumption to verify its validity as the project progresses.
5. Review and update the assumption log at key decision gates, such as before pilot testing or launch.

Core Elements

- Description of assumption
- Rationale or context behind the assumption
- Dependencies tied to the assumption
- Potential consequences if the assumption fails
- Review owner
- Status (Pending / Validated / Refuted)
- Date last reviewed

Checklist

1. Facilitate a structured assumptions discovery session.
2. Record assumptions using a clear and consistent format.
3. Link each assumption to deliverables or dependencies.
4. Assign assumption owners for ongoing validation.
5. Revalidate assumptions at key milestones or project shifts.
6. Document any assumptions proven false and adjust plans accordingly.
7. Use assumptions to inform your risk register proactively.

AI Considerations

- Use AI to detect unspoken assumptions in project briefs, meeting notes, and scripts.
- Generate structured assumption logs from rough workshop outputs.
- Auto-link assumptions to specific milestones or deliverables based on dependency analysis.
- Use AI to monitor assumption-related risks by tracking updates and inconsistencies across project documentation.
- Simulate project scenarios where critical assumptions fail, identify downstream impact before it happens.

Key Takeaways

Assumptions underpin nearly every project decision, yet left unexamined, they become hidden liabilities.

By documenting critical assumptions early and treating them as provisional hypotheses, instructional designers introduce a vital layer of transparency and adaptability into the planning process.

This step encourages proactive thinking: what are we counting on to be true, and what happens if it isn't?

Tools like if–then modelling, assumption audits, and dependency mapping turn guesswork into traceable inputs that can be challenged, validated, or revised as the project unfolds.

Well-managed assumptions help teams avoid surprises, adjust course quickly, and build more resilient learning experiences.

In ADDIE, this isn't just risk prevention, it's strategic foresight in action.

Evaluate Risk Impact and Probability

Why this is important

Identifying risks is only half the job, evaluating their **impact** and **likelihood** is what makes risk management actionable.

Without prioritisation, every risk looks equal, which leads to analysis paralysis or misallocated focus.

By assessing the potential severity (impact) of each risk and the chance it will occur (probability), you enable the project team to direct attention and resources to the most critical threats.

This clarity supports better mitigation planning, stakeholder alignment, and overall project stability.

Tips

- Use a **consistent risk rating scale** (e.g., 1–5 or Low/Medium/High) for both probability and impact to simplify comparison.
- Separate **subjective worry** from actual risk likelihood, focus on evidence, not emotion.
- Involve a cross-functional team to calibrate assessments, one person's "minor delay" may be another's "deal-breaker."
- Include **positive risks** (opportunities) if your project environment supports opportunistic planning.

Traps

- Overrating risks because of past trauma ("it happened before, so it must happen again").
- Underrating risks due to overconfidence in current resources or team capability.
- Failing to update ratings when circumstances change, especially after assumptions are disproven.
- Ignoring cumulative risk effects, three minor delays can equal one major delay.

Techniques

- **2×2 Risk Matrix**:
  Plot each risk based on its probability (Low–High) and impact (Low–High).
- **Weighted Risk Scoring**:
  Assign numeric scores to both dimensions and multiply to get a total risk rating.
- **Risk Heat Maps**:
  Visualise all risks colour-coded by threat level to support fast decision-making.
- **Scenario Analysis**:
  Explore "What if?" cases to understand how certain risks would unfold and interact.

Examples

- *High Impact, Low Probability:*
  "Data breach of learner results", unlikely but potentially catastrophic.
- *High Probability, Medium Impact:*
  "SME review delays due to workload", likely and would affect scheduling.
- *Low Impact, High Probability:*
  "Minor design revisions post-pilot", almost certain, but manageable.
- *Medium Impact, Medium Probability:*
  "LMS API fails to track completion rates correctly", plausible and annoying.

Risk and Assumption Analysis
Evaluate Risk Impact and Probability

**How it's done**	1. Take the full list of identified risks from your risk register.
	2. For each, assess:
	   - What would happen if the risk occurs (impact)?
	   - How likely is this to happen based on current evidence (probability)?
	3. Assign ratings using a 1–5 or Low–Medium–High scale.
	4. Calculate a total risk score (e.g., Impact × Probability).
	5. Categorise risks into bands (e.g., Critical, Watch, Low).
	6. Visualise findings in a matrix or dashboard and validate with the team.

**Core Elements**	• Clear definitions of impact levels (e.g., project delay, budget overrun, learner confusion) • Clear definitions of probability levels (based on past data, SME availability, tech reliability, etc.) • Standardised scoring system • Visualisation tool (matrix, heat map, bubble chart) • Risk prioritisation tags (e.g., Critical, Monitor, Ignore)
**Checklist**	1. Define and communicate the scoring system for impact and probability. 2. Review each risk from the register collaboratively. 3. Assign ratings and calculate overall risk scores. 4. Sort and categorise risks based on severity. 5. Visualise results in a matrix or heat map. 6. Share risk evaluation summary with key stakeholders. 7. Use evaluation to guide mitigation priorities. 8. Reassess ratings at key checkpoints or after major events.
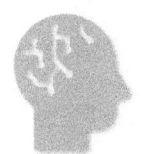**AI Considerations**	• Use AI to score risks based on similar historical project data and outcomes. • Auto-assign preliminary risk levels using machine learning models trained on impact narratives. • Generate interactive heat maps or visual dashboards of the current risk landscape. • Use predictive modelling to simulate multiple risks converging (compound risk analysis). • Flag risks with ratings that are inconsistent with project scope, assumptions, or timeline.
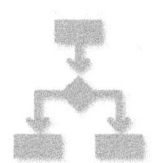**Key Takeaways**	Evaluating the impact and probability of identified risks transforms abstract concerns into actionable priorities. It provides structure to decision-making, ensuring that attention, resources, and mitigation strategies are focused where they matter most. By applying consistent rating scales, involving diverse perspectives, and visualising the risk landscape, teams gain clarity on which threats to manage proactively and which to simply monitor. This enables smarter trade-offs, more confident planning, and faster response when risks begin to materialise. Without risk evaluation, all threats appear equal, which paralyzes decision-making. With it, risk becomes a navigational aid, not just a hazard warning.

Plan Mitigation and Contingency Strategies

Why this is important

Identifying and evaluating risks is not enough. Without a response strategy, your team is merely informed, not protected. **Mitigation strategies** reduce the likelihood of risks occurring, while **contingency strategies** minimise the damage if risks do materialise.

These proactive planning mechanisms ensure that instructional projects stay on track even in the face of disruption.

Whether it's an SME dropout, platform failure, or unexpected stakeholder shift, having defined backup plans increases your agility, credibility, and delivery confidence.

Tips

- Focus mitigation efforts on **high-impact, high-probability** risks, not everything needs a plan.
- Develop **specific actions**, not generic "we'll figure it out" responses.
- Assign clear **ownership and timelines** for implementing mitigation tasks.
- Separate **preventive actions** (mitigation) from **responsive actions** (contingency) in your documentation.
- Communicate plans with stakeholders to build trust and reduce escalation when issues arise.

Traps

- Reusing old mitigation plans without checking if they still fit the current context.
- Ignoring resource requirements, many contingency plans fail because backup support wasn't available.
- Overplanning for low-risk, low-impact issues, wasting time and energy.
- Failing to trigger contingency plans because no one was assigned to monitor the early warning signs.

Techniques

- **Mitigation Planning Matrix**: List risk, prevention action, responsible person, due date, and monitoring signal.
- **Scenario Planning**: Run tabletop simulations ("What if SME drops out in Week 3?") to test response logic.
- **Trigger Definition**: Define what event or threshold activates a contingency plan (e.g., 3 missed SME meetings).
- **Tiered Mitigation**: Develop multiple fallback levels, e.g., Plan A (internal SME), Plan B (external consultant), Plan C (repurpose prior content).

Examples

- *Risk:* LMS integration delays
    - **Mitigation:** Schedule early LMS testing with placeholder content in Week 2
    - **Contingency:** Use standalone SCORM player or publish course as a downloadable PDF
- *Risk:* Script review bottlenecks
    - **Mitigation:** Pre-book SME review sessions during project planning
    - **Contingency:** Assign backup SME from same department
- *Risk:* Learner drop-off during self-paced modules
    - **Mitigation:** Add motivational check-ins and gamified progress bar
    - **Contingency:** Push reminders via SMS or learning coach

Risk and Assumption Analysis
Plan Mitigation and Contingency Strategies

How it's done

1. Review prioritised risk list (based on impact × probability).
2. For each major risk, define:
   - **Mitigation**, What action can reduce the chance of it happening?
   - **Contingency**, What action will be taken if it does happen anyway?
3. Assign responsibility and deadlines for mitigation tasks.
4. Define clear triggers or signals for when to activate contingency plans.
5. Document all plans in a shared and accessible register.
6. Communicate these strategies to the full team and key stakeholders.

Core Elements

- Risk statement
- Mitigation action and owner
- Contingency action and owner
- Triggers for contingency activation
- Timeline and checkpoints for each plan
- Status tracker (Planned / In Progress / Activated / Completed)

Checklist

1. Select risks requiring mitigation or contingency planning.
2. Define actionable mitigation steps for each.
3. Define fallback contingency plans with minimum disruption.
4. Assign owners and deadlines.
5. Identify and document trigger conditions.
6. Share mitigation and contingency register with team.
7. Revisit plans at phase transitions or after major risk developments.
8. Document the outcomes of any activated contingency plans for lessons learned.

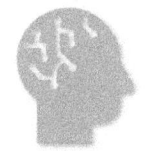

AI Considerations

- Use AI to generate mitigation suggestions based on risk type, delivery model, and available resources.
- Predict the cascading effects of a risk event using AI simulation (e.g., if SME drops out → delay → budget overrun).
- Trigger alerts when risk thresholds are breached or deadlines missed.
- Use AI to score the completeness and realism of proposed mitigation plans.
- Automatically match risk types with proven mitigation strategies from historical project databases.

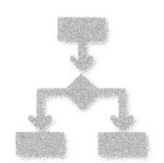

Key Takeaways

Mitigation and contingency planning transforms risk awareness into actionable protection. It's not enough to know what might go wrong, teams must be prepared to prevent what they can and respond decisively when needed.

Mitigation strategies reduce the likelihood of disruption, while contingency strategies soften the blow if risks do materialise.

Together, they give the project resilience, enabling it to bend without breaking.

By assigning ownership, defining triggers, and communicating these plans early, teams stay composed when the unexpected strikes.

Well-planned responses signal professionalism, increase stakeholder confidence, and ensure learning projects keep moving forward, even when conditions change.

Establish Ongoing Risk Monitoring

Why this is important

Risk management isn't a one-time event, it's a living discipline.

Once risks and assumptions have been identified, scored, and actioned, they must be **monitored continuously** to remain relevant.

Projects evolve, contexts shift, and new risks emerge.

Regular risk monitoring ensures that warning signs are not missed, assumptions remain valid, and contingency plans are activated early when needed.

This proactive oversight enhances team responsiveness, minimises surprise disruptions, and builds trust with stakeholders by showing that risk is being taken seriously.

Tips

- Integrate risk review into **existing project rituals**, don't treat it as a separate task.
- Appoint a **risk owner or monitor** for each active risk, not just the project manager.
- Use a **shared risk dashboard or register** that the whole team can update and access.
- Schedule **monthly or phase-gate reviews** to refresh assumptions and reassess exposure.
- Visualise risk movement (e.g., increased, reduced, resolved) over time to track project health.

Traps

- Ignoring new risks because they weren't in the original log, real-time vigilance is critical.
- Allowing outdated risks or assumptions to linger in registers unchallenged.
- Reviewing risk status reactively only after something has gone wrong.
- Treating risk monitoring as a compliance task, not an operational safeguard.

Techniques

- **Risk Review Meetings**: Include a standing risk check-in during weekly or milestone meetings.
- **Dynamic Risk Dashboards**: Use digital tools that auto-update when linked variables shift (e.g., timeline delays).
- **Traffic Light Systems**: Classify risks as Green (stable), Amber (watch), Red (urgent action needed).
- **Assumption Health Checks**: Run mini-audits on active assumptions at each ADDIE phase transition.

Examples

- *Weekly Status Report:*
  Includes section on Top 3 Active Risks and mitigation status.
- *Assumption Review:*
  "All learners have device access" revalidated before pilot rollout.
- *Dynamic Trigger:*
  LMS errors logged 3x in a week → automatically escalates LMS risk from Amber to Red.
- *Dashboard View:*
  Risks colour-coded and sorted by owner with timestamps and comments.

Risk and Assumption Analysis
Establish Ongoing Risk Monitoring

How it's done

1. Assign a **risk owner or monitor** for each medium- and high-priority risk.
2. Determine monitoring cadence (e.g., weekly, milestone-based, or real-time).
3. Set up a **shared risk log** or dashboard with status tracking and notes.
4. Incorporate risk status reviews into project meetings or reporting formats.
5. Reassess each assumption's validity at phase transitions or when conditions change.
6. Update risk scores and strategies based on observed indicators or team input.
7. Escalate risks that shift severity or that remain unresolved beyond their threshold.

Core Elements

- Updated risk register with live status
- Assigned risk monitors and reviewers
- Timeline or phase-based review points
- Assumption revalidation log
- Escalation protocol for unresolved or intensifying risks
- Risk trend tracking (e.g., improving, static, worsening)

Checklist

1. Assign monitors for each active risk and assumption.
2. Set monitoring cadence aligned with your project rhythm.
3. Use a dynamic tool or shared log for visibility.
4. Review and update each risk's status regularly.
5. Revalidate assumptions at key transition points.
6. Escalate any risks that meet trigger thresholds.
7. Document changes in status, actions taken, and outcomes.
8. Share updated risk status with all stakeholders at defined intervals.

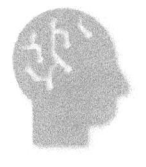

AI Considerations

- Use AI to track project signals (e.g., missed deadlines, slow feedback loops) that indicate escalating risks.
- Auto-summarise risk changes since last report and flag anomalies.
- Predict new risks based on trending variables (e.g., rising support tickets during pilot = likely usability risk).
- Generate real-time dashboards showing risk heat levels, ownership, and status.
- Use generative AI to compose stakeholder risk updates in concise, context-aware language.

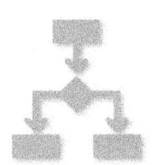

Key Takeaways

Risk management doesn't end with identification, it lives and evolves with the project.

Ongoing monitoring transforms risk logs from static documents into operational dashboards that inform real decisions and signal when to act.

By assigning ownership, integrating check-ins into project routines, and using dynamic tools for tracking, teams can stay ahead of emerging issues and adjust their strategies before problems escalate.

Assumptions are also subject to change and must be revalidated regularly to maintain project integrity.

Ongoing monitoring isn't about bureaucracy, it's a proactive discipline that boosts resilience, fosters transparency, and protects momentum when projects encounter turbulence.

Resource and Task Review

Overview

The **Resource and Task Review** step in the Analysis phase of the ADDIE model is essential for laying a solid foundation for the instructional design project.

This step involves a thorough evaluation of available resources, the identification of subject matter experts (SMEs), and a detailed analysis of learner tasks to ensure the content is well-informed and aligned with project objectives.

By addressing these elements early, instructional designers can identify gaps in materials or expertise, streamline content development, and ensure alignment with learner needs and project goals.

Key Sub-Steps are:

- **Identify SMEs**
  Locate and engage subject matter experts to provide authoritative knowledge and insights critical for content accuracy and relevance.
- **Conduct Task Analysis**
  Break down learner tasks into specific skills, behaviours, and knowledge areas to identify instructional targets and ensure practical, focused outcomes.

Outcomes

The outcomes of the **Resource and Task Review** step are to ensure that the instructional design process is equipped with high-quality resources, expertise, and a clear understanding of learner tasks.

Key outcomes include:

- **Identify and Engage Qualified SMEs**
  Secure access to subject matter experts who can validate and enrich the instructional content with accurate and relevant insights.
- **Evaluate Existing Resources for Quality and Relevance**
  Assess current materials and resources to determine their suitability for the project and identify areas that may require updates or enhancements.
- **Conduct a Thorough Task Analysis**
  Break down tasks into their essential components, focusing on the specific skills, knowledge, and behaviours learners need to develop.
- **Pinpoint Resource Gaps**
  Recognise any deficiencies in existing resources or expertise and develop a plan to address these gaps early in the process.
- **Facilitate Efficient Content Development**
  Streamline the content creation process by identifying reusable materials, eliminating redundancies, and focusing on actionable and relevant content.

Summary

The **Resource and Task Review** step is a cornerstone of the instructional design process, ensuring that the project is grounded in expertise and supported by high-quality resources.

By identifying subject matter experts, reviewing existing materials, and conducting a comprehensive task analysis, instructional designers can build a robust foundation for the project.

This step reduces risks such as misaligned objectives, content gaps, or outdated resources. It also supports the creation of relevant, learner-focused instruction that is actionable and effective.

With a clear understanding of available resources and learner requirements, instructional designers can confidently proceed to subsequent phases, ensuring alignment with project goals and learner success.

Resource and Task Review
Identify SMEs

Identify SMEs

 **Why this is important**	Subject Matter Experts (SMEs) are the source of truth in any learning project. They hold the deep operational, technical, or compliance knowledge that must be translated into accessible, engaging learning. Identifying the right SMEs early ensures design is accurate, relevant, and credible, and avoids last-minute firefighting or misinformation. Good SMEs don't just "know stuff", they also understand context, nuance, and the reality of how things get done. They can validate task flows, flag risks, and help shape authentic scenarios and assessments. If the wrong SMEs are chosen, or if their role is unclear, learning quality suffers, and rework increases.
 **Tips**	• Choose SMEs who are respected by peers and understand the 'why' behind the 'what' • Prioritise people who can articulate knowledge clearly and are open to collaboration • Where possible, nominate two SMEs, one for technical depth, one for practical context • Clarify early the scope of the SME role: contributor, reviewer, co-designer, or all three • Set expectations for availability, turnaround times, and communication styles • Provide SMEs with context on the learner audience and learning goals
 **Traps**	• Selecting SMEs based on job title rather than expertise or engagement • Assuming one SME can speak for all variations across business units or sites • Relying on SMEs who are too busy to contribute meaningfully • Allowing SMEs to overcontrol design or push irrelevant content • Failing to prepare SMEs for the learning process, leading to poor inputs • Not supporting SMEs with clear guidance, templates, or timelines
 **Techniques**	• Use a SME profile matrix, mapping candidates against availability, credibility, communication, and scope • Interview team leads to identify high performers who are also respected mentors • Confirm SME suitability by asking scenario-style questions about learner challenges • Co-develop a mini-charter with each SME outlining role, input points, and deliverables • Provide briefing packs or walkthroughs to orient SMEs to the course purpose and flow • Include SMEs in walk-throughs or early design prototypes to build ownership
 **Examples**	• A technical training project assigns one SME for content accuracy and another for real-world application • A compliance SME works with an instructional designer to translate legal requirements into learner-friendly language • A frontline leader is chosen as SME for a customer service module based on their coaching reputation and influence • Two SMEs are selected to reflect national and regional procedures, reducing the risk of location bias

Resource and Task Review
Identify SMEs

How it's done

1. Identify SME requirements based on content areas, audience context, and learning goals
2. Develop a shortlist of potential SMEs using manager recommendations and peer input
3. Vet candidates through informal interviews or task examples
4. Confirm SME availability, interest, and alignment to the project timeline
5. Brief SMEs on the course purpose, structure, and their specific role
6. Create an SME engagement plan, including communication cadence and sign-off points
7. Track SME contributions, feedback, and version history for transparency and consistency

Core Elements

- SME role definitions (e.g. contributor, reviewer, scenario builder)
- Criteria for SME selection, credibility, communication, availability
- Briefing materials and context for SMEs
- Defined input points across the ADDIE cycle
- Escalation paths if SME engagement is blocked
- A method for managing SME review and feedback cycles
- Recognition or credit for SME contribution

Checklist

1. Have the SME knowledge domains and contribution types been defined?
2. Are SME candidates evaluated on credibility, clarity, and collaboration?
3. Has each SME's role been agreed and documented?
4. Are timelines and input formats aligned with SME availability?
5. Are briefing materials provided to orient SMEs to the learning context?
6. Has SME feedback been tracked and versioned throughout the project?
7. Is there a plan for managing SME disengagement or delays?

AI Considerations

- Use AI to identify SME candidates based on communications data, previous projects, or expert tagging
- Generate SME briefing packs or role outlines using generative AI
- Use chatbots to simulate learner questions, helping SMEs understand the learner mindset
- Apply AI tools to summarise SME feedback and flag content discrepancies
- Automate scheduling, reminder emails, and document versioning for SME inputs
- Use AI transcription and summarisation to streamline SME interviews

Key Takeaways

The right SME makes content real, relevant, and respected.

The wrong SME, or a good one poorly managed, can derail timelines and distort quality. SME engagement is both a relationship and a system.

Get both right, and the learning shines.

Conduct Task Analysis

Why this is important

Conducting a thorough task analysis bridges the gap between identified learning needs and the creation of targeted, effective learning objectives.

It ensures that instructional design is anchored in the real-world tasks learners must perform to be successful in their roles.

By identifying and defining specific, measurable objectives based on these tasks, designers can focus content development on practical outcomes.

Understanding the prerequisites, those foundational skills or knowledge areas essential for task success, prevents learner frustration and enables scaffolded instruction.

Breaking tasks into logical, sequenced components reveals dependencies and informs activity design, while setting clear performance criteria helps establish expectations for quality, speed, and accuracy.

Additionally, assessing learner gaps related to each task sharpens focus and supports tailored interventions.

Contextual variables, such as the work environment or available resources, also influence how tasks should be taught and practiced.

Finally, aligning the task analysis with business goals ensures that learning outcomes support broader performance requirements, while documenting the entire process provides a reference for validation, review, and iteration.

Tips

- **Collaborate with SMEs**
  Working with subject matter experts (SMEs) provides valuable insights into task specifics and performance expectations.

- **Use Clear Performance Metrics**
  Define measurable standards for performance criteria, such as accuracy and speed, to assess task mastery.

- **Observe Task Performance**
  Observing tasks in their real context helps you understand any environmental or tool-related constraints.

- **Break Down Complex Tasks**
  Breaking down tasks into steps or subtasks clarifies dependencies and required skills.

- **Document Thoroughly**
  Comprehensive documentation of task analysis findings is essential for aligning design decisions with learning needs.

- **Prioritise Critical Tasks**
  Focus task analysis efforts on high-frequency, high-risk, or high-impact tasks, those most essential to performance and business outcomes.

Resource and Task Review
Conduct Task Analysis

Traps

- **Overlooking Prerequisites**
  Failing to identify foundational skills can lead to learning gaps if learners lack required background knowledge.

- **Ignoring Contextual Challenges**
  Not considering factors like work environment or resources may lead to unrealistic expectations.

- **Insufficient Stakeholder Involvement**
  Excluding stakeholders, such as SMEs and managers, can result in an incomplete or inaccurate task analysis.

- **Vague Performance Criteria**
  Ambiguous criteria make it difficult to assess learner proficiency accurately.

- **Incomplete Task Breakdown**
  Skipping over sub-tasks or dependencies can lead to instructional gaps and inefficient learning paths.

Techniques

- **Task Decomposition**
  Break tasks into smaller steps or subtasks to understand their sequence and dependencies better.

- **Performance Analysis Matrix**
  Use a matrix to outline tasks, required knowledge, skills, and associated performance criteria.

- **Contextual Observation**
  Observe tasks in their actual environment to understand contextual factors impacting performance.

- **Flowcharting**
  Visualise task steps and dependencies with flowcharts, highlighting decision points and critical actions.

- **Stakeholder Validation Sessions**
  Conduct validation sessions with SMEs and stakeholders to ensure the accuracy and relevance of the task analysis.

Examples

- *Learning Objective Identification*
  For a customer service role, define an objective such as "demonstrate effective problem-solving skills in resolving customer complaints.

- *Task Decomposition*
  For a technical support role, break down "troubleshoot software issues" into sub-tasks like identifying the problem, testing potential solutions, and implementing fixes.

- *Performance Criteria*
  Specify criteria such as "resolve customer inquiries within 5 minutes with 90% accuracy" for a call centre task.

- *Contextual Factors*
  For a field technician, factors may include outdoor environmental challenges or limited access to digital resources.

- *Prerequisites*
  Before training on advanced software, learners must understand basic operating system functions.

Resource and Task Review
Conduct Task Analysis

How it's done

- **Determine Essential Tasks**
  Identify the specific tasks learners need to perform in their roles by reviewing Learning Needs Assessment results and collaborating with SMEs. Compile a comprehensive list of essential tasks that align with job requirements.
- **Establish Clear Learning Objectives**
  Work with SMEs to articulate expected outcomes for each task, focusing on the knowledge, skills, and behaviours required. Create clear, measurable learning objectives to guide instructional design.
- **Break Down Complex Tasks**
  Decompose complex tasks into manageable sub-tasks by analysing their components, sequence, and required skills. This ensures learners can master tasks step by step.
- **Analyse Task Components**
  Examine the sequence, dependencies, and success factors for each task by collaborating with SMEs. Understand the steps, decisions, and problem-solving strategies involved in task performance.
- **Define Success Metrics**
  Establish measurable criteria for task success, such as quality standards, accuracy, or speed, with input from stakeholders. This provides clear performance expectations for learners.
- **Identify Foundational Knowledge and Skills**
  Determine the prerequisite knowledge or skills needed for task completion by consulting SMEs and reviewing Learning Needs Assessment findings.
- **Consider Contextual Factors**
  Assess environmental and situational factors that may impact task performance. Use observations, interviews, or surveys to gather insights into the context in which tasks are performed.
- **Document Task Analysis Findings**
  Compile a comprehensive record of task analysis results, including task descriptions, objectives, performance criteria, prerequisites, and contextual factors. Ensure this documentation is accessible to the instructional design team.
- **Validate Task Analysis Findings**
  Present task analysis results to SMEs and stakeholders for feedback. Refine the analysis as necessary to ensure accuracy and alignment with project goals.

Core Elements

- **Tasks Identified**
  A comprehensive list of required tasks based on Learning Needs Assessment and SME input.
- **Learning Objectives Defined**
  Clear and measurable objectives established for each task.
- **Tasks Broken Down**
  Complex tasks divided into manageable sub-tasks.
- **Task Components Analysed**
  Sequence, dependencies, and success factors identified for each task.
- **Performance Criteria Set**
  Measurable success metrics defined for task completion.
- **Prerequisites Identified**
  Foundational knowledge and skills documented.
- **Contextual Factors Assessed**
  Environmental and situational factors impacting tasks considered.
- **Findings Documented**
  Detailed documentation of task analysis results compiled.
- **Stakeholder Validation Completed**
  Task analysis findings reviewed and validated with stakeholders.

Resource and Task Review
Conduct Task Analysis

Checklist

1. Identify essential tasks based on Learning Needs Assessment and stakeholder input
2. Define clear, measurable learning objectives for each task
3. Break down complex tasks into manageable sub-tasks
4. Analyse the sequence, dependencies, and performance factors of each task
5. Establish performance criteria (e.g., accuracy, time, quality benchmarks)
6. Identify prerequisite knowledge, skills, or behaviours
7. Assess contextual and environmental factors affecting task performance
8. Document all findings in a structured, accessible format
9. Validate findings with SMEs and key stakeholders
10. Integrate task analysis insights into design planning and content development

AI Considerations

- **AI-Powered Task Extraction**
  Use NLP tools to scan SOPs, manuals, or policy documents and extract task lists, sequence steps, and implied skills.

- **Semantic Analysis for Performance Criteria**
  Apply AI to analyse recorded job performance data (e.g., call centre logs or field reports) to surface real-world performance benchmarks.

- **Automated Skill Gap Matching**
  Use AI to compare learner profiles or existing assessment data with task requirements to flag potential learning gaps.

- **Predictive Risk Analysis**
  Leverage AI to identify which tasks are most prone to failure, delay, or error based on historical performance or support requests.

- **AI-Generated Task Flow Diagrams**
  Automatically generate flowcharts or visual task sequences based on structured task inputs or recorded observations.

- **Digital Observations with AI Assistants**
  Use mobile AI tools to assist with real-time task observations, tagging behavioural data, or prompting checklists during job shadowing.

Key Takeaways

Effective task analysis bridges the gap between broad learning needs and specific, measurable learning objectives. It dissects complex job functions into teachable components, ensuring instructional content is anchored in real-world performance requirements.

By applying techniques like task decomposition, contextual observation, and stakeholder validation, instructional designers gain a clear map of what learners must know, do, and demonstrate.

This sub-step prevents the common pitfalls of assumption-driven design by grounding every instructional decision in observable behaviour, performance standards, and contextual realities.

Ultimately, it lays the foundation for a learning experience that is not only instructionally sound, but operationally relevant and strategically aligned with business goals.

Data and Evidence Audit

Conduct Task Analysis

Data and Evidence Audit

Overview

Data and Evidence Audit is the insight engine of the ADDIE process, the stage where assumptions are tested, patterns are surfaced, and decisions begin to take root in fact.

Rather than leaping into design based on stakeholder instinct or outdated perceptions, this step builds a robust foundation of validated insight.

It ensures that the team understands not just where performance problems appear, but why they exist, and whether they're training-related or not.

It also highlights what's missing, what needs updating, and what matters most to inform targeted, high-impact design.

Key sub-steps are:

- **Review Organisational Data Sources**: Analyse internal data sets, such as HR reports, compliance records, performance metrics, or support logs, to surface trends and strategic learning needs.
- **Assess Learner Performance Data**: Examine assessment results, behavioural data, and learner feedback to understand current capabilities, gaps, and transfer challenges.
- **Identify Gaps in Existing Evidence**: Map what's unknown or assumed and distinguish between tolerable gaps and those requiring new data collection or validation.
- **Validate Relevance and Recency of Data**: Confirm that datasets reflect current systems, structures, and roles, retiring obsolete inputs to avoid flawed design decisions.
- **Prepare Data Summary for Design Team**: Synthesize insights into a concise, actionable brief tailored to instructional planning, prioritising findings, surfacing assumptions, and flagging constraints.

Done well, this step shifts the foundation of design from speculation to strategy, ensuring every learning solution is both evidence-based and performance-aligned.

Outcomes

By the end of the Data and Evidence Audit phase, the team will have:

- **A mapped inventory of organisational data sources** relevant to the learning initiative, including system owners, formats, and limitations
- **A performance profile of the target audience**, based on current learner data, including knowledge, skill, and behavioural indicators
- **A clear list of evidence gaps**, distinguishing between acceptable assumptions and areas requiring further investigation
- **Validated, current data** that reflects today's roles, tools, and performance environment, with outdated inputs retired or annotated
- **A concise, design-ready data summary**, prioritised by relevance and tied to instructional and business objectives
- **Greater alignment between stakeholder goals, learner realities, and instructional intent**, based on factual insights rather than assumption

Summary

The Data and Evidence Audit ensures that the instructional design process starts with clarity, not conjecture.

By systematically analysing what the organisation knows, what learners can do, and what remains uncertain, this step eliminates guesswork and strengthens every downstream decision.

It replaces anecdotes with analytics, validates assumptions, and identifies where new insight is needed.

More importantly, it prepares the design team with a sharp, summarised insight package that links learner needs to business impact.

This is where strategic learning begins, not with a blank screen, but with a clear, validated picture of the reality instructional design is meant to improve.

Review Organisational Data Sources

Why this is important

Reviewing internal data sources ensures that learning projects are grounded in the actual performance and behavioural trends of the organisation, not guesswork.

Organisational data reveals the systemic challenges, recurring errors, or capability gaps that training might help address.

Ignoring these sources risks designing learning that is irrelevant, redundant, or poorly targeted.

By starting with what's already known, you position the project as both strategic and cost-effective.

Tips

- Engage stakeholders from HR, L&D, Ops, and IT, each holds a piece of the data puzzle.
- Prioritise data tied to performance goals, compliance obligations, or recent change initiatives.
- Look for both **quantitative (metrics, reports)** and **qualitative (survey comments, complaints)** sources.
- Be curious about outliers, they often point to root causes worth exploring.

Traps

- Assuming the data you find is comprehensive, many organisations have patchy or siloed data collection.
- Using data without understanding its collection method, flawed instruments = flawed insights.
- Overlooking outdated reports that no longer reflect current systems or roles.
- Confusing correlation with causation, just because two variables align doesn't mean one caused the other.

Techniques

- **Data Mapping Grid**: Organise sources by owner, format, update cycle, and relevance to learning goals.
- **Internal Discovery Interviews**: Ask leaders what data they rely on most when assessing team performance.
- **Kirkpatrick Crosswalk**: Map organisational data sources against Levels 3 and 4 of Kirkpatrick to identify training-relevant metrics.
- **Trend Heatmaps**: Visualise patterns of underperformance, turnover, or compliance failures over time.

Examples

- **HR Records:**
  Exit interview themes reveal confusion around safety procedures → training opportunity.
- *Helpdesk Logs:*
  Spike in support tickets for a new system after onboarding suggests gaps in initial training.
- *Performance Dashboards:*
  Consistent underperformance in specific regions points to manager capability issues.

How it's done

1. Create a master list of potential internal data sources (e.g., LMS, CRM, HRIS, survey tools, audit reports).
2. Meet with each system or data owner to identify what's available and relevant.
3. Request access or extracts for project-relevant data sets.
4. Analyse the data with a learning lens, what skills, behaviours, or knowledge gaps are implied?
5. Document all usable data sources, including metadata (last updated, frequency, source owner).

Data and Evidence Audit
Review Organisational Data Sources

 **Core Elements**	• Source name and type (quant/qual) • Data owner/contact • Relevance to learning goals or identified problems • Frequency of update • Limitations or access constraints • Summary of key findings
 **Checklist**	1. Identify internal systems containing performance or behavioural data. 2. Confirm access with relevant data owners. 3. Extract data relevant to learner profiles or training needs. 4. Evaluate data for completeness and bias. 5. Catalogue all sources in a structured audit log. 6. Highlight key insights or patterns tied to performance. 7. Share summary with the analysis team and SMEs. 8. Revalidate source relevance before design phase begins.
 **AI Considerations**	• Use AI to mine large datasets quickly (e.g., helpdesk tickets, survey comments) for recurring themes. • Auto-tag insights from unstructured data using NLP (e.g., policy confusion, tool misuse). • Generate initial audit reports summarising performance patterns. • Use AI visualisation tools to create dashboards that highlight training-relevant trends. • Correlate multiple datasets to surface hidden relationships between training and outcomes.
 **Key Takeaways**	Organisational data offers a treasure trove of insight if you know where to look. By systematically reviewing internal sources, instructional designers can anchor their learning initiatives in real performance patterns, behavioural trends, and operational needs. This ensures that training is targeted, relevant, and evidence-informed, not based on assumptions or hearsay. Engaging multiple departments and combining both quantitative and qualitative sources creates a more complete and actionable picture. When done well, this step positions learning as a strategic enabler rather than a reactive fix. When skipped, it risks delivering solutions to problems no one actually has.

Data and Evidence Audit
Assess Learner Performance Data

Assess Learner Performance Data

 **Why this is important**	Learner performance data provides a reality check on how well previous training initiatives have translated into knowledge, behaviour change, and measurable outcomes. By analysing this data, instructional designers can identify persistent gaps, strengths to build on, and where the previous efforts have succeeded or failed. It shifts the conversation from what learners should know to what they actually do or don't do well. This step not only sharpens the learning objectives but also strengthens the case for (or against) developing new interventions.
 **Tips**	• Review **both formative and summative data**, pre-tests, assessments, certifications, job observations, and workplace performance metrics. • Pay attention to **drop-off points**, where learners disengage, score poorly, or fail to apply knowledge. • Where direct performance data is unavailable, look for **proxy indicators** (e.g., error rates, task completion times, supervision requirements). • Collaborate with managers or team leads to validate whether data reflects **actual on-the-job proficiency**.
 **Traps**	• Mistaking **completion data** for competence, just because someone finished a course doesn't mean they learned. • Ignoring **low or inconsistent usage** of systems (LMS, assessments) that can mask poor performance. • Using aggregate data only, often the insights lie in **department-level or demographic splits.** • Relying solely on **multiple-choice quiz scores**, which often test recognition rather than real understanding or behaviour change.
  **Techniques**	• **Learner Performance Audit**: Collate assessment scores, application checklists, and feedback trends by role, cohort, or location. • **Comparative Analysis**: Compare high-performing teams against low-performing ones to surface skill differentials. • **Pre/Post Comparison**: Assess the change in learner performance after previous training cycles. • **Skill Gap Heatmaps**: Visualise learner proficiency across required capabilities to highlight clusters of weakness.
 **Examples**	• *Assessment Gaps:* 42% of learners failed the final module on customer conflict resolution, suggesting a gap in scenario-based learning. • *Application Data:* Supervisors report inconsistent use of incident reporting protocols even after compliance training, potential reinforcement gap. • *Quiz Analysis:* Average score is 87%, but 64% of learners got the same three questions wrong, pointing to systemic content misalignment.
 **How it's done**	1. Access learner data from LMS, assessment platforms, simulations, and observation checklists. 2. Filter data by learner group, job role, or time period to identify patterns. 3. Analyse for both **outcome quality** (scores, completions) and **behavioural transfer** (real-world application). 4. Correlate with business data where possible (e.g., sales performance, safety incident reduction). 5. Summarise key strengths, pain points, and opportunities to improve the learning experience.

Data and Evidence Audit
Assess Learner Performance Data

Core Elements

- Assessment scores (knowledge, skill-based)
- Completion rates and drop-off points
- Observed behaviour transfer in the workplace
- Learner engagement data (logins, time spent, revisit rates)
- Feedback or survey trends
- Variations by location, role, or tenure

Checklist

1. Identify relevant learner performance metrics from LMS and business systems.
2. Filter and segment data for relevant analysis (e.g., by team, region, tenure).
3. Compare performance before and after previous training interventions.
4. Evaluate evidence of behaviour transfer post-training.
5. Identify weak content areas using question/item-level analysis.
6. Document learner strengths and persistent challenges.
7. Validate findings with managers and facilitators.
8. Share insights with design team to inform objectives and modality choices.

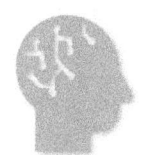
AI Considerations

- Use AI to flag unusual data patterns (e.g., unusually high scores in short time = potential guessing).
- Run sentiment analysis on open-ended learner feedback to identify recurring friction points.
- Auto-generate learner performance dashboards segmented by team, tenure, or job family.
- Link LMS data with business KPIs to detect training effectiveness.
- Recommend content remediation or adaptive pathways based on learner-level performance data.

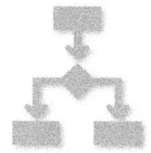
Key Takeaways

Learner performance data is a mirror, not just of how training was completed, but of whether it actually worked.

Analysing this data allows instructional designers to move from assumption to evidence, uncovering real gaps in knowledge, skill, or behavioural transfer.

By combining assessment results, usage trends, and workplace performance metrics, teams gain a nuanced understanding of what learners struggle with, what's sticking, and where reinforcement or redesign is needed.

Patterns of disengagement, repeated errors, or lack of application in the field are signals, not noise.

When this data is used well, it doesn't just inform course design; it elevates the credibility and impact of the entire learning function.

Data and Evidence Audit
Identify Gaps in Existing Evidence

 **Why this is important**	Even in data-rich environments, crucial insights are often missing. Gaps in evidence prevent instructional designers from fully understanding learner needs, performance barriers, or root causes of workplace issues. Identifying these gaps allows you to **ask the right questions**, gather the missing data, and ensure your learning solutions are built on a complete picture, not partial assumptions. This step strengthens the integrity of the entire ADDIE process and protects the learning strategy from flawed or unverified conclusions.
 **Tips**	• Compare your current data inventory against your learning goals, what do you still need to know to design well? • Prioritise **decision-critical gaps**, not every missing data point needs to be filled. • Use stakeholder interviews to surface "unknown unknowns", what people assume but haven't tested. • Frame data gaps as **research questions** (e.g., "Do team leaders understand how to coach underperformers?")
 **Traps**	• Believing "no data = no problem", a lack of evidence does not equal a lack of need. • Assuming qualitative feedback is less valuable than metrics, rich insight often hides in narrative. • Overengineering data collection efforts to fill every gap, focus only on what will move design forward. • Neglecting to log and revisit assumptions made in the absence of data.
 **Techniques**	• **Evidence Gap Matrix**: Cross-check each learning objective or problem area against available data, highlight empty cells. • **Root Cause Interviews**: Ask front-line managers and learners to describe barriers they face, gaps will surface naturally. • **Pre-Design Surveys**: Use pulse surveys or focus groups to test assumptions and clarify unknowns. • **Triangulation Checks**: If data sources conflict or don't align, you likely have an evidence quality or completeness issue.
 **Examples**	• *Available:* LMS data shows completion rates but no data on post-training behaviour. • *Gap:* No feedback from regional offices about onboarding effectiveness. • *Gap:* Inconsistent reporting across departments makes cross-team comparisons impossible. • *Partial:* Safety incident logs exist but lack detail on the role of human error vs. environmental conditions.

Data and Evidence Audit
Identify Gaps in Existing Evidence

How it's done

1. Review all existing data sources already gathered.
2. Map each one to specific design decisions or learner needs, what does each data set inform?
3. Identify decisions that still rely on gut feel, SME opinion, or assumption.
4. Categorise missing information as:
    - Unknown learner variables
    - Missing performance correlations
    - Unvalidated delivery constraints
5. Prioritise gaps that will impact instructional design, modality, or outcomes.
6. Plan how and whether each critical gap will be filled (interviews, surveys, pilots, etc.).

Core Elements

- Matrix of data coverage vs. learning design questions
- Categories of missing evidence (learner, performance, organisational, platform)
- Assumptions currently used in place of data
- Criticality rating (High/Medium/Low)
- Proposed method to address gap (if applicable)
- Owner and timeline for investigation

Checklist

1. Map all current data against learning objectives and performance questions.
2. Highlight areas with no supporting data or unverified assumptions.
3. Rank gaps by impact on design accuracy.
4. Decide whether each gap is tolerable or requires follow-up.
5. Assign data gathering methods for critical gaps (e.g., survey, SME validation, shadowing).
6. Record assumptions being made in lieu of evidence.
7. Communicate key gaps to the design and sponsor teams.
8. Update the audit log when gaps are filled or assumptions are tested.

AI Considerations

- Use AI to compare expected learning data points (from templates or benchmarks) against actual data inventory.
- Auto-tag incomplete datasets or misaligned metadata in audit logs.
- Summarise gaps and propose investigation questions using NLP.
- Generate draft focus group or survey questions based on missing variables.
- Recommend proxy metrics when ideal data is unavailable.

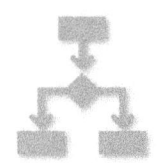
Key Takeaways

Identifying evidence gaps ensures that instructional design decisions are built on substance, not supposition.

Even in data-rich environments, critical insights can be missing, outdated, or assumed, and failing to surface those gaps invites blind spots into your learning strategy.

By mapping current data against what's needed to design effectively, you uncover which learner needs, behavioural patterns, or environmental factors still lack validation.

This process shifts teams from guessing to investigating, prompting smarter questions and more focused discovery efforts.

When gaps are acknowledged and prioritised, the integrity of the design process is preserved, and the solutions that follow are sharper, safer, and better aligned to real-world performance needs.

Data and Evidence Audit
Validate Relevance and Recency of Data

 **Why this is important**	Even the most comprehensive dataset can become misleading if it's outdated or no longer relevant to the current business context. Validating data ensures that learning solutions are designed based on **current conditions**, not expired assumptions or obsolete metrics. This is especially important in environments where systems, roles, regulations, or tools change rapidly. Ensuring recency and relevance protects against wasted effort, mismatched content, and eroded credibility with learners and stakeholders alike.	
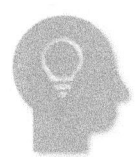 **Tips**	• Always check the **timestamp and update frequency** of datasets, when was it last refreshed? • Cross-verify whether the **organisational conditions** have changed since the data was captured (e.g., new systems, policy shifts). • Look for **trailing indicators**, does the data reflect lagging performance (e.g., past problems) or current behaviour? • Validate relevance with end users or SME interviews, sometimes numbers don't reflect lived realities.	
 **Traps**	• Assuming that historical data still applies, especially after restructures or leadership changes. • Treating regulatory compliance data as instructional proof without checking if requirements have changed. • Ignoring outdated assessments that no longer align with updated objectives or role descriptions. • Using pre-pandemic or pre-digital transformation data in rapidly evolving environments.	
 **Techniques**	• **Data Age Review**: Annotate each dataset with its last update date and intended review frequency. • **Relevance Scorecard**: Score each source based on how closely it aligns with the project's current learning goals. • **Stakeholder Reality Check**: Present high-level data insights to stakeholders and ask: "Is this still true today?" • **Change Log Comparison**: Align data collection dates with major organisational change logs or rollout calendars.	
 **Examples**	• *Recency Gap:* Learner survey data from two years ago collected under a now-defunct onboarding program. • *Relevance Gap:* Sales KPIs were redefined last quarter, making old sales enablement data non-comparable. • *Validated:* Safety compliance data from the past month directly tied to new audit procedures. • *Misleading:* Assessment pass rates up, but content has become easier, not learners more competent.	

Data and Evidence Audit
Validate Relevance and Recency of Data

**How it's done**	1. Catalogue each data source used or referenced in the needs analysis. 2. Document when it was last updated, by whom, and how often it is refreshed. 3. Validate relevance by checking whether job roles, systems, or policies have changed since the data was captured. 4. Conduct SME or stakeholder interviews to validate the operational reality behind the numbers. 5. Flag data sources that are outdated or no longer representative. 6. Replace, update, or annotate problematic data to avoid misinformed design decisions.
**Core Elements**	• Data source and owner • Last update timestamp • Frequency of updates • Relevance score (e.g., High / Medium / Low) • Validated or not validated • Summary of change context (if applicable) • Replacement or update plan
**Checklist**	1. Review last updated date for all datasets used. 2. Identify whether organisational or operational changes have occurred since data capture. 3. Score each dataset for relevance to current learner needs or business goals. 4. Validate findings with SMEs or stakeholders. 5. Annotate or exclude any data deemed stale or no longer representative. 6. Document recency and relevance findings in your data audit log. 7. Prioritise updates for high-impact but outdated data sources. 8. Communicate any limitations to the design team to avoid downstream misalignment.
**AI Considerations**	• Use AI to automatically tag datasets as outdated based on timestamp metadata. • Cross-reference job titles, policies, or workflows mentioned in the data with current organisational charts or systems. • Flag inconsistencies between old data trends and recent performance metrics. • Recommend prioritisation of datasets based on impact and update history. • Auto-suggest stakeholder interviews or content updates where data has aged beyond useful thresholds.
**Key Takeaways**	Data is only valuable if it reflects current reality. Validating the recency and relevance of datasets protects the design process from being led astray by obsolete information, expired metrics, or conditions that no longer apply. Outdated data can create false confidence, leading to poorly targeted learning solutions and eroding stakeholder trust. By checking timestamps, aligning data with recent organisational changes, and validating assumptions with SMEs, instructional designers ensure that every insight is timely and actionable. In fast-moving environments, this validation step isn't optional, it's a safeguard against designing for a world that no longer exists.

Prepare Data Summary for Design Team

Why this is important

The bridge between data analysis and instructional design is the data summary.

Without it, valuable insights risk being lost, misinterpreted, or simply not actioned.

A well-prepared summary ensures the design team can **translate data into learning architecture**, keeping the design focused on validated learner needs, organisational goals, and measurable performance outcomes.

It saves time, sharpens learning objectives, and reduces iteration by aligning the design team with the clearest possible picture of reality from day one.

Tips

- Focus on **what the data means**, not just what it says, design teams need context and implication, not just raw stats.
- Organise insights by **learner group, job role, or performance gap**, not by data source.
- Highlight **priorities and patterns**, not just observations, tell a story.
- Include a "What we don't know" section, gaps and assumptions are part of the evidence too.

Traps

- Dumping spreadsheets or raw graphs without interpretation.
- Making the summary too long or data-heavy, it must be digestible and design-ready.
- Excluding qualitative data because it's harder to summarise, stories and quotes bring insight to life.
- Using overly technical jargon that alienates creative or instructional team members.

Techniques

- **Insight Mapping**:
  Convert data points into statements like "Learners struggle with X," "Supervisors report confusion about Y."
- **Persona-Driven Summaries**:
  Frame findings around learner personas to guide tone, media, and pacing decisions.
- **Visual Highlighting**:
  Use infographics or dashboards to flag where performance is strong, weak, or variable.
- **Executive Summary Format**:
  Offer a one-page overview followed by deeper optional insights for design leads.

Examples

- *Priority Insight:*
  New hires consistently underperform in weeks 3–4 due to lack of contextual support materials.
- *Performance Pattern:*
  Region A outperforms Region B by 22% in system usage, correlated with local onboarding method.
- *Design Implication:*
  Add interactive walk-throughs and peer chat support to first four modules.
- *Gap Noted:*
  No current data on learners' mobile access, this assumption must be tested before finalising modality.

Data and Evidence Audit
Prepare Data Summary for Design Team

How it's done

1. Aggregate validated insights from all prior H3s (organisational data, learner performance, data gaps, recency checks).
2. Organise findings into categories that map directly to design decisions (e.g., behaviour gaps, modality preferences, role-specific needs).
3. Highlight confirmed needs, areas of opportunity, and known limitations.
4. Include illustrative quotes or examples where helpful.
5. Provide clear "Design Recommendations" or "Implications" at the end of each section.
6. Distribute the summary in an accessible format (slide deck, PDF, Notion page) with room for design team commentary.

Core Elements

- Executive summary of findings
- Prioritised learner needs and performance gaps
- Validated insights and supporting data
- Known data limitations and assumptions
- Recommended areas of focus for design
- Appendices or linked raw data (optional)
- Owner and version date for traceability

Checklist

1. Gather key insights from all data audit activities.
2. Translate raw data into design-relevant statements.
3. Group insights by learner profile or skill area.
4. Identify implications for content, modality, pacing, and assessment.
5. Include assumptions and data gaps as flags.
6. Create a summary format that is clear, visual, and navigable.
7. Review with SMEs or stakeholders for validation.
8. Deliver to the design team and review together in a formal handover session.

AI Considerations

- Use AI to auto-summarise large data sets into key learning implications.
- Generate learner persona summaries based on clustered behaviour or needs.
- Create infographics or visual dashboards highlighting performance gaps.
- Auto-flag contradictions or incomplete patterns in the data.
- Generate recommended instructional strategies aligned to the top three validated needs.

Key Takeaways

The data summary is the strategic handoff between analysis and design, it translates evidence into action. Without it, insights risk being buried in spreadsheets or misinterpreted, resulting in designs based on assumption rather than truth.

A well-crafted summary distils complex findings into clear, design-ready insights, highlighting not just what the data says, but what it means.

It organises information around learner needs, performance priorities, and instructional implications, while also flagging known gaps and assumptions.

When this step is done well, the design team moves faster, iterates less, and builds learning solutions that hit the mark from the outset.

Success Metrics Definition

Overview

Success Metrics Definition is where instructional design meets accountability. This step defines how success will be recognised, measured, and reported, not just from a learning perspective, but in terms of operational value and strategic impact. Without this clarity, learning efforts risk becoming activity without consequence.

Each sub-step contributes to building a metrics framework that is specific, measurable, stakeholder-aligned, and evaluation-ready:

- **Define Learning Success Criteria**: Translate learning objectives into observable, measurable indicators of success, shifting from vague verbs like "understand" to actionable behaviours that can be assessed.
- **Establish Business Impact Metrics**: Tie training outcomes to meaningful operational KPIs such as productivity, efficiency, compliance, or customer satisfaction. This anchors learning in organisational value.
- **Align Metrics to Stakeholder Expectations**: Engage business sponsors, managers, and learners to define what "success" looks like from their perspective, ensuring that the metrics tracked are relevant and defensible.
- **Select Evaluation Methods and Tools**: Choose the right mix of qualitative and quantitative methods, surveys, tests, observations, dashboards, that align with the type and level of impact being measured.
- **Plan Data Collection and Reporting Protocols**: Define how data will be collected, by whom, when, and how often, ensuring the evaluation strategy is sustainable, compliant, and stakeholder friendly.

Together, these actions ensure learning is positioned not as a cost, but as a performance multiplier, measured, managed, and optimised for continuous improvement.

Outcomes

By the conclusion of this step, the project team will have:

- **Defined learning success criteria** for each objective, with clear performance indicators
- **Mapped business impact metrics** to project goals, including baselines and target improvement levels
- **Captured and aligned stakeholder success expectations**, documented and validated across roles
- **Selected evaluation tools and methods**, matched to metrics and learner context
- **Developed a data collection and reporting protocol**, including frequency, roles, tools, and compliance safeguards
- **Established an evaluation framework** capable of supporting both continuous improvement and ROI justification

Summary

If you don't define success, you can't measure it, and if you can't measure it, you can't improve it.

Success Metrics Definition gives the project its scoreboard, ensuring learning is designed with outcomes in mind and evaluated with integrity.

This step turns learning into a measurable, strategic intervention.

It aligns instructional intent with business goals, secures stakeholder buy-in, and lays the foundation for demonstrating real-world impact.

When success is defined clearly and agreed collaboratively, training moves from "nice to have" to "non-negotiable."

Success Metrics Definition
Define Learning Success Criteria

Define Learning Success Criteria

Why this is important

Clear learning success criteria transform training from a creative endeavour into a **strategic intervention**.

Without precise definitions of what success looks like at the learning level, designers default to vague goals like "understand" or "know," which offer no basis for assessment or improvement.

Defining learning success ensures that objectives are measurable, aligned with performance goals, and realistic for the target audience.

It's also the only way to demonstrate impact and defend budget, time, or resource allocation.

Tips

- Use **Bloom's Taxonomy** or similar frameworks to define observable and measurable behaviours.
- Include **application-focused outcomes**, what should learners be able to do on the job?
- Tie each learning objective to **assessable criteria**, even if assessments are informal.
- Consider **qualitative evidence** (e.g., improved confidence or feedback scores) alongside quantitative metrics.

Traps

- Equating success with course completion or attendance, these are inputs, not outcomes.
- Using broad verbs like "understand" or "be familiar with", they cannot be reliably assessed.
- Defining success only in terms of what the business wants, without reference to what learners can realistically achieve.
- Ignoring transfer, learners may pass the course but fail to apply knowledge on the job.

Techniques

- **SMART Learning Objectives**: Specific, Measurable, Achievable, Relevant, Time-bound.
- **Backward Design**: Start with what you want to assess, then work backward to define the learning experience.
- **Success Criteria Matrix**: List each learning objective, desired performance, and assessment method.
- **Task Simulation Mapping**: Align learning success to actual job tasks and define observable indicators of mastery.

Examples

- *Weak:*
  "Learners will understand compliance procedures."
- *Strong:*
  "Learners will correctly complete the incident reporting form within 3 minutes, with no critical errors, in a simulated scenario."
- *Supplemental:*
  "Learners report 90% confidence in handling difficult customer conversations after role-play sessions."

How it's done

1. Review learning objectives and categorise them by knowledge, skills, or attitudes.
2. Define what successful demonstration looks like for each, what will the learner say, do, or produce?
3. Set performance thresholds where possible (e.g., 80% accuracy, 2-minute completion time).
4. Include both objective (assessment scores) and subjective (self-reported confidence) indicators.
5. Document success criteria in a format that guides both design and evaluation.

Success Metrics Definition
Define Learning Success Criteria

Core Elements

- Learning objective
- Desired observable behaviour
- Performance threshold (where applicable)
- Method of verification (assessment, observation, simulation)
- Aligned instructional strategy
- Success narrative for stakeholders

Checklist

1. Break down each objective into observable behaviours.
2. Define what "success" looks like for each behaviour.
3. Establish measurable thresholds or indicators.
4. Confirm that each criterion can be evaluated fairly and consistently.
5. Include both knowledge checks and application tasks where feasible.
6. Record success definitions in the design brief or project charter.
7. Review criteria with stakeholders and SMEs for realism.
8. Use these definitions to inform content structure and evaluation planning.

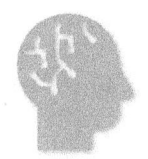
AI Considerations

- Use AI to rewrite vague objectives into action-oriented success statements.
- Generate learning success criteria based on past course completions and assessment patterns.
- Recommend assessment types aligned to each criterion (e.g., scenario for application, MCQ for recall).
- Detect missing success definitions in project documentation and prompt for clarification.
- Use AI to create learner performance dashboards mapped to each success metric.

Key Takeaways

Defining learning success criteria turns aspiration into accountability.

It enables instructional designers to build with intent, assess with confidence, and align learning outcomes with real performance goals.

Success criteria clarify what learners must demonstrate, how that will be measured, and what thresholds constitute mastery.

When properly framed, these criteria bridge the gap between learning and application, helping to ensure training isn't just consumed, but used.

Vague goals lead to vague results. Specific, observable, and measurable success definitions empower better design, sharper evaluation, and a stronger case for impact.

Success Metrics Definition
Establish Business Impact Metrics

Establish Business Impact Metrics

 **Why this is important**	Learning is not a goal, it's a means to achieve business outcomes. By establishing **business impact metrics**, you ensure that training initiatives are tied directly to organisational priorities like productivity, quality, efficiency, compliance, or customer satisfaction. This step translates the language of learning into the language of operations, finance, and strategy, making it easier to justify investment, gain stakeholder buy-in, and assess return on effort. It also focuses design choices on what actually moves the needle.
 **Tips**	• Identify the **business problem** the training aims to solve, missed KPIs, safety incidents, onboarding delays, etc. • Use metrics already tracked by the business where possible, this enhances credibility and reduces complexity. • Work with stakeholders to define **baseline performance levels** and set realistic improvement targets. • Think across levels, **individual, team, department, and enterprise-wide** metrics may all be relevant.
 **Traps**	• Selecting metrics that cannot be influenced by training (e.g., macroeconomic sales dips). • Defining too many metrics, this dilutes focus and clouds accountability. • Failing to confirm that baseline data exists for comparison. • Measuring things just because they're easy (e.g., completion rates), not because they matter.
 **Techniques**	• **Kirkpatrick Level 4 Mapping**: Define outcomes in terms of results, what business change should occur? • **Training-Business Link Chain**: Visualise how improved skills lead to changed behaviours and, ultimately, improved results. • **Stakeholder Co-Design Sessions**: Work with business leaders to align metrics with operational pain points. • **Balanced Scorecard Alignment**: Tie learning outcomes to pillars like financial, customer, process, and growth goals.
 **Examples**	• *Onboarding:* Reduce average time-to-competency from 8 weeks to 5 weeks. • *Sales:* Improve conversion rate on Product X by 12% in targeted region. • *Compliance:* Achieve 100% accurate completion of incident forms post-training. • *Customer Service:* Raise CSAT score by 0.5 points within 3 months of course rollout.

Success Metrics Definition
Establish Business Impact Metrics

 **How it's done**	1. Identify the **core business objectives** behind the training project. 2. Translate these objectives into measurable metrics (e.g., percentage change, cost reduction, time saved). 3. Confirm whether **baseline data** exists, if not, plan to establish it. 4. Define **targets** collaboratively with stakeholders, they must be ambitious yet credible. 5. Document all selected metrics, data owners, and timelines in a Business Impact Plan. 6. Reconfirm metrics before finalising evaluation tools or design strategy.
 **Core Elements**	• Business objective • Metric name and description • Baseline level and data source • Target improvement level • Metric owner • Timeline for measurement • Method of data collection and verification
 **Checklist**	1. Confirm the business challenge or opportunity driving the training need. 2. Select impact metrics that align with that challenge. 3. Validate that these metrics can realistically be influenced by learning. 4. Identify existing sources of measurement and responsible owners. 5. Set achievable target improvements (absolute or percentage). 6. Document all metric definitions and data logistics. 7. Communicate metrics clearly to the instructional team. 8. Schedule post-training reviews to assess progress against these metrics.
 **AI Considerations**	• Use AI to suggest impact metrics based on training type and business function. • Correlate past learning programs with downstream performance data to infer likely business impact. • Generate performance dashboards that include both learning and business metrics side by side. • Auto-flag metrics that lack clear data sources or owners. • Forecast impact using predictive models based on similar training interventions.
 **Key Takeaways**	Establishing business impact metrics ensures that learning is not an isolated activity but a strategic driver of organisational performance. It connects training outcomes to real-world improvements, in efficiency, compliance, quality, customer satisfaction, or cost. By aligning metrics with existing business priorities and data sources, learning teams gain credibility, improve stakeholder engagement, and create a defensible case for investment. It also sharpens the design focus by keeping everyone oriented around measurable, meaningful change. When learning speaks the language of business, it shifts from being a cost centre to a value engine.

Success Metrics Definition
Align Metrics to Stakeholder Expectations

Align Metrics to Stakeholder Expectations

 **Why this is important**	A beautifully crafted set of success metrics means little if they don't reflect what stakeholders actually care about. Stakeholders, from senior executives to operational leaders to frontline managers, each view success through different lenses. By explicitly aligning your learning and impact metrics with their expectations, you ensure support, relevance, and engagement throughout the project lifecycle. It also prevents painful post-launch surprises where stakeholders say, "That's not what we meant."
 **Tips**	• Identify **primary, secondary, and peripheral stakeholders**, each with their own success lens. • Ask direct questions like, "How will you know this training worked?" to extract real expectations. • Translate technical learning metrics into **stakeholder-friendly language** (e.g., "fewer complaints," "faster onboarding"). • Gain early agreement on what will be tracked, how it will be reported, and what constitutes success.
 **Traps**	• Assuming stakeholder goals are aligned, they rarely are. • Leaving success definition until after course delivery, this invites misalignment and disappointment. • Allowing loud voices to define all metrics, don't ignore quieter but equally important voices (e.g., learners). • Failing to document or circulate agreed success criteria, memory is fallible, expectations drift.
 **Techniques**	• **Stakeholder Expectations Map:** List each stakeholder and their definitions of success. • **Needs–Metric Matrix:** Cross-reference stakeholder pain points with proposed metrics. • **Expectation Interviews or Surveys**: Ask key stakeholders how they define success and what evidence they need. • **Co-signoff Process**: Require stakeholders to formally agree to the success framework before design begins.
 **Examples**	• *Executive Sponsor:* Wants to see a 10% reduction in onboarding time, metric = "Time to Competency" tracked monthly. • *Line Manager:* Wants to see fewer errors in safety documentation, metric = "Post-training audit pass rate." • *HR Partner:* Wants to track improved learner sentiment, metric = "Pulse survey confidence score post-training." • *Learner:* Wants easier access to support resources, metric = "Helpdesk ticket volume reduction" and self-reported clarity ratings.

Success Metrics Definition
Align Metrics to Stakeholder Expectations

 **How it's done**	1. Identify and map all relevant stakeholders across the business. 2. Facilitate structured conversations or surveys to collect each party's definition of success. 3. Translate expectations into measurable criteria wherever possible. 4. Reconcile conflicts or contradictions between stakeholder definitions. 5. Gain formal alignment through a documented "Success Agreement" or metrics charter. 6. Communicate success alignment across the design and evaluation teams.
 **Core Elements**	• Stakeholder name and role • Definition of success (in their words) • Mapped metric or proxy • Influence level (high/medium/low) • Agreed reporting method or cadence • Concerns or red flags
 **Checklist**	1. Identify all stakeholders relevant to the learning initiative. 2. Collect their success definitions via structured interviews or forms. 3. Translate expectations into metrics or observable results. 4. Resolve conflicting expectations or surface trade-offs. 5. Confirm alignment through documentation and formal signoff. 6. Share aligned success criteria with design, dev, and evaluation teams. 7. Build stakeholder-specific insights into post-launch reporting. 8. Revisit expectations periodically if business context changes.
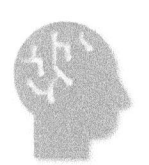 **AI Considerations**	• Use AI to summarise stakeholder interviews and extract recurring success themes. • Match stated expectations to likely metrics or measurement approaches. • Detect contradictions or vague language in success definitions. • Auto-generate stakeholder-specific report templates based on their success focus. • Suggest alignment phrases or framing that satisfies multiple stakeholders with one metric (e.g., "efficiency" as time + accuracy).
 **Key Takeaways**	Aligning success metrics to stakeholder expectations ensures your learning project remains relevant, supported, and strategically credible. Different stakeholders care about different outcomes, what matters to an executive may differ from what a line manager or learner prioritises. By actively surfacing and reconciling these expectations early, you build trust, gain buy-in, and prevent post-launch misalignment. Translating metrics into the language each audience understands, and agreeing on what success looks like upfront, transforms learning from a siloed effort into a shared objective. When stakeholder-defined success becomes your compass, your solution earns greater impact and enduring support.

Success Metrics Definition
Select Evaluation Methods and Tools

Select Evaluation Methods and Tools

 **Why this is important**	Defining metrics is just the starting line, measuring them effectively requires thoughtful **evaluation methods** and the right **tools**. This step ensures that success isn't just declared, but demonstrated, using valid, reliable, and scalable approaches. Whether you're assessing knowledge retention, behavioural change, or business impact, your chosen tools must suit the level of evaluation, the audience, and the available resources. This also establishes your evidence trail for continuous improvement and stakeholder reporting.	
 **Tips**	<ul><li>Match your method to the **Kirkpatrick level** being measured (reaction, learning, behaviour, results).</li><li>Use **mixed methods**, combine quantitative (scores, metrics) with qualitative (comments, observations) to capture a full picture.</li><li>Consider tools that integrate with existing systems (e.g., LMS analytics, business dashboards, survey platforms).</li><li>Keep **data ethics** in mind, inform learners how their data will be used and maintain confidentiality.</li></ul>	
 **Traps**	<ul><li>Relying only on learner satisfaction surveys (smile sheets), they tell you how learners felt, not what they learned.</li><li>Overcomplicating evaluation plans, tools should be **usable, interpretable, and sustainable**.</li><li>Choosing tools without consulting IT, privacy, or business systems teams.</li><li>Designing evaluations that don't allow for comparative analysis (e.g., no pre-data or no control groups).</li></ul>	
 **Techniques**	<ul><li>**Evaluation Method Matrix**: Map each metric to a method/tool combo (e.g., "knowledge gain" → quiz; "confidence" → Likert scale).</li><li>**Pre/Post Testing**: Measure growth by comparing before/after knowledge or attitude data.</li><li>**360° Feedback Tools**: For leadership or behavioural objectives, gather feedback from peers, managers, and reports.</li><li>**Performance Observation Checklists**: Use structured rubrics to assess on-the-job behaviour post-training.</li></ul>	
 **Examples**	<ul><li>*Learning Gain:* Pre/post knowledge quiz via LMS, auto-graded with instant feedback.</li><li>*Behavioural Change:* Supervisor observations using tablet-based checklist 30 days post-training.</li><li>*Sentiment Shift:* Pulse survey emailed to learners and line managers 2 weeks after course.</li><li>*Business Impact:* CRM dashboard shows support call volume drop in regions where training was deployed.</li></ul>	

Success Metrics Definition
Select Evaluation Methods and Tools

 **How it's done**	1. Review all defined learning and business success metrics. 2. Choose a **primary method** for measuring each one (e.g., test, survey, observation, system log). 3. Select or configure tools that can collect, store, and report on that data effectively. 4. Align with IT, privacy, and HR to ensure compliance. 5. Pilot test your evaluation tools for clarity, reliability, and ease of use. 6. Document your full Evaluation Framework for the project team and stakeholders.
 **Core Elements**	• Metric being evaluated • Evaluation method (test, survey, observation, etc.) • Tool or platform (LMS, Google Forms, Power BI, custom system) • Data owner and frequency of collection • Reporting format and recipients • Notes on data privacy or user transparency
 **Checklist**	1. Map each success metric to a valid evaluation method. 2. Select or develop tools that fit the method, audience, and environment. 3. Align evaluation design with stakeholder expectations and privacy policies. 4. Test the tools for reliability, clarity, and user accessibility. 5. Document roles for who will administer, analyse, and act on the data. 6. Build evaluation tool access into your learning ecosystem (e.g., LMS links, email follow-ups). 7. Validate tools with a sample group or during pilot testing. 8. Include tool setup and access in the project timeline.
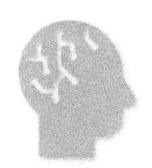 **AI Considerations**	• Use AI to generate draft surveys, rubrics, or quiz questions from learning objectives. • Automatically score and analyse free-text responses with sentiment or topic clustering. • Recommend optimal evaluation methods based on delivery modality and metric type. • Predict potential survey fatigue or low response rates and suggest mitigation strategies. • Auto-format collected data into stakeholder-specific reports or dashboards.
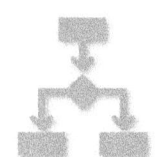 **Key Takeaways**	Defining success is only meaningful if it can be measured reliably, and that's where evaluation methods and tools come in. This step transforms intention into evidence, ensuring that impact is tracked with precision, not guesswork. The right combination of methods and tools allows teams to measure learning gains, behavioural shifts, and business outcomes across multiple levels. By aligning tools with metrics, systems, privacy expectations, and usability needs, you ensure evaluation is not only possible, but practical and credible. When evaluation is thoughtfully planned and seamlessly integrated, it becomes a powerful engine for improvement, accountability, and storytelling that stakeholders believe.

Success Metrics Definition
Plan Data Collection and Reporting Protocols

Plan Data Collection and Reporting Protocols

Why this is important

Having clear metrics and evaluation tools is essential, but without a structured **data collection and reporting plan**, measurement efforts fall apart.

This step defines how, when, by whom, and to whom data will be collected and communicated.

It ensures that success isn't just tracked, but continuously surfaced, interpreted, and used to inform decisions.

Done well, this step builds a performance narrative that supports iteration, stakeholder confidence, and long-term impact tracking.

Tips

- Align data collection timing with key project phases (e.g., immediately post-course, 30 days later, quarterly).
- Automate data collection wherever possible to minimise manual effort and human error.
- Define a **reporting cadence** that matches stakeholder attention spans, not all data needs weekly updates.
- Create a single **source of truth** for performance data to avoid misalignment.

Traps

- Collecting too much data "just in case", it burdens the team and reduces insight.
- Forgetting to secure permissions or privacy approvals for learner data usage.
- Creating reports no one reads or acts on, vanity dashboards waste resources.
- Over-focusing on front-end metrics (e.g., completions) without back-end behaviour or impact data.

Techniques

- **Data Collection Schedule**:
  A calendar that details what data is collected when, and by whom.
- **Role-Based Data Matrix**:
  Map each data point to its collector, validator, and recipient.
- **Push-Pull Reporting Design**:
  Push summary insights to execs, allow deeper pull-based access for analysts.
- **Reporting Templates**:
  Standardise layouts (e.g., performance against targets, traffic lights, recommendations).

Examples

- *Learning Data:*
  Completion rates, test scores, and feedback collected via LMS and reported monthly to L&D team.
- *Behaviour Data:*
  Supervisor observation data collected via mobile forms 14 days post-training and reported to Ops Managers.
- *Business Impact:*
  Quarterly metrics pulled from CRM and HRIS systems to assess training ROI.
- *Reporting Protocol:*
  Monthly dashboard emailed to stakeholders + quarterly review presentation with visual highlights.

Success Metrics Definition
Plan Data Collection and Reporting Protocols

 **How it's done**	1. List all data points needed to track success metrics (learning, behaviour, business). 2. Assign **data owners** and collectors for each point. 3. Establish timelines and triggers for collection (e.g., post-assessment, 30-day check-ins). 4. Define reporting formats, frequency, and recipients. 5. Create templates and automation where possible (e.g., BI dashboards, email reports). 6. Include compliance and data privacy checks in the protocol. 7. Test reporting systems during the pilot or soft-launch phase. 8. Continuously refine protocols based on feedback and metric movement.
 **Core Elements**	• Data point description and source • Collection method and responsible role • Timing (e.g., immediate, delayed, recurring) • Reporting format (dashboard, PDF, presentation) • Audience and frequency of reporting • Data privacy notes and approval logs • Tool or platform used (e.g., LMS, Power BI, Excel, Formstack)
 **Checklist**	1. Define every success metric's data source and collection method. 2. Assign responsible roles for collection and validation. 3. Create a calendar of data events (collection, reporting, review). 4. Design templates for reports and dashboards. 5. Confirm data access rights, storage security, and compliance with regulations. 6. Automate reporting wherever possible. 7. Pilot test your protocol with a sample group or pre-launch run. 8. Build a review cadence to keep reports actionable and up to date.
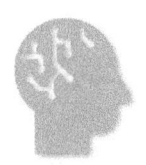 **AI Considerations**	• Use AI to monitor learning systems for threshold triggers (e.g., score dips, delayed completions). • Auto-generate reports in stakeholder-friendly language and visuals. • Summarise large data sets and flag trends or outliers. • Suggest new report sections based on evolving stakeholder questions or observed gaps. • Auto-schedule data pulls and email briefings using AI-driven scheduling assistants.
 **Key Takeaways**	Success metrics only drive value when they're consistently captured, interpreted, and shared. A well-structured data collection and reporting plan ensures that evaluation is not just possible, but operationalised, turning isolated data points into an ongoing performance narrative. By defining what data is collected, when, by whom, and how it will be reported, you give shape to the measurement process and ensure it aligns with project rhythms and stakeholder needs. The right protocols also protect data integrity, uphold privacy, and prevent reporting from becoming a disconnected afterthought. When data flows with purpose and precision, insights become actionable, and learning earns its place at the table of strategic decision-making.

Instructional Goal Definition

The **Instructional Goal Definition** in the Analysis phase of the ADDIE model is a critical element for establishing the instructional framework.

This step ensures clarity and alignment between the course's purpose and the needs of both learners and stakeholders.

By defining objectives, crafting an engaging course description, and creating a logical progression of content, instructional designers build a solid foundation for successful learning outcomes.

This step serves as a guide for content development, ensuring the instructional materials flow logically and support learners as they progress toward achieving their goals.

Key Sub-Steps are:

- **Define Course Objectives**
  Define what learners should achieve by the end of the course, focusing on measurable and actionable goals.

- **Description of Course**
  Provide a concise yet comprehensive summary of the course's purpose, key topics, and relevance to learners.

- **Behavioural Objectives**
  Define specific actions or behaviours learners should be able to demonstrate upon completing the course, ensuring objectives are observable, measurable, and aligned with overall course goals.

- **Review Existing Materials**
  Evaluate and assess current instructional resources to determine their relevance, accuracy, and alignment with course objectives, identifying areas for improvement or enhancement.

- **Learning Hierarchy**
  Organise the content in a logical sequence, progressing from foundational concepts to advanced skills to ensure a cohesive learning journey.

Overview

Instructional Goal Definition
Plan Data Collection and Reporting Protocols

Outcomes

The outcomes of the **Course Description and Goals** step are to create a roadmap for the course that aligns with learner needs and organisational priorities.

Key outcomes include:

- **Define Clear and Measurable Course Objectives**
  Develop specific learning outcomes that clearly articulate what learners will achieve. Use frameworks like SMART (Specific, Measurable, Achievable, Relevant, Time-bound) for precision and focus.

- **Craft an Engaging and Informative Course Description**
  Write a course summary that highlights its purpose, benefits, and key topics, providing learners with a clear understanding of its relevance and value.

- **Develop a Logical Learning Hierarchy**
  Structure the content to progress in complexity, ensuring each concept builds on the previous one for a seamless and effective learning experience.

- **Align Objectives with Learner and Organisational Needs**
  Ensure that the course's goals meet both the learners' needs and broader organisational objectives, balancing relevance and practicality.

- **Set Expectations for Learning Outcomes and Assessments**
  Clearly communicate what learners will accomplish, how they will be assessed, and what is expected of them throughout the course.

Summary

The **Course Description and Goals** step lays the groundwork for a well-structured, learner-focused instructional design.

By establishing clear objectives, crafting a compelling course description, and organising content in a logical hierarchy, this step ensures both learners and stakeholders are aligned on the course's purpose and expectations.

This step mitigates potential challenges, such as disorganised content or unclear objectives, by providing a structured blueprint for the course.

Learners benefit from understanding what they will achieve and how the course will help them progress, while instructional designers gain clarity in how to structure materials and assessments.

A well-executed **Course Description and Goals** step guarantees a smooth, cohesive learning experience that fosters engagement, comprehension, and satisfaction, laying the foundation for impactful outcomes.

Instructional Goal Definition
Define Course Objectives

Define Course Objectives

 **Why this is important**	Defining course objectives sets the compass for the entire instructional journey. Objectives clarify the intended outcomes for learners, inform assessment design, and guide the choice of instructional strategies and content. They also ensure alignment between learner needs, organisational goals, and measurable outcomes. Poorly defined objectives lead to vague expectations, disengaged learners, and ineffective training.
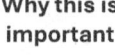 **Tips**	• Use action verbs to define observable and measurable outcomes. • Align each objective with broader organisational or business goals. • Consult SMEs to confirm performance relevance and accuracy. • Keep objectives focused, one idea per objective. • Use Bloom's Taxonomy to scaffold cognitive complexity.
 **Traps**	• Writing objectives that are too broad or vague to assess. • Using passive verbs like "understand" or "be aware of" without qualifiers. • Creating too many objectives, diluting focus and overloading content. • Failing to consider assessment methods during objective formulation. • Writing objectives that are not directly linked to job or performance needs.
 **Techniques**	• **Bloom's Taxonomy**: Framework for creating tiered cognitive objectives. • **SMART criteria**: Ensures objectives are Specific, Measurable, Achievable, Relevant, and Time-bound. • **Backward Design**: Start with desired outcomes and work backwards to content. • **Verb Tables**: Reference lists of observable actions grouped by cognitive level. • **Objective Mapping**: Align objectives with content, activities, and assessments.
 **Examples**	• "Identify three common causes of electrical equipment failure." • "Demonstrate correct lifting technique in accordance with company safety policy." • "Create a basic report using standard data analysis tools." • "Differentiate between active and passive fire control systems." • "List the steps required to initiate a shutdown protocol."

Instructional Goal Definition
Define Course Objectives

How it's done

- **Articulate Desired Outcomes**
  Collaborate with SMEs to identify the key knowledge, skills, and behaviours learners should demonstrate upon course completion. Ensure these outcomes are aligned with the success criteria for the target role or goal.

- **Select Measurable Action Verbs**
  Use clear, action-oriented verbs aligned with Bloom's Taxonomy to define expected learner behaviours. This ensures objectives are precise and measurable.

- **Align Objectives with Identified Needs**
  Review learning needs assessments to validate that each objective addresses a specific need or gap identified during the analysis phase.

- **Define Assessment Criteria**
  Specify how each objective will be evaluated, using measurable criteria such as performance standards, accuracy levels, or specific outcomes. This ensures clarity in expectations and assessment.

- **Seek Stakeholder Feedback**
  Present objectives to SMEs, managers, and other stakeholders for review. Refine the objectives based on their input to ensure they are practical, relevant, and aligned with organisational goals.

- **Organise Objectives Logically**
  Sequence objectives in a progression that supports skill development, building from foundational knowledge to more complex applications.

- **Document Final Objectives**
  Record a comprehensive list of the finalised objectives, including associated criteria. This serves as a guide for course development and instructional planning.

- **Cross-Check with Learner Profiles**
  Verify that objectives are relevant, achievable, and tailored to the needs of the target audience. Adjust objectives as needed to accommodate diverse learner backgrounds and preferences.

Core Elements

- **Course Outcomes Defined**
  Clear and measurable course outcomes are articulated, providing focus for the learning experience.

- **Action Verbs Selected**
  Objectives use precise, action-oriented verbs to specify desired learner behaviours.

- **Objectives Aligned with Needs**
  Learning objectives address the gaps and needs identified during analysis.

- **Measurable Criteria Set**
  Each objective includes specific criteria for assessment or evaluation.

- **Stakeholder Review Completed**
  Objectives are reviewed and refined based on input from SMEs and other stakeholders.

- **Logical Sequence Established**
  Objectives are ordered in a logical progression to support skill development.

- **Objectives Documented**
  A comprehensive list of objectives is recorded to guide instructional planning.

- **Alignment with Learner Profiles**
  Objectives are reviewed to ensure they are achievable and relevant for the target audience.

Instructional Goal Definition
Description of the Course

Checklist

1. Articulate desired knowledge, skills, and behaviours aligned with role outcomes
2. Select measurable, observable action verbs using Bloom's Taxonomy
3. Validate alignment with learning needs and gaps
4. Specify assessment criteria for each objective
5. Seek SME and stakeholder review for practicality and accuracy
6. Organise objectives in logical instructional sequence
7. Finalise and document objectives with clear formatting
8. Cross-check for relevance to learner profiles and diversity

AI Considerations

- Use AI tools to suggest Bloom-aligned action verbs based on course goals
- Generate SMART-formatted versions of draft objectives for review
- Use LLMs to rewrite vague objectives into measurable statements
- Analyse job descriptions to derive task-linked learning outcomes
- Detect duplicated or overlapping objectives across multiple modules

Key Takeaways

Defining course objectives is not a formality, but a foundational act of instructional architecture. Clear, measurable objectives create alignment between learner needs, business outcomes, and instructional design.

They translate learning gaps into teachable outcomes and shape everything downstream, from content development to assessment design.

When built using frameworks like Bloom's Taxonomy and SMART criteria, objectives become more than statements, they become performance contracts.

This sub-step ensures instructional intent is explicit, stakeholder-aligned, and learner-focused, providing a reliable blueprint for course development and meaningful evaluation.

Neglecting this step risks instructional drift, vague expectations, and diminished learning impact.

Description of the Course

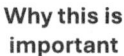

Why this is important

A well-crafted course description lays the foundation for instructional clarity, learner engagement, and overall course coherence. It begins with clearly defining what learners should know or be able to do by the end of the course, these goals and objectives serve as guiding beacons for all design decisions.

Establishing a structured framework of modules, lessons, and topics ensures logical sequencing and flow, helping learners build knowledge progressively.

Identifying core content areas and aligning them tightly with the objectives maintains relevance and focus.

Instructional methods must also be selected thoughtfully to match the learners' needs and the nature of the subject matter.

Equally important is the design of assessment strategies that measure learner progress meaningfully through both formative and summative checkpoints.

Accessibility and inclusivity cannot be afterthoughts, they must be embedded from the start to ensure all learners, regardless of background or ability, can engage fully.

Lastly, aligning the course with the realities of the learning environment, including technical platforms and available resources, helps eliminate barriers and sets the course up for smooth delivery and learner success.

Tips

- **Start with Learning Objectives**
  Use learning objectives as a foundation to shape course content, instructional methods, and assessments.

- **Organise Content for Progression**
  Sequence content from simple to complex to facilitate progressive learning.

- **Consider Audience Needs**
  Tailor content, methods, and assessments based on an understanding of the target audience's preferences, backgrounds, and prior knowledge.

- **Use Diverse Instructional Methods**
  Incorporate varied instructional methods (e.g., discussions, simulations, multimedia) to enhance engagement and support different learning styles.

- **Ensure Accessibility**
  Design the course with accessibility standards in mind, making content available for learners with diverse needs.

Traps

- **Overloading Content**
  Avoid excessive content that can overwhelm learners; focus on essential topics that align with course objectives.

- **Ignoring Audience Analysis**
  Failing to consider the target audience's characteristics and needs can result in misaligned content.

- **Lack of Alignment**
  Ensure that all course elements, content, assessments, instructional methods, are directly aligned with learning objectives.

- **Neglecting Real-World Application**
  If content lacks relevance to real-world situations, learners may struggle to see its value or applicability.

- **Overemphasis on One Instructional Method**
  Relying too heavily on a single method (e.g., lectures) can disengage learners; instead, vary methods to keep learners engaged.

Instructional Goal Definition
Description of the Course

Techniques

- **Content Mapping**
  Create a visual map of the course's main topics, subtopics, and key points to ensure a logical structure and flow.
- **Backward Design**
  Start by defining desired learning outcomes, then develop content and assessments to support those outcomes.
- **Audience Analysis Surveys**
  Use surveys or interviews to understand the target audience's demographics, prior knowledge, and learning preferences.
- **Use of Bloom's Taxonomy**
  Apply Bloom's Taxonomy to develop content and assessments that address various cognitive levels, from basic recall to advanced application.
- **Feedback Loops**
  Implement feedback sessions with stakeholders and SMEs during course development to refine content and strategies.

Examples

- *Course Overview Example*
  A project management course overview might state
  "This course provides learners with foundational skills in project planning, scheduling, and risk management."
- *Course Structure Example*
  A sales training course might be organised into three modules
  'Product Knowledge,' 'Sales Techniques,' and 'Customer Engagement Strategies.'
- *Learning Objectives Example*
  For a safety course
  "Learners will be able to identify workplace hazards and outline appropriate response protocols."
- *Content Outline Example*
  A course on leadership might include topics such as 'Communication Skills,' 'Conflict Resolution,' and 'Decision Making.'
- *Assessment Strategy Example*
  For a coding course, assessment methods might include quizzes on programming concepts, practical coding assignments, and a final project

Instructional Goal Definition
Description of the Course

How it's done

- **Articulate Learning Objectives**
  Collaborate with SMEs and stakeholders to define specific learning objectives and desired competencies. Ensure the objectives align with organisational goals and learner needs.

- **Develop a Course Outline**
  Create a comprehensive outline of course topics and subtopics. Structure the content in a logical sequence to support comprehension and retention, ensuring each topic builds on the previous one.

- **Analyse Learner Needs**
  Understand the characteristics and preferences of the intended audience by conducting surveys, interviews, or focus groups. Evaluate demographics, prior knowledge, and learning preferences to inform course design.

- **Assess the Learning Environment**
  Evaluate the technical and physical environments where the course will be delivered. Ensure delivery platforms, resources, and accessibility features are compatible with the course requirements.

- **Select Instructional Methods**
  Choose methods that suit the learning objectives and audience, such as lectures, simulations, case studies, or discussions. Match delivery methods to content complexity and learner engagement needs.

- **Create Learning Materials**
  Develop or curate resources such as multimedia, handouts, case studies, and assessments. Ensure all materials align with the course objectives and enhance learning.

- **Plan Assessments**
  Design formative and summative assessments, including quizzes, exams, projects, or performance tasks. These assessments should effectively measure learner progress and provide actionable feedback.

- **Organise Course Structure**
  Divide the course into modules or units, creating a roadmap that progressively guides learners through the content. Ensure the structure is clear and promotes logical skill development.

- **Check Alignment**
  Review all course components, including objectives, content, instructional methods, and assessments, to confirm alignment with the intended learning outcomes. Make adjustments as needed.

- **Evaluate the Course Description**
  Ensure the course description accurately reflects its objectives, structure, and content. Solicit feedback from SMEs and stakeholders, incorporating their insights into the final version.

Instructional Goal Definition
Description of the Course

Core Elements	• **Course Goals Defined** Specific learning objectives are established to guide the course. • **Content Outline Created** A comprehensive outline includes topics, subtopics, and supporting materials. • **Audience Analysed** Learner characteristics, needs, and preferences are evaluated. • **Learning Environment Assessed** Delivery platforms and resources are confirmed to support the course. • **Instructional Methods Selected** Methods chosen are tailored to objectives and audience needs. • **Learning Materials Developed** Resources are aligned with content and learning objectives. • **Assessment Strategies Designed** Formative and summative assessments are planned to evaluate learner progress. • **Course Structure Established** Modules or units are clearly organised to provide a logical progression. • **Alignment Checked** Objectives, content, methods, and assessments are reviewed for coherence. • **Stakeholder Review Completed** Feedback from SMEs and stakeholders is incorporated into the final course design.
Checklist	1. Clearly communicates course purpose and audience 2. Summarises format, outcomes, and key features 3. Uses tone appropriate to learner context 4. Avoids internal jargon or unexplained acronyms 5. Fits within LMS or catalogue character limits 6. Reviewed by neutral party for clarity and engagement 7. Reflects finalised scope and learning objectives 8. Updated to match current content version and delivery model
 **AI Considerations**	• Generate first-pass course descriptions using GPT-based tools • Use tone-checkers to shift between formal and conversational language • Apply keyword enhancement for SEO and catalogue relevance • Use AI personas to simulate learner expectations and reactions • Scan and compare peer course listings for uniqueness
 **Key Takeaways**	A well-structured course description is more than a summary; it's a strategic foundation that aligns learning intent with delivery. This sub-step consolidates learning objectives, instructional strategies, content structure, and assessment plans into a unified blueprint. It ensures every component, from course flow to learner engagement, is logically sequenced, pedagogically sound, and aligned with both learner profiles and organisational outcomes. By integrating backward design, audience insights, and stakeholder validation, the course description becomes a central reference point for development and communication. Done well, it improves clarity, consistency, and learner readiness, anchoring the course in purpose, precision, and real-world relevance.

Behavioural Objectives

Why this is important

Defining clear behavioral objectives is essential for shaping effective, measurable, and outcomes-driven learning experiences.

These objectives articulate the specific performance or behavioral changes learners are expected to demonstrate upon course completion, making the intended learning outcomes explicit for both designers and participants.

By establishing measurable criteria, each objective becomes observable and assessable, enabling accurate evaluation of learner progress.

Effective behavioral objectives are anchored in the findings of the learning needs assessment and task analysis, ensuring that instruction targets real gaps in knowledge, skills, or attitudes.

When grounded in real-world application, these objectives help learners transfer new skills directly into their roles, improving job performance.

Action-oriented language using strong verbs enhances clarity and ensures the focus remains on what learners will *do*, not just what they will *know*.

Incorporating objectives across cognitive, affective, and psychomotor domains creates a holistic learning experience, while prioritising them in a logical sequence supports a structured progression from foundational understanding to advanced competence.

Tips

- **Choose Clear Action Verbs**
  Use precise verbs like "analyse," "demonstrate," "apply," and "evaluate" to avoid ambiguity in learner expectations.

- **Align with Real Tasks**
  Design objectives that mirror actual tasks learners will perform in their roles, ensuring relevance and application.

- **Define Success Criteria**
  Specify conditions and success criteria for each objective to provide clear performance benchmarks.

- **Involve Stakeholders in Review**
  Involve subject matter experts and stakeholders in reviewing objectives for accuracy and relevance.

- **Be Adaptable**
  Keep objectives flexible enough to accommodate diverse learning environments, backgrounds, and learning styles.

Traps

- **Vague Objectives**
  Avoid using broad terms that lack clarity and specificity, such as "understand" or "learn," which are difficult to measure.

- **Misalignment with Learning Needs**
  Ensure objectives address the actual needs and gaps identified during the needs assessment and task analysis.

- **Ignoring Real-World Relevance**
  Objectives that lack practical application may disengage learners and reduce learning effectiveness.

- **Overcomplicating Hierarchy**
  Organising objectives hierarchically is important but avoid creating unnecessary complexity that could confuse learners.

- **Neglecting Affective Domain**
  Focusing solely on cognitive skills can overlook the importance of attitudes and motivation, especially in fields where these are critical.

Instructional Goal Definition
Behavioural Objectives

Techniques

- **Use Bloom's Taxonomy**
  Apply Bloom's taxonomy to ensure a range of cognitive, affective, and psychomotor objectives, covering all learning dimensions.
- **SMART Criteria**
  Use the SMART framework (Specific, Measurable, Achievable, Relevant, Time-bound) to define objectives that are clear and actionable.
- **Action Verb Lists**
  Refer to a list of action verbs to accurately describe desired learner behaviours and avoid ambiguity.
- **Hierarchy Mapping**
  Create a hierarchy map to organise objectives based on complexity, moving from basic skills to advanced applications.
- **Stakeholder Feedback Sessions**
  Host feedback sessions with stakeholders to validate and refine objectives, ensuring alignment and relevance.

Examples

- *Learning Outcomes Clarity*
  Learners will be able to "analyse data trends to make informed decisions in a business context."
- *Measurable Criteria*
  "Demonstrate ability to troubleshoot technical issues with 90% accuracy within a simulated environment."
- *Real-World Application*
  Learners will "apply customer service principles to resolve client issues effectively during live role-playing scenarios."
- *Action-Oriented Language*
  "Evaluate case studies," "demonstrate problem-solving techniques," "apply negotiation strategies."
- *Hierarchical Objectives*
  - **Basic Level**
    Identify key components of the software interface.
  - **Intermediate Level**
    Demonstrate use of software features to perform tasks.
  - **Advanced Level**
    Analyse software data to optimise workflow processes.

Instructional Goal Definition
Behavioural Objectives

How Its Done

- **Review Findings from Learning Needs Assessment and Task Analysis**
  Examine insights from previous assessments to identify specific gaps in learner knowledge, skills, and performance. Clarify which behavioural objectives are essential for addressing these identified needs.

- **Identify Target Audience**
  Define the characteristics, prior knowledge, and skill levels of the target learners. Tailor behavioural objectives to align with their backgrounds and abilities.

- **Define Learning Outcomes**
  Articulate specific learning outcomes using action-oriented language that specifies observable behaviours. These outcomes address desired behavioural changes or improvements.

- **Select Action Verbs**
  Choose precise and measurable action verbs, such as "analyse," "apply," and "demonstrate," to clearly define expected learner actions.

- **Specify Conditions and Criteria**
  Define the performance conditions under which learners demonstrate behaviours and establish the assessment criteria and standards for success.

- **Organise Objectives Hierarchically**
  Arrange objectives in a logical sequence, progressing from foundational skills to more complex applications. This guides learners through skill mastery effectively.

- **Ensure Alignment with Learning Goals**
  Confirm that all behavioural objectives align with broader course and learning goals to maintain cohesion and focus.

- **Review and Refine**
  Seek feedback from stakeholders, including SMEs and educators, to ensure objectives are accurate, relevant, and achievable. Refine them based on input received.

- **Document Behavioural Objectives**
  Compile a comprehensive list of behavioural objectives, detailing action verbs, conditions, criteria, and hierarchical organisation for reference and instructional design.

Core Elements

- **Learning Outcomes Defined**
  Behavioural objectives are clearly stated, addressing specific performance improvements.

- **Action Verbs Selected**
  Objectives use action-oriented verbs (e.g., analyse, demonstrate) to specify behaviours.

- **Measurable Criteria Established**
  Each objective includes measurable indicators to assess learner performance.

- **Conditions Specified**
  Context and criteria for successful behaviour demonstration are defined.

- **Hierarchical Organisation Created**
  Objectives are organised by complexity, progressing from foundational to advanced skills.

- **Alignment with Learning Goals Confirmed**
  Objectives align with the overall course or programme goals.

- **Stakeholder Feedback Collected**
  Feedback from relevant stakeholders is incorporated into the objectives.

- **Behavioural Objectives Documented**
  A complete list of finalised objectives is documented for reference.

Instructional Goal Definition
Behavioural Objectives

Checklist

- Verbs are specific, observable, and assessable
- Each objective includes context or performance conditions
- Criteria for successful performance are clearly stated
- Objectives align with on-the-job tasks and behaviours
- Avoids non-measurable terms like "understand" or "appreciate"
- Objectives are discrete, not compound
- Validated by SMEs and reviewed for relevance
- Structured to support assessment design

AI Considerations

- Rewrite weak or vague objectives into clear, measurable form
- Identify gaps or redundancies across learning objectives
- Suggest performance conditions or success criteria for each behaviour
- Use job-role data or competency frameworks to auto-generate starter objectives
- Align objectives with assessment questions using AI tagging

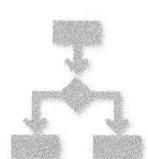
Key Takeaways

Behavioural objectives are the precision tools of instructional design, they translate broad intentions into observable, assessable learner actions.

This sub-step transforms learning needs into concrete, measurable statements that define what learners must do to demonstrate mastery.

By integrating Bloom's Taxonomy, SMART principles, and stakeholder validation, instructional designers ensure that objectives are relevant, achievable, and performance-focused.

Structured hierarchically, behavioural objectives support logical skill progression and allow for targeted assessment design.

Done well, they eliminate ambiguity, drive instructional clarity, and anchor the entire course in real-world application and measurable success.

Review Existing Materials

Why this is important

Reviewing existing materials is a critical step that ensures instructional design efforts build on what already works, rather than reinventing the wheel.

It begins with evaluating the relevance and accuracy of available content in relation to the defined learning objectives and learner needs.

This review helps identify where current materials align well and where there are gaps that require new development.

Assessing quality through the lens of instructional design principles, such as clarity, learner engagement, and usability, provides insights into what can be retained, revised, or discarded.

Optimising the use of existing resources can save time and reduce duplication of effort, allowing the project team to focus efforts strategically.

Gathering feedback from stakeholders adds another layer of insight, highlighting strengths and pointing to improvement opportunities.

Legal and ethical compliance is also paramount, ensuring that all materials meet accessibility standards and respect copyright obligations.

Finally, documenting the outcomes of this review offers a clear roadmap for content development and supports informed decision-making throughout the design process.

Tips

- **Involve Key Stakeholders Early**
  Engage subject matter experts, instructors, and learners in the review process for a well-rounded perspective.
- **Use a Consistent Evaluation Framework**
  Apply a consistent set of criteria for evaluating content, design, and technology to ensure thoroughness and objectivity.
- **Prioritise Gap Identification**
  Focus on gaps that directly impact learning outcomes, as these will guide necessary updates.
- **Document Legal Considerations**
  Keep clear records of any permissions or restrictions related to copyright or intellectual property for future reference.
- **Encourage Open Feedback**
  Create an environment where stakeholders feel comfortable sharing honest feedback about the existing materials.

Traps

- **Overlooking Stakeholder Feedback**
  Ignoring feedback from key stakeholders can lead to overlooking critical issues or areas for improvement.
- **Failing to Assess Quality Thoroughly**
  Rushing through quality evaluation may result in retaining outdated or ineffective materials.
- **Ignoring Alignment Issues**
  Not ensuring alignment with current learning objectives and instructional goals can lead to irrelevant or unhelpful content.
- **Neglecting Legal and Ethical Review**
  Overlooking compliance can result in copyright or accessibility violations, affecting the course's credibility and inclusivity.
- **Over-reliance on Existing Content**
  Using old materials without critical evaluation may lead to outdated or irrelevant information that weakens the instructional quality.

Instructional Goal Definition
Review Existing Materials

Techniques

- **SWOT Analysis**
  Use a Strengths, Weaknesses, Opportunities, and Threats framework to evaluate the current materials in relation to instructional goals. This helps surface both what works and what may need revision or removal.

- **Stakeholder Feedback Surveys**
  Distribute structured surveys or conduct interviews with SMEs, instructors, and learners to gather qualitative insights on clarity, engagement, usability, and content gaps.

- **Content Mapping**
  Create a visual content map that aligns existing materials to specific learning objectives or competency areas. This makes it easier to identify overlaps, redundancies, and missing pieces.

- **Instructional Quality Rubric**
  Apply a detailed rubric to assess materials across dimensions such as instructional clarity, learner engagement, visual design, accuracy, and alignment to adult learning principles.

- **Legal and Ethical Compliance Checklist**
  Review each material against copyright permissions, accessibility standards (e.g., WCAG), and cultural sensitivity guidelines to ensure ethical and inclusive use.

- **Version Control and Metadata Tagging**
  Track document versions and use metadata tagging (e.g., topic, media type, date created) to manage content libraries efficiently and streamline future audits or reuse efforts.

- **AI-Assisted Content Review**
  Use natural language processing (NLP) tools to extract topics, scan for redundancy, assess tone and complexity, and identify alignment with learning outcomes.

Examples

- *Content Review*
  Reviewing an onboarding manual to determine if it accurately reflects current company policies and procedures.

- *Alignment Assessment*
  Assessing existing safety training materials to ensure they meet updated regulatory standards.

- *Gap Identification*
  Discovering that existing customer service training lacks sections on handling digital inquiries, a critical skill in the current role.

- *Feedback Incorporation*
  Incorporating feedback from a learner survey showing that the current material is too text-heavy and lacks engagement.

- *Legal Compliance*
  Ensuring that an eBook used in training is accessible to learners with disabilities, including those requiring screen readers

Instructional Goal Definition
Review Existing Materials

How it's done

- **Gather Existing Materials**
  Collect all relevant instructional materials, including documents, presentations, videos, manuals, and other past training resources. Ensure all potentially useful resources are included in the review.
- **Evaluate Content**
  Assess the relevance, accuracy, and completeness of the materials to confirm alignment with the identified learning objectives. Focus on whether the content meets current educational needs.
- **Analyse Instructional Design**
  Examine the structure, clarity, and engagement of the materials. Review the effectiveness of instructional strategies used and their alignment with the desired learning outcomes.
- **Conduct a Technological Review**
  Evaluate the usability, accessibility, compatibility, and functionality of platforms or tools used in the materials. Ensure that technological components support learner needs effectively.
- **Collect Stakeholder Feedback**
  Engage learners, SMEs, and instructors through surveys, interviews, or focus groups. Use their insights to inform the evaluation and identify areas for improvement.
- **Identify Gaps**
  Compare the existing content with the current learning needs to identify missing or inadequate content and instructional design elements requiring improvement.
- **Check Legal and Ethical Compliance**
  Verify that materials adhere to copyright laws, intellectual property standards, accessibility requirements, and cultural sensitivity guidelines. Ensure compliance with organisational policies.
- **Document Findings and Recommendations**
  Compile a detailed report outlining the strengths, weaknesses, and actionable recommendations for improving the materials. Include supporting evidence from the review process.
- **Suggest Revisions or Enhancements**
  Provide specific recommendations to revise or enhance the instructional materials. Suggestions should focus on improving relevance, engagement, and quality.
- **Present to Stakeholders**
  Organise a meeting or presentation to share findings and recommendations. Collaborate with stakeholders to discuss the proposed enhancements and agree on next steps.

Core Elements

- **Materials Collected**
  All relevant instructional resources are compiled for review.
- **Content Evaluated**
  Existing content is assessed for relevance, accuracy, and completeness.
- **Instructional Design Analysed**
  The structure, clarity, and engagement of materials are reviewed.
- **Technological Review Completed**
  Usability, accessibility, and compatibility of platforms and tools are verified.
- **Stakeholder Feedback Collected**
  Feedback from SMEs, learners, and instructors is documented.
- **Gaps Identified**
  Areas requiring content or design improvements are highlighted.
- **Legal and Ethical Compliance Verified**
  Copyright, accessibility, and cultural sensitivity are checked.
- **Findings Documented**
  Results and actionable recommendations are summarised in a report.
- **Recommendations Provided**
  Specific suggestions for revisions or enhancements are outlined.
- **Presentation to Stakeholders Scheduled**
  Findings and proposed improvements are prepared for stakeholder review.

Instructional Goal Definition
Review Existing Materials

Checklist

1. All available content sources have been gathered and catalogued
2. Assets reviewed for accuracy, relevance, and instructional value
3. Evaluated against learning objectives and current needs
4. Reuse/revise/retire decisions clearly documented
5. SME validation performed on retained materials
6. Gaps identified for new content development
7. Audio/video content assessed for production quality and currency
8. Organised in a central, accessible repository

AI Considerations

- Use AI to scan content libraries for duplicates or overlaps
- NLP to extract key topics and align to objectives
- Auto-classify materials by relevance and media type
- Compare multiple versions of documents to detect changes
- Transcribe audio/video content for searchable review

Key Takeaways

Reviewing existing materials is a critical filtering step that separates what should be retained, revised, or retired.

It ensures instructional content is accurate, up to date, instructionally sound, and aligned with current learning needs and business priorities.

This sub-step avoids redundant effort, uncovers usable assets, and flags critical content or design gaps that must be addressed in development.

By applying structured techniques, such as content mapping, stakeholder feedback, and legal compliance checks, designers ensure resources are pedagogically effective, ethically compliant, and performance-relevant.

A well-executed review lays the groundwork for efficient design decisions and maximises the value of existing investments.

Learning Hierarchy

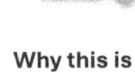

Why this is important

Establishing a well-defined learning hierarchy is essential for creating a structured, logical, and effective learning experience.

It begins with identifying the prerequisite knowledge or skills learners need in order to engage meaningfully with course content.

By sequencing learning objectives from simple to complex, the course design promotes a natural progression that supports cognitive development and long-term retention.

Each layer of the hierarchy must align with the overarching course goals to ensure that every step contributes to the desired outcomes.

Mapping this progression helps learners build on foundational concepts before tackling more advanced material, fostering deeper understanding and application.

Taking into account learner characteristics, such as prior knowledge, skill levels, and learning preferences, further refines the sequencing and makes the learning journey more accessible and relevant.

Finally, the learning hierarchy should be continuously reviewed and adjusted based on feedback from stakeholders, subject matter experts, and pilot testing, ensuring that it remains responsive to learner needs and instructional effectiveness.

Tips

- **Start with Basic Concepts**
  Ensure learners master foundational skills before advancing to complex topics.
- **Use Bloom's Taxonomy as a Guide**
  Progress from knowledge and comprehension to application, analysis, and synthesis to support cognitive development.
- **Consider Cognitive Load**
  Break down complex tasks and introduce them gradually to prevent learner overwhelm.
- **Align Content and Objectives**
  Ensure each topic and activity directly contributes to achieving the learning objectives.
- **Iterate and Refine**
  Regularly review and adjust the learning hierarchy based on pilot feedback and stakeholder input.

Traps

- **Overlooking Prerequisites**
  Failing to identify necessary prerequisites can create gaps in learners' understanding, making advanced concepts harder to grasp.
- **Ignoring Logical Progression**
  Presenting content out of sequence can confuse learners and hinder the development of deeper understanding.
- **Overloading Learners with Complexity**
  Introducing complex skills too early may overwhelm learners and reduce retention.
- **Disregarding Learner Diversity**
  Not considering different skill levels and backgrounds can lead to gaps or irrelevant instruction for some learners.
- **Neglecting Feedback**
  Ignoring feedback from stakeholders and SMEs may result in an ineffective or poorly structured learning hierarchy.

Instructional Goal Definition
Learning Hierarchy

Techniques

- **Content Mapping**
  Create a visual map that links each learning objective and topic to ensure a logical, progressive flow.
- **Backward Design**
  Start with the end goals and work backward to sequence objectives and topics effectively.
- **Learning Pathways**
  Develop pathways based on learner skill levels or areas of specialisation to address diverse learning needs.
- **Stakeholder Review Sessions**
  Conduct sessions with SMEs and stakeholders to review the learning hierarchy for logical progression and relevance.
- **Progressive Scaffolding**
  Build complexity gradually by providing scaffolding in early stages and reducing support as learners progress.

Examples

- *Prerequisites*
  For a digital marketing course, prerequisite skills might include basic computer literacy and understanding of internet usage.
- *Sequenced Objectives*
  In a coding course, the hierarchy might start with 'Basic Syntax' before advancing to 'Control Structures' and then to 'Functions and Loops.'
- *Alignment with Course Goals*
  In a safety training course, the learning hierarchy might progress from recognising hazards to implementing risk mitigation strategies.
- *Mapped Learning Activities*
  For an advanced project management topic, activities could include initial concept discussions, followed by hands-on case studies and simulations.
- *Refinement Based on Feedback*
  After pilot testing, an introductory data analysis course may need to adjust the pacing of advanced statistical concepts based on learner feedback.

Instructional Goal Definition
Learning Hierarchy

How it's done

- **Gather and Assess Materials**
  Collect and evaluate existing instructional materials to understand the scope, content, and hierarchical structure. This provides a foundation for designing a logical progression of learning objectives.

- **Define Learning Goals and Objectives**
  Collaborate with SMEs and stakeholders to outline the course's overall learning goals and specific objectives. Clearly articulate desired outcomes to guide the learning hierarchy.

- **Break Down Objectives into Subtopics**
  Identify domains or subtopics within the objectives, outlining relationships and prerequisites. Organise the content so that learners progress logically from foundational to more complex concepts.

- **Sequence Learning Objectives**
  Arrange objectives in a structured and progressive order, considering cognitive load and the appropriate learning pace. Ensure that each step builds on prior knowledge for effective skill development.

- **Plan Supporting Activities**
  Design learning activities tailored to each objective. Match instructional strategies, such as lectures, discussions, or simulations, to the complexity and purpose of each objective.

- **Select Instructional Methods**
  Choose methods that align with the hierarchical progression, using varied approaches like hands-on activities, multimedia, or case studies. Tailor methods to the needs of each level and the audience.

- **Evaluate Learner Needs**
  Conduct surveys or assessments to understand the prior knowledge, skill levels, and potential barriers of the target audience. Incorporate these insights to ensure accessibility and relevance.

- **Refine the Hierarchy**
  Present the learning structure to SMEs, stakeholders, and pilot groups. Use their feedback to iterate and improve the organisation, ensuring it meets learning goals effectively.

Core Elements

- **Prerequisites Identified**
  Foundational skills or knowledge for course progression are established.

- **Learning Objectives Sequenced**
  Objectives are ordered logically, progressing from simple to complex.

- **Content Alignment Verified**
  Course content supports and aligns with each learning objective.

- **Learning Pathways Mapped**
  A clear content flow allows learners to build on previous knowledge seamlessly.

- **Activities and Methods Mapped**
  Instructional methods and activities are matched to each hierarchical level.

- **Learner Needs Addressed**
  Characteristics and needs of the target audience are considered in the hierarchy.

- **Feedback Incorporated**
  Stakeholder and SME input is used to refine the learning structure.

- **Documented for Reference**
  The hierarchical structure, objectives, and sequence are recorded for instructional planning.

Instructional Goal Definition
Learning Hierarchy

Checklist

1. Prerequisites identified for each skill or concept
2. Content sequenced from basic to advanced logic
3. Similar concepts clustered to support cognitive flow
4. Validated by SMEs for job-task alignment
5. Visual hierarchy or learning map created
6. Sequence aligns with learner capability and pace
7. Updated during development to reflect design evolution
8. Dependencies or prerequisites documented

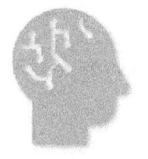
AI Considerations

- Generate concept maps or dependency diagrams from topic lists
- Suggest optimal instructional flow based on learner profiles
- Analyse sequencing in existing materials for logic gaps
- Use AI tutors to simulate learner pathways through the hierarchy
- Identify prerequisite concepts using semantic analysis

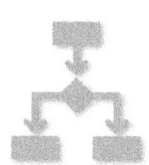
Key Takeaways

The learning hierarchy transforms a list of objectives into a coherent, progressive journey, enabling learners to move from foundational understanding to advanced application with confidence.

This sub-step defines prerequisite knowledge, sequences learning experiences, and aligns instructional strategies with learner capability and cognitive load.

By integrating audience analysis, backward design, and stakeholder validation, it ensures that the instructional flow is both logical and learner-centric.

A well-structured hierarchy scaffolds mastery, minimises confusion, and accelerates learning impact, providing a strategic blueprint that underpins content design, activity planning, and assessment alignment.

Learner and Needs Analysis

Overview

The **Learner and Needs Analysis** step in the Analysis phase of the ADDIE model is pivotal for designing learner-centred, effective instruction.

This stage ensures a deep understanding of the learners' characteristics, motivations, and challenges, as well as the specific learning needs required to achieve the desired outcomes.

By bridging the gap between the learners' current state and the intended goals, this step enables the creation of targeted, impactful content.

Key Sub-Steps are:

- **Develop Learner Profile**
  Collect demographic and psychographic data, including age, cultural influences, prior knowledge, and motivations, to create a detailed picture of the learners.
- **Conduct Learning Needs Analysis**
  Identify gaps between current and desired knowledge, skills, or behaviours, focusing on areas that require development.

Outcomes

The outcomes of the Learner and Needs Analysis step ensure the instructional design aligns with learner needs and objectives.

Key Outcomes include:

- **Understand Learner Demographics and Psychographics**
  Gather comprehensive information about learners' backgrounds, prior experiences, motivations, and potential barriers to learning.
  Create a holistic profile that informs design decisions.
- **Identify Learning Gaps and Needs**
  Analyse the difference between the learners' current knowledge, skills, or behaviours and the desired outcomes.
  Pinpoint areas requiring development to focus instructional efforts.
- **Define Clear, Measurable Behavioural Objectives**
  Develop specific, observable goals that learners should achieve, providing a framework for instructional content and assessment.
- **Align Instruction with Learner Needs**
  Ensure learning objectives and instructional content directly address identified gaps, making the course relevant and effective.
- **Prepare for Customised Instructional Approaches**
  Use data from the learner profile and needs analysis to select strategies and methods that resonate with the audience, fostering engagement and retention.

Summary

The **Learner and Needs Analysis** step is fundamental to creating impactful instructional design by ensuring the course is relevant, targeted, and learner focused.

By developing detailed learner profiles, identifying gaps between current and desired states, and defining behavioural objectives, instructional designers can lay the groundwork for content that is engaging, effective, and actionable.

A structured and thorough approach during this step avoids common pitfalls like misaligned content or ineffective strategies.

It provides a clear roadmap for the instructional design process, ensuring the course meets learners' needs and achieves its intended outcomes. This step is not just a foundation but a guidepost for creating a meaningful and transformative learning experience.

Learner and Needs Analysis
Develop Learner Profile

Develop Learner Profile

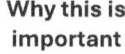

Why this is important

Developing a detailed learner profile is foundational to designing instruction that truly resonates with the target audience.

It starts with clearly defining who the learners are, their age, education level, job roles, cultural background, and other demographic factors that influence how they engage with learning.

Understanding their specific needs, preferences, motivations, and prior knowledge allows for the creation of instructional experiences that are both relevant and impactful.

These insights directly inform the choice of content formats, instructional strategies, and assessment methods, enabling designers to tailor learning in ways that feel personalised and purposeful.

A robust learner profile also promotes engagement by aligning content with what matters most to learners, while ensuring that diverse needs, including accessibility and cultural considerations, are respected and addressed.

Ultimately, the learner profile guides content development, helping to shape a course that is inclusive, focused, and fit for purpose.

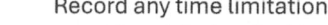

Tips

- **Use Multiple Data Sources**
  Gather learner information through a variety of methods (surveys, interviews, pre-assessments) to build a comprehensive profile.

- **Assess Learning Styles Early**
  Understand learners' preferred ways of engaging with content to tailor delivery formats and instructional techniques.

- **Account for Diversity**
  Consider cultural and linguistic backgrounds to make content inclusive and relevant for all learners.

- **Capture Motivational Drivers**
  Understanding what motivates learners can enhance engagement and completion rates.

- **Document Constraints**
  Record any time limitations, accessibility needs, or environmental preferences to ensure these factors are considered during design.

Traps

- **Overgeneralising Learner Characteristics**
  Avoid making assumptions based on superficial demographic data; drill down into specifics of motivations, goals, and learning preferences.

- **Ignoring Prior Knowledge**
  Neglecting to consider learners' existing knowledge can result in content that is too advanced or too basic.

- **Failing to Address Constraints**
  Ignoring constraints such as time availability or learning environments can negatively impact engagement and completion.

- **Overlooking Cultural Sensitivity**
  Not considering cultural backgrounds can lead to instructional materials that may feel alienating or irrelevant to certain learners.

- **Not Revisiting Learner Profiles**
  Learner profiles should be updated periodically, especially for long-term or evolving projects.

Learner and Needs Analysis
Develop Learner Profile

Techniques

- **Surveys and Questionnaires**
  Use surveys to gather demographic data, learning preferences, and motivational factors from a large group of learners.
- **Interviews and Focus Groups**
  Conduct interviews or focus groups for in-depth insights into learners' backgrounds, goals, and learning preferences.
- **Learning Style Assessments**
  Employ standardised learning style assessments to identify whether learners prefer visual, auditory, kinaesthetic, or multimodal approaches.
- **Pre-assessment Tests**
  Use pre-assessments to gauge learners' prior knowledge and experience with the subject matter.
- **Cultural and Linguistic Analysis**
  Analyse cultural and linguistic backgrounds to ensure content aligns with diverse learner contexts and is inclusive.

Examples

- *Demographics*
  Learners aged 25-35, with a college degree, predominantly working professionals looking to advance in their careers.
- *Learning Styles*
  60% visual, 20% auditory, 20% kinaesthetic learners identified through learning style assessments.
- *Prior Knowledge*
  Most learners have a basic understanding of the subject, with gaps in advanced concepts and practical applications.
- *Motivation*
  Learners are motivated by career progression and the desire to apply new skills in their current roles.
- *Preferences and Constraints*
  Many learners prefer mobile-friendly content due to time constraints and frequent travel for work.

Learner and Needs Analysis
Develop Learner Profile

How it's done

- **Collect Demographic Information**
  Gather data on age, gender, education, occupation, and other relevant demographics using surveys, interviews, or existing records. This provides foundational insights into the learner group.

- **Assess Learning Styles**
  Determine learners' preferred learning styles, such as visual, auditory, or kinaesthetic, using assessments or questionnaires. Understanding these preferences supports effective instructional design.

- **Evaluate Prior Knowledge and Experience**
  Use pre-assessments or interviews to gauge learners' existing knowledge and skills related to the course subject. This ensures content builds appropriately on their current level.

- **Explore Motivations and Goals**
  Identify learners' motivations for participating in the course and their specific objectives through surveys or focus groups. This information helps align course content with learner expectations.

- **Identify Preferences and Constraints**
  Document learners' preferences, such as preferred learning environments, and constraints, such as time limitations or accessibility requirements. Use surveys and interviews to gather this data.

- **Consider Cultural and Linguistic Background**
  Collect information on cultural and linguistic factors to ensure course content is inclusive, relevant, and accessible to a diverse audience.

- **Compile Learner Profile**
  Organise all collected data into a comprehensive profile that includes demographics, learning styles, prior knowledge, motivations, preferences, and cultural backgrounds. This serves as a detailed reference for course design.

- **Analyse Learner Profile**
  Review the compiled learner profile for patterns, trends, and common characteristics. Use this analysis to guide instructional design decisions and create a learner-centred course.

Core Elements

- **Demographics Collected**
  Relevant demographic information, such as age, gender, and education, is gathered.

- **Learning Styles Identified**
  Preferred learning styles are assessed using surveys or questionnaires.

- **Prior Knowledge Evaluated**
  Existing knowledge and skills are measured to inform course design.

- **Motivations and Goals Explored**
  Learners' motivations and objectives are identified and documented.

- **Preferences and Constraints Documented**
  Preferences and constraints, such as time or accessibility needs, are recorded.

- **Cultural and Linguistic Background Considered**
  Content inclusivity and relevance are ensured by accounting for cultural and linguistic factors.

- **Learner Profile Compiled**
  All collected data is consolidated into a comprehensive learner profile document.

- **Learner Profile Analysed**
  Trends and patterns are reviewed to guide instructional design decisions.

Learner and Needs Analysis
Develop Learner Profile

 **Checklist**	1. Gather demographic data (e.g., age, education, language proficiency, job role) 2. Identify learner roles and map them to course relevance 3. Assess prior knowledge, skill level, and experience range 4. Determine preferred learning styles or modalities where appropriate 5. Explore motivation drivers and possible engagement challenges 6. Identify constraints (e.g., time, access to technology, reading level) 7. Create representative learner personas or profiles 8. Validate profiles with SME or HR to ensure accuracy and realism
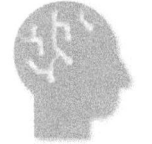 **AI Considerations**	• Use AI clustering tools to segment learners into persona groups • Extract learner traits and preferences from past training analytics • NLP tools can summarise survey and interview inputs into persona drafts • Simulate learner responses to content using AI-based personas • AI can generate empathy maps and scenario profiles to guide design
 **Key Takeaways**	A well-developed learner profile is the cornerstone of learner-centred design. It captures the realities of who the learners are, not just demographically, but cognitively, motivationally, and contextually. This sub-step ensures that instructional design decisions are grounded in real-world data, not assumptions. By understanding learner backgrounds, styles, goals, and constraints, designers can craft experiences that resonate, engage, and deliver measurable outcomes. Tools like surveys, interviews, pre-assessments, and AI-driven analytics help surface actionable insights that shape content relevance, accessibility, and tone. A thoughtful learner profile doesn't just guide course development, it elevates it, turning content into connection and design into impact.

Learner and Needs Analysis
Conduct Learning Needs Analysis

Conduct Learning Needs Analysis

Why this is important

Conducting a learning needs analysis is critical to ensuring that instructional solutions are purposeful, targeted, and aligned with both learner development and organisational priorities. It begins with the clear definition of learning objectives that support strategic business outcomes and desired performance standards.

By assessing the current competencies of the target audience, instructional designers can establish a baseline to compare against expected performance.

This comparison reveals performance gaps, areas where learning interventions can make the greatest impact. Prioritising these gaps helps allocate resources effectively and ensures that training efforts are focused where they are truly needed.

A thorough analysis also explores the root causes behind these gaps, whether they stem from knowledge deficits, environmental barriers, or organisational constraints.

Aligning the findings with broader business goals reinforces the strategic value of the learning initiative, while consideration of learner preferences ensures that the learning experience is not only relevant but also engaging and effective.

Tips

- **Involve Stakeholders Early**
  Engaging managers, SMEs, and learners early ensures alignment with organisational priorities and adds valuable insights.
- **Use Mixed Data Collection Methods**
  Combining surveys, interviews, and observations offers a well-rounded perspective on learning needs.
- **Focus on Root Causes**
  Look beyond symptoms to identify underlying issues affecting performance; this helps in designing more effective solutions.
- **Prioritise Needs**
  Address high-impact learning needs first to maximise the training programme's organisational value.
- **Document and Review Regularly**
  Document the LNA process and review it periodically to adjust to changes in organisational needs.

Traps

- **Overlooking Stakeholder Input**
  Neglecting key stakeholders can lead to misaligned objectives and diminished support for the programme.
- **Ignoring Root Causes**
  Addressing only the symptoms of performance issues, rather than root causes, may lead to ineffective learning interventions.
- **Relying Solely on Quantitative Data**
  Quantitative data is valuable but often lacks context; qualitative data adds depth and helps interpret numbers meaningfully.
- **Failing to Align with Business Goals**
  Not linking learning needs to organisational objectives can result in a lack of support or funding for the initiative.
- **Underestimating Continuous Improvement**
  An LNA should be revisited regularly, as business needs and job roles evolve over time.

Learner and Needs Analysis
Conduct Learning Needs Analysis

Techniques

- **Surveys and Questionnaires**
  Use structured surveys to gather quantitative data on current competencies, learning preferences, and self-assessed skill gaps.
- **Interviews and Focus Groups**
  Conduct interviews or focus groups with stakeholders and learners to gather qualitative insights and context.
- **Root Cause Analysis Tools**
  Use tools like the "5 Whys" or Fishbone Diagrams to drill down into the root causes of performance gaps.
- **Performance Reviews and Job Analysis**
  Analyse job descriptions, performance reviews, and task analyses to understand the demands of each role.
- **SWOT Analysis**
  Conduct a SWOT (Strengths, Weaknesses, Opportunities, Threats) analysis to understand organisational factors impacting learning needs.

Examples

- *Learning Objectives*
  Develop a learning programme to improve problem-solving skills among mid-level managers, with clear objectives tied to real-world applications.
- *Current Competencies*
  Sales team members have strong communication skills but show gaps in product knowledge and technical skills.
- *Performance Gaps*
  Frontline customer service agents lack proficiency in using new software, impacting response times and customer satisfaction.
- *Root Causes*
  Identified issues include limited software training, high turnover in technical support, and outdated resources.
- *Training Needs*
  Conduct a two-day intensive workshop on software skills for customer service agents and provide ongoing support through an online help centre.

Learner and Needs Analysis
Conduct Learning Needs Analysis

How it's done

- **Stakeholder Engagement**
  Identify key stakeholders, including managers, SMEs, HR personnel, and employees. Engage them to gather input on learning priorities, expected outcomes, and alignment with organisational goals.

- **Define Learning Goals and Objectives**
  Clarify the goals of the Learning Needs Analysis (LNA) and establish specific learning objectives. Ensure these objectives align with business goals and outline measurable performance outcomes.

- **Select Data Collection Methods**
  Choose suitable methods such as surveys, interviews, or job/task analyses. Develop data collection tools tailored to the audience and organisational context for effective information gathering.

- **Data Gathering**
  Collect comprehensive data on current skills, job roles, and organisational needs from multiple sources. This ensures a holistic view of the current competency landscape.

- **Data Analysis**
  Analyse the collected data to identify trends, patterns, and discrepancies in knowledge and performance. Use this analysis to uncover areas requiring improvement.

- **Identify Performance Gaps**
  Compare current skills and competencies against desired standards and outcomes. Highlight gaps that need to be addressed through targeted learning interventions.

- **Root Cause Analysis**
  Conduct a root cause analysis to identify underlying issues contributing to performance gaps. This step ensures that solutions address the core problems rather than symptoms.

- **Prioritise Learning Needs**
  Rank learning needs based on their organisational impact, urgency, and feasibility. Refine this prioritisation with input from stakeholders to focus on the most critical areas.

- **Report and Recommendations**
  Compile findings into a comprehensive report. Include actionable recommendations and propose learning strategies to address identified needs effectively.

- **Continuous Monitoring and Evaluation**
  Establish a process for ongoing monitoring and evaluation of learning needs. Ensure that learning interventions remain relevant as business requirements evolve over time.

Learner and Needs Analysis
Conduct Learning Needs Analysis

Core Elements

- **Stakeholders Engaged**
  Managers, SMEs, HR personnel, and employees are involved in the LNA process.
- **Learning Goals Defined**
  Objectives and performance outcomes are clearly outlined and aligned with organisational priorities.
- **Data Collection Methods Selected**
  Suitable methods, such as surveys or interviews, are chosen to gather relevant data.
- **Data Gathered**
  Information on current skills, roles, and needs is collected from diverse sources.
- **Data Analysed**
  Patterns, trends, and performance gaps are identified through data analysis.
- **Performance Gaps Identified**
  Documented gaps between current and desired performance levels guide learning priorities.
- **Root Causes Analysed**
  Underlying causes of performance gaps are thoroughly examined and recorded.
- **Learning Needs Prioritised**
  Needs are ranked by impact, urgency, and feasibility, with stakeholder input.
- **Report and Recommendations Prepared**
  Findings and actionable suggestions are compiled into a comprehensive report.
- **Monitoring Process Established**
  A plan for continuous review and adjustment of learning needs is implemented.

Checklist

1. Identify current vs desired performance for target roles
2. Collect data from multiple sources: interviews, surveys, observations, job data
3. Analyse gaps in knowledge, skills, or attitudes affecting performance
4. Prioritise learning needs based on frequency, severity, or business impact
5. Distinguish between training needs and non-training issues (e.g., motivation, tools)
6. Validate findings with SMEs and performance managers
7. Document needs in actionable format for design planning
8. Ensure alignment of learning needs with organisational objectives

AI Considerations

- AI tools can detect learning gaps from unstructured data (e.g. feedback, reviews)
- Predict high-impact learning needs from past training outcomes
- Use LLMs to synthesise interview transcripts into need summaries
- AI models can cross-check existing training libraries against current needs
- Segment needs by role, region, or experience level using data clustering

Key Takeaways

A rigorous Learning Needs Analysis (LNA) is the foundation for purposeful instructional design. It connects business goals to learner realities by identifying performance gaps, uncovering root causes, and defining specific, measurable learning objectives.

This sub-step moves beyond assumptions and anecdotal inputs, using data-driven insights from surveys, interviews, and job analyses to prioritise what truly matters.

By aligning learning needs with strategic outcomes, and distinguishing between training and non-training issues, designers ensure that interventions are targeted, efficient, and impactful.

A well-executed LNA delivers more than a report, it delivers a mandate for change, grounded in evidence and tailored to real-world performance improvement.

Feasibility and Cost Analysis

Overview

The **Feasibility and Cost Analysis** step in the Analysis phase of the ADDIE model evaluates whether the instructional design project is realistic and achievable within the constraints of budget, resources, and time. This step ensures that the project aligns with organisational priorities and delivers a strong return on investment (ROI).

Through a detailed examination of costs, benefits, and resource needs, stakeholders can make informed decisions about project viability, resource allocation, and risk mitigation.

Key Sub-Steps are:

- **Cost Effectiveness Analysis**
  Assess the balance between the project's anticipated costs and benefits to determine its overall value and ROI.

- **Feasibility Assessment**
  Evaluate the practicality of the project by analysing resource availability, potential constraints, and alignment with organisational goals to ensure successful implementation within defined parameters.

Outcomes

The outcomes of the **Feasibility and Cost Analysis** step are focused on ensuring financial and resource-based alignment with project goals.

Key outcomes include:

- **Assess Project Viability**
  Evaluate whether the project can realistically be delivered within budget, resource, and time constraints.

- **Conduct Cost-Benefit Analysis**
  Compare anticipated project costs with expected benefits to ensure the ROI justifies the investment.

- **Determine Resource Allocation Needs**
  Identify specific resources required, such as personnel, technology, and materials, ensuring their availability aligns with project demands.

- **Provide Financial Justification for Project Approval**
  Develop a clear, data-driven case demonstrating the financial benefits and strategic alignment of the project to secure stakeholder buy-in.

- **Identify Financial Risks and Mitigation Strategies**
  Highlight potential financial challenges and propose strategies to address them, safeguarding the project's viability.

Summary

The **Feasibility and Cost Analysis** step is critical to ensuring that instructional design projects are financially sustainable, resource-efficient, and aligned with organisational goals.

By carefully examining costs, anticipated benefits, and resource requirements, instructional designers and stakeholders can make informed decisions that maximise ROI and minimise risks.

This analysis reduces the likelihood of issues such as budget overruns or resource mismanagement. Techniques like cost-benefit analysis, scenario planning, and ROI calculations provide a solid foundation for financial decision-making.

By aligning project expectations with realistic constraints, this step lays the groundwork for a strategically sound instructional solution that delivers value and meets organisational objectives.

Cost Effectiveness Analysis

Why this is important

Conducting a cost effectiveness analysis is essential for determining the financial viability and strategic value of an instructional program.

This process starts by identifying all cost components, such as personnel, technology, and materials, to build a complete picture of investment requirements.

Evaluating the cost-benefit ratio helps compare these expenditures against anticipated gains, including improvements in productivity, efficiency, or reduced future training needs. It also enables the forecasting of return on investment (ROI), providing tangible metrics that support the business case for learning.

By analysing these factors early, instructional designers and stakeholders can identify opportunities to optimise resource allocation, maintain quality while reducing redundancy, and ensure that the program delivers value without unnecessary spend.

Long-term viability is also a key consideration, requiring assessment of the total cost of ownership, including ongoing maintenance, updates, and scalability.

Ultimately, a well-executed cost effectiveness analysis provides stakeholders with clear, data-driven insights to support informed decision-making and responsible use of learning budgets.

Tips

- **Use Industry Benchmarks**
  Compare costs and ROI against similar projects in your industry to gauge competitiveness and efficiency.

- **Prioritise High-Impact Investments**
  Focus on elements that offer the greatest ROI, such as technology upgrades or streamlined content delivery methods.

- **Involve Stakeholders**
  Engage SMEs, project sponsors, and financial analysts early to ensure accurate estimates and realistic assumptions.

- **Leverage Existing Resources**
  Explore ways to repurpose existing materials or platforms to reduce development and implementation costs.

- **Document Clearly**
  Present cost analysis findings in an organised format to enhance understanding and decision-making.

Traps

- **Underestimating Costs**
  Failing to account for hidden or indirect costs, such as ongoing support or content updates, can lead to budget overruns.

- **Ignoring Long-Term Costs**
  Focusing only on initial costs without considering long-term expenses like maintenance can skew the analysis.

- **Overlooking Alternatives**
  Neglecting to explore alternative solutions may result in higher-than-necessary expenditures.

- **Unrealistic ROI Expectations**
  Overestimating benefits or underestimating risks can mislead stakeholders and undermine credibility.

- **Failing to Monitor Risks**
  Ignoring potential cost risks, such as inflation or delays, can compromise the financial integrity of the programme.

Feasibility and Cost Analysis
Cost Effectiveness Analysis

Techniques

- **Cost-Benefit Analysis (CBA)**
  Quantify the anticipated benefits of the programme (e.g., productivity gains, cost savings) and compare them to projected costs.
- **ROI Calculations**
  Use ROI formulas to determine the ratio of net benefits to total costs.
- **Total Cost of Ownership (TCO)**
  Estimate all costs, including development, implementation, and maintenance, to capture the full financial picture.
- **Sensitivity Analysis**
  Assess how changes in key factors (e.g., enrolment, resource costs) impact the financial outcomes of the programme.
- **Benchmarking**
  Compare your programme's costs and benefits against industry standards to contextualise your analysis.

Examples

- *Cost-Benefit Analysis*
  An online leadership course costing $100,000 to develop is estimated to save $50,000 annually in reduced travel expenses for in-person training.
- *ROI Calculation*
  A sales training programme costing $75,000 improves team productivity, yielding an additional $150,000 in annual revenue, resulting in a 200% ROI.
- *TCO Example*
  A digital onboarding programme has initial development costs of $80,000 and annual maintenance costs of $10,000 over five years, totalling $130,000.
- *Cost-Saving Opportunity*
  Switching from a custom LMS to an open-source platform saves $15,000 in annual licensing fees.
- *Sensitivity Analysis*
  Enrolment decreases by 20%, reducing revenue projections, prompting adjustments to delivery methods to maintain cost-effectiveness.

Feasibility and Cost Analysis
Cost Effectiveness Analysis

How it's done

- **Categorise Costs**
  Break down all potential costs associated with the programme into categories such as personnel, technology, materials, facilities, and outsourcing. This step provides a clear structure for financial analysis.

- **Estimate Costs**
  Use benchmarks, historical data, and expert insights to estimate costs for each component accurately. This ensures reliable projections for all expense categories.

- **Calculate Total Costs**
  Sum all direct and indirect expenses to determine the total financial investment required for the programme. Include long-term costs like maintenance and updates.

- **Conduct Cost-Benefit Analysis**
  Compare the total projected costs with anticipated benefits, such as productivity gains or cost savings. Evaluate the cost-benefit ratio to assess the programme's financial viability.

- **Identify Cost-Saving Opportunities**
  Explore ways to reduce expenses without compromising quality. Options may include utilising open educational resources (OER), renegotiating vendor contracts, or leveraging in-house expertise.

- **Forecast ROI**
  Calculate the return on investment (ROI) by comparing the total costs with the estimated financial or productivity benefits. This provides insights into the programme's value.

- **Compile Findings**
  Summarise costs, benefits, ROI, and recommendations in a clear, comprehensive report. This document serves as a key resource for stakeholder decision-making.

- **Validate with Stakeholders**
  Share findings with SMEs and stakeholders to gather feedback. Refine calculations and assumptions based on their insights to ensure accuracy and relevance.

Core Elements

- **Costs Categorised**
  All cost components, including direct and indirect expenses, are identified and structured.

- **Accurate Estimates Provided**
  Costs are estimated using reliable data sources and expert insights.

- **Total Costs Calculated**
  Comprehensive financial projections are completed.

- **Benefits Quantified**
  Expected benefits, such as cost savings or productivity gains, are clearly defined.

- **Cost-Benefit Ratio Evaluated**
  A thorough cost-benefit analysis ensures financial viability.

- **ROI Forecasted**
  Return on investment is calculated to assess the programme's value.

- **Cost-Saving Opportunities Identified**
  Potential savings are explored without impacting quality.

- **Long-Term Costs Considered**
  Maintenance and update costs are included in the analysis.

- **Stakeholder Feedback Incorporated**
  Findings are refined based on stakeholder input.

- **Documentation Completed**
  Results and recommendations are documented for clear decision-making.

Feasibility and Cost Analysis
Cost Effectiveness Analysis

Checklist

1. Identify all potential cost components (development, delivery, licensing, SME time)
2. Estimate costs for each delivery option (e.g., online, in-person, blended)
3. Define expected learning outcomes or performance improvements
4. Quantify potential benefits (e.g., productivity gain, error reduction, compliance impact)
5. Calculate cost per learner or cost per outcome achieved
6. Compare projected ROI across multiple implementation scenarios
7. Include hidden costs (maintenance, tech support, content updates)
8. Present findings in a decision-ready format for stakeholders

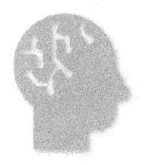
AI Considerations

1. Use AI models to simulate ROI under varying learner engagement and pass rates
2. Generate side-by-side cost-benefit scenarios using AI-powered spreadsheets
3. Predict ongoing maintenance costs from historical data
4. Use AI to extract cost benchmarks from industry reports or legacy data
5. Summarise findings into visual dashboards or infographics for decision-makers

Key Takeaways

The **Cost Effectiveness Analysis** sub-step in the Feasibility and Cost Analysis phase of the ADDIE model evaluates the financial viability of an instructional programme by assessing costs, benefits, and potential ROI.

By categorising costs, quantifying benefits, and exploring cost-saving opportunities, instructional designers provide stakeholders with a transparent understanding of the programme's financial implications.

Using techniques like cost-benefit analysis, ROI calculations, and sensitivity analysis, instructional designers ensure data-driven decisions that align with organisational goals.

Avoiding pitfalls such as underestimating costs or overlooking long-term expenses ensures a realistic and comprehensive analysis.

Presenting findings in a clear and compelling format fosters informed decision-making and stakeholder buy-in, ultimately ensuring the programme's financial and strategic success.

Feasibility and Cost Analysis
Feasibility Assessment

Why this is important

A feasibility assessment is a critical checkpoint that helps determine whether a proposed instructional project is achievable, sustainable, and strategically worthwhile. It begins by evaluating the project's viability within the constraints of available resources, budget, and time.

This assessment also ensures that the initiative aligns with organisational goals, providing measurable value and reinforcing strategic direction.

By identifying the human, technological, and material resources required for success, the process helps teams plan realistically and avoid overextension.

At the same time, potential constraints, such as operational risks, cultural barriers, or infrastructure limitations, can be identified and addressed early.

A comprehensive feasibility assessment equips stakeholders with the information needed to make informed decisions about project approval, scope adjustments, or alternative solutions, ultimately reducing the risk of wasted effort and increasing the likelihood of a successful outcome.

Tips

- **Engage Stakeholders Early**
  Collaborate with key decision-makers to align feasibility assessments with organisational priorities.
- **Use Realistic Assumptions**
  Base your feasibility assessment on practical and achievable assumptions rather than ideal scenarios.
- **Prioritise Transparency**
  Clearly communicate findings, including any limitations or uncertainties in the assessment.
- **Incorporate Flexibility**
  Account for potential changes in scope, timeline, or resources to accommodate unforeseen circumstances.
- **Leverage Historical Data**
  Refer to past projects or benchmarks to validate feasibility conclusions and provide context.

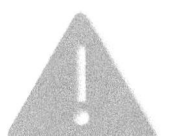

Traps

- **Overlooking Hidden Costs**
  Failure to account for indirect or unexpected expenses can result in budget overruns.
- **Underestimating Risks**
  Ignoring potential challenges or barriers can lead to unrealistic feasibility conclusions.
- **Limited Stakeholder Input**
  Excluding key stakeholders from the process may result in misaligned goals and impractical recommendations.
- **Bias Toward Approval**
  Assessments that favour proceeding without thorough evaluation can lead to poorly planned projects.
- **Neglecting Long-Term Considerations**
  Focusing solely on short-term feasibility may ignore sustainability or scalability issues.

Feasibility and Cost Analysis
Feasibility Assessment

Techniques

- **SWOT Analysis**
  Evaluate strengths, weaknesses, opportunities, and threats to provide a balanced feasibility assessment.
- **Resource Mapping**
  List and categorise all required resources, including personnel, tools, and budgetary needs.
- **Scenario Planning**
  Explore multiple feasibility scenarios to account for different risks or constraints.
- **Stakeholder Workshops**
  Conduct collaborative sessions to gather diverse perspectives and validate assumptions.
- **Gap Analysis**
  Identify discrepancies between current capabilities and project requirements to better assess feasibility.

Examples

- *Feasible Scenario*
  A project with well-defined outcomes, sufficient budget, and available personnel is deemed feasible.
- *Risky Scenario*
  A project that requires technology upgrades not currently available within the organisation presents significant challenges.
- *Scalable Initiative*
  A course redesign that uses existing content while incorporating new interactive elements ensures feasibility within time and cost constraints.
- *Non-Viable Project*
  A programme requiring excessive hiring beyond current budget and recruitment timelines is deemed infeasible.

How it's done

- **Define Project Scope and Objectives**
  Collaborate with stakeholders to clearly articulate the goals, boundaries, and desired outcomes for the feasibility assessment. This provides a focused framework for evaluation.
- **Analyse Available Resources**
  Review existing personnel, technology, and budget to understand the current capabilities available for project implementation.
- **Identify Constraints and Risks**
  Evaluate potential limitations, such as budgetary restrictions, time constraints, or technological gaps. Highlight any challenges that could impact the project's feasibility.
- **Evaluate Alignment with Organisational Goals**
  Ensure the project aligns with broader strategic initiatives and delivers measurable value to the organisation.
- **Conduct Cost and Resource Analysis**
  Estimate the financial and material resources required for successful implementation, providing detailed projections for stakeholders.
- **Develop Scenarios and Recommendations**
  Create best-case, worst-case, and most likely scenarios based on available data. Use these scenarios to offer actionable recommendations and assess project viability.
- **Document and Present Findings**
  Compile a comprehensive report that summarises feasibility conclusions, identifies risks, and provides recommendations. Present this report to stakeholders for review and input.
- **Incorporate Feedback**
  Refine the feasibility assessment based on stakeholder input and any additional data, ensuring the final recommendations are accurate and practical.

Feasibility and Cost Analysis
Feasibility Assessment

Core Elements

- **Project Scope Defined**
  Clear and specific project goals and boundaries are articulated.
- **Resource Inventory Completed**
  Existing resources, including personnel and technology, are documented and reviewed.
- **Risks and Constraints Identified**
  All potential barriers and limitations are evaluated.
- **Cost Estimates Prepared**
  Financial requirements are accurately calculated and included in the assessment.
- **Alignment Verified**
  Project goals are confirmed to align with organisational objectives and strategies.
- **Feasibility Scenarios Developed**
  Multiple scenarios are prepared to assess feasibility under varying conditions.
- **Stakeholder Feedback Incorporated**
  Input from key stakeholders is integrated into the final assessment.
- **Feasibility Report Finalised**
  Findings and recommendations are documented and presented for decision-making.

Checklist

1. Assess organisational readiness (leadership support, culture, resourcing)
2. Confirm technical infrastructure availability and compatibility
3. Evaluate availability and willingness of SMEs or facilitators
4. Review alignment with business priorities and timing constraints
5. Identify any regulatory, legal, or compliance constraints
6. Explore content development or sourcing feasibility (internal or external)
7. Flag risks related to learner access, engagement, or scalability
8. Prepare a feasibility report with risk mitigation and go/no-go recommendation

AI Considerations

- Use AI to scan project plans and flag resource or timing conflicts
- Generate feasibility checklists dynamically based on delivery mode and audience
- Analyse stakeholder sentiment from comms or surveys using NLP
- Model risks to feasibility using historical project data
- Auto-generate risk registers and mitigation plans based on feasibility criteria

Key Takeaways

Feasibility Assessment is a critical sub-step in the Feasibility and Cost Analysis process of the ADDIE model's Analysis phase It evaluates whether a project can realistically be implemented within existing constraints of resources, budget, and time.

By thoroughly analysing risks, resources, and alignment with organisational goals, instructional designers provide stakeholders with actionable recommendations that balance potential benefits against limitations. Techniques like SWOT analysis, resource mapping, and stakeholder workshops ensure a comprehensive and accurate evaluation.

Effective Feasibility Assessment contributes to project success by identifying and mitigating risks early. It ensures resources and efforts are directed towards viable, impactful initiatives, ultimately enabling organisations to make informed and strategic decisions.

Part 2: The **DESIGN** phase

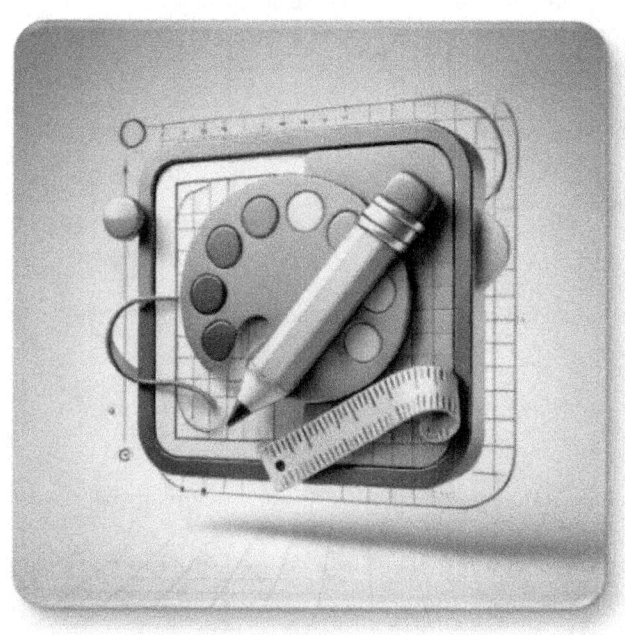

The **Design phase** is the architectural core of ADDIE. It is where analysis becomes structure and vision becomes blueprint.

Instructional designers make deliberate decisions about how learning will be structured, sequenced, delivered, and evaluated.

This is not about decoration but instructional integrity, clarity of intent, and purposeful alignment with objectives, learner profiles, organisational context, and available technologies.

The Design phase is the architectural core of ADDIE. It is where analysis becomes structure and vision becomes blueprint. Instructional designers make deliberate decisions about how learning will be structured, sequenced, delivered, and evaluated.

This is not about decoration but instructional integrity, clarity of intent, and purposeful alignment with objectives, learner profiles, organisational context, and available technologies.

Informed by Analysis, Design defines instructional strategy, selects learning modalities, and builds the scaffolding for engagement, practice, reflection, and transfer.

Lessons and modules are mapped, sequenced, and storyboarded, with media strategies chosen to explain, simulate, or immerse. Accessibility and inclusion are embedded from the outset, ensuring a wide range of learner needs are met.

Design also sets tone, pacing, and interaction style, anticipates learner behaviour, and engineers moments of challenge and discovery. Assessment and evaluation are integral, with success measures identified early and mechanisms for feedback and iteration built in.

AI brings opportunities for adaptive sequencing, personalisation, and multilingual localisation.

The technology stack is addressed early, ensuring platform constraints, authoring tools, and analytics are considered. Strong design documentation provides clarity for developers, SMEs, and stakeholders, acting as a bridge between planning and production.

Done well, this phase converts conceptual promise into structured potential and ensures Development builds something both technically sound and instructionally powerful.

Learning Experience Design

Overview

The **Learning Experience Design** step in the Design phase of the ADDIE model focuses on creating a structured blueprint for instructional content. This framework ensures the course is well-organised, accessible, and aligned with learning objectives, enhancing the overall learner experience. By establishing a logical sequence and leveraging appropriate delivery platforms, this step sets the stage for impactful and engaging instruction.

Key Sub-Steps are:

- **Define Conceptual Structure**
  Define the overall flow and organisation of course content, ensuring a logical progression that reinforces learning objectives.
- **Lesson Breakdown**
  Segment the course into lessons or modules, making the content easier to digest and fostering step-by-step learning.
- **Develop Lesson Storyboarding**
  Develop detailed outlines or visuals for each lesson to map the instructional flow and key elements, guiding content creation.
- **Select and Configure LMS**
  Select a platform to manage content delivery, track learner progress, and administer assessments.
- **Select and Configure LXP**
  If applicable, choose an LXP to provide curated, personalised, and social learning features that enhance engagement and retention.

Outcomes

The outcomes of **The Learning Experience Design** step focus on creating an organised structure that aligns with learning goals and maximises learner engagement.

Key outcomes include:

- **Establish a Clear Conceptual Structure**
  Create a logical content flow where each element builds on prior knowledge, reinforcing the learning objectives.
- **Create Manageable Lessons and Modules**
  Divide content into lessons or modules to simplify progression and reduce cognitive load.
- **Develop Detailed Lesson Storyboards**
  Outline the sequence, visuals, and key points of each lesson to ensure consistency, coherence, and engagement.
- **Select the Right Delivery Platform (LMS or LXP)**
  Identify a delivery platform that aligns with the learning environment and project requirements to enhance learner support and content accessibility.
- **Design for Engagement and Accessibility**
  Build the framework with a focus on fostering engagement and meeting the needs of diverse learners, using platform tools effectively.

Summary

The **Learning Experience Design** step is integral to designing a learner-focused and cohesive instructional experience.

By defining a clear conceptual structure, segmenting content into manageable modules, and leveraging storyboarding, instructional designers create a roadmap that supports effective learning progression.

Selecting an appropriate LMS or LXP enhances the framework by providing a platform for seamless content delivery, learner tracking, and engagement tools.

This structured approach mitigates risks such as disorganised content or unclear learning paths, ensuring a well-designed instructional experience that aligns with learner needs and organisational objectives.

Through careful planning and the use of robust tools, the Instructional Framework step builds the foundation for a successful course that is both accessible and impactful.

Learning Experience Design
Define Conceptual Structure

Define Conceptual Structure

Why this is important

A well-defined conceptual structure is the foundation of any effective instructional design.

It ensures that learning objectives are clear and measurable, that content is logically sequenced, and that instructional strategies are aligned with both learner needs and course outcomes.

Without this structure, courses risk becoming fragmented, confusing, or overloaded.

By establishing scope and sequence, selecting appropriate instructional methods, and integrating media and technology purposefully, designers create a seamless learning flow that supports engagement, comprehension, and progression.

This step also enables the development of relevant assessments and feedback mechanisms, ensuring that learning is not only well-planned but also measurable and meaningful.

Tips

- **Begin with the End in Mind**
  Use backward design to ensure all components align with the desired learning outcomes.
- **Leverage Active Learning**
  Include activities that encourage learners to apply knowledge and interact with peers and instructors.
- **Test Media for Accessibility**
  Ensure that all media elements meet accessibility standards and are compatible with learners' devices.
- **Keep Navigation Intuitive**
  Use clear headings, breadcrumbs, and progress indicators to make navigation straightforward.
- **Iterate with Stakeholders**
  Collaborate with SMEs and stakeholders regularly to refine content, strategies, and flow.

Traps

- **Overcomplicating Navigation**
  Complex pathways or unclear instructions can frustrate learners and detract from the learning experience.
- **Ignoring Learner Preferences**
  Neglecting to account for diverse learner needs or preferences may reduce engagement and effectiveness.
- **Overloading Content**
  Including excessive or irrelevant material can overwhelm learners and dilute the course's focus.
- **Using Ineffective Media**
  Poorly chosen or overused media elements can distract rather than enhance learning.
- **Lack of Feedback Mechanisms**
  Without timely feedback, learners may struggle to gauge their progress or areas for improvement.

Techniques

- **Content Mapping**
  Use a content map to visualise and structure topics, subtopics, and their relationships.
- **Flowcharting**
  Design flowcharts to represent the instructional flow and navigation structure visually.
- **Bloom's Taxonomy Framework**
  Align content and activities with cognitive levels, progressing from basic knowledge to application and evaluation.
- **Storyboarding**
  Create storyboards to plan media integration, instructional flow, and interactivity.
- **Pilot Testing**
  Conduct pilot sessions to gather feedback on navigation, activities, and technology before full implementation.

Learning Experience Design
Define Conceptual Structure

Examples

- **Instructional Goal**
  "By the end of this module, learners will demonstrate effective conflict resolution techniques in workplace scenarios."

- **Content Scope and Sequence**
  Start with "Understanding Conflict Types," progress to "Techniques for Resolution," and conclude with "Role-Playing Scenarios."

- **Instructional Strategy**
  Use problem-based learning (PBL) by presenting real-life case studies for learners to analyse and resolve.

- **Engaging Activities**
  Include a simulation where learners mediate a conflict between fictional team members.

- **Media Integration**
  Use an interactive video with clickable decision points to navigate different conflict outcomes.

How it's done

- **Define Goals and Objectives**
  Collaborate with SMEs to outline clear learning goals and create measurable objectives. These objectives guide content development, instructional strategies, and assessment design.

- **Organise Content Scope and Sequence**
  Identify key topics and arrange them in a logical progression, starting with foundational knowledge and building towards more complex concepts to support effective learning.

- **Select Instructional Strategies**
  Choose instructional approaches, such as direct instruction, simulations, or collaborative activities, that align with the learning objectives and the target audience's needs.

- **Design Learning Activities**
  Create engaging activities, including discussions, case studies, and simulations, to promote interaction and practical application of course content.

- **Integrate Media**
  Incorporate diverse media formats, such as text, videos, and interactive elements, to enhance accessibility and engagement while tailoring the media to the course content.

- **Develop Assessments and Feedback**
  Design both formative and summative assessments, such as quizzes, projects, or peer reviews, that measure learner progress and align with course objectives. Include constructive feedback mechanisms.

- **Create Instructional Flow**
  Plan seamless transitions between modules or lessons. Use clear navigation aids and pathways to ensure learners can easily follow the course structure.

- **Integrate Technology Solutions**
  Select and configure technological tools, such as Learning Management Systems (LMS) or Learning Experience Platforms (LXP), that support content delivery, engagement, and assessment needs. Ensure these tools align with the course's instructional goals.

Learning Experience Design
Define Conceptual Structure

Core Elements

- **Goals and Objectives Defined**
  Clear and measurable objectives are established for each module to guide learners towards specific outcomes.
- **Logical Content Sequencing**
  Topics are arranged to build progressively from foundational knowledge to advanced skills.
- **Instructional Strategies Aligned**
  Strategies are chosen to meet the objectives and address audience needs effectively.
- **Interactive and Engaging Activities**
  Activities encourage learner interaction, practical application, and critical thinking.
- **Media Formats Tailored**
  Accessible and engaging media formats are integrated to enhance the learning experience.
- **Assessments with Feedback**
  Assessments are designed to align with objectives and include mechanisms for providing constructive feedback.
- **User-Friendly Navigation**
  Instructional flow and navigation tools are intuitive and help learners transition seamlessly between modules.
- **Technology Compatibility**
  Platforms and tools are configured to support content delivery, engagement, and assessment requirements.

Checklist

1. Identify overarching themes or learning strands
2. Group content into logical categories or modules
3. Ensure structure aligns with performance goals and learner flow
4. Sequence themes to reflect increasing complexity or workplace application
5. Validate structure with SMEs and instructional designers
6. Document structure in a concept map, matrix, or diagram
7. Confirm instructional alignment with learning objectives
8. Review structure for consistency, balance, and cohesion

AI Considerations

- Generate concept maps or learning strands from raw content using LLMs
- Use AI to cluster related topics and suggest logical groupings
- Analyse learning objectives to identify implicit themes or connections
- Simulate learner pathways through conceptual structures for usability testing
- Detect gaps or overlaps in concept distribution across modules

Key Takeaways

This **Define Conceptual Structure** sub-step in the Design phase, establishes a solid blueprint for instructional delivery. It ensures content, strategies, and activities are aligned with learning objectives while meeting audience needs and technological capabilities.

By leveraging techniques such as content mapping, Bloom's Taxonomy, and pilot testing, instructional designers can create courses that are engaging, effective, and learner centric.

Avoiding common pitfalls, such as content overload or neglecting accessibility, ensures a smooth and inclusive learning experience.

A well-defined conceptual structure fosters engagement, retention, and successful learning outcomes, laying the foundation for impactful instruction.

Lesson Breakdown

Why this is important

Breaking a course into clear, purposeful lessons is essential for creating an effective learning experience. Lessons serve as the building blocks of instruction, each with defined learning objectives that align with the overall course goals.

When content is segmented and sequenced thoughtfully; learners are more likely to stay engaged, retain information, and build skills progressively.

Logical lesson flow supports cognitive processing by reducing overload and promoting connections between new and prior knowledge.

By incorporating appropriate instructional strategies, meaningful activities, and built-in assessments, each lesson becomes a self-contained yet interconnected unit of learning.

Moreover, planning at the lesson level allows for better resource allocation, adaptability to learner needs, and opportunities for personalisation.

A well-structured lesson breakdown creates a roadmap for both designers and learners, ensuring clarity, momentum, and instructional integrity throughout the course.

Tips

- **Focus on Key Takeaways**
  Prioritise essential concepts and skills in each lesson to avoid overwhelming learners.
- **Engage with Real-World Examples**
  Use scenarios and case studies to contextualise learning objectives and boost relevance.
- **Use Multimedia Wisely**
  Integrate videos, graphics, and interactive elements to enhance engagement without distracting from the content.
- **Layer Complexity Gradually**
  Start with foundational knowledge and progressively introduce advanced topics.
- **Solicit Stakeholder Feedback**
  Involve SMEs and stakeholders in the lesson breakdown process to ensure alignment and accuracy.

Traps

- **Overloading Content**
  Cramming too much information into a single lesson can overwhelm learners and hinder retention.
- **Neglecting Engagement**
  Failing to include interactive elements can lead to disengagement and passive learning.
- **Inconsistent Objectives**
  Misaligned lesson objectives and activities can confuse learners and reduce course effectiveness.
- **Skipping Assessments**
  Lack of assessments makes it difficult to track learner progress and identify gaps in understanding.
- **Ignoring Accessibility**
  Overlooking diverse learner needs can limit inclusivity and hinder participation.

Learning Experience Design
Lesson Breakdown

Techniques

- **Backward Design**
  Start by defining desired learning outcomes and design lesson activities and assessments to achieve them.
- **Chunking**
  Break content into smaller sections to make it easier for learners to process and retain information.
- **Storyboarding**
  Create visual representations of lesson flow, including activities, media, and assessments.
- **Scaffolding**
  Provide support and gradually reduce it as learners gain proficiency, ensuring mastery of complex topics.
- **Gamification**
  Use gamified elements, such as quizzes or challenges, to make lessons interactive and fun.

Examples

- *Lesson Objective Example*
  "By the end of this lesson, learners will be able to identify the steps of conflict resolution and apply them in workplace scenarios."
- *Content Segmentation Example*
  A lesson on "Effective Communication" could include topics such as "Active Listening," "Nonverbal Communication," and "Providing Feedback."
- *Instructional Strategy Example*
  For a coding lesson, use problem-based learning with real-world programming challenges.
- *Learning Activity Example*
  Pair learners in role-playing exercises to practice negotiation techniques.
- *Assessment Example*
  A sales training lesson could include a quiz on product features followed by a simulation where learners pitch the product to a mock client.

Learning Experience Design
Lesson Breakdown

How it's done

- **Define Lesson Objectives**
  Collaborate with stakeholders to establish measurable outcomes that align with overall course goals and address learner needs. These objectives provide a clear focus for each lesson.

- **Break Down Content**
  Segment the course content into manageable lesson units, organising topics in a logical sequence to facilitate smooth progression from foundational knowledge to more complex concepts.

- **Select Instructional Strategies**
  Choose effective methods for delivering lesson content, such as simulations, discussions, or direct instruction. Tailor strategies to the complexity of the content and the needs of the learners.

- **Design Activities**
  Develop engaging exercises to reinforce learning, incorporating approaches like group projects, role-plays, or interactive media that promote active participation and practical application.

- **Plan Assessments**
  Create quizzes, projects, or assignments for each lesson, ensuring these assessments are directly aligned with lesson objectives and effectively measure understanding.

- **Allocate Resources**
  Prepare the necessary materials and technology to support lesson delivery. This includes multimedia, handouts, and any tools required for activities or instruction.

- **Test Lesson Flow**
  Review the lesson structure for coherence, ensuring all elements align with objectives and learner needs. Conduct pilot testing with a sample audience to identify areas for improvement.

- **Refine and Adjust**
  Incorporate feedback from pilot testing and make necessary adjustments. Focus on maintaining engagement, accessibility, and alignment with the lesson's objectives.

Learning Experience Design
Lesson Breakdown

Core Elements

- **Objectives Defined**
  Measurable and clear outcomes are established for each lesson.
- **Content Segmentation**
  Topics are divided into manageable and logically ordered units.
- **Effective Strategies**
  Instructional methods align with the lesson's objectives and learner requirements.
- **Interactive Activities**
  Activities are designed to actively engage learners and reinforce understanding.
- **Aligned Assessments**
  Assessments are thoughtfully crafted to measure learning outcomes accurately.
- **Resource Preparation**
  Required materials, multimedia, and tools are prepared and readily available.
- **Flow and Coherence Tested**
  Lesson structures are reviewed and pilot-tested to ensure alignment and engagement.
- **Adaptability Incorporated**
  Lessons are refined to address diverse learner needs and feedback.

Checklist

1. Divide course into clear, manageable lessons or modules
2. Ensure each lesson addresses specific learning objectives
3. Define lesson purpose, duration, and delivery format
4. Confirm instructional flow within each lesson (intro, core, wrap-up)
5. Assign activities, resources, and assessments to each lesson
6. Sequence lessons based on dependency and learner progression
7. Validate with SMEs for completeness and logic
8. Document lesson breakdown in an instructional design document

AI Considerations

- Auto-suggest lesson boundaries based on content analysis
- Recommend lesson lengths based on cognitive load data
- Generate learning outcomes-to-lesson mapping matrices
- Flag unassigned objectives or underrepresented concepts
- Simulate time-on-task per lesson to optimise pacing

Key Takeaways

The Lesson Breakdown sub-step in the Design phase, is essential for organising course content into structured, engaging, and effective units. By clearly defining objectives, aligning activities and assessments with outcomes, and preparing resources, instructional designers ensure that lessons are coherent and accessible.

Using strategies like chunking, scaffolding, and backward design, designers create lessons that support smooth progression and active learning

Regular feedback and iteration further enhance the quality and relevance of the lessons, ensuring learners can engage with the content and achieve desired outcomes effectively.

Develop Lesson Storyboarding

Why this is important

Storyboarding is a critical bridge between instructional design and course development. It transforms abstract ideas into a concrete visual plan that captures how learning will unfold.

A well-crafted storyboard aligns directly with the learning objectives, structures content in a logical sequence, and integrates assessment, multimedia, and interactivity from the outset. It ensures that every instructional element is purposeful and that the learner experience remains coherent, accessible, and engaging.

By planning early and visually, designers can anticipate issues, secure stakeholder input, and streamline the production process, saving time, reducing rework, and enhancing the quality of the final course.

In short, storyboarding provides the clarity and control needed to deliver a well-designed learning experience.

Tips

- **Start with the Objectives**
  Always map each storyboard element to specific learning objectives.
- **Use Visual Storyboarding Tools**
  Tools like PowerPoint, Visio, or specialized software (e.g., Storyboard That) can streamline the process.
- **Include Placeholder Media**
  Mark where images, videos, or animations will go to maintain focus during the design process.
- **Iterate and Test**
  Pilot the storyboard with a small group to gather feedback on flow and engagement.
- **Focus on Transitions**
  Ensure seamless transitions between sections to avoid breaking learner immersion.

Traps

- **Overloading the Storyboard**
  Including too much detail can complicate development and overwhelm learners.
- **Ignoring Accessibility**
  Overlooking accessibility can exclude learners with disabilities.
- **Neglecting Engagement**
  Failing to include interactive or practical elements can make the lesson static and uninspiring.
- **Skipping Feedback**
  Not consulting stakeholders or SMEs may lead to misalignment with goals.
- **Underestimating Time Constraints**
  Unrealistic pacing can leave learners feeling rushed or frustrated.

Techniques

- **Layered Design Mapping**
  Use a multi-layered storyboard to separate instructional elements (e.g., narration, visuals, interactions) so that content, media, and functionality can be reviewed independently.
- **Narration Scripting with Timing**
  Script narration line by line and estimate timing to align audio with visuals and transitions for better learner pacing and engagement.
- **Interaction Prototyping**
  Design and test sample interactions (like click-to-reveal or branching scenarios) using simple tools to validate learner experience before committing to full development.
- **Storyboard Templates**
  Create reusable templates for different lesson types (e.g., scenarios, tutorials, assessments) to maintain consistency and speed up design.
- **Collaborative Review Cycles**
  Use shared platforms or slide decks to gather real-time feedback from SMEs and stakeholders, ensuring the storyboard meets both content accuracy and instructional intent.

Learning Experience Design
Develop Lesson Storyboarding

Examples

- *Learning Objective Example*
  "Learners will analyse three customer service scenarios and identify appropriate conflict resolution strategies."
- *Storyboard Flow Example*
  Start with an introduction video, present content in a slide deck, include a discussion forum, and end with a case-study assessment.
- *Interactive Element Example*
  Include a drag-and-drop activity where learners match actions to conflict scenarios.
- *Assessment Example*
  Use a quiz with immediate feedback to test understanding of the content presented.
- *Media Integration Example*
  Insert a video demonstrating best practices for resolving customer complaints, followed by a reflective activity.

How it's done

- **Review Learning Objectives**
  Revisit lesson objectives to ensure they are clear and aligned with the overall instructional goals. Use these objectives as the foundation for all storyboard elements.
- **Outline Lesson Structure**
  Define the sequence of instructional elements, including the lesson's introduction, main content, activities, and conclusion. Use sketches or digital tools to visually outline the flow.
- **Identify Key Content**
  Highlight essential topics and concepts to include, using concise descriptions or bullet points for each section to maintain focus and clarity.
- **Plan Interactivity**
  Incorporate opportunities for learner engagement by designing interactive elements such as simulations, polls, or group discussions to enhance participation.
- **Incorporate Multimedia**
  Select appropriate media, including images, videos, and audio, to complement the content. Mark placeholders in the storyboard for integrating these elements seamlessly.
- **Design Assessments**
  Create both formative and summative assessments that align with lesson objectives. Include opportunities for immediate feedback to support learning.
- **Ensure Accessibility**
  Review all storyboard elements to ensure compliance with accessibility standards. Add features such as alt text, captions, and adaptable navigation to support diverse learners.
- **Seek Feedback**
  Share the storyboard with SMEs and stakeholders, gathering their input to refine content, flow, and interactivity. Revise the storyboard based on feedback to ensure alignment and effectiveness.

Learning Experience Design
Develop Lesson Storyboarding

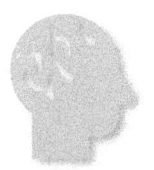
Core Elements

- **Objectives Aligned**
  All storyboard elements are mapped to specific learning objectives, ensuring clarity and relevance.
- **Organised Content**
  The lesson flow is clearly defined, progressing logically from introduction to conclusion.
- **Engaging Elements**
  Interactive features, such as discussions, polls, and simulations, are included to maintain learner interest.
- **Multimedia Integration**
  Placeholder media, including videos and images, are identified and aligned with lesson content.
- **Assessments Included**
  Assessments are strategically incorporated and linked to objectives, with feedback options included.
- **Accessibility Prioritised**
  All elements meet accessibility standards, supporting diverse learner needs.
- **Feedback Incorporated**
  Revisions are made based on stakeholder and SME input to refine the storyboard.
- **Documentation Completed**
  The storyboard is finalised and prepared for the development phase.

Checklist

1. Create consistent templates for screen-by-screen or slide-by-slide layout
2. Include narration, visuals, interactivity, and media cues per screen
3. Align each element to specific learning objectives
4. Identify required assets (e.g., images, animations, videos)
5. Confirm transitions and learner navigation logic
6. Version control applied for iterative development
7. Storyboards reviewed by design team and SMEs
8. Final storyboard approved for production or authoring tool handover

AI Considerations

- Generate storyboard drafts from lesson plans and scripts
- Use AI to suggest visuals or interactions based on text content
- Check consistency across storyboards (voice, layout, tone)
- Generate narration pacing estimates and animation timing
- Convert storyboard text to visual mock-ups using AI tools

Key Takeaways

Lesson storyboarding is a foundational practice in effective course design.

It ensures alignment between objectives, content, and delivery by visually mapping each element of the lesson before development begins.

This structured approach enhances coherence, engagement, and accessibility while providing clear direction to content creators, media producers, and technical developers.

By incorporating feedback loops and accessibility planning early, storyboarding reduces costly rework and sets a strong foundation for high-quality, learner-centred instruction.

Learning Experience Design
Select and Configure LMS

Select and Configure LMS

Why this is important

Selecting and configuring the Learning Management System (LMS) is a foundational step in the design phase that directly impacts the learner experience, instructional delivery, and course success.

A well-chosen LMS should support the course's learning objectives by offering features that enhance engagement, simplify navigation, track progress, and provide timely feedback.

Designers must ensure content compatibility with the LMS platform and align the configuration with accessibility requirements, mobile responsiveness, and user expectations.

Strategic LMS setup allows for automation, analytics, and scalability, ensuring the learning environment is not only functional but also adaptable and future ready. Getting the LMS right from the start enables smooth deployment and long-term effectiveness.

Tips

- **Explore LMS Features Early**
  Familiarise yourself with the LMS capabilities during the design phase to identify opportunities for enhanced engagement and functionality.
- **Design for Mobile Access**
  Ensure all content is mobile-friendly for learners accessing the LMS via smartphones or tablets.
- **Leverage Automation**
  Use automated features like reminders, grading, and certification to save time and improve efficiency.
- **Simplify Navigation**
  Keep the LMS interface intuitive and user-friendly, minimising barriers to learner engagement.
- **Test Frequently**
  Pilot test course elements within the LMS to ensure seamless integration and functionality before launch.

Traps

- **Overcomplicating the Interface**
  Complex navigation and excessive customisation can overwhelm learners and detract from usability.
- **Ignoring LMS Limitations**
  Designing content or activities that exceed the LMS's capabilities may result in technical issues.
- **Lack of Accessibility Compliance**
  Overlooking accessibility features can exclude learners with disabilities.
- **Forgetting Analytics Setup**
  Neglecting to configure tracking and reporting tools may result in lost insights into learner progress and engagement.
- **Underestimating Mobile Usage**
  Failing to optimise content for mobile users can limit accessibility and engagement.

Techniques

- **Feature Mapping**
  Create a checklist of LMS features and match them against course delivery needs to ensure alignment and compatibility.
- **Responsive Design**
  Use responsive content creation tools to ensure materials adapt to different devices and screen sizes.
- **Modular Structure**
  Build courses using a modular design to facilitate updates, reusability, and scalability within the LMS.
- **Gamification**
  Utilise LMS gamification features, such as badges, leaderboards, or progress tracking, to enhance motivation.
- **Interactive Tools**
  Incorporate LMS tools like forums, quizzes, and multimedia to create dynamic and engaging content.

Learning Experience Design
Select and Configure LMS

Examples

- **LMS Feature Integration Example**
  Use an LMS quiz builder to create interactive assessments that provide instant feedback.
- **Responsive Design Example**
  Design a training course that adjusts seamlessly for desktop, tablet, and mobile viewing.
- **Gamification Example**
  Implement a badge system to reward learners for completing milestones within the LMS.
- **Tracking and Reporting Example**
  Configure the LMS to track metrics like completion rates, assessment scores, and time spent on activities.
- **Accessibility Example**
  Ensure videos hosted on the LMS include captions and transcripts to accommodate diverse learners.

How it's done

- **Identify LMS Features**
  Review the capabilities of the selected LMS, including content hosting, assessments, reporting, and interactivity tools. Create a comprehensive list of features that align with the course requirements.
- **Plan Content Integration**
  Design content in compatible formats (e.g., SCORM, xAPI, multimedia) and test uploads to ensure seamless integration within the LMS.
- **Optimise Navigation**
  Structure course modules and resources logically for intuitive access, using consistent naming conventions and organising materials for ease of use.
- **Configure Assessments**
  Set up quizzes, assignments, and grading criteria in the LMS, leveraging automation tools to streamline grading and provide instant feedback to learners.
- **Enable Analytics**
  Configure tracking tools to capture learner engagement and performance data. Develop dashboards for real-time monitoring and actionable reporting.
- **Ensure Accessibility**
  Review LMS settings and content to ensure compliance with accessibility standards such as WCAG. Include features like alt text, captions, and adjustable font sizes to accommodate diverse learner needs.
- **Pilot Test Courses**
  Test courses within the LMS to identify technical issues or functionality gaps. Gather feedback from testers and make necessary adjustments to enhance usability and effectiveness.
- **Prepare Support Resources**
  Develop comprehensive learner guides or FAQs that include walkthroughs, contact details, and troubleshooting tips to assist learners in navigating the LMS.

Learning Experience Design
Select and Configure LMS

Core Elements

- **LMS Features Identified**
  A clear list of LMS capabilities relevant to the course has been documented.
- **Content Compatibility Tested**
  All materials are tested for seamless integration and functionality.
- **Navigation Optimised**
  Course structure and navigation are user-friendly and intuitive.
- **Assessments Configured**
  Quizzes and assignments are set up with clear instructions and automated grading.
- **Analytics Enabled**
  Tools for tracking and reporting learner engagement are configured.
- **Accessibility Ensured**
  LMS content and settings comply with accessibility standards, ensuring inclusivity.
- **Pilot Tested**
  Courses are tested with feedback incorporated for final adjustments.
- **Support Resources Available**
  Learner guides and troubleshooting resources are ready for use.

Checklist

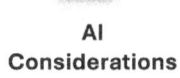

1. Define LMS requirements (SCORM, xAPI, quizzes, user tracking, reporting)
2. Evaluate available platforms against technical and business needs
3. Test sample content uploads and user flows
4. Confirm compatibility with learner devices and browsers
5. Configure course structure, enrolment rules, and completion logic
6. Integrate with HR systems or other platforms as needed
7. Pilot test with learners or facilitators
8. Finalise admin and user documentation for deployment

AI Considerations

- Use AI tools to compare LMS feature sets based on your requirements
- Analyse user logs or past LMS data to inform configuration choices
- Simulate learner journeys for different enrolment scenarios
- Generate admin help guides or user walkthroughs using AI
- Flag common usability issues or error patterns from historic LMS data

Key Takeaways

Selecting and configuring an LMS is not simply a technical task, it is a strategic design decision that directly influences learner engagement, content accessibility, and course effectiveness.

By aligning platform capabilities with instructional needs, designers ensure that content delivery is seamless, scalable, and inclusive.

A well-configured LMS supports assessment, automation, mobile access, and analytics, while also meeting accessibility standards. Pilot testing and learner support resources round out the setup, ensuring a smooth experience for all users.

When done right, LMS configuration becomes an enabler of high-quality learning, operational efficiency, and long-term adaptability.

Select and Configure LXP

Why this is important

Selecting and configuring a Learning Experience Platform (LXP) is a strategic move that shifts learning from structured delivery to dynamic, personalised exploration.

Unlike a traditional LMS, an LXP enables the creation of tailored learning pathways aligned with each learner's goals, preferences, and performance data. It empowers users to take greater ownership of their development, exploring content at their own pace and curating resources that resonate with them.

When configured effectively, an LXP enhances engagement through social features, peer learning, and collaborative tools that foster community and interaction.

The platform's ability to integrate external content, such as curated articles, videos, and microlearning, expands the learning ecosystem well beyond internal courses.

Meanwhile, built-in analytics offer deep insights into learner behaviour and progress, supporting continuous improvement and better decision-making.

A well-implemented LXP becomes more than a content hub, it becomes a living environment for continuous, self-directed learning.

Tips

- **Focus on User Experience**
  Keep the platform intuitive and learner-friendly, minimising friction in navigation and access.
- **Curate High-Quality Content**
  Include a mix of internal and external resources to create a rich learning ecosystem.
- **Use Recommendations**
  Leverage the LXP's AI-driven recommendation engines to suggest personalised content to learners.
- **Encourage Collaboration**
  Utilise discussion forums, peer reviews, and team activities to foster a sense of community.
- **Test Across Devices**
  Ensure the platform functions smoothly on desktops, tablets, and mobile devices.

Traps

- **Overloading Content**
  Including too many resources can overwhelm learners and dilute focus on core objectives.
- **Ignoring Personalisation**
  Failing to tailor learning paths undermines the LXP's potential for individualised learning.
- **Underutilising Analytics**
  Not leveraging data insights can result in missed opportunities to refine the learning experience.
- **Neglecting Accessibility**
  Overlooking accessibility features can exclude learners with disabilities.
- **Lack of Clear Objectives**
  Failing to align content and platform features with learning goals can confuse learners and reduce effectiveness.

Learning Experience Design
Select and Configure LXP

Techniques

- **Personalised Pathways**
  Use learner profiles and AI-driven algorithms to guide individuals through relevant content and activities.
- **Gamification**
  Incorporate gamified elements such as badges, leaderboards, and challenges to boost motivation and participation.
- **Content Curation**
  Blend internal training materials with external resources, like TED Talks, industry webinars, or articles, for diverse learning options.
- **Social Learning**
  Integrate features for peer-to-peer interactions, knowledge sharing, and collaborative projects.
- **Microlearning**
  Design bite-sized modules for quick, focused learning opportunities that fit into busy schedules.

Examples

- *Personalised Learning Path Example*
  A sales training course suggests additional negotiation skills modules based on a learner's low performance in a related assessment.
- *Social Learning Example*
  A group of employees collaborates on a project using the LXP's discussion board and shared document features.
- *Content Recommendation Example*
  After completing a cybersecurity module, the LXP recommends an advanced webinar on ethical hacking.
- *Gamification Example*
  Learners earn badges for completing modules and see their progress on a leaderboard, encouraging friendly competition.
- *Analytics Utilisation Example*
  Administrators use data from the LXP to identify content that has the highest completion rates and optimise future learning paths.

Learning Experience Design
Select and Configure LXP

How it's done

- **Evaluate LXP Capabilities**
  Assess the platform's features, such as personalisation, analytics, and social tools. Document functionalities that align with course objectives and learner needs.

- **Design Learning Pathways**
  Develop personalised learning pathways using learner profiles and goals, leveraging AI-driven tools to guide learners through relevant content and activities.

- **Curate Content**
  Blend internal training materials with up-to-date external resources to ensure a diverse and engaging mix of high-quality content tailored to learning objectives.

- **Integrate Social Features**
  Incorporate tools like discussion forums, group activities, and peer feedback to foster collaboration, engagement, and knowledge sharing among learners.

- **Set Up Analytics Dashboards**
  Configure tracking and reporting tools to monitor learner engagement and progress. Use analytics insights to refine content and optimise learning outcomes.

- **Test Content Integration**
  Pilot test content within the LXP to verify smooth functionality and alignment with learning objectives. Gather feedback and make adjustments to enhance usability and effectiveness.

- **Ensure Accessibility**
  Ensure all platform features and content comply with accessibility standards, including alt text, captions, and scalable interfaces, to support diverse learner needs.

- **Promote Self-Directed Learning**
  Enable tools that allow learners to explore and curate their own resources, such as bookmarking, creating playlists, and sharing materials with peers.

Core Elements

- **LXP Features Identified**
  Ensure core functionalities align with learning objectives.

- **Learning Pathways Designed**
  Create personalised paths tailored to individual learner goals.

- **Content Curated**
  Combine internal and external resources effectively.

- **Social Features Integrated**
  Incorporate collaborative tools to foster interaction.

- **Analytics Configured**
  Set up dashboards for real-time tracking of progress and engagement.

- **Accessibility Verified**
  Confirm compliance with accessibility standards across all content and features.

- **Pilot Testing Completed**
  Validate the functionality and relevance of content with tester feedback.

- **Learner Autonomy Enabled**
  Activate tools that encourage self-directed exploration and resource sharing.

-

Learning Experience Design
Select and Configure LXP

Checklist

1. Define LXP use cases (personalised learning, social sharing, AI recommendations)
2. Evaluate platforms for scalability, UX, and integration capabilities
3. Align LXP functionality with organisational learning culture
4. Configure learning pathways, tags, and content curation rules
5. Test AI-driven recommendations and adaptive learning features
6. Set up analytics dashboards for learner insights
7. Integrate with LMS and content repositories where applicable
8. Provide orientation or microlearning to onboard users to the LXP

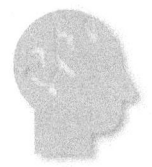
AI Considerations

- Use AI to model learning journeys and trigger recommendations
- Analyse learner behaviour to personalise content feeds
- Auto-tag uploaded content for discoverability
- Use AI to generate personalised nudges, learning goals, and reminders
- Run simulations to test adaptive pathways for various learner types

Key Takeaways

The Learning Experience Platform (LXP) sub-step in the Design phase, leverages advanced tools to craft a personalised, engaging, and adaptable learning environment.

Through the curation of diverse content, integration of social learning features, and utilisation of analytics, LXPs empower learners to take control of their learning journey.

By avoiding common challenges like content overload and neglecting accessibility, instructional designers ensure inclusivity and focus.

A well-structured LXP strategy enhances engagement, fosters collaboration, and supports continuous learning aligned with organisational objectives. This thoughtful integration of tools and strategies provides rich, meaningful experiences that drive learner success and overall program impact.

Gamification and Interactivity Planning

The **Gamification and Interactivity Planning** step in the Design phase focuses on embedding purposeful engagement strategies into the learning experience. By aligning game elements and interactivity with instructional intent, this step enhances learner motivation, focus, and retention, while avoiding gimmicks or cognitive overload. It ensures that all engagement features support the content flow and serve measurable outcomes.

Key Sub-Steps are:

- **Define Engagement Objectives**
  Clarify the purpose of gamification and interactivity to ensure every engagement element supports a specific learning goal.

- **Select Gamification Elements**
  Choose appropriate game mechanics (e.g. points, badges, challenges) that match learner needs and content structure.

- **Design Interactive Experiences**
  Build active learning components that require learner input, decision-making, or exploration.

- **Map Engagement to Content Flow**
  Integrate gamified and interactive elements at key points in the learning sequence to reinforce and guide progress.

- **Test for Usability and Cognitive Load**
  Evaluate the design to ensure interactivity enhances learning without causing confusion or fatigue.

- **Integrate Feedback and Motivation Loops**
  Provide meaningful feedback, progress indicators, and rewards that reinforce effort and achievement.

- **Align Tools and Platforms**
  Confirm that your LMS, LXP, or delivery environment can support the required engagement features effectively.

Overview

Gamification and Interactivity Planning
Select and Configure LXP

Outcomes

The outcomes of the **Gamification and Interactivity Planning** step focus on strategically embedding game mechanics and interactive features into the learning experience to enhance engagement and support learning goals.

Key Outcomes Include:

- **Clarify Engagement Objectives**
  Establish a clear purpose for incorporating gamification and interactivity to ensure every feature aligns with the course's instructional intent.
- **Select Meaningful Game Elements**
  Identify specific gamification mechanics (e.g. points, rewards, levels) that are appropriate for the audience and content type.
- **Design Interactive Experiences**
  Plan interactions that require learner input and decision-making to promote active engagement and knowledge retention.
- **Map to Instructional Flow**
  Ensure that gamified and interactive features are embedded logically within the course structure and reinforce progression.
- **Minimise Cognitive Load**
  Validate that interactive components are intuitive, purposeful, and do not overwhelm learners with complexity.
- **Incorporate Feedback Loops**
  Design feedback and motivation mechanisms that support progress tracking and sustain learner momentum.
- **Ensure Technical Compatibility**
  Align engagement strategies with platform capabilities to ensure seamless integration and delivery.

Summary

Gamification and Interactivity Planning turns learning into a two-way conversation, where every click, decision, and action reinforces skill, confidence, and insight.

When designed with purpose, interactivity enhances rather than distracts, and gamification becomes a vehicle for transformation, not just entertainment. This step brings neuroscience, UX, learning theory, and storytelling together to elevate engagement from gimmick to strategy.

Whether you're creating a safety simulation, leadership path, or compliance series, learners will only stay with you if they *feel* the learning. This phase ensures that they do.

Define Engagement Objectives

Why this is important

Before selecting any game elements or interactive components, it's essential to define *why* engagement is being pursued in the first place. Gamification without purpose becomes gimmickry. Engagement objectives focus design efforts on meaningful outcomes, whether it's increasing motivation, reinforcing behaviours, encouraging reflection, or sustaining attention across modules. This clarity ensures that interactivity serves learning, not ego or aesthetics.

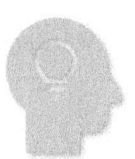
Tips

- Identify specific **learner states or behaviours** you want to change or reinforce.
- Distinguish between **extrinsic (rewards)** and **intrinsic (mastery, autonomy, purpose)** engagement.
- Map engagement goals to **learning moments**, e.g., pre-assessment warm-ups, difficult transitions, or application points.
- Interview learners or use past course feedback to understand where drop-offs or disengagement typically occur.

Traps

- Mistaking entertainment for engagement, learners can be amused and still disengaged.
- Defining vague goals like "make it fun" or "add a game" without a clear instructional target.
- Using the same engagement objective across all audiences or modules, nuance matters.
- Ignoring accessibility, not all learners are motivated by competition or visuals.

Techniques

- **Engagement Objective Matrix**:
  Define what type of engagement is needed (attention, motivation, exploration, repetition) and where.
- **Persona Mapping**:
  Connect objectives to learner profiles and their likely motivational triggers.
- **Cognitive Load Checkpoints**:
  Decide where learners will need stimulation versus reflection.
- **Motivation Model Frameworks**:
  Use theories like Self-Determination Theory, ARCS Model, or Flow Theory to define engagement types.

Examples

- *Attention Hook*:
  "Use gamified timer to drive urgency during compliance scenario challenge."
- *The Learning Experience Design* "Award badges for each correct step in incident escalation protocol to encourage correct sequencing."
- *Confidence Boost*:
  "Micro-successes in branching dialogue reinforce communication confidence after each decision."

How it's done

1. Review the learning objectives and determine where learners are likely to struggle or disengage.
2. Identify what type of engagement is needed at each learning stage, motivation, reinforcement, challenge, feedback.
3. Write specific, measurable engagement goals aligned to those needs.
4. Document these goals as design anchors to validate gamification and interactivity choices later.

Gamification and Interactivity Planning
Define Engagement Objectives

Core Elements

- Engagement need (e.g., motivation, challenge, feedback)
- Target audience or learner persona
- Trigger point within course structure
- Intended behavioural or emotional outcome
- Alignment to learning objective
- Measurement proxy (if any)

Checklist

1. Review learner personas and behavioural goals.
2. Identify potential engagement drop-off points.
3. Define what type of engagement is required and why.
4. Write SMART engagement objectives linked to learning goals.
5. Validate objectives with stakeholders or SMEs.
6. Use these objectives to evaluate all proposed gamification/interactivity later.

AI Considerations

- Use AI to suggest likely engagement gaps based on content flow or past learner analytics.
- Generate engagement objective prompts tailored to Bloom's level and learner profile.
- Simulate learner personas interacting with the proposed flow to reveal motivation dips.
- Recommend ideal motivational styles (e.g., autonomy vs. reward) based on AI-inferred learner preferences.

Key Takeaways

Defining engagement objectives is a foundational step in planning purposeful gamification and interactivity.

Rather than adding game elements for entertainment, engagement objectives clarify the *why*, ensuring that interactive features directly support motivation, retention, behavioural change, or reflection.

Clear objectives help instructional designers target specific learner needs, map engagement to key learning moments, and avoid the trap of gimmick-driven design.

When aligned with learner personas, motivational theory, and instructional goals, engagement becomes a tool for transformation, not distraction.

By documenting and validating these objectives early, designers create a strategic blueprint for interactivity that is both measurable and meaningful.

Gamification and Interactivity Planning
Select Gamification Elements

Select Gamification Elements

Why this is important

Choosing the right gamification elements is where instructional strategy meets creative execution. These elements, such as points, badges, leaderboards, progress bars, or challenge levels, create structured feedback loops that reinforce learning, drive motivation, and sustain attention. Selecting the wrong elements can confuse, annoy, or distract learners. Selecting the right ones creates meaningful engagement that supports, not competes with, instructional outcomes.

Tips

- Align game elements directly to **engagement objectives** and learner personas, don't assume every learner wants to compete.
- Use **minimal viable gamification**, start simple, then layer complexity if needed.
- Consider **progression mechanics** (levels, streaks, unlocking content) to build momentum across modules.
- Differentiate between **game mechanics** (what learners do) and **game dynamics** (how it feels).

Traps

- Overloading the course with too many game features, this creates noise and fatigue.
- Using competitive elements (e.g., leaderboards) in cultures that value collaboration or privacy.
- Ignoring learner feedback on previous gamified modules, especially where disengagement was caused by gimmickry.
- Forgetting to **reward the right behaviours**, make sure points and recognition are tied to learning value, not speed or luck.

Techniques

- **Gamification Mechanics Map:**
  Align each game element to an instructional purpose or engagement outcome.
- **Game Element Inventory:**
  Score potential mechanics based on their alignment to learner types (e.g., achiever, explorer, socialiser, avoider).
- **Progression Mapping:**
  Define how learners will experience reward, challenge, or feedback across the journey.
- **Feedback Loop Design:**
  Ensure each game mechanic includes timely, meaningful feedback.

Examples

- *Points*:
  Learners earn points for correct answers and lose points for missed questions in a scenario challenge.
- *Badges*:
  A "Quick Resolver" badge is awarded for completing the de-escalation simulation without triggering more than one escalation step.
- *Progress Bars*:
  Each module shows a visual indicator of progression through scenario stages, reinforcing persistence.
- *Unlockables*:
  Bonus reflection activities are unlocked after a learner completes 3 challenges in a row without help.

Gamification and Interactivity Planning
Select Gamification Elements

How it's done

1. Review your engagement objectives and learner personas.
2. Select game elements that support specific types of motivation (achievement, feedback, curiosity, etc.).
3. Map each selected element to a place in the learning flow, where will it appear and what will it reinforce?
4. Define the rules, triggers, and outcomes for each mechanic.
5. Document all selected elements and test them in early design wireframes or storyboards.

Core Elements

- Selected game mechanic (e.g., badges, levels, challenges)
- Purpose (what it reinforces or rewards)
- Trigger condition (when it appears)
- Feedback method (visual, audio, text, etc.)
- Placement within the learning path
- Link to behavioural or learning objective

Checklist

1. Identify a short list of game elements that support your engagement goals.
2. Match each element to a learner type and motivation driver.
3. Map element placement across the course flow.
4. Define rules and feedback conditions for each mechanic.
5. Ensure accessibility and device compatibility.
6. Validate that each element supports, not distracts from, the learning objectives.
7. Include a rationale for each selected element in the design spec.
8. Prototype or simulate key elements for early feedback.

AI Considerations

- Use AI to recommend game mechanics based on learner persona analysis and engagement patterns.
- Auto-generate badge names, challenge descriptions, or level titles based on course themes.
- Simulate learner reactions to different mechanics using conversational AI personas.
- Monitor learner interaction with gamified features post-launch to suggest optimisations.

Key Takeaways

Selecting gamification elements is not about adding bells and whistles, it's about choosing the right mechanics to support the learner journey.

When tied to clearly defined engagement objectives and learner personas, elements like points, progress bars, or unlockable content create purposeful feedback loops that motivate and reinforce learning behaviours.

Overuse, misalignment, or cultural mismatch can lead to fatigue or disengagement. The most effective gamified designs start with a few well-placed elements, each with a defined purpose, clear trigger conditions, and feedback mechanisms that enhance rather than distract.

A thoughtful gamification strategy turns interactivity into instructional value, and ensures that learners remain engaged for the right reasons.

Design Interactive Experiences

Why this is important

Interactivity transforms learners from passive recipients into active participants.

Done well, interactive experiences deepen understanding, promote decision-making, and sustain attention.

This focuses on crafting *meaningful interactivity*, not just clicking for clicking's sake.

Whether it's through scenarios, drag-and-drop activities, real-time feedback, or simulated environments, the goal is to design learning moments that feel relevant, engaging, and cognitively activating.

Tips

- Tie each interactive moment directly to a **learning objective** or required behaviour.
- Use a **mix of interactivity types**, not every interaction needs to be elaborate; some can be light-touch.
- Ensure interactions have **clear purpose and feedback**, what happens after the learner clicks or chooses?
- Design for **scalability and accessibility**, what works on desktop must also work on mobile and with assistive tech.

Traps

- Overusing interaction to "make it interesting", learners can detect padding or filler.
- Using generic interactions (e.g., click-to-reveal trivia) that don't support application or reflection.
- Failing to test interactivity across devices and browsers, what works in authoring tools doesn't always translate.
- Designing for interactivity before instructional flow, the learning should lead the interaction, not the reverse.

Techniques

- **Interaction Mapping**:
  Place each interaction on a storyboard map with its instructional function and learner action.
- **Decision Tree Flowcharts**:
  Build out paths for branching scenarios and capture possible learner responses.
- **Progressive Reveal Mechanics**:
  Use timed or triggered reveals to simulate unfolding real-world complexity.
- **Guided Feedback Loops**:
  Include layered feedback (e.g., hints, reinforcement, correction) based on learner input.

Examples

- *Scenario*:
  Learners must choose how to respond to a difficult customer. Each choice branches to a unique consequence.
- *Exploration*:
  A digital equipment panel lets learners click each button to see its function and consequence.
- *Drag-and-Drop*:
  Learners match safety procedures to risk scenarios, receiving immediate visual confirmation.
- *Hotspots*:
  Clicking on parts of a machine reveals related risks and required PPE.

Gamification and Interactivity Planning
Design Interactive Experiences

How it's done

1. Review the instructional flow and mark where interactivity will enhance learning outcomes.
2. Choose interaction types based on content complexity, cognitive load, and learner preferences.
3. Write decision prompts and responses that reflect real-life ambiguity and consequence.
4. Embed meaningful feedback into each interaction, not just "correct/incorrect" but why.
5. Prototype interactions and review them with SMEs and sample learners.
6. Optimise for speed, clarity, and responsiveness before full integration.

Core Elements

- Type of interaction (e.g., branching, simulation, drag-drop, click-reveal)
- Instructional goal of interaction
- Learner task and input
- Feedback type and trigger
- Location in course flow
- Accessibility requirements and platform constraints

Checklist

1. Align each interaction with a specific instructional purpose.
2. Select interaction types that match content difficulty and learner profile.
3. Script realistic options and layered feedback.
4. Map interaction into the storyboard or design document.
5. Prototype and test on multiple devices and browsers.
6. Ensure all interactivity complies with accessibility guidelines (e.g., WCAG).
7. Incorporate interaction timing and flow pacing into design.
8. Gather early feedback and refine for clarity and relevance.

AI Considerations

- Use AI to suggest interactive formats based on content type and learner goals.
- Auto-generate distractors or alternate responses in scenario-based interactions.
- Analyse learner performance to adapt future interactions dynamically (adaptive learning).
- Simulate walkthroughs of interactive paths to detect flow issues or dead ends.
- Recommend interaction pacing based on predicted cognitive load and engagement levels.

Key Takeaways

Designing interactive experiences is about crafting purposeful, learner-driven moments that elevate engagement and deepen understanding.

When aligned with learning objectives and thoughtfully placed within the course flow, interactivity reinforces decision-making, promotes reflection, and creates opportunities for real-world application.

Effective interactive design goes beyond surface-level clicks, it involves feedback, flow, and cognitive relevance.

The most impactful experiences are intuitive, scalable, and inclusive across devices and abilities.

By prototyping early, testing thoroughly, and using data to refine, instructional designers can create meaningful interactivity that transforms learning from passive consumption to active participation.

Gamification and Interactivity Planning
Map Engagement to Content Flow

 **Why this is important**	Even the best-designed gamification and interactivity elements will fail if they're placed randomly or disrupt the instructional rhythm. Mapping engagement elements to the course's content flow ensures that the *right interaction happens at the right moment*. This maintains cognitive momentum, supports learner motivation, and aligns engagement with the pedagogical intent. It also prevents overloading or underwhelming the learner at critical points in the journey.
 **Tips**	• Begin with the **learning journey**, not the game, overlay engagement onto established learning arcs. • Identify **high-value zones** for interaction: knowledge checks, transitions, simulations, reflection points. • Consider **emotional pacing**, when learners need encouragement, relief, or a challenge boost. • Use **visual journey mapping** to align content segments, engagement goals, and game mechanics.
  **Traps**	• Dropping gamification elements into the course without tying them to content transitions or performance moments. • Front-loading or clustering all interactivity in one module, spread it intelligently across the experience. • Assuming every module needs equal gamification, some content may require calm reflection instead. • Failing to monitor **engagement drop-off points** from past courses to inform placement.
 **Techniques**	• **Engagement Flowchart**: Plot the entire course journey and place interactive/gamified components along it. • **Tension Mapping**: Identify when learners will be cognitively stretched or emotionally disengaged, use gamification strategically to lift energy. • **"Push–Pull" Placement**: Balance mandatory engagement (quizzes, feedback) with optional discovery (explorables, unlockables). • **Reward Distribution Mapping**: Plan how and when feedback, badges, or unlocks occur to maintain interest and fairness.
 **Examples**	• *Scenario Challenge*: Placed midway through a module to apply learned concepts before moving into a higher complexity section. • *Badge Award*: Tied to module completion + achieving 85% or higher on scenario response scores. • *Confidence Pulse*: Micro-feedback loop placed at the end of each module to gather learner sentiment. • *Interactive Map*: Used during onboarding to allow new hires to explore departments in any order while collecting mission tokens.

Gamification and Interactivity Planning
Map Engagement to Content Flow

How it's done

1. Lay out the course structure as a journey, module by module, or experience by experience.
2. Mark areas of high cognitive challenge or emotional dip.
3. Overlay the previously chosen gamification and interactive components where they will support learning momentum.
4. Ensure every engagement touchpoint links back to an objective or skill checkpoint.
5. Prototype and user-test the engagement flow, are there lulls, spikes, or confusion points?
6. Adjust sequence and frequency to create a balanced rhythm across the experience.

Core Elements

- Course flow structure or storyboard
- Key transition or application points
- Engagement element type and location
- Learner emotion or cognitive load forecast
- Feedback or reward cadence
- Flow validation notes from pilot or SME review

Checklist

1. Create a visual or tabular course flow map.
2. Identify natural breakpoints, decision points, and application moments.
3. Overlay chosen gamification and interactivity elements.
4. Ensure pacing allows time for reflection, exploration, and mastery.
5. Validate alignment between content, interaction, and feedback.
6. Monitor for engagement "dead zones" and adjust as needed.
7. Simulate or walkthrough the journey with SMEs or learners.
8. Finalise map as a shared artefact for developers and reviewers.

AI Considerations

- Use AI to analyse course scripts and recommend where interaction will most likely boost engagement.
- Auto-generate engagement flow maps based on cognitive complexity or pacing models.
- Predict drop-off points using historical LMS data and suggest game elements to offset them.
- Simulate learner journeys and flag over-clustering or missed engagement opportunities.
- Recommend reward placement patterns based on predicted learner satisfaction curves.

Key Takeaways

Effective engagement isn't just about adding interactive elements, it's about placing them with intent.

Mapping engagement to the content flow ensures that gamification and interactivity align with the rhythm of learning, supporting both cognitive and emotional progression. This strategy avoids overloading learners at the wrong time or introducing distractions where focus is needed.

By planning for peaks and dips in attention and challenge, designers can sustain motivation, encourage reflection, and amplify outcomes.

Engagement mapping transforms the course from a sequence of content into a compelling learner journey, one that feels responsive, intuitive, and meaningful from start to finish.

Test for Usability and Cognitive Load

Why this is important

A gamified or interactive learning experience can fail *not* because the ideas were wrong, but because the execution overwhelmed or confused the learner.
Testing for usability and **cognitive load** ensures that interactivity is intuitive, smooth, and supportive, not mentally draining or frustrating.
This safeguards learner attention, protects accessibility, and fine-tunes the learning experience so it *feels as good as it functions*.

Tips

- Test early, and repeat at key milestones. Even rough wireframes or draft screens can uncover usability issues before they become costly.
- Use **diverse user groups**, including low-literacy, ESL, or neurodiverse learners if relevant.
- Ask testers to "think aloud", hearing how they navigate reveals friction you may not see.
- Evaluate not just what works technically, but how it *feels* emotionally and cognitively to use.

Traps

- Skipping usability testing to stay on schedule, this usually causes rework later.
- Assuming that designers or SMEs can accurately test usability, they're too close to the content.
- Ignoring cognitive overload caused by stacking too many stimuli (sound, motion, choices, colours).
- Failing to check accessibility (e.g., keyboard navigation, screen reader compatibility, motion reduction settings).

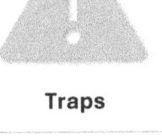
Techniques

- **5-User Heuristic Testing**:
  Run usability sessions with just 5 participants, enough to catch 80% of issues.
- **Cognitive Walkthroughs**:
  Ask users to explain what they expect at each point and whether it happens.
- **Load Observation Rubric**:
  Watch for signs of overload, long pauses, repeated attempts, skipped content.
- **Usability Feedback Cards**:
  Give users quick rating cards to score elements on clarity, confidence, and fatigue.

Examples

- *Scenario Confusion*:
  Learners in testing couldn't tell which response option was selected, UI redesign required.
- *Load Spike*:
  Interactive timeline had 12 events with small fonts, testers skimmed without comprehension.
- *Over-Motivation*:
  Too many badges were awarded too quickly, feedback felt meaningless and cluttered.
- *Accessibility Miss*:
  Drag-and-drop activities didn't support keyboard input, excluding some learners.

How it's done

1. Build a clickable prototype or minimum viable version of your interactive module.
2. Recruit diverse learners, or representatives, for usability testing.
3. Facilitate test sessions focused on navigation clarity, feedback comprehension, and workload.
4. Observe learner reactions, pauses, confusion, and comments.
5. Analyse findings for patterns and thresholds, where do most users struggle or disengage?
6. Revise design for simplification, clarity, and learner flow, then retest.

Gamification and Interactivity Planning
Test for Usability and Cognitive Load

Core Elements

- Prototype or demo version
- User test participant group and personas
- Testing script or tasks
- Observation sheet and success criteria
- Identified usability issues and fixes
- Cognitive load feedback and adjustments
- Accessibility compliance notes

Checklist

1. Develop a prototype of the interactive or gamified section.
2. Plan usability testing with diverse learner types.
3. Observe learners as they engage, document where confusion or overload occurs.
4. Collect qualitative feedback on confidence, clarity, and engagement.
5. Check for excessive decision points or redundant interactions.
6. Evaluate accessibility features and test screen reader and keyboard compatibility.
7. Revise designs based on patterns, not just individual feedback.
8. Retest or validate improvements before final integration.

AI Considerations

- Use AI to simulate learner journeys and highlight potential overload zones.
- Auto-generate heatmaps or interaction logs during usability testing.
- Transcribe and summarise learner feedback for faster iteration.
- Recommend simplification of wording, layout, or branching paths where cognitive friction is detected.
- Benchmark time-on-task data against content complexity to detect mismatch.

Key Takeaways

Testing for usability and cognitive load ensures that interactive experiences support learning rather than sabotage it.

Even well-intentioned designs can cause confusion or overload if they are not intuitive, accessible, or emotionally aligned with the learner's pace.

By observing real users, listening to their thought processes, and analysing interaction patterns, designers can uncover friction points that would otherwise go unnoticed.

This process validates design decisions, protects inclusivity, and refines the experience for clarity and flow. Usability testing is not an optional polish, it is a critical safeguard for learning impact, accessibility, and long-term engagement.

Integrate Feedback and Motivation Loops

Why this is important

Gamification without feedback is like a game without a scoreboard, directionless and unrewarding.

Motivation loops transform engagement into progression, while feedback loops ensure learners know where they stand and how to improve.

Together, they reinforce behaviour, build confidence, and create emotional traction with the content.

These loops are critical for sustaining attention and building a sense of mastery and momentum throughout the learning experience.

Tips

- Provide **immediate feedback** on learner actions, success or failure should never be ambiguous.
- Use **layered feedback**: quick nudges for minor choices, deeper feedback for complex scenarios.
- Reinforce **progress visually**, progress bars, unlocked badges, and completed steps all cue satisfaction.
- Include **motivational triggers** at key moments: "You're halfway through," "You've earned a break," or "Next challenge unlocked."

Traps

- Giving only right/wrong answers, this shuts down deeper reflection or exploration.
- Over-praising minor achievements, this can dilute the perceived value of genuine progress.
- Creating feedback that's too vague ("Good job!") or robotic ("Correct."), specific and humanised responses matter.
- Forgetting to reward effort or strategy, not just outcomes, especially in branching scenarios or complex decisions.

Techniques

- **Feedback Taxonomy:**
  Use a structured model to vary feedback types (confirmatory, elaborative, comparative, reflective).
- **Loop Balancing:**
  Ensure positive motivation loops are balanced with meaningful challenges, avoid constant praise.
- **Gamified Reflection Prompts:**
  Embed quick journaling or reflection wins:
  "What would you do differently next time?"
- **Social Reinforcement:** Let learners earn recognition or share progress (if appropriate) with peers or facilitators.

Gamification and Interactivity Planning

Integrate Feedback and Motivation Loops

Examples

- *Micro-Feedback*:
  "Correct, you spotted the compliance breach before escalation."
- *Motivation Pulse*:
  After 3 modules completed:
  "You're making great progress, 70% of learners stop here, but you're ahead!"
- *Challenge Response*:
  "You chose to delay the incident report. Here's how that plays out, and how it impacts trust."
- *Progress Loop*:
  "You've unlocked a bonus scenario, this one builds on what you mastered earlier."

How it's done

1. Review each gamified element or interaction and define the type of feedback it should generate.
2. Design feedback that is **immediate, clear, and tied to behaviour or decision quality**.
3. Layer motivational cues throughout the learner journey, early momentum, midpoint encouragement, final payoff.
4. Build in variety: some feedback should inform, others should challenge or surprise.
5. Ensure that feedback is contextual, tied to the learning goal and learner choice.
6. Pilot test and refine based on user engagement patterns and sentiment.

Core Elements

- Action or interaction trigger
- Feedback content and tone (supportive, corrective, reflective)
- Timing (immediate, delayed, cumulative)
- Motivation cue (visual, textual, gamified)
- Link to success criteria or performance benchmark
- Repetition thresholds or encouragement cycles

Checklist

1. Define feedback points for every interactive decision or performance checkpoint.
2. Write context-sensitive feedback for both success and failure outcomes.
3. Insert motivational prompts at emotional "valleys" in the learning arc.
4. Provide feedback that links behaviour to consequence, not just outcome.
5. Use progress visualisation elements to reinforce momentum.
6. Integrate social or self-comparison only if culturally appropriate.
7. Localise tone and language of feedback to suit audience maturity.
8. Test emotional impact of feedback in pilot sessions.

Gamification and Interactivity Planning
Integrate Feedback and Motivation Loops

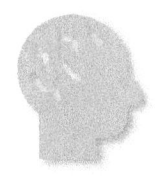

AI Considerations

- Use AI to dynamically generate personalised feedback based on learner input and path taken.
- Track motivation metrics (engagement dips, time-on-task) to auto-trigger encouragement loops.
- Suggest tailored challenge levels based on performance history, keep the "flow zone" alive.
- Recommend improvement tips based on past learners with similar performance profiles.
- Auto-adapt feedback tone to learner sentiment or pacing.

Key Takeaways

Feedback and motivation loops are essential components of meaningful gamification. They transform interactivity into momentum by showing learners where they stand, how far they've come, and what they can do next.

When designed well, feedback loops clarify actions and reinforce learning, while motivation loops inspire continued effort and emotional engagement.

These systems must be thoughtful, never robotic or excessive, and should reward strategy, effort, and growth as much as outcomes.

By embedding a mix of immediate, layered, and reflective feedback, instructional designers ensure that learners stay oriented, energised, and committed from start to finish.

Gamification and Interactivity Planning
Align Tools and Platforms

Align Tools and Platforms

Why this is important

No matter how creative or pedagogically sound your gamified learning plan is, it will fall apart without the right tools and delivery infrastructure.

This step ensures that all gamification and interactivity elements are technically feasible within your chosen learning platforms (LMS, LXP, authoring tools, or custom apps).

Aligning tools and platforms early avoids costly rework, clunky user experiences, and failed expectations during deployment.

Tips

- Map **each gamification element to platform capability**, e.g., does your LMS support XP points or conditional branching?
- Use tools that offer **interoperability**, SCORM, xAPI, or LTI compatibility allows smoother integration.
- Include **IT, digital learning, or platform admins** in early planning sessions.
- Prototype small components in the platform *before* building the full course, don't assume feature parity.
-

Traps

- Designing gamified elements that can't be supported by the platform's engine or interface.
- Using too many disconnected tools, learners should not need to log in multiple times or switch contexts.
- Ignoring platform analytics capabilities, you'll need these to measure interaction success and usage.
- Failing to test how platform limitations affect mobile responsiveness, accessibility, or offline access.

Techniques

- **Platform Capability Audit**:
  Create a grid showing each tool's ability to support points, badges, leaderboards, timers, simulations, branching, etc.
- **Tool–Content Fit Assessment**:
  Evaluate whether the authoring tool (e.g., Storyline, Rise, Evolve) supports your desired game mechanics.
- **Single Sign-On (SSO) Testing**:
  Ensure a frictionless login experience across all platforms used.
- **Data Compatibility Mapping**:
  Plan how engagement data will be stored, analysed, and reported across systems.

Examples

- *Authoring Tool Use*:
  Articulate Storyline used to build branching scenarios with visual feedback and gamified scoring.
- *LMS Integration*:
  Moodle used to trigger badge awards based on conditional activities and completion logic.
- *Progressive Web App*:
  Custom module built in React for drag-and-drop sequencing with AI-based hints, then embedded into the LXP via LTI.
- *Analytics*:
  xAPI data sent from gamified scenario to LRS (Learning Record Store) for heatmap analysis.

Gamification and Interactivity Planning
Align Tools and Platforms

How it's done

1. List all proposed gamification and interactivity features.
2. Cross-reference this list with your delivery platform's technical capabilities.
3. Identify gaps and assess whether custom development or tool substitution is needed.
4. Consult with IT or learning systems teams about integration, compatibility, and future maintenance.
5. Prototype key interactions and test across devices and environments.
6. Finalise toolset choices and document the rationale, constraints, and setup steps.

Core Elements

- Feature/tool matrix (what's needed vs. what's available)
- Platform constraints (e.g., browser requirements, mobile responsiveness, security policies)
- Integration pathways (e.g., LTI, SCORM, xAPI)
- Analytics capabilities
- Support and update ownership (who manages what post-launch)
- Custom development requirements, if any

Checklist

1. Identify all gamification and interactivity elements to be deployed.
2. Audit current LMS/LXP/authoring tools for compatibility.
3. Prototype critical features before committing to design.
4. Confirm accessibility, mobile-friendliness, and multilingual support.
5. Align tool choices with IT policy and cybersecurity standards.
6. Document tool responsibilities and maintenance pathways.
7. Test end-to-end learner experience across all systems.
8. Create a contingency plan for platform gaps or failures.

AI Considerations

- Use AI to assess tool compatibility based on historical success with similar features.
- Auto-scan course design for features unsupported by the target platform.
- Recommend authoring tool plugins or API connectors to fill capability gaps.
- Optimise platform data exports for analysis and ROI tracking.
- Simulate end-user experience in different platforms to flag likely engagement issues.

Key Takeaways

Even the most creative gamification and interactivity plans will fail if they're not supported by the chosen tools and platforms. Aligning instructional intent with technical feasibility ensures that learner experiences are smooth, scalable, and trackable.

This alignment prevents rework, reduces complexity for learners, and safeguards the integrity of the design.

By auditing capabilities early, testing prototypes across environments, and involving IT stakeholders from the start, designers can avoid technical surprises and maintain full control over engagement delivery.

The result is a cohesive, functional learning environment that works as well behind the scenes as it does on screen.

Assessment Design

Overview

The **Assessment Design** step in the Design phase of the ADDIE model is dedicated to creating tools and strategies to evaluate learners' progress and understanding. This step ensures that assessments align with learning objectives and provide valid, reliable evidence of knowledge acquisition and skill development.

Effective assessment design involves planning evaluation strategies and developing diverse assessment types to address various cognitive levels and practical applications. By incorporating formative and summative assessments, this step supports ongoing feedback and end-of-course evaluation to ensure comprehensive learning outcomes.

Key Sub-Steps are:

- **Evaluation Design**
  Plan assessment methods and frequency to track learner progress and measure outcomes effectively, incorporating both formative (ongoing) and summative (final) evaluations.

- **Assessment Items**
  Create tasks such as quizzes, projects, or simulations aligned with course objectives, providing meaningful and measurable insights into learner performance.

Outcomes

The outcomes of the Assessment Design step focus on ensuring that assessments are purposeful, aligned, and supportive of diverse learning goals.

Key outcomes include:

- **Align Assessments with Learning Objectives**
  Ensure each assessment correlates directly with course objectives to measure learner progress accurately.

- **Incorporate Formative and Summative Assessments**
  Use formative assessments for ongoing feedback and summative assessments for final evaluation of learning achievements.

- **Develop Clear, Well-Defined Assessment Items**
  Craft concise, unambiguous questions and tasks that focus on specific learning goals.

- **Use Diverse Assessment Techniques**
  Incorporate varied methods such as multiple-choice questions, open-ended tasks, scenario-based exercises, and project work to evaluate a range of skills and cognitive abilities.

- **Provide Constructive Feedback Mechanisms**
  Design assessments that deliver actionable, specific feedback to foster reflection and encourage learning growth.

Summary

The **Assessment Design** step is essential for ensuring that learners' progress is accurately evaluated and aligned with course objectives. By creating assessments that are varied, clear, and purposeful, instructional designers provide learners with fair opportunities to demonstrate their understanding and skills.

Using tools such as Bloom's Taxonomy, rubrics, and scenario-based exercises enables the design of assessments that measure both foundational knowledge and higher-order thinking. Incorporating formative and summative assessments ensures ongoing feedback and final evaluation, supporting a well-rounded learning experience.

By following best practices in assessment design, instructional designers can avoid pitfalls like poorly aligned learning objectives or unclear tasks. A robust assessment strategy not only measures learner achievement effectively but also reinforces learning and fosters continuous improvement.

Evaluation Design

Why this is important

Evaluation planning begins by **defining clear goals** for assessing the instructional materials. These goals typically focus on evaluating the effectiveness of the learning experience, the level of learner engagement, the usability of the course interface, and the degree to which content aligns with the intended learning outcomes.

Once the goals are set, the next step is to **develop measurable criteria** that can be used to judge the quality and impact of the instruction. These criteria should be specific, observable, and aligned with both the learning objectives and the broader organisational goals.

With evaluation criteria in place, designers then **select appropriate methods** for gathering evidence. This may include a mix of surveys, usability testing, structured interviews, and focus groups, chosen to suit the instructional context and the resources available.

Designing the evaluation requires **developing effective instruments** to capture meaningful feedback. These may include questionnaires, Checklists, rubric-based scoring tools, or observation protocols that ensure data collected is reliable, valid, and actionable.

A structured approach to **pilot testing** follows, where the evaluation plan is put into action with a representative learner group. This phase includes defining participant roles, setting timelines, and outlining how data will be collected, managed, and reviewed.

Finally, the evaluation cycle concludes with a focus on **incorporating feedback**. Insights gathered from the evaluation are used to refine and improve the instructional materials, driving continuous improvement and ensuring that future learners benefit from a more engaging and effective learning experience.

Tips

- **Collaborate with Stakeholders**
  Involve subject matter experts (SMEs), instructors, and learners early in the evaluation design process for diverse insights.

- **Align with Objectives**
  Ensure all evaluation methods and criteria are directly tied to the learning objectives and course goals.

- **Pilot Test Instruments**
  Test evaluation tools with a small group to confirm their effectiveness and clarity before full implementation.

- **Focus on Usability**
  Include usability testing as part of the evaluation to ensure instructional materials are intuitive and learner friendly.

- **Use Mixed Methods**
  Combine quantitative (e.g., surveys) and qualitative (e.g., focus groups) approaches for a well-rounded evaluation.

- **Incorporate Cognitive Load Principles**
  Structure content to avoid overload by chunking material and spacing out complex concepts.

Assessment Design
Evaluation Design

Traps

- **Overcomplicating the Process**
  Complex evaluation plans can overwhelm participants and yield unclear results.
- **Neglecting Learner Perspectives**
  Failing to include learner feedback may overlook critical usability and engagement issues.
- **Lack of Clear Protocols**
  Unclear instructions can lead to inconsistent data collection and unreliable results.
- **Focusing Only on Strengths**
  Ignoring weaknesses in instructional materials prevents meaningful improvement.
- **Underestimating Time and Resources**
  Inadequate planning for pilot testing can result in incomplete evaluations.
- **Designing for the Designer, Not the Learner**
  Building complex structures that impress SMEs but overwhelm learners can reduce usability and retention.

Techniques

- **Backward Design**
  Start with evaluation goals and work backward to design instruments and methods.
- **Criteria Mapping**
  Map each evaluation criterion to specific learning objectives for clarity and alignment.
- **Think-Aloud Protocols**
  Use this technique during usability testing to capture real-time learner feedback.
- **Benchmarking**
  Compare instructional materials against industry standards or similar courses for context.
- **Cognitive Walkthroughs**
  Step through the design as if you were a learner to identify confusion points or navigation issues early.

Examples

- *Evaluation Criteria Example*
  Assess learner engagement by measuring time spent on tasks and completion rates.
- *Pilot Testing Example*
  Invite a group of 10 learners to test a course module and provide feedback through surveys and focus groups.
- *Usability Testing Example*
  Observe learners navigating a course module, noting areas of confusion or difficulty.
- *Feedback Integration Example*
  Use pilot test results to refine lesson flow, adjust activities, and add multimedia elements for improved engagement.
- *Learning Path Visualisation*
  Provide learners with a visual roadmap of their journey through the course, reinforcing structure and purpose.

Assessment Design
Evaluation Design

How it's done

1. **Define Evaluation Criteria**
   Work with stakeholders to establish clear, measurable criteria for assessing the effectiveness, engagement, and usability of instructional materials. Ensure these criteria align with the learning objectives and goals of the course.
2. **Select Evaluation Methods**
   Identify appropriate evaluation methods, such as expert reviews, learner surveys, or usability tests, based on the depth of feedback required and the available resources.
3. **Develop Evaluation Instruments**
   Create well-structured tools, such as surveys, Checklist
4. **Plan Pilot Testing**
   Draft a comprehensive pilot testing plan that includes objectives, participant roles, timelines, logistics, and data collection strategies to evaluate the materials in a realistic setting.
5. **Prepare Testing Protocols**
   Develop clear and consistent protocols for data collection to ensure reliability across all evaluation activities. Provide participants with detailed instructions to minimise variability.
6. **Analyse Evaluation Data**
   Collect and review feedback from evaluation activities, identifying trends, strengths, and weaknesses. Use this data to pinpoint areas requiring improvement.
7. **Incorporate Feedback into Refinements**
   Apply findings from the evaluation to refine the instructional materials. Collaborate with stakeholders to validate changes and confirm improvements align with learning objectives.
8. **Document Findings**
   Summarise the evaluation results in a detailed report. Highlight key insights, actionable recommendations, and next steps, providing stakeholders with a clear overview of outcomes and decisions.

Core Elements

- **Criteria Defined**
  Evaluation criteria are directly aligned with learning objectives and goals.
- **Methods Selected**
  Evaluation methods suit the desired depth of feedback and resource availability.
- **Pilot Testing Planned**
  Testing is organised with clear objectives, roles, and timelines.
- **Protocols Prepared**
  Data collection is standardised with detailed instructions.
- **Data Analysed**
  Evaluation results are reviewed for actionable insights and improvement areas.
- **Findings Documented**
  A comprehensive report is prepared for stakeholders, detailing results and recommendations.

Checklist

1. Define the purpose of evaluation (e.g., learning, performance, compliance)
2. Align evaluation types (formative, summative, diagnostic) with learning objectives
3. Identify target levels of Kirkpatrick or equivalent model
4. Determine data collection methods (e.g., tests, surveys, observation)
5. Establish success thresholds and metrics for evaluation
6. Assign responsibilities for evaluation design, delivery, and analysis
7. Ensure ethical and accessible evaluation practices
8. Document the evaluation plan, tools, and reporting requirements
9. Simulate learner navigation through the structure to identify flow or logic issues

Assessment Design
Evaluation Design

151

AI Considerations

- Use AI to generate evaluation plans aligned to learning goals
- Auto-suggest appropriate evaluation levels (e.g., Kirkpatrick L1–L4)
- Analyse historical data to define realistic success thresholds
- Generate feedback forms or surveys from content objectives
- AI can automate analysis of open-ended learner feedback
- Use AI to generate variant learning sequences for different learner personas (e.g. beginner vs advanced)

Key Takeaways

The Evaluation Design sub-step in the Design phase, is crucial for systematically assessing the quality and effectiveness of instructional materials.

By establishing clear criteria, selecting appropriate methods, and conducting thorough pilot testing, instructional designers ensure that materials meet their intended goals.

A strong evaluation design fosters collaboration with stakeholders and provides valuable insights for refining and improving course materials. Thoughtful planning and robust analysis maximise the impact of instructional content, ensuring that learners achieve desired outcomes and that the course delivers measurable value.

A strong conceptual structure not only supports instruction but also enables scale, personalisation, and long-term learning success.

Assessment Items

Why this is important

Assessment items form the backbone of any meaningful evaluation strategy.

They must align directly with the course's learning objectives to ensure that what is being measured reflects what was taught.

Well-designed assessment items promote both validity and reliability, accurately and consistently gauging learner performance across various contexts and attempts.

Equally important is fairness and accessibility, assessment tasks should be free from bias, inclusive of diverse learner needs, and deliverable across platforms and devices.

To support deeper learning, assessment items should reflect a range of cognitive levels, from foundational recall to complex problem-solving and application.

When crafted carefully, assessments not only measure understanding but also provide actionable feedback that helps learners improve, reflect, and achieve mastery.

Tips

- **Begin with Objectives**
  Base each assessment item on a specific learning objective to maintain alignment and focus.
- **Diversify Item Types**
  Use a mix of multiple-choice, short-answer, essays, and performance tasks to assess different skills.
- **Pilot Test**
  Trial assessment items with a small group to identify issues with clarity or difficulty.
- **Use Rubrics**
  Develop rubrics for open-ended tasks to ensure consistent and objective grading.
- **Consider Accessibility**
  Design items that accommodate learners with disabilities, using alternative formats or assistive technologies.

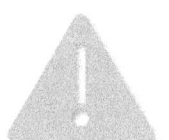

Traps

- **Misalignment with Objectives**
  Items that do not directly measure the intended learning outcomes will result in irrelevant evaluations.
- **Overly Complex Wording**
  Confusing language can lead to misinterpretation of questions by learners.
- **Bias in Content**
  Unintentional cultural, gender, or regional biases can unfairly disadvantage certain learners.
- **Neglecting Feedback**
  Assessments without feedback fail to support learner improvement and growth.
- **Ignoring Practicality**
  Overly complex or time-consuming items may not be feasible within the instructional context.

Techniques

- **Backward Design**
  Start with learning objectives and design assessment items to measure those outcomes.
- **Cognitive Load Balance**
  Distribute items across Bloom's taxonomy, addressing knowledge, comprehension, application, and higher-order thinking.
- **Scenario-Based Questions**
  Use real-world scenarios to create authentic and engaging assessment items.
- **Adaptive Assessment**
  Incorporate technology to adjust item difficulty based on learner responses.
- **Peer Review**
  Have colleagues or SMEs review assessment items to ensure quality and relevance.

Assessment Design
Assessment Items

Examples

- *Multiple-Choice*
  A question asks learners to identify the best solution to a workplace problem, requiring analysis and application.
- *Short-Answer*
  Learners explain a concept in their own words, testing comprehension and clarity.
- *Performance Task*
  Learners design a project plan, demonstrating application of key skills.
- *Scenario-Based Item*
  Given a case study, learners analyse the situation and recommend actionable solutions.
- *Rubric Example*
  A detailed scoring guide outlines criteria for grading an essay, including clarity, depth of analysis, and relevance.

How it's done

1. **Review Learning Objectives**
   Ensure each assessment item is clearly aligned with specific learning objectives by mapping them in a matrix to maintain focus and relevance.
2. **Select Assessment Types**
   Incorporate a variety of assessment formats, such as formative (e.g., quizzes, reflections) and summative (e.g., exams, projects), to cater to diverse learning goals and learner preferences.
3. **Develop Assessment Items**
   Write clear, precise questions or prompts that use active verbs to measure intended outcomes effectively. Avoid ambiguous or overly complex language to ensure learners understand expectations.
4. **Create Rubrics**
   Develop detailed scoring guides for open-ended tasks, specifying performance levels with clear descriptors to standardise grading and provide transparent feedback.
5. **Pilot Test Assessments**
   Test assessment items with a sample group of learners, gathering feedback to identify issues such as unclear wording or unintentional biases. Make revisions to improve accuracy and fairness.
6. **Ensure Accessibility**
   Review all items for inclusivity and accessibility, adhering to universal design principles. Provide alternative formats or tools, such as screen readers or extended time, to support diverse learner needs.
7. **Integrate Assessments with Technology**
   Design assessment items compatible with the chosen platform, leveraging LMS features like auto-grading, adaptive pathways, and analytics to enhance efficiency and learner engagement.
8. **Document and Store Assessment Items**
   Maintain an organised repository of all items and rubrics, tagging them for easy retrieval and future use in similar instructional contexts.

Assessment Design
Assessment Items

Core Elements

- **Objective Alignment**
  All assessment items align directly with the intended learning objectives.
- **Diverse Item Types**
  A range of formats (e.g., multiple-choice, short-answer, case studies) assesses different skills effectively.
- **Clear Language**
  Questions are concise, precise, and easy to understand, reducing confusion.
- **Rubrics Ready**
  Comprehensive scoring rubrics are developed for open-ended or subjective items.
- **Bias-Free Content**
  Items are reviewed for cultural, linguistic, or other biases to ensure fairness.
- **Accessibility Ensured**
  Accommodations and universal design principles make assessments inclusive for all learners.
- **Pilot Testing Complete**
  Items are validated through testing with feedback integrated to refine accuracy and usability.
- **Feedback Mechanisms**
  Systems are in place to provide learners with actionable feedback to support their learning.

Checklist

1. Items clearly linked to behavioural and learning objectives
2. Include a balanced mix of item types (MCQ, drag-drop, scenario-based, etc.)
3. Avoid bias, ambiguity, and overly complex language
4. Include distractors that are plausible but clearly incorrect
5. Define scoring logic, passing criteria, and feedback for each item
6. Validate questions with SMEs and pilot with sample learners
7. Randomisation and pooling considered where applicable
8. Review for alignment, coverage, and fairness before deployment

AI Considerations

- Generate draft assessment items from learning objectives
- Use AI to classify questions by Bloom's Taxonomy or difficulty level
- Simulate learner responses to evaluate distractor effectiveness
- Auto-generate feedback explanations for both correct and incorrect options
- Analyse question bank coverage for redundancy or gaps

Key Takeaways

The Assessment Items sub-step in the Design phase, ensures robust, fair, and meaningful evaluations of learner progress.

Through alignment with objectives, a variety of item types, and a focus on clarity and accessibility, Instructional designers create assessments that accurately measure learning outcomes.

Pilot testing and iterative refinements enhance reliability, while tools like rubrics and adaptive technologies streamline evaluation.

These efforts culminate in assessments that not only validate learning but also empower learners and inform stakeholders about the effectiveness of the instructional design.

Media and Content Strategy

Overview

The **Media and Content Strategy** step in the Design phase of the ADDIE model is focused on selecting, structuring, and presenting media and content to maximise learner engagement and comprehension.

This step is integral to delivering content that is informative, interactive, visually appealing, and aligned with the course objectives.

By incorporating thoughtful media choices, clear organisation, and supportive visuals, this step ensures that the instructional content is both accessible and engaging, catering to diverse learning preferences and needs.

Key Sub-Steps are:

- **Media Selection**
  Choose media types (e.g., video, audio, animations, text) that align with learning objectives and enhance engagement.
- **Courseware Design**
  Structure and organise course content logically, ensuring it supports effective learning progression.
- **Graphic Design**
  Develop visuals, diagrams, and infographics to simplify complex concepts and add visual appeal.
- **Links to References**
  Provide curated external resources that deepen understanding and encourage self-directed learning.
- **Accessibility Standards Review**
  Ensure that all course elements comply with accessibility guidelines, such as WCAG, by incorporating features like alt text, captions, and keyboard navigation to create an inclusive learning environment that accommodates diverse learner needs.

Media and Content Strategy
Assessment Items

Outcomes

The outcomes of the Media and Content Strategy step are centred on creating an engaging, cohesive, and learner-focused instructional experience.

Key outcomes include:

- **Align Media with Learning Objectives**
  Select media that complements and reinforces instructional goals, addressing specific learning needs effectively.

- **Design Logical and Engaging Courseware**
  Organise content into a clear structure that enhances flow and guides learners through the material intuitively.

- **Enhance Understanding with Visuals**
  Incorporate graphics, infographics, and other visual aids to clarify complex information and boost retention.

- **Provide External Learning Resources**
  Link to relevant references or additional materials to extend learning opportunities and support deeper exploration.

- **Ensure Accessibility**
  Adhere to accessibility standards by including features such as captions for videos, alt text for images, and compatibility with assistive technologies.

Summary

The Media and Content Strategy step is fundamental to creating an engaging and effective learning experience. By selecting appropriate media, structuring content logically, incorporating supportive visuals, and linking to relevant references, instructional designers ensure that the course is aligned with its objectives and resonates with learners.

A well-executed strategy avoids common pitfalls, such as overloading learners with unnecessary media or presenting disorganised content, by focusing on balance and cohesion. This approach not only supports learner engagement but also enhances comprehension, retention, and satisfaction, delivering an impactful and accessible learning environment.

By balancing media elements and aligning them with the course's instructional goals, the Media and Content Strategy step ensures a streamlined, impactful learning journey tailored to the needs of all learners.

Media and Content Strategy
Media Selection

Media Selection

Why this is important

Selecting the right media is essential for achieving effective learning outcomes.

Well-chosen media formats help communicate key concepts clearly and reinforce the instructional content, making learning more memorable and impactful.

Beyond clarity, engaging and interactive media play a crucial role in capturing learners' attention and sustaining their interest throughout the course. It is equally important to ensure that all media choices meet accessibility standards, so that every learner, including those with disabilities, can engage fully and equitably with the content.

The selected media should also support real-world application by contextualising concepts through examples, scenarios, or simulations that mirror actual workplace or life situations.

Finally, good media selection makes optimal use of available resources, balancing quality and cost to deliver experiences that are aligned with both instructional goals and project constraints.

Tips

- **Match Media to Objectives**
  Ensure each media type serves a defined instructional purpose by directly aligning it with the learning objective it supports.

- **Conduct Audience Analysis**
  Choose media formats that reflect your audience's needs, considering their learning preferences, access to technology, and digital fluency.

- **Prioritise Accessibility**
  Build in accessibility from the outset, use captions, alt text, transcripts, and screen-reader-friendly layouts to support diverse learner needs.

- **Plan Media Integration**
  Develop a clear integration plan showing how each media element complements the instructional flow and reinforces key concepts.

- **Leverage Existing Resources**
  Audit existing media assets for potential reuse or adaptation to reduce development time and optimise budget without sacrificing quality.

Traps

- **Overloading Learners**
  Using too much media or including elements that are not instructionally relevant can overwhelm learners and dilute the core message.

- **Ignoring Technical Constraints**
  Selecting media formats that are incompatible with the delivery platform or learners' devices can disrupt access and usability.

- **Neglecting Accessibility**
  Failing to incorporate accessibility features, such as captions, alt text, and keyboard navigation, can exclude users and may lead to non-compliance with accessibility standards.

- **Underestimating Costs**
  Overly ambitious or custom media production plans can quickly exceed available budgets and slow down project timelines.

- **Misaligned Media**
  Using media that does not directly support the learning objectives can create confusion and reduce the instructional impact of the course.

- **Inconsistent Style or Quality**
  Mixing different visual or audio styles without a cohesive strategy can create a fragmented learning experience and reduce credibility.

Media and Content Strategy
Media Selection

Techniques

- **Storyboard Integration**
  Use storyboards to map out the instructional flow and pinpoint where media elements will be introduced to support learning objectives.

- **Apply Multimedia Learning Principles**
  Incorporate evidence-based principles such as dual-channel processing, coherence, and modality effects to enhance comprehension and retention.

- **Content Chunking with Media Mapping**
  Break complex content into manageable segments and assign appropriate media types to each chunk to reinforce clarity and learner focus.

- **Rapid Prototyping**
  Build low-fidelity or sample versions of media assets to test usability, engagement, and instructional value before committing to full-scale production.

- **Blended Media Strategy**
  Combine complementary media formats, such as text, audio, video, and interactive elements, to accommodate diverse learner needs and preferences.

Examples

- *Video Tutorials*
  Step-by-step demonstrations of a technical process to aid comprehension.

- *Interactive Simulations*
  A virtual lab environment for learners to experiment with concepts safely.

- *Infographics*
  A visual summary of complex data to simplify understanding.

- *Case Study Animations*
  Animated scenarios presenting real-world challenges and solutions.

- *Audio Narrations*
  Story-driven lessons with voiceovers to guide learners through the content.

- *Media-First Design for Key Concepts*
  For difficult or abstract topics, start with media concepts (like an animation or demo) and build the narrative or activity around it to anchor understanding.

Media and Content Strategy
Media Selection

How it's done

1. **Understand Learning Objectives**
   Review learning objectives to determine appropriate media types and map specific media elements to each objective, ensuring alignment and clarity.

2. **Conduct Audience Analysis**
   Gather data on learner preferences and technology habits through surveys or focus groups to refine media selection and enhance engagement.

3. **Evaluate Resource Availability**
   Assess internal and external resources for media production, including budget considerations and time constraints, to ensure feasibility.

4. **Select Media Types**
   Choose media formats that align with the content's instructional purpose and the learner profile. Use media strategically to address content gaps or enhance difficult concepts through visual, auditory, or experiential elements.

5. **Test Media Formats**
   Pilot media elements with a sample audience to evaluate usability, engagement, and accessibility. Refine based on feedback to optimise the learner experience.

6. **Ensure Accessibility**
   Implement accessibility features such as captions, alt text, and scalable interfaces. Test all media for compliance with accessibility standards to accommodate diverse learner needs.

7. **Document a Media Plan**
   Develop a comprehensive media plan outlining selected media types, their purpose, and their placement within the course structure for seamless integration.

8. **Plan for Media Maintenance**
   Identify any media elements that may require future updates due to changing content, technology, or branding, and document version control procedures accordingly.

Core Elements

- **Alignment**
  Ensure all media directly support the learning objectives and add value to the instructional content.

- **Engagement**
  Select engaging media elements that capture and maintain learner interest.

- **Accessibility**
  Include captions, alt text, and alternative formats to comply with accessibility standards and promote inclusivity.

- **Compatibility**
  Verify that all media formats are compatible with delivery platforms and learner devices.

- **Pilot Testing**
  Use pilot testing to evaluate media clarity, engagement, and accessibility. Refine based on learner feedback to improve overall impact.

- **Budget Adherence**
  Keep media production within established budgetary constraints.

- **Resource Allocation**
  Allocate sufficient resources for the development and integration of media into the course.

Media and Content Strategy
Media Selection

Checklist

1. Identify content types requiring visual, audio, or interactive media
2. Align media formats with learning objectives and delivery mode
3. Consider learner access, bandwidth, and device constraints
4. Evaluate media for cognitive load and clarity
5. Select media that support inclusivity and diverse learning styles
6. Review licensing and intellectual property rights if using third-party assets
7. Pilot media selections with sample learners where feasible
8. Document media selection rationale for design consistency

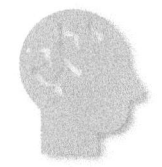
AI Considerations

- Use AI to recommend media formats based on learning goals
- Analyse past learner preferences or completion data to inform choices
- Use text-to-video/image generators to prototype assets
- Suggest cost-effective media alternatives (e.g. animation vs. live-action)
- Flag media-heavy designs that may impact bandwidth or access equity

Key Takeaways

The Media Selection sub-step in the Design phase, is integral to creating impactful learning experiences. By carefully aligning media with objectives and audience needs, instructional designers ensure content is engaging, accessible, and effective.

Through thoughtful planning, testing, and refinement, media elements enhance the overall instructional environment while accommodating technological, budgetary, and accessibility considerations.

A well-executed media strategy bridges the gap between content delivery and learner engagement, driving successful outcomes.

Media and Content Strategy
Courseware Design

Courseware Design

Why this is important

A well-designed courseware structure must align directly with the learning objectives defined during the Analysis phase. This alignment ensures that each instructional element serves a clear educational purpose and contributes to the achievement of measurable outcomes. When objectives and design are tightly connected, learners experience more focused, purposeful instruction that avoids unnecessary or distracting content.

Incorporating engaging and interactive elements into courseware is essential for maintaining learner interest and motivation. When learners are actively involved through scenarios, simulations, and responsive feedback, they are more likely to retain knowledge and apply it effectively. Engagement transforms passive consumption into active learning, which deepens understanding and improves outcomes.

Logical flow and progression within the courseware support cognitive scaffolding. By structuring the content so that each segment builds upon the previous one, learners can assimilate complex material more effectively. A well-sequenced journey enables learners to grow their knowledge step-by-step, reinforcing comprehension and confidence as they advance through the material.

Accessibility is a critical consideration in modern learning environments.

Inclusive courseware ensures that individuals with disabilities or diverse learning needs are not disadvantaged. Designing with accessibility in mind, from captioning and readable fonts to keyboard navigation and screen reader compatibility, creates a welcoming learning environment for all users, fostering equity and compliance with global standards.

Lastly, the integration of appropriate technology enriches the learning experience by delivering content through platforms and tools that are intuitive and seamless. Leveraging technology effectively enables scalability, responsiveness, and interactivity, which are all essential in today's digital-first training environments. Whether it's through LMS compatibility, multimedia support, or AI-enhanced adaptivity, smart use of technology transforms static learning into dynamic engagement.

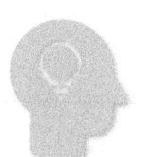

Tips

- **Start with Storyboarding**
  Start with structured storyboarding. It allows you to plan interactions, visual flow, and media placement with precision and alignment.

- **Prioritise User Experience**
  Keep navigation intuitive and design a clean, responsive interface for ease of use.

- **Incorporate Feedback Loops**
  Embed opportunities for learners to provide feedback and reflect on their progress.

- **Keep It Modular**
  Develop content in modular units to facilitate updates and adapt to different learning pathways.

- **Test Early and Often**
  Test early and repeat at key milestones. Even rough wireframes or draft screens can uncover usability issues before they become costly.

Traps

- **Overcomplicating Design**
  Avoid adding unnecessary features that can overwhelm learners or distract from the content.

- **Ignoring Accessibility**
  Failing to meet accessibility standards can exclude learners and result in non-compliance.

- **Neglecting Alignment**
  Mismatched courseware and learning objectives can lead to ineffective learning outcomes.

- **Underestimating Resource Needs**
  Overlooking time, budget, or technical constraints can compromise courseware quality.

- **Inconsistent Content**
  Lack of standardisation in visuals, tone, or design can confuse learners and detract from the experience.

Media and Content Strategy
Courseware Design

Techniques

- **Chunking**
  Divide content into manageable sections to prevent cognitive overload and enhance retention.
- **Gamification**
  Include elements like badges, points, or leaderboards to increase motivation and engagement.
- **Visual Hierarchy**
  Use design elements such as colour, size, and spacing to guide learners' attention to key areas.
- **Scaffolding**
  Gradually build complexity in content and activities to support skill and knowledge acquisition.
- **Rapid Prototyping**
  Create quick prototypes to test design concepts with stakeholders and iterate based on feedback.

Examples

- *Interactive Modules*
  A self-paced course broken into modules with quizzes and multimedia elements to test comprehension.
- *Case-Based Learning*
  Learners solve real-world problems using scenarios presented through videos and simulations.
- *Accessible Content*
  Courseware includes closed captions, alternative text for images, and transcripts for audio materials.
- *Gamified Learning*
  A sales training programme with progress tracking, rewards for milestones, and role-play simulations.
- *Mobile-Friendly Design*
  A responsive course interface optimised for learning on smartphones and tablets.

How it's done

1. **Align with Learning Objectives**
   Begin by reviewing the learning objectives to ensure that all courseware content, activities, and assessments directly support the desired outcomes.
2. **Create a Content Map**
   Organise modules, lessons, and subtopics into a logical sequence that builds on prior knowledge, providing a clear structure for learners to follow.
3. **Design Interactive Elements**
   Develop quizzes, simulations, and other interactive components to reinforce learning objectives and promote active learner engagement.
4. **Integrate Multimedia**
   Incorporate visuals, videos, animations, and other multimedia elements that enhance comprehension and maintain learner interest.
5. **Prioritise Accessibility**
   Ensure the courseware complies with accessibility standards by including features such as captions, alt text, and compatibility with screen readers to accommodate diverse learner needs.
6. **Prototype Development**
   Create a working model of the courseware for stakeholder review. Use feedback to refine and improve the design before finalising.
7. **Quality Assurance**
   Perform usability testing and thorough content reviews to identify and resolve technical or instructional issues, ensuring a polished and effective learning experience.

Media and Content Strategy
Courseware Design

Core Elements

- **Alignment**
  All courseware content and activities should align directly with the stated learning objectives.
- **Engagement**
  Use interactive elements and multimedia to keep learners motivated and actively involved.
- **Accessibility**
  Ensure that courseware meets accessibility standards, allowing all learners to participate equally.
- **Consistency**
  Maintain uniformity in visuals, tone, and navigation throughout the course for a cohesive experience.
- **Feedback Integration**
  Include mechanisms for learners to provide and receive feedback to enhance the learning process.
- **Technology Compatibility**
  Verify that the courseware functions seamlessly across all intended devices and platforms.
- **Quality Testing**
  Conduct rigorous testing to ensure instructional quality and usability before deployment.

Checklist

1. Structure aligns with conceptual framework and learning hierarchy
2. Consistent navigation, visual layout, and instructional flow applied
3. Interactive elements support active engagement and feedback
4. Templates used for visual and instructional consistency
5. Chunking and pacing optimised for attention and retention
6. Content reviewed for clarity, tone, and accessibility
7. Style guide applied for fonts, colour, tone, and terminology
8. Stakeholders review design before build phase

AI Considerations

- Auto-generate courseware layouts based on storyboard or script inputs
- Suggest user interface flows optimised for learner engagement
- Scan for consistency of terminology, tone, and visual branding
- Predict learner drop-off points and recommend adjustments
- Convert raw text into structured course screen drafts

Key Takeaways

The Courseware Design sub-step in the Design phase, is essential for creating engaging learner-focused materials.

By ensuring alignment with objectives, incorporating accessibility and multimedia, and refining through iterative feedback, instructional designers can deliver impactful courseware.

This process not only meets diverse learner needs but also achieves organisational goals, providing scalable and effective learning solutions.

Graphic Design

Why this is important

Graphic design is critical to supporting the achievement of learning objectives. When visual elements are intentionally aligned with key outcomes, they do more than decorate, they clarify, reinforce and elevate the learning experience. A well-designed graphic highlights essential concepts and provides visual cues that guide learner attention to what matters most.

Good graphics also enhance comprehension. Visuals can simplify complex ideas by turning abstract or detailed information into clear, digestible formats.

Diagrams, charts, icons and annotated illustrations help learners understand relationships, processes and structures that may be difficult to explain with text alone. This visual support reduces cognitive load and makes it easier to absorb and retain information.

Engagement is another major benefit. Visually appealing and thoughtfully placed graphics spark interest, stimulate curiosity and help maintain motivation throughout the course. Where appropriate, interactive or animated elements can add energy and focus, making the learning journey feel more dynamic and responsive.

Accessibility must be built into all visual design decisions. Graphics should be inclusive and comply with accessibility standards to ensure they can be understood and used by learners with visual, cognitive or motor impairments.

This includes the use of high contrast, clear labelling, alternative text, and avoiding reliance on colour alone to convey meaning.

Finally, consistency in visual styling reinforces the professionalism and coherence of the courseware. A unified graphic approach, through colour palettes, font usage, iconography and layout choices, creates a strong visual identity that supports the tone and structure of the course. Consistency helps learners stay focused and reduces distractions, making the content easier to navigate and trust.

Tips

- **Use Storyboards**
  Plan the placement and purpose of each graphic to ensure alignment with the learning content.

- **Leverage Templates**
  Use design templates to maintain consistency in style and layout across all visuals.

- **Consider Colour Psychology**
  Use colours strategically to evoke desired emotions and direct learner attention.

- **Test for Readability**
  Ensure text within graphics is legible across various screen sizes and resolutions.

- **Keep It Simple**
  Avoid overloading visuals with unnecessary details or text to maintain clarity and focus.

Traps

- **Ignoring Accessibility**
  Neglecting alternative text, colour contrast, or scalable designs can exclude learners with disabilities.

- **Overcomplication**
  Complex graphics can confuse rather than clarify, detracting from the learning experience.

- **Inconsistent Design**
  Using varying styles or colour schemes across graphics can disrupt the learner's focus and reduce cohesion.

- **Using Low-Quality Images**
  Poor resolution can appear unprofessional and detract from learner engagement.

- **Lack of Relevance**
  Graphics that don't directly relate to the content can distract or confuse learners.

Media and Content Strategy
Graphic Design

Techniques

- **Chunking**
  Break down complex information into smaller, visual segments for better retention.
- **Data Visualisation**
  Use charts, graphs, or infographics to represent numerical or statistical data meaningfully.
- **Iconography**
  Develop or use icons to symbolise concepts or actions clearly and consistently.
- **Interactive Elements**
  Add clickable elements, hotspots, or animations to foster engagement.
- **Universal Design Principles**
  Follow principles like balance, alignment, and proximity to ensure visual appeal and functionality.

Examples

- *Diagrams*
  Process flow diagrams illustrating steps in a workflow or procedure.
- *Infographics*
  Visual representation of data comparing training effectiveness before and after implementation.
- *Illustrations*
  Custom drawings to depict scenarios or concepts that are abstract or hard to photograph.
- *Icons and Symbols*
  Standardised icons to represent actions like "Save," "Download," or "Submit."
- *Interactive Graphics*
  Hotspot-enabled images where learners click to explore different parts of a system or process.

How it's done

1. **Identify Visual Needs**
   Collaborate with subject matter experts to pinpoint concepts requiring visual representation. Focus on areas where visuals will simplify or enhance the learning content.
2. **Develop Storyboards**
   Create detailed drafts of graphic placements within the instructional flow, using sketches or design tools to ensure visuals align seamlessly with the content.
3. **Design Graphics**
   Utilise graphic design software to produce visuals that are clear, engaging, and aligned with the principles of effective design.
4. **Test Accessibility**
   Ensure all graphics meet accessibility standards by including alt text, captions, or descriptive audio, and confirming compliance with contrast and readability requirements.
5. **Review and Iterate**
   Share draft visuals with stakeholders for feedback. Refine designs based on their input to improve clarity, relevance, and alignment with learning objectives.
6. **Finalise Integration**
   Incorporate approved graphics into the instructional materials, ensuring they align with the content flow and are technically compatible with the delivery platform.

Media and Content Strategy
Graphic Design

Core Elements

- **Alignment**
  Graphics must directly support learning objectives and enhance understanding.
- **Clarity**
  Visuals should be free of unnecessary elements and easy to interpret.
- **Consistency**
  Maintain a uniform design style across all graphics for a cohesive look and feel.
- **Accessibility**
  Graphics should comply with standards, incorporating features like alt text and appropriate contrast.
- **Engagement**
  Use visuals to capture learner attention and sustain interest.
- **Relevance**
  Ensure that each graphic meaningfully contributes to the instructional content.
- **Quality**
  Graphics should be high resolution and optimised for use across various devices.

Checklist

1. Visual elements align with content, tone, and learner expectations
2. Graphics support comprehension and reduce cognitive load
3. Visuals are culturally appropriate and inclusive
4. Standardised iconography and styles applied across modules
5. All graphics optimised for performance (size, format, resolution)
6. Alt text provided for all non-decorative images
7. Templates used to maintain visual coherence
8. Graphic designs reviewed for clarity, relevance, and accessibility

AI Considerations

- Generate placeholder graphics, icons, or layouts from prompts
- Auto-check colour contrast ratios for accessibility compliance
- Suggest visual metaphors or diagrams based on text input
- Analyse graphics for cultural bias or visual overload
- Optimise image sets for speed, resolution, and cross-device compatibility

Key Takeaways

The Design Graphics sub-step in the Design Phase, is essential for creating impactful visual elements that simplify complex concepts, engage learners, and support learning objectives.

By adhering to design principles, prioritising accessibility, and incorporating feedback through iterative refinement, instructional designers can craft visuals that transform instructional materials into engaging and inclusive learning experiences.

Links to References

Why this is important

Providing clear and accessible links to references plays a key role in establishing the credibility, depth and integrity of courseware. Referencing source materials not only acknowledges the work of others, it signals to learners that the content is grounded in evidence, aligned with industry standards or scholarly thinking, and open to further exploration.

Links to references also support learner autonomy. They give learners the opportunity to explore topics in more detail, validate claims, or follow up with additional reading based on their own curiosity or needs. This ability to extend learning beyond the course encourages self-directed growth and fosters a deeper intellectual engagement with the material.

From a compliance and ethical standpoint, transparent referencing helps to avoid plagiarism and respects copyright and intellectual property laws. It reflects best practice in academic and corporate training environments, especially where regulated or technical subject matter is involved.

In addition, including links to reputable references allows instructional designers to keep content lean and focused. Rather than overloading the main course narrative with lengthy justifications or background detail, links provide a clean way to separate essential knowledge from optional enrichment. This helps reduce cognitive load while still catering to diverse learning styles.

Finally, references contribute to the overall user experience. When links are clearly presented, well labelled, and consistently formatted, they become a navigational aid rather than a distraction. Effective referencing is not just about content, it's also about trust, transparency and professionalism.

Tips

- **Verify Sources**
  Always vet the credibility of linked resources to maintain the integrity of the instructional material.
- **Use Multimedia**
  Include videos, articles, case studies, and interactive tools to appeal to diverse learners.
- **Provide Context**
  Briefly describe why a resource is included and how it aligns with learning objectives.
- **Update Regularly**
  Periodically review links to ensure they remain relevant and functional.
- **Centralise Access**
  Offer a single repository or section within the course for all references to simplify navigation.

Traps

- **Overloading Learners**
  Too many links can overwhelm learners; prioritise quality over quantity.
- **Broken or Outdated Links**
  Regularly check to avoid frustration from non-functional or obsolete references.
- **Irrelevant Resources**
  Ensure all links directly support the learning objectives to avoid distracting learners.
- **Ignoring Accessibility**
  Failing to provide accessible resources can exclude some learners.
- **Lack of Feedback Mechanism**
  Not gathering learner feedback can lead to missed opportunities for improvement.

Media and Content Strategy
Links to References

Techniques

- **Thematic Categorisation**
  Group resources by topic or module to streamline navigation and enhance relevance.
- **Interactive Resource Integration**
  Incorporate quizzes or activities linked to references to promote active engagement.
- **Contextual Linking**
  Embed links within lesson content where they are most relevant, rather than listing them separately.
- **Dynamic Resource Lists**
  Use technology to track learner interaction with resources and adjust offerings based on usage patterns.
- **Annotation Tools**
  Provide annotations or highlights on key points within linked documents or articles to focus learner attention.

Examples

- *Video Tutorials*
  A YouTube playlist on specific tools or techniques related to the lesson topic.
- *Case Studies*
  A PDF link to a real-world case study that demonstrates the application of theoretical principles.
- *Interactive Simulations*
  A link to a web-based simulation where learners can experiment with concepts in action.
- *Expert Talks*
  TED Talks or industry webinars offering deeper insights into the subject matter.
- *Collaborative Resources*
  Links to discussion forums or collaborative platforms where learners can share insights.

How it's done

1. **Identify and Curate Resources**
   Collaborate with subject matter experts to locate credible, high-quality resources that align with the course's learning objectives. Evaluate each resource for relevance and reliability before compiling them into a comprehensive reference list.
2. **Ensure Accessibility**
   Review all resources to ensure compliance with accessibility standards by incorporating features such as captions, alternative text, and accessible formats.
3. **Integrate into Content**
   Embed links seamlessly within instructional materials at relevant points to provide additional context and relevance. Ensure the integration does not disrupt the flow of the content.
4. **Provide Context**
   Accompany each resource with a brief summary or description explaining its purpose, significance, and relevance to the lesson or course objectives.
5. **Monitor Usage**
   Utilise analytics tools to track learner interactions with the resources. Measure key metrics such as click through rates, time spent on linked materials, and overall engagement.
6. **Gather Feedback**
   Collect insights from learners about the usefulness and relevance of the references through surveys or feedback forms. Use this information to refine and enhance the resource list.
7. **Maintain and Update**
   Periodically review the resources to ensure they remain accurate and up to date. Address broken links, replace outdated materials, and expand the resource list to keep it dynamic and relevant.

Media and Content Strategy
Links to References

169

Core Elements

- **Relevance**
  Resources must directly support course objectives and learning outcomes.
- **Functionality**
  All links should be functional, accurate, and up to date.
- **Accessibility**
  Resources should accommodate diverse learner needs with features such as captions and alt text.
- **Diversity**
  Offer a variety of resources, including articles, videos, and interactive tools, to cater to different learning preferences.
- **Context**
  Provide concise descriptions for each resource to clarify its purpose and enhance its usability.
- **Feedback**
  Use learner input to improve the relevance and quality of the resources over time.
- **Maintenance**
  Regularly review and refresh the resource list to maintain its accuracy and effectiveness.

Checklist

1. Review all content and media for compliance with WCAG 2.1 or equivalent
2. Provide alt text for all images and descriptive labels for interactivity
3. Ensure keyboard navigability and screen reader compatibility
4. Use accessible colour palettes and contrast ratios
5. Avoid flashing or seizure-triggering animations
6. Include transcripts for audio and captions for video
7. Design for neurodiverse learners with simple layouts and clear instructions
8. Test accessibility using automated and manual tools

AI Considerations

- Use AI tools to auto-scan for WCAG compliance issues
- Generate alt text and captions based on image/audio content
- Simulate navigation using screen reader emulators
- Flag layout or interaction designs that may confuse neurodiverse users
- Generate accessibility checklists tailored to chosen media and platforms

Key Takeaways

The Links to References sub-step is essential for enriching instructional content by connecting learners with supplementary materials that enhance their understanding and engagement.

By curating, contextualising, and integrating resources thoughtfully, instructional designers can create a dynamic and accessible learning experience.

Regular updates and learner feedback ensure that resources remain valuable and aligned with course objectives, fostering deeper exploration and supporting diverse learning needs.

Accessibility Standards Review

Why this is important

Reviewing accessibility standards is essential to ensuring that all learners can fully participate in the learning experience, regardless of ability. By confirming alignment with recognised frameworks such as the Web Content Accessibility Guidelines (WCAG), designers can be confident that course materials are inclusive and usable across a wide range of learner needs and preferences.

Accessibility reviews promote an inclusive learning environment by removing barriers that may prevent learners with visual, auditory, cognitive or motor impairments from engaging with content. This means not just compliance with technical requirements, but thoughtful design that reflects empathy and consideration for diverse user experiences.

These reviews also play a crucial role in identifying gaps where the course may fall short of accessibility expectations. By proactively evaluating content, navigation, multimedia elements and interaction patterns, design teams can uncover issues before they impact learners, making it easier to implement timely and effective adjustments.

There is also a strong legal and ethical imperative. Many jurisdictions require digital learning materials to meet defined accessibility standards, and failing to do so may expose an organisation to risk. Beyond the legal aspect, inclusive design demonstrates a commitment to social responsibility and reinforces the organisation's values.

Lastly, prioritising accessibility directly enhances the overall learner experience. When learning is easy to navigate, intuitive to interact with, and readable by assistive technologies, it benefits everyone, not just those with diagnosed disabilities. Accessible design leads to more consistent engagement, higher satisfaction, and broader reach across the intended audience.

Tips

- **Use Established Standards**
  Follow guidelines such as WCAG to ensure a clear and measurable framework for accessibility.
- **Test with Assistive Technologies**
  Ensure compatibility with screen readers, voice recognition software, and other assistive tools.
- **Engage SMEs in Accessibility**
  Collaborate with accessibility experts to validate your design and materials.
- **Prioritise User Feedback**
  Collect insights from learners with disabilities to identify practical improvements.
- **Integrate Accessibility Early**
  Incorporate accessibility considerations from the start of the design process to avoid costly retrofitting.

Traps

- **Overlooking Key Features**
  Failing to include alt text, captions, or keyboard navigation can make content inaccessible to some learners.
- **Assuming Accessibility Equals Usability**
  Accessibility standards must be applied effectively to ensure ease of use.
- **Relying Solely on Automated Tools**
  Automated checks may miss nuanced accessibility issues that require human assessment.
- **Ignoring Diverse Disabilities**
  Designing for one type of disability may inadvertently exclude others.
- **Delaying Accessibility Reviews**
  Postponing reviews until late stages can result in costly changes and missed deadlines.

Media and Content Strategy
Accessibility Standards Review

Techniques

- **WCAG Compliance Checklist**
  Use to systematically review adherence to accessibility guidelines.
- **Simulated User Testing**
  Test the course with real or simulated users employing assistive technologies.
- **Contrast and Colour Tools**
  Use tools to ensure text and background combinations meet contrast ratio standards.
- **Accessible Media Creation**
  Include captions, transcripts, and descriptive audio in all multimedia materials.
- **Iterative Design Reviews**
  Conduct regular accessibility reviews at different stages of course development.

Examples

- *Accessible Video Content*
  A course video with accurate captions and audio descriptions ensures inclusivity.
- *Keyboard Navigation*
  Designing navigation that can be fully accessed using only a keyboard caters to motor-impaired learners.
- *Screen Reader Compatibility*
  Materials structured with proper headings and labels are easily navigable for screen reader users.
- *Contrast Standards Met*
  Using high-contrast text ensures readability for visually impaired learners.
- *Accessible Assessments*
  Interactive quizzes with alternative formats for input enhance inclusivity.

How it's done

1. **Review Applicable Accessibility Standards**
   Start by familiarising yourself with relevant guidelines such as WCAG or equivalent standards applicable to your course. These guidelines form the benchmark for accessibility compliance.
2. **Audit Course Materials for Compliance**
   Conduct a comprehensive review of all course content, multimedia elements, and navigation features to identify any potential accessibility issues.
3. **Identify Gaps in Accessibility**
   Document areas where the course does not meet required accessibility standards. Common gaps include missing alt text, lack of captions, and poorly designed navigation paths.
4. **Incorporate Assistive Technology Testing**
   Test the course for compatibility with assistive technologies like screen readers, keyboard navigation, and voice recognition software to ensure usability for all learners.
5. **Engage Accessibility SMEs**
   Work with subject matter experts in accessibility to validate your findings and gather recommendations for improving the course's inclusivity.
6. **Implement Necessary Changes**
   Address identified gaps by adding features like alternative text, closed captions, scalable fonts, or enhanced navigation options.
7. **Test Revised Content**
   Reassess the updated materials to confirm that the changes effectively resolve the identified issues and meet accessibility standards.
8. **Document Compliance Efforts**
   Maintain detailed records of all accessibility reviews, adjustments, and testing outcomes to demonstrate compliance and support future evaluations.

Media and Content Strategy
Accessibility Standards Review

Core Elements

- **Standards Reviewed**
  Familiarity with WCAG or similar guidelines ensures a structured approach to accessibility.
- **Audit Completed**
  All course elements, including multimedia and navigation, must be reviewed for compliance.
- **Assistive Technology Tested**
  Testing tools like screen readers and voice recognition software ensures compatibility with assistive technologies.
- **Gaps Addressed**
  Issues such as missing captions, improper navigation, or non-inclusive design must be resolved.
- **SME Validation**
  Accessibility experts provide critical validation and recommendations.
- **Updated Materials Tested**
  Revised content must undergo further testing to verify compliance and usability.
- **Documentation Maintained**
  Comprehensive records support accountability and enable continuous improvement.

Checklist

1. Review all content and media for compliance with WCAG 2.1 or equivalent
2. Provide alt text for all images and descriptive labels for interactivity
3. Ensure keyboard navigability and screen reader compatibility
4. Use accessible colour palettes and contrast ratios
5. Avoid flashing or seizure-triggering animations
6. Include transcripts for audio and captions for video
7. Design for neurodiverse learners with simple layouts and clear instructions
8. Test accessibility using automated and manual tools

AI Considerations

- Use AI tools to auto-scan for WCAG compliance issues
- Generate alt text and captions based on image/audio content
- Simulate navigation using screen reader emulators
- Flag layout or interaction designs that may confuse neurodiverse users
- Generate accessibility checklists tailored to chosen media and platforms

Key Takeaways

The Accessibility Standards Review is an essential sub-step in the Analysis phase of the ADDIE model, ensuring that instructional materials are inclusive and compliant with standards such as WCAG.

Proactively addressing accessibility enhances usability for all learners while avoiding costly retrofits. By leveraging expert insights, assistive technology testing, and iterative reviews, instructional designers can create engaging, inclusive, and legally compliant learning experiences.

Accessibility and Inclusion Strategy

Overview

The **Accessibility and Inclusion Strategy** step in the Design phase ensures that all learners, regardless of ability, background, or context, can fully engage with the learning experience. This step embeds inclusive thinking into every design decision, aligning with global accessibility standards and promoting equity through intentional, learner-centred design.

Key Sub-Steps are:

- **Define Inclusion Principles**
  Establish foundational values that shape inclusive learning design from the outset, not as an afterthought.
- **Address Diverse Learner Needs**
  Design for variability across cognitive, physical, linguistic, emotional, and cultural dimensions.
- **Culturally Sensitive Design**
  Ensure content, examples, and imagery reflect a respectful, globally aware perspective.
- **Inclusive Language and Visuals**
  Use wording and media that affirms dignity, avoids bias, and supports clarity for all learners.
- **Align with Global Accessibility Standards**
  Apply internationally recognised guidelines (e.g. WCAG 2.2) to guarantee legal compliance and universal usability.

Outcomes

The outcomes of the *Accessibility and Inclusion Strategy* step focus on ensuring that learning content is inclusive, respectful, and accessible to all learners, regardless of ability, background, or context.

Key Outcomes Include:

- **Establish Inclusion Principles**
  Define the foundational values and frameworks that will guide inclusive design decisions throughout the project.
- **Design for Learner Diversity**
  Identify and address varied cognitive, physical, cultural, and linguistic needs within the target audience.
- **Embed Cultural Sensitivity**
  Ensure that examples, imagery, and references reflect a globally respectful and context-aware perspective.
- **Use Inclusive Language and Visuals**
  Eliminate bias and enhance clarity by applying inclusive terminology and accessible visual conventions.
- **Apply Accessibility Standards**
  Align course design with recognised global standards (e.g. WCAG 2.2) to meet both compliance and usability expectations.

Summary

The Accessibility and Inclusion Strategy phase transforms learning from something that merely *reaches people* into something that *embraces them*.

It is where universal design, empathy, and technical rigour intersect to create equitable experiences for all learners, including those who are often underserved or overlooked.

It isn't just about avoiding exclusion; it's about actively building inclusion. When learners can see themselves in the content, navigate without barriers, and engage on their terms, learning becomes not only more effective, but more human.

Define Inclusion Principles

Why this is important

Defining inclusion principles is not just an exercise in ethics or optics, it is a strategic foundation that shapes every aspect of learning design. Without clearly articulated principles, efforts to promote accessibility or equity risk becoming reactive, fragmented, or purely cosmetic.

Inclusion must be intentional, embedded from the outset, and evident in both design choices and learner experience.

Strong inclusion principles guide design teams in navigating complex cultural, linguistic and neurodiverse contexts. They help reconcile competing needs, avoid unconscious bias, and ensure that every learner feels respected, recognised and represented.

Rather than defaulting to broad corporate DEI statements, these principles translate values into tangible decisions, such as how learners are depicted, how content is delivered, and how voice and choice are embedded in the learning process.

When done well, inclusion principles shift the entire project posture from compliance to care. They influence how scenarios are framed, how learners interact with the material, and how success is defined across different learner groups.

They provide a moral and creative compass for teams making difficult trade-offs under time or budget pressure.

Critically, inclusion principles also help teams stay responsive. As learner expectations evolve and new barriers emerge, well-framed principles allow for adaptive design without losing cohesion. They act as living guides, not static statements, that can be evaluated, tested and improved over time through feedback and reflection.

At their best, inclusion principles unlock innovation. They push teams to think beyond the typical learner profile and explore new modes of engagement, language use, representation and empowerment. In doing so, they ensure that the learning journey is not just accessible, but meaningful, for everyone.

Tips

- Co-create principles with learner-facing stakeholders or representatives.
- Focus on *empowerment* and *agency*, not just compliance or accommodation.
- Translate abstract values into concrete design implications.

Traps

- Relying on vague or generic DEI statements without mapping them to instructional design decisions
- Assuming one-size-fits-all principles work across cultures, industries, or learner types.
- Failing to update principles based on learner feedback or evolving social context.

Techniques

- Develop a **Design Equity Charter** with 4–6 learner-first values.
- Conduct a **"Principle in Action" review** of past content to evaluate how inclusion has (or hasn't) shown up.
- Embed principles into **design reviews and quality assurance checkpoints**.

Accessibility and Inclusion Strategy
Define Inclusion Principles

Examples

- *Principle*:
  "Learners should see themselves represented in content."
  Action:
  Every scenario includes diverse characters across age, ethnicity, and roles.
- *Principle*:
  "Content should accommodate multiple modes of access."
  Action:
  Every core module is available in audio, text, and visual summary format.

How it's done

1. Facilitate a collaborative session with key stakeholders and representative learners.
2. Draft a small set of high-impact inclusion principles tailored to your audience.
3. Map each principle to design behaviours or output standards.
4. Socialise the principles across your instructional design, media, and tech teams.
5. Include them as a standing reference in content sign-offs.

Core Elements

- Inclusion value (e.g., Representation, Choice, Voice, Equity)
- Audience-specific interpretation
- Design implications
- Behavioural signals
- QA checkpoints

Checklist

1. Define 4–6 core inclusion principles that reflect your learner population.
2. Link each principle to practical design behaviours.
3. Document principles in the design brief or ID template.
4. Review past courses for alignment or gaps.
5. Train design and media teams on principle integration.
6. Revisit principles annually or after major feedback events.

AI Considerations

- Use AI to draft or refine principles based on audience data and DEI benchmarks.
- Scan existing content to surface alignment or violations of stated principles.
- Generate learner-centric descriptions of each principle for user onboarding.
- Summarise stakeholder interviews into principle themes.

Key Takeaways

Inclusion principles are not optional extras; they form the ethical and strategic backbone of accessible learning design.

When clearly defined, these principles help instructional teams make consistent, values-driven decisions throughout the course development process.

Effective inclusion frameworks go beyond compliance by actively supporting learner empowerment, autonomy, and a sense of belonging.

Co-creating these principles with learner representatives enhances authenticity, relevance, and cultural sensitivity.

To ensure consistent implementation, values must be translated into observable behaviours, design standards, and quality assurance touchpoints.

Most importantly, inclusion principles must be treated as living artefacts; reviewed regularly, refined through feedback, and embedded across teams and workflows.

Address Diverse Learner Needs

Why this is important

Instructional design must account for the full spectrum of learner diversity, not just physical ability, but cognitive, cultural, emotional, linguistic, and technological.

A course that fails to meet these varied needs alienates learners, increases dropout rates, and undermines the intended learning outcomes.

Addressing diverse learner needs is an act of respect, equity, and practical wisdom.

Tips

- Start with a **learner spectrum map**, identify key dimensions of diversity within your target group.
- Use **universal design for learning (UDL)** principles to create content that supports variability in how learners perceive, engage with, and express knowledge.
- Provide **multiple means of representation**, for example, pair audio with visuals, or provide transcripts with video.
- Build in **optional support** (e.g., glossaries, examples, help prompts) so learners can choose what they need.

Traps

- Designing for an "average learner" that doesn't really exist.
- Assuming digital literacy or access is uniform across your audience.
- Mistaking equality for equity, giving everyone the same thing isn't the same as giving each person what they need.

Techniques

- **Learner Persona Expansion**:
  Go beyond job role or age, include reading ability, tech comfort, and learning preference.
- **Access Pathway Audits**:
  Identify all the ways learners will engage (devices, times, locations) and plan accordingly.
- **Built-in Flexibility**:
  Allow learners to toggle formats, difficulty levels, or navigation routes.

Examples

- *Cognitive Load*:
  Chunked content with optional deep dives for advanced learners.
- *Linguistic Diversity*:
  Simplified English version paired with localised terms and audio narration.
- *Tech Variability*:
  A mobile-friendly version of the course that works offline.
- *Neurodiversity Support*:
  Visual timelines and predictable layouts for learners who thrive on structure.

How it's done

1. Conduct a diversity scan or use existing demographic/psychographic learner data.
2. Identify barriers to access, from bandwidth to reading level to language nuance.
3. Embed flexible, optional supports that let learners personalise their experience.
4. Test early designs with a diverse group of pilot learners.
5. Capture feedback patterns and revise accordingly.

Accessibility and Inclusion Strategy
Address Diverse Learner Needs

Core Elements

- Learner variability map (e.g., sensory, linguistic, emotional, cognitive, digital)
- Personalisation and adaptation options
- Delivery constraints (e.g., remote access, low bandwidth)
- Flexibility built into design
- Accessibility support (captions, transcripts, visual aids)

Checklist

1. Identify diverse learner characteristics (language, tech access, neurodiversity, etc.).
2. Build optional supports and format alternatives.
3. Use UDL guidelines for perception, action, and engagement.
4. Provide easy switching between content modes (text/audio/video).
5. Validate that content is understandable across literacy levels.
6. Pilot with diverse learners and review feedback for patterns.
7. Embed user guidance or help prompts for optional features.

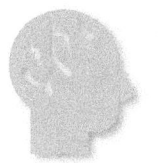
AI Considerations

- Use AI to analyse learner data and recommend personalisation features.
- Automatically generate alternate content formats (text, audio, simplified language).
- Detect potential barriers based on learner interaction logs.
- Offer adaptive learning paths based on real-time learner behaviour.
- Translate and localise content using AI-powered multilingual support.

Key Takeaways

An effective **Accessibility and Inclusion Strategy** goes beyond compliance to foster genuine learner equity. By recognising and addressing the wide spectrum of learner diversity, cognitive, cultural, emotional, linguistic, physical, and digital designers create inclusive experiences that support all learners to succeed.

Using Universal Design for Learning (UDL) principles, flexible access options, and optional supports allows learners to engage in ways that suit their needs and preferences. This reduces friction, increases satisfaction, and strengthens outcomes.

Testing early with diverse learners ensures that hidden barriers are exposed and resolved before full rollout. AI tools can assist by personalising learning paths, generating alternate content formats, and identifying patterns in learner behaviour that may signal inclusion gaps.

Ultimately, designing for diversity is both a strategic advantage and a moral imperative. It ensures that learning reaches everyone it was intended for, and that no one is left behind because of avoidable obstacles.

Culturally Sensitive Design

Why this is important

Learning does not happen in a vacuum.
Culture influences how learners interpret meaning, relate to authority, respond to feedback, and engage with visual or linguistic cues.
Without cultural sensitivity, even well-designed content can be alienating or misunderstood.
Culturally sensitive design ensures that your learning experience resonates globally while respecting local norms, identities, and values.

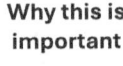
Tips

- Use **localisation, not just translation**, adapt tone, context, examples, and visual cues to fit the learner's environment.
- Include **regional reviewers or cultural advisors** to screen for unintentional bias or offence.
- Be mindful of **symbols, gestures, idioms, humour, and metaphors**, they often don't translate well.
- Provide **customisable content blocks** or alternate examples for global audiences.

Traps

- Using U.S.-centric or Western metaphors, calendars, currencies, or workplace norms.
- Overcorrecting and slipping into tokenism or stereotyped representation.
- Ignoring intra-cultural differences (e.g., urban vs rural learners in the same country).

Techniques

- **Culture Lens Review**:
  Systematically assess imagery, tone, language, and examples through a cultural lens.
- **Dual Track Storyboarding**:
  Design global core content and localised variants in parallel.
- **Symbol Sensitivity Checklists**:
  Validate icons, colours, gestures, and attire used in visuals.

Examples

- *Visuals*:
  Replacing handshake imagery in a module intended for cultures where this isn't customary.
- *Language*:
  Rewriting "kill two birds with one stone" to "achieve two goals at once."
- *Time References*:
  Replacing "Friday beers" with "team wind-down activity."
- *Narratives*:
  Adjusting leadership scenarios to reflect collectivist vs individualist workplace norms

How it's done

1. Define key cultural regions or clusters in your audience base.
2. Review all visuals, copy, and examples through each cluster's lens.
3. Consult with SMEs, native speakers, or local trainers for insight.
4. Make tone, style, and example choices intentional and respectful.
5. Provide flexibility, where possible, for region-specific swaps in content.

Accessibility and Inclusion Strategy
Culturally Sensitive Design

Core Elements

- Regional norms and communication styles
- Tone and language preferences
- Symbol and gesture validation
- Example substitution bank
- Localised visuals or scenarios
- Cultural SMEs or review partners

Checklist

1. Identify cultural regions or segments in your learner audience.
2. Conduct a culture lens review of all copy, visuals, and metaphors.
3. Adapt humour, references, and examples to suit local norms.
4. Validate colours, hand gestures, and character representation.
5. Offer flexibility for swapping regionally specific content blocks.
6. Involve native speakers or cultural experts in the review.
7. Conduct pilot reviews with sample learners from different regions.

AI Considerations

- Use AI-powered localisation tools to adjust tone and cultural framing.
- Flag idioms, figures of speech, or images likely to misfire across cultures.
- Suggest region-specific equivalents for case studies or metaphors.
- Simulate how learners from different cultures may interpret course elements.
- Optimise navigation instructions and help text for non-native English users.

Key Takeaways

Culturally sensitive design is essential for creating inclusive learning experiences that resonate across geographic, linguistic, and social boundaries. It ensures that content is not only understandable but also respectful, relatable, and free from unintended bias.

Culture influences how people perceive authority, respond to tone, engage with storytelling, and interpret visual and verbal cues.

Ignoring these dimensions can lead to confusion, alienation, or even offence, undermining learning effectiveness and learner trust.

By adopting a culture lens, involving regional reviewers, and offering flexible content variants, instructional designers can create learning that speaks authentically to diverse audiences. AI tools can assist by flagging potential cultural missteps and helping to localise tone and references.

Done well, culturally sensitive design promotes global reach without sacrificing local relevance. It allows learning to land meaningfully in every context, reinforcing the credibility and value of the instructional message.

Inclusive Language and Visuals

Why this is important

Language and visuals are never neutral, they shape how learners feel, relate, and engage. Inclusive language affirms dignity and avoids exclusion.

Inclusive visuals reflect the diversity of the learner audience, making everyone feel seen, valued, and respected.

When content omits or misrepresents certain groups, it silently signals who belongs, and who doesn't. This ensures your learning speaks to *everyone*.

Tips

- Use **gender-neutral terms** (e.g., "they," "firefighter," "partner," "chairperson").
- Show **diverse representation** across age, ability, ethnicity, body type, and cultural background.
- Write in **plain, respectful language**, avoid jargon, slurs, or emotionally loaded phrases.
- Let learners opt-in to share identity-related info, never assume pronouns or demographics.

Traps

- Relying on stock imagery that defaults to white, able-bodied, thin, young models.
- Using language that unintentionally reinforces bias (e.g., "manpower," "crazy idea," "guys").
- Making diversity a one-off feature rather than a consistent thread.
- Overcorrecting by stereotyping underrepresented groups or being performatively inclusive.

Techniques

- **Language Audit**:
  Use tools or peer review to check for gendered, ableist, ageist, or racially charged terms.
- **Visual Inclusion Grid**:
  Evaluate your graphic library across 6–8 dimensions of human diversity.
- **Authenticity Review**:
  Ask real learners if they feel reflected and respected in what they see and read.

Examples

- *Language*:
  "Employees must complete their tasks" vs. "Each man must complete his task."
- *Visuals*:
  A wheelchair user included in a project team illustration, not as a special case but a team member.
- *Tone*:
  "You're invited to learn more, at your own pace" instead of "You must complete this training now."

How it's done

1. Draft content with inclusive defaults, avoid assumptions about gender, age, or background.
2. Choose visual assets that showcase natural diversity without overemphasis.
3. Conduct a language bias scan, both manually and using digital tools.
4. Validate image libraries using diversity checklists or tools like the Gender Spectrum Visual Index.
5. Involve learners or DEI reps in final review before publishing.

Accessibility and Inclusion Strategy
Inclusive Language and Visuals

**Core Elements**	• Gender-neutral terms • Diversity in visuals • Inclusive tone of voice • Authenticity (avoiding stereotypes) • Accessibility of colour contrast and icon meaning • Representation in scenarios and examples
**Checklist**	1. Use gender-neutral and people-first language throughout. 2. Remove idioms and loaded expressions (e.g., "blind spot," "crazy," "man up"). 3. Evaluate every image for authentic diversity across multiple attributes. 4. Provide alternate text for images that reflects content meaning, not just appearance. 5. Avoid defaulting to male names or characters, use balanced examples. 6. Test with learners from different groups and adjust based on feedback. 7. Maintain a curated, inclusive image library for repeated use. 8. Ensure consistent representation in visuals *and* language across modules.
**AI Considerations**	• Use AI-powered language analysis tools to flag non-inclusive terms. • Generate alternate text descriptions that are both accurate and respectful. • Recommend visual content tags (e.g., diversity, inclusion, equity) for image libraries. • Suggest gender-balanced names, job roles, and character backstories for scenarios. • Run sentiment analysis on text to detect unintended bias or alienation.
Key Takeaways	Inclusive language and visuals aren't just about compliance; they are a design choice that communicates who belongs in the learning space. By deliberately choosing words and images that reflect diversity, avoid stereotypes, and affirm dignity, designers can create content that resonates with all learners. This not only improves engagement but also builds trust, reduces cognitive friction, and signals psychological safety. Inclusion should be consistent and authentic, woven throughout the course rather than confined to token examples. Done well, it allows every learner to feel seen, respected, and invited into the learning experience.

Align with Global Accessibility Standards

Why this is important

Compliance with accessibility standards isn't just a legal box to tick, it's a commitment to providing equitable access to learning for all individuals, including those with visual, auditory, cognitive, and motor impairments. Global standards like **WCAG 2.2**, **Section 508 (USA)**, and **EN 301 549 (EU)** offer concrete, measurable guidance for making digital learning accessible. Aligning your instructional design with these frameworks ensures *legitimacy, inclusivity, and scalability*.

Tips

- Familiarise yourself with the **four WCAG principles**: Perceivable, Operable, Understandable, and Robust (POUR).
- Choose tools and authoring platforms that **bake in accessibility compliance** by default.
- Build accessibility **into the design process**, not as a post-production check.
- Regularly **test courses using assistive technology** (screen readers, keyboard-only navigation).

Traps

- Assuming the LMS or authoring tool handles accessibility automatically.
- Forgetting to test real user scenarios (e.g., dyslexia, colour blindness, keyboard users).
- Misusing accessible tools (e.g., using alt text for decoration rather than description).
- Only testing one type of accessibility (e.g., visual) and ignoring cognitive or auditory needs.

Techniques

- **Accessibility Checklist Development**:
  Create a compliance-aligned internal checklist (WCAG, Section 508, etc.).
- **Manual Testing + Automation**:
  Use both screen reader testing and automated tools like Axe, WAVE, or Lighthouse.
- **Role-based Access Simulations**:
  Review your course from the perspective of different assistive device users.
- **Captioning + Transcription Standards**:
  Develop house standards for consistent application.

Examples

- *Alt Text*:
  All meaningful images include concise, functional descriptions.
- *Keyboard Access*:
  All interactions (e.g., buttons, sliders, modals) are usable without a mouse.
- *Transcripts*:
  All video and audio content have downloadable text equivalents.
- *Colour Contrast*:
  Visual content passes AA or AAA contrast thresholds for readability.

How it's done

1. Determine which compliance framework applies to your audience or geography.
2. Embed relevant accessibility criteria into your storyboard and development templates.
3. Choose tools and LMS features that support WCAG-aligned output.
4. Conduct periodic compliance audits during development, not just at the end.
5. Document conformance and remediation plans in your project repository.

Accessibility and Inclusion Strategy
Align with Global Accessibility Standards

Core Elements

- Relevant accessibility standards (WCAG 2.2, Section 508, EN 301 549)
- Authoring and delivery platform capabilities
- Testing protocols (manual, assistive tech, automation)
- Accessible content elements (alt text, transcripts, captions, keyboard paths)
- Documentation and audit trail

Checklist
1. Identify the accessibility compliance framework(s) applicable to your audience.
2. Ensure your tools, platforms, and authoring environments support the required standards.
3. Use colour combinations that pass WCAG AA or AAA contrast levels.
4. Provide alt text for all meaningful images.
5. Include captions and transcripts for all multimedia.
6. Enable full navigation via keyboard and test functionality.
7. Validate accessible interactions (e.g., drag-drop alternatives, skip links).
8. Conduct manual audits using screen readers and AI-assisted tools.
9. Maintain a living accessibility log for each course build.
10. Involve users with disabilities in pilot testing when possible.

AI Considerations
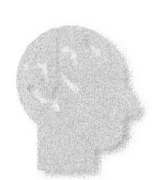
- Use AI to automatically scan and flag accessibility violations in layouts, colours, or text structure.
- Auto-generate image alt text and verify clarity for screen readers.
- Evaluate contrast and readability using machine learning models.
- Simulate user experience for learners using assistive technologies.
- Generate accessible versions of content (e.g., plain language summaries, audio narration, captioned video).

Key Takeaways

Aligning your design with global accessibility standards ensures that learning is inclusive, legally compliant, and future ready.

Standards like WCAG 2.2, Section 508, and EN 301 549 provide clear benchmarks for making content usable by all learners, regardless of ability.

By integrating accessibility from the start, through design templates, platform selection, testing protocols, and audit trails, you avoid costly rework and demonstrate a commitment to equity. Accessibility isn't just about checking boxes, it's about crafting learning that welcomes everyone.

When done consistently, it improves usability for all learners, enhances engagement, and strengthens the credibility of your learning offering.

AI Integration Planning

The **AI Integration Planning** step in the Design phase lays the groundwork for effective and responsible use of AI within learning programs. By planning AI implementation with intent, teams can unlock its full potential while avoiding ethical, technical, or pedagogical pitfalls. This step ensures that AI elements add value to the learning experience, operate within defined boundaries, and evolve responsibly through feedback and oversight.

Key Sub-Steps are:

Overview

- **Define AI Use Cases**
  Identify where and how AI can meaningfully enhance the learning experience, aligned with instructional goals.

- **Assess Infrastructure Readiness**
  Evaluate whether existing platforms, tools, and data environments can support the desired AI functions.

- **Define Human–AI Roles**
  Clarify how AI will support, not replace, instructional designers, SMEs, and facilitators.

- **Prototype and Validate AI-Enhanced Elements**
  Build and test AI-powered features with learners to confirm they are usable, valuable, and aligned with learning objectives.

- **Establish Monitoring and Continuous Improvement**
  Put systems in place to evaluate AI performance, collect feedback, and adapt over time to stay effective and ethical.

AI Integration Planning
Align with Global Accessibility Standards

Outcomes

The outcomes of the *AI Integration Planning* step focus on designing the responsible, strategic use of AI to enhance the learning experience without compromising ethics, clarity, or instructional alignment.

Key Outcomes Include:

- **Identify AI Use Cases**
  Clarify where AI can meaningfully support instructional goals, such as content personalisation, analytics, or learner support.

- **Evaluate Platform Readiness**
  Confirm whether the technical infrastructure can support the proposed AI functionality reliably and securely.

- **Address Ethical and Privacy Concerns**
  Anticipate risks like bias, data misuse, or learner distrust, and plan strategies to mitigate them proactively.

- **Define Human-AI Collaboration**
  Establish clear boundaries and relationships between automated processes and human-led instructional responsibilities.

- **Validate AI-Enhanced Features**
  Pilot AI-powered elements with real users to assess usefulness, usability, and alignment with learner expectations.

- **Set Up Ongoing Monitoring**
  Build feedback loops and performance metrics to track AI impact and evolve usage over time.

Summary

AI Integration Planning is the backbone of responsible innovation in digital learning. It turns inspiration into integration, aligning AI capabilities with instructional goals, learner needs, and platform realities.

This phase goes beyond automation, it's about amplification, intelligence, and inclusion. By embedding AI thoughtfully, transparently, and ethically, you empower your learning programs to scale with integrity and evolve with agility.

The future of learning isn't AI versus humans, it's humans working smarter *with* AI. And this is where that future begins.

Define AI Use Cases in Learning Design

Why this is important

The growing role of AI in instructional design offers both opportunity and complexity. Defining use cases early provides clarity, scope control, and purpose. Without this step, AI may be used haphazardly, introducing risks or inefficiencies.

Clearly articulating where AI adds value, and where it doesn't, ensures thoughtful adoption aligned with learning goals, not just tech trends.

Tips

- Begin with **instructional pain points** (e.g., time-consuming tasks, low learner engagement), these reveal strong AI opportunities.
- Use **simple language** to describe AI roles so stakeholders understand them without technical jargon.
- Match use cases to **project phase and need**, e.g., AI for storyboarding, assessment generation, feedback optimisation, or learner support.
- Consider both **designer-side** AI (tools that help your team) and **learner-facing** AI (like chatbots or recommendation engines).

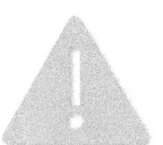

Traps

- Overpromising what AI can do, especially in nuanced tasks like assessment or behaviour prediction.
- Choosing AI tools before identifying real use cases.
- Assuming one use case works across all audiences, industries, or cultures.
- Treating AI as a replacement for human insight, creativity, or judgement.

Techniques

- **Use Case Canvas**:
  A structured document defining the problem, AI function, expected benefit, and boundaries.
- **Team AI Brainstorming**:
  Invite designers, SMEs, and tech leads to co-create a shortlist of high-impact use cases.
- **Learning Journey Mapping**:
  Plot potential AI touchpoints along the learner and content creation path.

Examples

- *Content Design*:
  Use GPT to co-draft scenario scripts, then edit for alignment and voice.
- *Assessment*:
  Generate alternate versions of quiz questions for randomisation.
- *Learner Support*:
  Integrate AI chatbots to answer FAQs or explain concepts in plain language.
- *Analytics*:
  Use AI to detect at-risk learners based on performance and behaviour patterns.

How it's done

1. Review your course goals, learner profile, and instructional workflows.
2. Identify friction points that AI could ease, such as repetitive writing, long feedback cycles, or manual analytics.
3. Brainstorm 6–8 possible AI applications, grouped into design-side and learner-side categories.
4. Validate each use case by asking: *Does it improve learning quality, speed, or scalability?*
5. Document each approved use case clearly with scope, success indicators, and limits.

AI Integration Planning
Define AI Use Cases in Learning Design

Core Elements

- Use case name and description
- Targeted user or workflow
- Intended instructional benefit
- Scope and boundary conditions
- Dependencies (e.g., tech stack, data access)
- Human oversight or handoff points

Checklist

1. List key instructional challenges that could benefit from AI support.
2. Identify at least one AI use case for each course development phase (design, develop, deliver).
3. Separate back-end (designer use) and front-end (learner experience) applications.
4. Evaluate each use case for instructional value, not just novelty.
5. Set parameters around each AI function to avoid scope creep.
6. Gain stakeholder alignment before progressing to tool selection.

AI Considerations

- Use AI to draft and refine the use case documentation itself.
- Deploy AI personas or simulations to test the usefulness of each proposed application.
- Use analytics from previous projects to uncover hidden use case opportunities.
- Employ AI to recommend similar use cases based on your domain and learning goals.

Key Takeaways

Defining AI use cases in learning design ensures that AI is applied with purpose, not hype.

By identifying where AI can meaningfully reduce friction, increase scale, or enhance learner experience, instructional designers can focus on value-driven innovation.

Separating designer-side and learner-facing applications helps clarify priorities and avoid overreach.

This step also sets boundaries, outlining where human oversight is essential and where AI can operate autonomously.

Thoughtful use case definition prevents scope creep, aligns teams, and supports measurable outcomes. When done well, it builds the foundation for a sustainable, ethical, and effective AI integration strategy in learning design.

Assess Technical Feasibility and Tool Compatibility

Why this is important

Even the most promising AI use case will fail if the underlying infrastructure can't support it.

Assessing technical feasibility ensures your AI integrations are practical, scalable, and compliant with organisational and platform constraints.

This step guards against wasted time, misaligned investments, and poor user experience, ensuring that chosen AI tools enhance, rather than obstruct, the learning process.

Tips

- Check for **platform compatibility** with LMS/LXP and content authoring tools (e.g., SCORM, xAPI, LTI integration).
- Engage **IT, cybersecurity, and data governance teams early**, especially when using third-party AI tools.
- Review **privacy, data residency, and IP implications** when AI generates or stores learner data.
- Choose tools with **APIs or modular design** to allow flexibility across different projects.

Traps

- Selecting AI tools without verifying technical fit or compliance standards.
- Assuming a tool that works in marketing or HR will work in L&D without adaptation.
- Overloading the tech stack with AI features that aren't scalable or user tested.
- Ignoring vendor lock-in or limitations in AI models (e.g., fixed knowledge cutoff, lack of domain alignment).

Techniques

- **Tool Feasibility Matrix**:
  Evaluate shortlisted tools against criteria like integration ease, security, compliance, learning benefit, and cost.
- **Risk–Reward Heat Mapping**:
  Plot use cases by feasibility and potential instructional value.
- **Sandbox Testing**:
  Create isolated environments to test compatibility before full-scale integration.
- **Stakeholder Readiness Assessment**:
  Survey technical and instructional teams on familiarity, concerns, and support needs.

Examples

- *Assessment Tool*:
  AI-powered quiz generator integrates with your LMS via LTI, approved by IT but limited to multiple-choice formats.
- *Feedback Bot*:
  GPT-based chatbot functions well in authoring tools like Rise and Evolve but requires strict API controls.
- *Voiceover*:
  AI voice generator works beautifully with Storyline but produces regional accents that may not suit the target learner group.

AI Integration Planning
Assess Technical Feasibility and Tool Compatibility

How it's done

1. List the AI tools aligned to each use case.
2. For each, gather documentation on integrations, input/output formats, and supported standards.
3. Meet with IT and legal stakeholders to check for approval constraints (data privacy, storage, vendor policies).
4. Conduct controlled tests using actual course components.
5. Document limitations and configuration requirements for each tool.
6. Shortlist tools that offer both instructional value and infrastructure compatibility.

Core Elements

- Tool name and vendor
- Required integrations and protocols (LTI, xAPI, SCORM, API keys)
- Technical support level
- Security and data handling model
- Compatibility with design and delivery platforms
- Known limitations or constraints

Checklist

1. Identify target AI tools per use case.
2. Check compatibility with LMS, LXP, and authoring environments.
3. Validate compliance with organisational IT, legal, and security policies.
4. Conduct sandbox testing on key tools.
5. Rate each tool across feasibility, supportability, and flexibility.
6. Shortlist tools that meet both instructional and technical standards.
7. Flag integration risks early and update project timelines accordingly.
8. Document tool approval path and required setup/configuration steps.

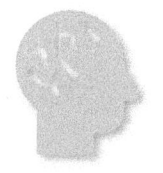
AI Considerations

- Use AI to scan technical documentation for integration points and compliance flags.
- Auto-score tool candidates using custom feasibility criteria.
- Analyse historical support tickets or tool usage patterns for scalability indicators.
- Recommend platform-specific plugins or connectors to reduce friction.
- Assist with generating technical specs or requests for vendor clarifications.

Key Takeaways

Assessing technical feasibility and tool compatibility is critical to turning AI use cases into real, working solutions.

No matter how compelling the concept, AI tools must align with your existing platforms, security protocols, and learner needs. This step ensures that instructional value is not undermined by technical gaps, poor integration, or compliance issues.

By involving IT, legal, and platform stakeholders early, and validating tools in controlled environments, you reduce risk, avoid rework, and maintain confidence in your AI strategy.

Compatibility isn't just a backend concern; it's essential to delivering smooth, scalable, and effective learning experiences.

Ensure Ethical and Transparent AI Use

Why this is important

AI brings immense potential to instructional design, but it also introduces risks, from algorithmic bias and misinformation to privacy violations and learner mistrust.

Ensuring ethical and transparent use is essential to maintain trust, equity, and accountability in the learning environment.

This is not just a matter of compliance, it's about upholding human-centred values in the design and delivery of learning experiences.

Tips

- Be explicit about **what the AI is doing, when, and why**, both for instructional teams and learners.
- Review AI content or decisions for **bias, misrepresentation, or unintended harm**.
- Avoid AI applications that **predict learner behaviour** without clear consent or safeguards.
- Keep a **human in the loop**, AI should assist, not replace, critical instructional decisions.

Traps

- Using generative AI outputs without human review, especially in assessments or sensitive content.
- Failing to disclose AI-generated feedback or content to learners.
- Relying on opaque AI models where rationale or data sources cannot be explained.
- Ignoring the long-term data implications of AI-generated learner insights or behaviour logs.

Techniques

- **AI Ethics Canvas**:
  A planning tool that prompts ethical consideration across data, use, and consequences.
- **Bias Review Panels**:
  Have diverse reviewers examine AI-generated content for stereotyping or skew.
- **Transparency Statements**:
  Embed short disclosures about AI use in onboarding or learner interfaces.
- **Consent Management**:
  Let learners opt in (or out) of AI-personalised pathways or data-driven adaptivity.

Examples

- *Assessment Feedback*:
  AI suggests feedback but notes, "This response was generated using an AI tutor model and reviewed by a learning designer."
- *Scenario Content*:
  AI-generated case study is reviewed to ensure it doesn't reflect racial or gender bias.
- *Adaptive Path*:
  Learner is offered a tailored path with an explanation: "This was suggested based on your recent quiz performance, using AI pattern recognition."

How it's done

1. Define the ethical scope for AI use across design, development, and delivery.
2. Identify potential risk zones, bias, misinformation, opacity, surveillance.
3. Establish review protocols and define human oversight responsibilities.
4. Create learner-facing transparency statements explaining where AI is used.
5. Log all AI decisions or generated elements that influence learner progression or evaluation.
6. Train design and development teams on AI ethics and best practice guidelines.

AI Integration Planning
Ensure Ethical and Transparent AI Use

 **Core Elements**	- Purpose and role of AI in each use case - Human–AI decision boundaries - Bias and fairness checks - Learner consent and visibility - Transparency protocols - Content review and sign-off trails
 **Checklist**	1. Define ethical guidelines for each AI use case. 2. Ensure AI-generated content or actions are reviewed by a human. 3. Create a transparency statement for learner-facing AI. 4. Document how and where AI will impact learner experience or outcomes. 5. Check for bias in datasets or AI outputs. 6. Offer opt-in/opt-out options for AI-based personalisation. 7. Involve diverse perspectives in content validation. 8. Keep a compliance log of AI decisions that impact grading or learner support.
 **AI Considerations**	- Use AI to generate and refine ethics checklists or transparency blurbs. - Apply AI-based bias detection on scripts, visuals, or datasets. - Create simulated learner personas to test fairness across use cases. - Auto-flag inconsistencies in tone, representation, or inclusivity in AI-generated content. - Support human reviewers with AI-generated summaries of content risks or flagged patterns.
Key Takeaways	**Ethical and transparent AI use is essential** to protect learner trust, preserve instructional integrity, and uphold fairness across diverse learning contexts. While AI can accelerate content creation, personalise learning, and improve feedback, it must be applied with care and oversight. Transparency about how AI is used, and where human judgement remains critical, reinforces accountability and avoids confusion or mistrust. Ethical implementation also means checking for bias, securing informed consent, and ensuring that AI-driven features don't unintentionally exclude or disadvantage learners. By building in transparency, review, and human involvement from the start, instructional designers can harness AI's power without compromising their responsibility to the learner.

Design Human–AI Collaboration Workflows

Why this is important

AI is not a replacement for instructional designers, SMEs, or facilitators, it's a collaborator.

Effective learning design requires clear workflows where humans and AI interact in complementary, intentional ways.

This balance maximises productivity while preserving quality, oversight, and creativity.

Without a defined collaboration model, AI can either be underused or misused, leading to confusion, errors, or rework.

Tips

- Define which steps in your workflow are **AI-assisted**, **AI-led**, or **human-only**.
- Ensure humans retain control over high-stakes content (e.g., assessments, compliance messaging, feedback tone).
- Use AI for **first drafts, analysis, or pattern recognition**, and humans for interpretation, emotional nuance, and judgment.
- Train your team not just on AI tools, but on **when and how to hand off tasks to/from AI**.

Traps

- Over-automating early in the design process, bypassing strategic thinking.
- Creating parallel workflows (AI vs human) that don't align, causing friction or duplication.
- Failing to log AI decisions or contributions, especially in high-impact areas.
- Relying on AI outputs without human validation, assuming they're "ready to publish."

Techniques

- **Workflow Mapping**:
  Create a swim lane diagram to visualise when and how humans and AI interact at each phase.
- **Role Designation**:
  Define who oversees AI usage, reviews content and resolves discrepancies.
- **Triage Approach**:
  Let AI handle repetitive or high-volume tasks, while humans manage nuance and complexity.

Examples

- *Storyboard Creation*:
  AI drafts outline based on SME notes, instructional designer refines tone, logic, and pacing.
- *Scenario Writing*:
  AI generates branching structure; designer adjusts dialogue to match real-world dynamics.
- *Feedback Generation*:
  AI provides initial feedback on quiz responses, with human moderation for tone and clarity.

How it's done

1. Map the learning design lifecycle, from analysis through to delivery.
2. Identify AI opportunities at each phase (e.g., script writing, visual creation, learner support).
3. Designate touchpoints where humans take over or validate AI output.
4. Establish naming conventions and version control to track human and AI contributions.
5. Train the team in collaboration etiquette, when to use AI, when not to, and how to escalate concerns.
6. Embed human–AI workflows in SOPs, style guides, or project templates.

AI Integration Planning
Design Human–AI Collaboration Workflows

Core Elements

- Phase-by-phase task delegation
- Human oversight checkpoints
- Collaboration principles (e.g., respect, review, refinement)
- Documentation and audit trails
- Team responsibilities and permissions
- Feedback and refinement loops

Checklist

1. Identify AI opportunities across the design, development, and delivery lifecycle.
2. Map human–AI touchpoints using a swim lane or matrix format.
3. Define who owns each step of the process, both human and AI.
4. Establish approval gates for AI-generated content.
5. Train the team on tools *and* handoff logic.
6. Document collaboration workflows in project templates or SOPs.
7. Assign a quality owner for each AI output area.
8. Monitor time saved vs time spent reviewing or revising AI contributions.

AI Considerations

- Use AI to visualise workflow maps or generate RACI matrices for task ownership.
- Build AI checklists into authoring tools to prompt handoff moments.
- Monitor AI-generated work for changes in tone, accuracy, or style drift over time.
- Auto-summarise workflow changes based on project logs.
- Simulate learner reactions to AI-generated interactions to test emotional impact.

Key Takeaways

Designing human–AI collaboration workflows ensures that AI is used intentionally, not indiscriminately.

Clear task delegation, oversight checkpoints, and defined handoff points protect the integrity of instructional design while improving efficiency.

AI is most effective when it complements, not replaces, human strengths such as judgment, emotional nuance, and instructional intent.

Without structured collaboration, teams risk confusion, duplicated effort, or publishing unchecked content.

By embedding these workflows into SOPs, templates, and team training, you create a repeatable model that maximises AI's strengths while safeguarding learning quality.

The result is a design process that is faster, smarter, and still distinctly human.

Prototype and Validate AI-Enhanced Elements

Why this is important

Even well-mapped AI strategies can fall apart in execution if they're not tested under real-world conditions. Prototyping allows you to validate that your AI integrations actually *work*, functionally, pedagogically, and ethically, before you commit to scale.

It's where theoretical planning meets actual learner experience. This step ensures your AI-enhanced elements deliver value, not just novelty.

Tips

- Prototype **one use case at a time**, isolate variables so you know what's working.
- Include **instructional designers, SMEs, and real learners** in your testing pool.
- Measure both **usability and impact**: Does it help? Is it accurate? Is it worth the time saved?
- Test on **multiple devices, platforms, and user profiles** (e.g., low bandwidth, screen readers).

Traps

- Skipping prototyping because "it's just a small feature."
- Testing with internal team only, real learners may behave differently.
- Overlooking emotional response, AI features can unintentionally feel impersonal or alienating.
- Rushing into full-scale implementation based on superficial feedback.

Techniques

- **A/B Testing**:
  Compare human-created vs AI-enhanced content side by side.
- **Pilot Focus Groups**:
  Gather qualitative and emotional feedback on AI-powered features.
- **Prototyping Tools**:
  Use low-fidelity mockups or slide-based simulations before investing in complex builds.
- **Micro-Validation Loops**:
  Build AI tools into a test course and gather analytics from early access users.

Examples

- *Scenario Branching*:
  AI generates dialogue; users rate realism and tone.
- *Auto-Feedback on Quizzes*:
  Learners are asked whether the feedback helped them improve or felt robotic.
- *Content Generation*:
  SME reviews an AI-generated lesson draft for accuracy, nuance, and instructional value.
- *Chatbot Pilot*:
  Deployed on a single FAQ module to test whether learner questions are answered effectively.

How it's done

1. Choose a single AI-enhanced feature to pilot (e.g., adaptive quiz, AI tutor, visual generator).
2. Build a prototype, ideally integrated with your actual platform or environment.
3. Conduct structured testing with a diverse group of users.
4. Collect both qualitative feedback and usage data (time saved, errors caught, learner confusion).
5. Debrief with your team and revise before expanding.
6. Document what worked, what didn't, and what to watch out for in rollout.

AI Integration Planning
Prototype and Validate AI-Enhanced Elements

 **Core Elements**	• Target AI feature • Prototype environment and scope • Testing participant pool • Evaluation criteria (instructional, UX, ethical) • Revision and improvement cycle • Sign-off process before scale-up
 **Checklist**	1. Select one AI-enhanced feature to pilot. 2. Build a working prototype in a sandbox or live course. 3. Define success metrics: engagement, accuracy, usefulness, trust. 4. Test with at least 3–5 diverse user profiles. 5. Capture both behavioural data and open-ended feedback. 6. Compare against human-created or baseline alternatives. 7. Revise based on findings and document implications for broader rollout. 8. Repeat for other use cases in priority order.
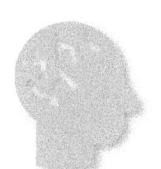 **AI Considerations**	• Use AI to generate usability testing protocols or learner survey questions. • Auto-collect sentiment from open-ended pilot feedback. • Suggest refinements based on interaction patterns or low engagement flags. • Analyse clickstream and dwell time to predict feature effectiveness. • Simulate different learner types (e.g., low confidence, neurodivergent) interacting with the prototype.
 **Key Takeaways**	Prototyping AI-enhanced elements is essential to ensure they deliver instructional value, usability, and alignment with learning objectives before full-scale deployment. It allows teams to surface and resolve technical, pedagogical, or ethical issues early, saving time and reducing risk. Testing with real learners provides critical insight into how AI features are perceived whether they support or hinder engagement, and what refinements are needed. A well-executed prototype phase helps maintain trust in AI-enabled learning by grounding innovation in real-world feedback and human-centered design.

Establish Monitoring and Continuous Improvement Processes

Why this is important

AI integrations aren't set-and-forget, they require ongoing monitoring, evaluation, and refinement.

As AI tools evolve and learner expectations shift, your implementations must remain accurate, effective, and ethically aligned.

Continuous improvement ensures AI remains a trusted asset in the learning experience, not a black box or a liability.

Tips

- Define **what success looks like** for each AI feature: accuracy, time savings, learner satisfaction, engagement, etc.
- Establish **feedback channels** that include learner reactions, designer reviews, and system logs.
- Schedule **periodic reviews** (monthly, quarterly) for AI outputs and behaviours, especially if models are learning over time.
- Involve **cross-functional teams** in AI governance: L&D, IT, Compliance, DEI, and even Legal.

Traps

- Failing to track long-term impact of AI, leading to unnoticed drift, bias, or user distrust.
- Treating AI performance as invisible or secondary to traditional metrics.
- Assuming learner satisfaction means instructional success, always cross-validate with learning outcomes.
- Overloading L&D teams with technical monitoring tasks better handled by analytics tools.

Techniques

- *AI KPI Dashboards*:
  Display real-time metrics for AI interactions, completions, flagged errors, etc.
- *Output Audits*:
  Randomly sample AI-generated elements (e.g., feedback, responses, recommendations) for quality checks.
- *Learner Pulse Surveys*:
  Include periodic AI-specific questions to gauge ussefulness and clarity.
- *Continuous Learning Loops*:
  Feed evaluation findings into model updates or content improvement tasks.

Examples

- *Analytics Integration*:
  LMS dashboard includes AI-touched content interaction rates and learner opt-outs.
- *Audit Protocol*:
  Quarterly review of AI-generated quizzes to ensure continued relevance and difficulty calibration.
- *Alert System*:
  AI model logs abnormal learner behaviours (e.g., high retry rates) and triggers human review.
- *Post-Launch Survey*:
  Asks learners, "Did you find the AI assistant helpful and clear? Why or why not?"

AI Integration Planning
Establish Monitoring and Continuous Improvement Processes

How it's done

1. Set AI-specific KPIs aligned to your learning goals and technical capabilities.
2. Create a monitoring schedule (weekly/monthly/quarterly) depending on use case risk.
3. Build dashboards or reports to centralise AI impact and performance metrics.
4. Assign owners for reviewing and responding to flagged issues.
5. Involve stakeholders in quarterly improvement cycles, what should be tweaked, removed, or expanded?
6. Document changes and outcomes for traceability.

Core Elements

- Key AI performance indicators (KPIs)
- Feedback collection mechanisms (learners, facilitators, system logs)
- Audit protocols
- Escalation processes
- Ownership and accountability matrix
- Documentation standards for traceability

Checklist

1. Define KPIs for each AI integration (accuracy, time saved, satisfaction, etc.).
2. Build a dashboard or reporting tool to track these KPIs.
3. Schedule periodic AI content audits with SME or designer oversight.
4. Collect learner and stakeholder feedback specifically about AI experiences.
5. Define escalation procedures for problematic AI behaviour or output.
6. Document changes and link them to outcomes.
7. Review AI compliance and ethical fit at least quarterly.
8. Update governance documents and workflows as AI evolves.

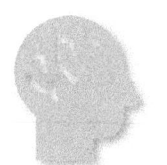
AI Considerations

- Use AI to summarise learner feedback into insight clusters.
- Detect shifts in usage patterns or engagement metrics in real time.
- Recommend content updates based on low-performing AI features.
- Automate the generation of quarterly audit reports.
- Forecast risk areas using predictive analytics based on learner interaction data.

Key Takeaways

Ongoing monitoring and refinement are essential to ensure AI remains a reliable, ethical, and high-performing element of instructional delivery.

Without structured oversight, AI tools can drift from their original purpose, degrade in quality, or introduce bias over time.

By setting clear KPIs, collecting learner feedback, and auditing outputs regularly, design teams can maintain alignment with learning goals and continuously enhance the learner experience.

This sub-step turns AI from a one-time feature into a responsive, evolving partner in long-term instructional success.

Pilot Testing Preparation

Overview

The **Pilot Testing Preparation** step in the Design phase of the ADDIE model ensures that a course is rigorously tested in a controlled environment before its full-scale implementation. This step allows instructional designers to identify and address potential issues, gather feedback, and fine-tune the course to better meet the needs of the target audience.

By conducting a well-structured pilot test, designers can verify the course's content, structure, and delivery, ensuring alignment with learning objectives and organisational goals. The feedback collected during this phase informs targeted adjustments, enhancing the course's overall effectiveness and learner satisfaction.

Key Sub-Steps are:

- **Identify Pilot Test Learners**
  Select a representative group of learners reflective of the target audience to ensure feedback is relevant and actionable.

- **Pilot Test Design & Evaluation**
  Plan how the pilot will be conducted, including evaluation methods such as surveys, interviews, or observational data collection.

- **Prepare Content for Pilot Testing**
  Prepare for any necessary customisations to meet the pilot group's needs, tailoring content or delivery methods as needed to enhance relevance and effectiveness.

Outcomes

The outcomes of the Pilot Testing Preparation step are focused on validating the course and ensuring its readiness for broader implementation.

Key outcomes include:

- **Validate Course Content and Delivery Methods**
  Confirm that the instructional design and delivery align with learning objectives and resonate with the intended audience.

- **Collect Constructive Learner Feedback**
  Use the pilot test to gather insightful feedback from participants, highlighting both strengths and areas for improvement.

- **Identify Specific Improvement Areas**
  Use pilot data to pinpoint elements requiring adjustment, such as content clarity, learner engagement, or accessibility.

- **Test Feedback Mechanisms**
  Ensure feedback tools, such as surveys or focus group discussions, effectively capture meaningful and comprehensive insights.

- **Implement Refinements Based on Outcomes**
  Make targeted adjustments to course content and structure based on feedback, optimising the course for engagement, comprehension, and retention.

Summary

The **Pilot Testing Preparation** step is a critical component of the Design phase, providing a structured approach to testing and refining the course before its full release. By selecting a representative group of learners, designing effective evaluation methods, and addressing feedback through targeted refinements, instructional designers ensure the course is well-prepared to meet its objectives.

This step mitigates risks such as misaligned content or technical issues, fostering confidence in the course's readiness for launch. Through feedback-driven adjustments, the Pilot Testing Preparation step enhances the instructional quality, ensuring a smooth rollout and maximising the course's impact on learners and organisational goals.

Identify Pilot Test Learners

Why this is important

Identifying the right learners for pilot testing ensures that the feedback gathered is both relevant and actionable.

Selecting a representative subset of the target audience helps validate whether the content resonates as intended, while ensuring diversity among pilot participants captures a broad range of perspectives across demographics, prior knowledge, and learning preferences.

This approach improves the reliability of feedback on content clarity, accessibility, and instructional effectiveness.

It also provides insight into how well the course performs under real-world conditions before full deployment.

Tips

- **Diversify Participants**
  Aim for a balanced mix of demographics, skill levels, and accessibility needs to reflect the broader target audience.
- **Communicate Clearly**
  Provide participants with detailed information about the pilot test objectives, timeline, and their role in the process.
- **Engage Early**
  Build rapport with participants by involving them early and emphasising the importance of their feedback.
- **Focus on Feedback**
  Prepare specific questions to guide participants in providing constructive feedback.

Traps

- **Overlooking Accessibility**
  Failing to include learners with diverse needs can result in a lack of inclusivity in the final materials.
- **Selection Bias**
  Choosing participants who are overly familiar with the content or process can skew feedback.
- **Underestimating Logistics**
  Neglecting scheduling or resource planning can lead to delays or technical difficulties.
- **Generalised Feedback**
  Accepting vague or overly positive feedback without actionable insights can hinder improvement.

Techniques

- **Survey Distribution**
  Use surveys to pre-screen and recruit participants based on predefined criteria.
- **Focus Groups**
  Organise focus groups to collect qualitative feedback and discuss learner experiences in-depth.
- **Role Simulation**
  Assign specific roles to participants that align with the intended target audience to simulate realistic scenarios.
- **Accessibility Testing**
  Include participants with varying accessibility needs to identify and address potential barriers.

Pilot Testing Preparation
Identify Pilot Test Learners

Examples

- *Scenario 1*
  A corporate eLearning module is piloted with 10 employees from different departments, ensuring diverse roles and experiences.
- *Scenario 2*
  A virtual classroom platform pilot involves learners with different levels of digital literacy to evaluate usability.
- *Scenario 3*
  A training programme for teachers includes participants from urban and rural schools to assess adaptability to different teaching environments.
- *Scenario 4*
  A compliance training course includes learners with visual impairments to test accessibility features like screen reader compatibility.

How it's done

1. **Define Pilot Objectives**
   Start by specifying the aspects of the instructional materials to be evaluated, such as usability, content clarity, or alignment with learning objectives. Clearly defining objectives ensures the pilot test remains focused and effective.

2. **Segment the Audience**
   Group potential learners based on relevant criteria like demographics, skill levels, or professional backgrounds to ensure a representative test audience.

3. **Recruit Participants**
   Develop a recruitment plan targeting a diverse pool of learners. Use methods such as invitations, advertisements, or personal outreach to gather participants.

4. **Set Selection Criteria**
   Establish key characteristics that participants must meet, ensuring the sample accurately reflects the target audience's diversity and needs.

5. **Coordinate Logistics**
   Plan and organise the necessary schedules, resources, and technology for the pilot test. Confirm that all logistical aspects, such as venue bookings or online platform setups, are in place.

6. **Prepare Feedback Tools**
   Design surveys, questionnaires, or interview templates to collect structured and actionable feedback from participants.

7. **Communicate Expectations**
   Provide participants with clear instructions about their roles, the evaluation process, and the importance of their feedback. This ensures participants are well-prepared and engaged.

8. **Monitor and Follow-Up**
   Track participation during the pilot and address any issues promptly. Follow up with participants to ensure feedback is submitted in a timely and complete manner.

Pilot Testing Preparation
Identify Pilot Test Learners

Core Elements

- **Objectives Defined**
  Ensure the pilot's focus aligns with the overall goals of the instructional design process.
- **Representative Sample**
  Select participants that reflect the diversity of the target audience.
- **Selection Criteria Established**
  Use clear guidelines for participant selection to maintain objectivity.
- **Logistics Coordinated**
  Schedules, venues, and required technology are organised and functional.
- **Feedback Tools Designed**
  Surveys and templates are tailored to collect detailed and actionable responses.
- **Expectations Communicated**
  Clear instructions are given to participants to promote meaningful engagement.
- **Monitoring Ensured**
  Participation is tracked, and issues are resolved promptly.
- **Feedback Gathered**
  All feedback is collected and reviewed for insights into material effectiveness.

Checklist

1. Define criteria for pilot participants (roles, experience, tech access)
2. Select a representative sample of the target learner population
3. Confirm availability and willingness to participate
4. Communicate expectations, time commitment, and feedback process
5. Ensure diversity in region, role, and background where applicable
6. Maintain documentation of pilot group selection rationale
7. Obtain required approvals (e.g., from HR or business leaders)
8. Provide orientation or guidance prior to pilot launch

AI Considerations

- Use AI to segment existing learners into representative groups
- Analyse past performance or feedback to identify ideal pilot candidates
- Predict learner engagement risk or dropout likelihood
- Generate selection matrices or personas based on learner data
- Suggest balanced samples to minimise bias in pilot results

Key Takeaways

Identifying pilot test learners is a pivotal step in refining instructional materials.

By selecting a diverse and representative group, instructional designers can obtain meaningful feedback on the course's clarity, accessibility, and effectiveness.

Through clear communication, structured planning, and diligent monitoring, the pilot phase ensures the final materials are optimised to meet the needs of the target audience, delivering impactful and inclusive learning outcomes.

Pilot Test Design & Evaluation

Why this is important

A well-structured pilot test provides critical insight into how effectively the instructional materials achieve their intended goals.

By clearly defining the scope and evaluation criteria, designers can assess content clarity, learner engagement, technical usability, and alignment with learning objectives.

Using a mix of feedback methods, such as surveys, focus groups, or usability testing, helps capture both quantitative and qualitative data for a well-rounded view.

This structured evaluation not only highlights strengths and weaknesses but also informs targeted refinements that improve the course's instructional integrity, learner experience, and overall effectiveness.

Tips

- **Start with Objectives**
  Clearly outline what aspects of the instructional materials you want to evaluate.
- **Collaborate with Stakeholders**
  Engage subject matter experts and stakeholders to define evaluation criteria.
- **Use Multiple Methods**
  Combine quantitative (e.g., surveys) and qualitative (e.g., interviews) methods for a comprehensive evaluation.
- **Simplify Feedback Tools**
  Make evaluation instruments easy to understand and complete.
- **Iterate Regularly**
  Incorporate feedback iteratively throughout the pilot test phase.

Traps

- **Misaligned Criteria**
  Failing to align evaluation criteria with learning objectives leads to irrelevant feedback.
- **Overcomplicated Instruments**
  Complex evaluation tools may discourage participant engagement.
- **Neglecting Diversity**
  Lack of participant diversity can result in biased or incomplete insights.
- **Insufficient Communication**
  Poor communication of the evaluation process may confuse participants.
- **Ignoring Ethics**
  Overlooking privacy or consent issues could compromise participant trust and data integrity.

Techniques

- **Thematic Analysis**
  Use open-ended feedback to identify recurring themes or issues.
- **Usability Testing**
  Observe participants interacting with the materials to identify navigation or accessibility challenges.
- **Focus Groups**
  Facilitate discussions to gain deeper insights into learner experiences.
- **Pre-and Post-Assessments**
  Measure knowledge or skill improvements to evaluate content effectiveness.
- **A/B Testing**
  Compare different versions of content or activities to identify more effective approaches.

Pilot Testing Preparation
Pilot Test Design & Evaluation

Examples

- *Scenario 1*
  Use a survey to measure learner engagement, clarity, and usability of a corporate compliance training module.
- *Scenario 2*
  Conduct focus groups to gather qualitative feedback on an eLearning course for healthcare professionals.
- *Scenario 3*
  Observe participants completing tasks in a software simulation to identify usability issues.
- *Scenario 4*
  Compare learning outcomes between interactive and static instructional methods using pre-and post-assessments.

How it's done

1. **Define Evaluation Objectives**
   Establish specific goals for the evaluation, such as assessing content clarity, learner engagement, technical functionality, or accessibility. Clear objectives ensure the evaluation remains focused and aligned with learning outcomes.
2. **Establish Evaluation Criteria**
   Define measurable standards for evaluation, such as content accuracy, ease of navigation, learner satisfaction, and accessibility compliance. Collaborate with stakeholders to ensure these criteria reflect both learner and organisational priorities.
3. **Select Evaluation Methods**
   Determine the most appropriate methods for collecting feedback, such as surveys, focus groups, usability testing, or interviews. Consider the nature of the content and the type of insights needed when choosing methods.
4. **Design Evaluation Instruments**
   Develop tools like surveys, and Checklists
5. **Plan Data Collection Procedures**
   Organise logistics for collecting data, including scheduling pilot sessions, distributing evaluation instruments, and ensuring participants understand their roles. Communication is key to ensuring smooth execution.
6. **Conduct Pilot Tests**
   Run the pilot test with a representative group of learners and stakeholders. Collect feedback on various aspects, such as usability, engagement, and technical functionality.
7. **Analyse Results**
   Interpret the collected data using statistical or thematic analysis methods. Identify trends, strengths, weaknesses, and areas requiring improvement.
8. **Prepare Reports**
   Summarise evaluation findings in a structured report. Highlight key insights, strengths, identified gaps, and actionable recommendations for refining instructional materials.

Pilot Testing Preparation
Pilot Test Design & Evaluation

Core Elements

- **Objectives Aligned**
  Evaluation objectives are clearly defined and linked to learning outcomes.
- **Criteria Set**
  Measurable evaluation criteria are established in collaboration with stakeholders.
- **Methods Appropriate**
  Evaluation methods match the nature of the feedback needed and participant demographics.
- **Instruments Well-Designed**
  Tools for data collection are clear, user-friendly, and aligned with evaluation goals.
- **Ethics Ensured**
  Informed consent and data privacy are maintained throughout the process.
- **Representative Participants**
  Pilot test includes a diverse and representative sample of learners.
- **Findings Actionable**
  Data is analysed to extract meaningful insights and identify trends.
- **Recommendations Clear**
  Results are summarised in a comprehensive report with practical suggestions for improvement.

Checklist

1. Define goals for the pilot (e.g., usability, accuracy, engagement)
2. Establish evaluation criteria (e.g., time-on-task, error rates, feedback quality)
3. Choose feedback collection methods (surveys, interviews, observation)
4. Prepare structured tools for capturing quantitative and qualitative data
5. Include mechanisms for capturing technical issues or learner confusion
6. Set timing and scope of pilot to simulate real delivery
7. Debrief learners and facilitators post-pilot
8. Summarise results in a decision-ready format for course refinement

AI Considerations

- Generate pilot feedback surveys and Likert-style evaluation tools
- Use AI to summarise qualitative feedback from open-ended responses
- Analyse error logs or user clicks to detect usability issues
- Identify patterns in learner navigation or confusion
- Auto-generate pilot summary reports with key metrics and insights

Key Takeaways

A well-designed pilot test evaluation is essential for ensuring instructional materials are effective, engaging, and aligned with both learner and organisational goals.

By focusing on inclusivity, clear communication, and ethical practices, instructional designers can refine their materials to address identified gaps.

This iterative process lays the foundation for a successful course launch, ensuring positive learner outcomes and organisational impact.

Pilot Testing Preparation
Prepare Content for Pilot Testing

Prepare Content for Pilot Testing

Why this is important

Preparing content for pilot testing ensures that the instructional materials are complete, coherent, and aligned with the learning objectives.

It involves refining structure, flow, media, interactivity, and assessments so that they can be tested in conditions that reflect the intended learner environment.

This step also verifies accessibility and inclusivity, enabling all learners to engage meaningfully with the content.

By integrating feedback mechanisms and ensuring that transitions, tools, and delivery formats function smoothly, designers reduce the risk of disruption during testing and increase the reliability of the feedback collected for final improvements.

Tips

- **Start with Objectives**
  Use clear, measurable objectives to guide all design decisions.
- **Consider the Audience**
  Tailor strategies and media to the needs, preferences, and abilities of the target learners.
- **Build Interactivity**
  Incorporate elements like quizzes, discussions, or simulations to actively engage learners.
- **Use Accessible Design**
  Follow accessibility standards to ensure inclusivity for all learners.
- **Iterate and Refine**
  Review and update the design plan based on feedback from stakeholders or pilot testing.

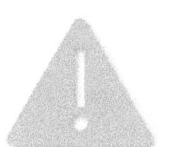

Traps

- **Overloading Content**
  Avoid including too much content in a single module, which can overwhelm learners
- **Ignoring Accessibility**
  Neglecting accessibility can exclude some learners and limit the effectiveness of the materials
- **Misaligned Strategies**
  Choosing instructional methods that do not support the learning objectives
- **Disjointed Flow**
  Poor transitions between topics or activities can disrupt learner engagement and understanding
- **Static Design**
  Rigid materials lacking interactivity or flexibility can hinder engagement and adaptability.

Techniques

- **Storyboarding**
  Map out the content structure, flow, and media integration for clarity
- **Backward Design**
  Begin with desired outcomes and design activities and assessments to achieve them
- **Chunking**
  Break content into manageable segments to improve understanding and retention
- **Universal Design for Learning (UDL)**
  Use multiple means of representation, engagement, and expression to address diverse learner needs
- **Rapid Prototyping**
  Create initial versions of instructional materials to gather feedback and refine them iteratively.

Pilot Testing Preparation
Prepare Content for Pilot Testing

Examples

- *Scenario 1*
  Developing a compliance training course with interactive scenarios to simulate decision-making in real-world situations
- *Scenario 2*
  Designing an eLearning module on software skills with video tutorials, hands-on simulations, and quizzes for assessment
- *Scenario 3*
  Creating a blended learning programme combining in-class discussions with multimedia-rich online materials
- *Scenario 4*
  Implementing gamified learning activities in a virtual classroom environment to boost motivation and participation.

How it's done

1. **Review Analysis Findings**
   Start by examining data on learner needs, objectives, and environmental constraints to inform design decisions. This ensures the instructional materials are tailored to the target audience and aligned with the learning environment.
2. **Define Objectives**
   Develop specific, measurable learning objectives that directly address the identified needs. These objectives serve as the foundation for all design elements, guiding the structure and content of the materials.
3. **Select Strategies**
   Choose instructional methods such as case studies, simulations, or group activities that best support the learning objectives and engage the target audience.
4. **Outline Content**
   Organise topics into logical modules with clear sequencing and transitions. Ensure content flows naturally to facilitate understanding and retention.
5. **Choose Media**
   Identify suitable media formats, including text, videos, and interactive simulations, to effectively support the learning objectives and maintain learner interest.
6. **Plan Interactivity**
   Design engaging interactive elements like quizzes, discussions, or simulations to foster active participation and deeper understanding of the material.
7. **Design Assessments**
   Develop formative and summative assessments that align with the learning objectives, providing opportunities to measure learner progress and understanding.
8. **Address Accessibility**
   Incorporate accessibility features such as alt text, captions, and screen reader compatibility to ensure inclusivity and compliance with accessibility standards.
9. **Integrate Feedback**
   Establish mechanisms for providing constructive feedback to learners, helping them identify areas for improvement and reinforcing their understanding.
10. **Finalise Flow**
    Ensure smooth transitions between topics, activities, and assessments, creating a coherent and intuitive learning experience.

Pilot Testing Preparation
Prepare Content for Pilot Testing

Core Elements

- **Learning Objectives Defined**
  Objectives guide all design elements and align with identified learner needs.
- **Instructional Strategies Selected**
  Methods match content complexity and learner preferences.
- **Content Structured**
  Modules are logically sequenced with clear transitions.
- **Media and Interactivity**
  Engaging elements are included to maintain interest and support learning.
- **Accessibility**
  Materials meet inclusion standards with features like captions and alt text.
- **Assessments Aligned**
  Evaluation tools match learning objectives and measure outcomes effectively.
- **Flow and Coherence**
  The instructional flow supports understanding and retention.
- **Delivery Environment Considered**
  Materials are compatible with the planned delivery platform.
- **Iterative Refinement**
  Feedback from pilot testing informs continuous improvement.

Checklist

1. Ensure all learning materials are complete, functional, and formatted for delivery
2. Conduct technical checks on courseware across target platforms/devices
3. Validate that assessments, interactivities, and branching logic work as intended
4. Finalise instructions and support documents for learners and facilitators
5. Ensure all accessibility elements are in place (captions, alt text, navigation)
6. Load and test content in the target LMS or delivery platform
7. Review version control and lock updates during the pilot window
8. Establish support channels for pilot learners (e.g., help desk or feedback loop)

AI Considerations

- Run automated QA scripts to check for broken links or missing media
- Use AI to simulate different learner journeys through the content
- Auto-flag inconsistencies in layout, style, or instruction text
- Generate support documentation (FAQs, quick guides) based on content
- Use AI to verify accessibility compliance before launch

Key Takeaways

Preparing content for pilot testing ensures instructional materials are well-designed, accessible, and aligned with learning objectives.

By combining thoughtful strategies, engaging media, and robust assessments, instructional designers create impactful and inclusive learning experiences.

Adhering to accessibility standards, reviewing content flow, and integrating feedback during iterative refinement enhance the overall quality and usability of the materials, supporting successful learning outcomes in various environments.

Pre-Production Logistics

Overview

The **Pre-Production Logistics** step in the Design phase prepares the instructional design for smooth transition into development. It ensures that production is deliberate, well-sequenced, and aligned with both the instructional strategy and project constraints. By setting clear workflows and treatment guidelines, this step minimises rework, delays, and ambiguity during development and deployment.

Key Sub-Steps are:

- **Establish Production Blueprint**
  Create a master document that defines instructional materials, responsibilities, and development workflow.

- **Schedule Production**
  Develop a timeline with clearly sequenced tasks, assigned resources, and built-in checkpoints to track progress.

- **Format and Treat Lessons**
  Apply consistent layout, media placement, and navigation styles to ensure clarity, usability, and alignment with learning goals.

Outcomes

The outcomes of the **Pre-Production Logistics** step focus on translating design into executable, trackable development workflows, ensuring clarity, efficiency, and alignment before build begins.

Key Outcomes Include:

- **Create a Production Blueprint**
  Document the full scope of development activities, roles, asset requirements, and review checkpoints to guide execution.

- **Develop a Realistic Production Schedule**
  Sequence production tasks with clear deadlines, resource assignments, and built-in buffer periods.

- **Standardise Lesson Formatting and Treatment**
  Define consistent layout, styling, and navigation approaches that align with instructional design and learner expectations.

Summary

Pre-Production Logistics is not merely a checklist of administrative tasks, it is a strategic handover zone between the creative work of instructional design and the technical precision of production. It prevents friction by aligning expectations, finalising specifications, and orchestrating the timing of people, tools, and deliverables.

Well-executed logistics at this stage reduce rework, avoid bottlenecks, and accelerate the development of high-quality learning materials. It ensures that design intent is preserved in execution, and that all stakeholders, from designers to voice actors to LMS admins, are working from the same playbook.

This phase acts as a project stabiliser, converting creative decisions into structured, executable workflows.

Establish Production Blueprint

 **Why this is important**	A clear production blueprint acts as the master guide for translating instructional design into tangible deliverables. Without it, development becomes reactive, inconsistent, and prone to delays. This blueprint aligns all stakeholders around the scope, sequence, content treatment, roles, and review cycles required to bring the course to life. It provides structure, avoids miscommunication, and ensures that production is intentional, not improvised.
 **Tips**	• Treat the blueprint as a living document that evolves with design refinements. • Use visual mapping tools to outline dependencies and asset flows. • Make it accessible to all contributors, designers, developers, SMEs, and reviewers. • Include both macro (module-level) and micro (screen/slide-level) guidance. • Align blueprint milestones with your overall production schedule.
 **Traps**	• Skipping this step and relying on informal briefs leads to chaos later. • Overloading the blueprint with technical specs makes it unreadable. • Omitting responsibilities or review checkpoints increases rework. • Failing to update the blueprint during scope changes causes misalignment.
  **Techniques**	• Create a modular production map with separate tracks for content, media, assessments, and interactivity. • Use collaborative tools like Miro, Lucidchart, or Notion for dynamic editing and commenting. • Incorporate icons, colour codes, and templates to increase clarity and speed up adoption. • Include delivery specifications (e.g., screen size, SCORM version) early in the plan.
  **Examples**	• *A two-page production plan:* showing which SMEs review which slides and by when. • *A flowchart outlining dependencies:* between animation, narration, and screen build. • *A template assigning each course:* asset to a team member with delivery deadlines. • *A shared Google Doc:* listing every media file, script, and interaction element needed.
 **How it's done**	1. Begin by mapping the full instructional structure, modules, lessons, screens, and flagging required assets for each. Identify production roles and assign owners to each deliverable. 2. Define timelines and interdependencies (e.g., narration before video, storyboard before graphics). 3. Set quality control checkpoints. 4. Review the draft blueprint with the full team and revise collaboratively. 5. Lock in the version and publish it in a shared workspace.

Pre-Production Logistics
Establish Production Blueprint

Core Elements

- Production scope and deliverables clearly defined
- Roles and responsibilities documented
- Timeline with dependencies and milestones
- Asset lists and treatment notes
- Review and approval checkpoints
- Shared access and version control

Checklist

1. Have all deliverables been itemised and mapped to the course structure?
2. Are roles, responsibilities, and deadlines clearly assigned?
3. Does the blueprint align with your LMS or platform constraints?
4. Are quality review gates identified and documented?
5. Is the blueprint stored where all stakeholders can access the current version?

AI Considerations

- AI can help auto-generate initial blueprint drafts based on your storyboard or learning objectives.
- It can also tag content types and flag missing elements (e.g., a screen with no assessment).
- Tools like AI-powered project planners or natural language processors can monitor blueprint updates and alert stakeholders of scope creep or unassigned tasks.
- Just ensure AI doesn't override human judgment, blueprint validation must remain a team effort.

Key Takeaways

A production blueprint bridges the gap between design and development. It reduces confusion, aligns teams, and accelerates delivery by making roles, requirements, and timelines transparent.

Without it, even the best-designed course risks falling apart in execution.

With it, development flows with clarity, confidence, and control.

Schedule Production

Why this is important

A well-structured production schedule ensures that tasks are executed efficiently, resources are allocated appropriately, and timelines are met without compromising quality.

It enables clear sequencing of dependencies, supports coordination across teams, and provides visibility for stakeholders.

Incorporating quality assurance and buffer periods into the timeline helps mitigate risks and allows for adjustments when challenges arise.

Ultimately, an effective schedule transforms design intent into operational momentum, keeping the project on track, on budget, and ready for smooth handover to development.

Tips

- **Use Project Management Tools**
  Leverage software like Trello, Asana, or MS Project to plan, track, and adjust the schedule dynamically.
- **Engage Stakeholders Early**
  Involve team members and stakeholders in the planning process to ensure alignment and commitment.
- **Set Milestones**
  Break the project into smaller milestones to monitor progress and stay on track.
- **Allocate Buffer Time**
  Include buffer periods for unexpected delays or revisions in the schedule.
- **Communicate Regularly**
  Maintain open communication channels for updates and issue resolution.

Traps

- **Overly Ambitious Timelines**
  Avoid setting unrealistic deadlines that lead to burnout or missed quality standards.
- **Ignoring Dependencies**
  Failing to account for task dependencies can cause delays and disrupt workflow.
- **Underestimating Resources**
  Ensure resource needs are accurately assessed to prevent bottlenecks.
- **Skipping QA**
  Not allocating sufficient time for quality assurance can result in substandard materials.
- **Lack of Documentation**
  Poor documentation can cause miscommunication and missed tasks.

Techniques

- **Critical Path Method (CPM)**
  Identify the sequence of critical tasks that must be completed on time to avoid project delays.
- **Agile Scheduling**
  Use iterative cycles to adjust schedules based on ongoing progress and feedback.
- **Gantt Charts**
  Create visual timelines to illustrate task durations, dependencies, and progress.
- **Resource Levelling**
  Adjust schedules to avoid overloading any team member or resource.
- **Timeboxing**
  Allocate fixed time slots for each task to maintain focus and efficiency.

Pre-Production Logistics
Schedule Production

Examples

- *Scenario 1*
  Scheduling the production of multimedia content, allocating two weeks for video creation and one week for editing and QA.
- *Scenario 2*
  Sequencing content creation to align with media production, ensuring written materials are completed before video scripts are recorded.
- *Scenario 3*
  Assigning subject matter experts to review content drafts within 48 hours to keep the project on track.
- *Scenario 4*
  Incorporating a one-week buffer before the final launch to resolve any unforeseen issues.

How it's done

1. **Break Down Tasks**
   Start by identifying specific production tasks such as content writing, media creation, and integration. This ensures clarity on what needs to be accomplished and helps allocate responsibilities effectively.

2. **Develop Timelines**
   Create detailed timelines with start and end dates for each task, including key milestones. This establishes a clear roadmap for project completion.

3. **Assign Resources**
   Allocate human, technical, and financial resources to tasks based on requirements. Ensure resources are matched with the necessary expertise and availability.

4. **Sequence Activities**
   Organise tasks in a logical order, taking into account dependencies and workflow. This prevents delays and ensures a smooth progression of activities.

5. **Set Deadlines**
   Establish realistic deadlines for each task and communicate them clearly to all team members. This keeps the team focused and aligned with project goals.

6. **Plan Quality Assurance**
   Schedule review and approval steps at critical points in the production process to maintain high standards and address issues promptly.

7. **Monitor Progress**
   Use project management tools to track the completion of tasks, identify bottlenecks, and ensure the project stays on track.

8. **Update Schedule**
   Regularly update the schedule to reflect changes, progress, or unforeseen challenges. This ensures that the plan remains accurate and actionable.

9. **Document Plan**
   Maintain detailed records of the production schedule, task assignments, and dependencies. This documentation provides clarity and serves as a reference for stakeholders.

Pre-Production Logistics
Schedule Production

Core Elements

- **Production Timeline Finalised**
  A clear and realistic schedule with defined start and end dates for each task is established and approved.
- **Task Dependencies Mapped**
  Logical sequencing of tasks is outlined to reflect dependencies and ensure efficient workflow.
- **Resource Allocation Confirmed**
  Personnel, tools, and budget resources are assigned to each production task based on capacity and expertise.
- **Milestones and Checkpoints Defined**
  Key progress markers and quality assurance gates are built into the schedule to track progress and trigger reviews.
- **Buffer Time Built In**
  Contingency periods are included to accommodate delays, last-minute changes, or rework without derailing timelines.
- **Stakeholder Commitments Secured**
  All contributors, reviewers, and decision-makers are aligned on availability, deadlines, and responsibilities.
- **Schedule Documented and Shared**
  The production schedule is recorded in a shared, version-controlled environment and communicated to all stakeholders.

Checklist

1. Finalise all content and design elements for production readiness
2. Define production tasks (e.g., recording, authoring, animation, reviews)
3. Create a detailed production schedule with task durations and dependencies
4. Assign responsibilities and secure availability of SMEs, designers, narrators, etc.
5. Confirm availability of tools, licenses, and technical resources
6. Include review, rework, and QA phases in the schedule
7. Monitor progress against milestones with regular updates
8. Build in contingency time for unexpected delays or revisions

AI Considerations

- Generate project timelines based on content volume and resource availability
- Use AI to allocate production tasks based on skillsets and dependencies
- Simulate potential bottlenecks using AI-driven Gantt or Kanban tools
- Predict risk areas based on past production delays
- Auto-generate task lists from storyboard or design documents

Key Takeaways

The **Schedule Production** step in the ADDIE model's Design Phase turns planning into actionable tasks with defined timelines, resources, and review points.

A clear and structured schedule ensures efficient production of high-quality instructional materials, while tools and regular updates help manage progress and adapt to challenges.

By integrating flexibility, quality assurance, and effective communication, this process supports the timely delivery of materials that align with instructional objectives.

Lesson Formatting and Treatment

Why this is important

Consistent lesson formatting is essential to ensure that learning content is clear, engaging, and accessible across all delivery platforms.

When formatting aligns with instructional goals, it creates a structured flow that enhances comprehension and reduces cognitive load.

Proper layout, navigation, and media placement help guide learners intuitively through the material, while formatting for accessibility ensures that all users, including those with disabilities, can fully participate.

Embedding feedback loops, visual cues, and interaction standards into the formatting also reinforces learner engagement and supports effective progress tracking.

Ultimately, well-executed formatting translates instructional design into a cohesive, high-impact learning experience.

Tips

- **Keep It Consistent**
  Maintain consistent formatting elements, such as font size, style, and colour scheme, throughout the lesson.
- **Chunk the Content**
  Break lessons into smaller, manageable sections or modules to improve retention and reduce cognitive overload.
- **Use Visual Aids**
  Include charts, graphs, and images to visually represent key concepts and enhance understanding.
- **Integrate Multimedia**
  Add videos, audio clips, or animations to make the content more dynamic and engaging.
- **Provide Navigation Cues**
  Use clear headings, subheadings, and transitions to guide learners through the material.

Traps

- **Overloading Information**
  Including too much content in a single lesson can overwhelm learners and reduce retention.
- **Ignoring Accessibility**
  Failing to accommodate learners with disabilities can limit inclusivity and compliance with accessibility standards.
- **Inconsistent Design**
  Variations in formatting can distract learners and detract from the overall learning experience.
- **Lack of Engagement**
  Omitting interactive or engaging elements may result in learner disinterest or passive participation.
- **Poor Alignment**
  Mismatching lesson format with learning objectives can hinder the achievement of desired outcomes.

Techniques

- **Storyboard Your Lessons**
  Create a visual outline of the lesson format to ensure logical flow and alignment with objectives.
- **Apply Chunking**
  Divide content into distinct sections with clear boundaries to improve learner focus and understanding.
- **Leverage Universal Design for Learning (UDL)**
  Design materials that are flexible and adaptable to a wide range of learning preferences.
- **Interactive Activities**
  Incorporate quizzes, polls, or simulations to actively involve learners and reinforce concepts.
- **Accessibility Tools**
  Use tools like screen readers, alt text for images, and captioning for videos to ensure accessibility.

Pre-Production Logistics
Lesson Formatting and Treatment

Examples

- *Scenario 1*
  A training module on workplace safety is divided into three sections hazard identification, prevention strategies, and emergency response. Each section includes interactive quizzes and real-world examples.
- *Scenario 2*
  An eLearning lesson on coding basics uses videos to explain concepts, followed by coding exercises learners can complete in an embedded IDE.
- *Scenario 3*
  A classroom lesson on ecosystems includes diagrams of food chains, group activities to build their own ecosystem models, and a reflection worksheet.
- *Scenario 4*
  An online history course lesson is formatted with timelines, key event summaries, and short video reenactments to bring historical events to life.

How it's done

1. **Review Learning Objectives**
   Begin by ensuring that all lesson content aligns with the intended learning outcomes and objectives. This keeps the instructional design focused and purposeful.
2. **Organise Content**
   Sequence information logically, grouping related topics to ensure coherence and flow. This makes the material easier for learners to understand and navigate.
3. **Design Modules**
   Break the lesson into smaller, manageable sections or modules to enhance usability and learner engagement.
4. **Integrate Media**
   Select and incorporate appropriate media formats, such as videos, images, and text, to complement and enrich the lesson content.
5. **Develop Interactivities**
   Include exercises, quizzes, discussions, or other interactive elements to actively engage learners and reinforce their understanding.
6. **Ensure Accessibility**
   Ensure all materials are accessible, incorporating alternative formats and ensuring compatibility with assistive technologies to accommodate diverse learner needs.
7. **Create Visual Aids**
   Design charts, diagrams, and other visual tools to simplify and illustrate complex concepts effectively.
8. **Test and Revise**
   Pilot the lesson with a sample audience to identify potential issues. Use feedback to refine the format, ensuring it meets learning objectives and user expectations.

Pre-Production Logistics
Lesson Formatting and Treatment

Core Elements

- **Alignment**
  The lesson format must align with the established learning objectives.
- **Structure**
  Content is divided into logical, manageable modules or sections.
- **Engagement**
  Multimedia elements and interactive activities enhance learner engagement.
- **Accessibility**
  Materials include alternative formats and support for assistive technologies.
- **Visual Appeal**
  Visual aids are thoughtfully designed to clarify and enhance understanding.
- **Consistency**
  Design elements, including fonts and colours, are uniform throughout.
- **Navigation**
  Clear and intuitive headings, transitions, and navigation cues are incorporated.
- **Cross-Platform Compatibility**
  Lessons are tested to ensure functionality across various devices and platforms.
- **Documentation**
  Guidelines for the lesson format are thoroughly documented.

Checklist

1. Apply consistent formatting templates to all lessons/modules
2. Ensure typography, colour schemes, layout, and visual styles match the design guide
3. Standardise placement of objectives, activities, and feedback elements
4. Optimise formatting for screen size, device, and delivery platform compatibility
5. Review for accessibility compliance (e.g., contrast, font size, navigation structure)
6. Ensure consistent tone, terminology, and instructional style across lessons
7. Conduct formatting QA on multiple devices or platforms
8. Version-lock formatted content for publishing or development

AI Considerations

- Use AI to scan for formatting inconsistencies across modules
- Auto-adjust layout for different devices (responsive formatting previews)
- Generate style guides or enforce brand compliance using formatting rules
- Summarise formatting errors and generate fix recommendations
- Apply tone and terminology alignment across lessons using NLP consistency tools

Key Takeaways

The **Lesson Formatting and treatment** step is critical for ensuring instructional materials are well-structured, engaging, and accessible.

By focusing on alignment with objectives, logical organisation, and inclusivity, instructional designers create effective learning experiences that cater to diverse needs.

Testing and refining the format based on feedback further enhance the quality and usability of the lessons, establishing a strong foundation for impactful instruction.

Part 3: The **DEVELOPMENT** phase

The **Development phase** is the production powerhouse of the ADDIE model, where all the conceptual scaffolding and careful planning of the earlier phases are transformed into tangible, high-quality learning assets. This is where strategy becomes substance.

Building on the design blueprint, this phase involves the **creation, assembly, and integration** of all course materials, scripts, visuals, multimedia elements, user interfaces, assessments, guides, and delivery frameworks.

Every component is crafted with precision to meet the instructional, accessibility, and aesthetic standards set in the Design phase.

But in ADDIE on Steroids, development is not just a hand-off to production. It is an iterative, intelligence-assisted process powered by AI tools, agile workflows, and continuous feedback loops.

This allows for rapid prototyping, early detection of quality issues, and precise adaptation to learner needs and platform requirements.

This phase includes **content writing, shot listing, media creation, and full courseware assembly**, followed by **usability testing and pilot readiness reviews**.

Multiple stakeholders, Instructional Designers, Subject Matter Experts (SMEs), media producers, AI agents, and even pilot learners, are involved in reviewing, refining, and validating outputs.

A key innovation in this enhanced Development phase is the strategic use of **generative AI**. From drafting narration scripts and branching scenarios to generating alt text and synthesising voiceovers, AI helps accelerate production without compromising quality.

Dedicated steps in this phase help teams define AI boundaries, validate ethical use, and ensure version control across tools.

The **Development phase is not the finish line**, but it is the critical foundation that determines whether your learning solution is viable, scalable, and ready for real-world delivery. The polish applied here directly impacts learner engagement, retention, and ROI. And thanks to the structured checklists, conditional logic tags,

AI readiness scans, and quality assurance steps embedded in this book, your outputs won't just be "done", they'll be deployment-ready and data-informed.

In this phase, your guiding principle is not just "build it" but **"build it right then test it ruthlessly."** Because what comes next is Implementation, and Implementation will not forgive half-baked outputs.

Content Development

The **Content Development** step in the Development phase of the ADDIE model focuses on producing instructional materials that are engaging, clear, and aligned with the course's learning objectives. This phase involves crafting scripts, preparing shot lists for media production, and creating supporting materials like learner guides and manuals.

The objective is to ensure that all content elements are purposeful, cohesive, and supportive of the desired learner outcomes. By combining multimedia, written documentation, and structured planning, this step delivers high-quality resources that enhance comprehension and engagement.

Overview

Key Sub-Steps are:

- **Write Content Scripts**
  Develop scripts for video and audio content that are clear, concise, and aligned with course objectives while maintaining learner engagement.

- **Prepare Shot List**
  Organise video production with detailed shot lists specifying camera angles, scene composition, lighting, and other visual elements.

- **Document Manual and Guides**
  Create supporting written materials such as learner guides or manuals to reinforce content and provide ongoing learner support.

The outcomes of the **Content Development** step are to produce structured, engaging, and learner-focused materials that align with course goals.

Key outcomes include:

- **Develop Purposeful Scripts**
  Write clear, concise scripts for multimedia content that directly support learning objectives and maintain learner interest.

- **Organise Media Production**
  Use shot lists to streamline video production, ensuring that visual elements align with instructional goals and reduce production inefficiencies.

- **Prepare Comprehensive Supporting Documents**
  Develop user-friendly guides, manuals, or supplementary materials that support learners and enhance understanding of course content.

- **Ensure Consistency Across Content**
  Align all content elements under a unified design and style to maintain coherence and reinforce key messages.

- **Cater to Engagement and Accessibility**
  Use engaging multimedia and ensure compliance with accessibility standards (e.g., captions, alt text) to address the needs of a diverse learner audience.

Outcomes

The **Content Development** step is pivotal in transforming instructional plans into learner-ready materials.

By focusing on detailed script writing, well-structured shot lists, and supporting documentation, instructional designers ensure that the course content is both engaging and aligned with the learning objectives.

This process helps to avoid common issues like inconsistent messaging or disorganised materials by following best practices, such as collaborative planning and thorough reviews. The result is a cohesive, accessible, and visually appealing course that provides learners with a seamless and impactful educational experience.

Summary

Content Development
Write Content Scripts

Write Content Scripts

Why this is important

Well-crafted scripts form the backbone of effective multimedia learning experiences.

A clear, concise script ensures that the instructional message is delivered with precision and supports the intended learning outcomes.

Aligning the script with course objectives helps maintain focus and relevance throughout. Scripts written in an engaging, conversational tone can capture attention and sustain learner interest, while tailoring the language and style to the target audience enhances relatability and comprehension.

Incorporating storytelling techniques promotes retention and makes the content more memorable.

Most importantly, the script must seamlessly integrate with visual and audio elements to create a cohesive, immersive learning experience.

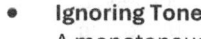

Tips

- **Know Your Audience**
  Understand the target audience's background, prior knowledge, and learning goals to craft relevant and relatable scripts.
- **Be Conversational**
  Use a friendly and conversational tone to make the script engaging and approachable.
- **Keep It Concise**
  Focus on essential information and avoid overloading learners with unnecessary details.
- **Emphasise Key Points**
  Highlight important concepts or takeaways through repetition, tone variation, or visuals.
- **Incorporate Visual Cues**
  Align the script with planned visuals to create a seamless narrative flow.

Traps

- **Overloading Content**
  Including too much information can overwhelm learners and detract from the core message.
- **Overcomplicated Language**
  Using jargon or complex terminology may confuse learners and reduce comprehension.
- **Ignoring Tone**
  A monotonous or overly formal tone can disengage learners.
- **Misaligned Visuals**
  Scripts that don't sync with visuals can create confusion and disrupt the learning experience.
- **Lack of Accessibility**
  Scripts that exclude captions or alternative formats may alienate learners with diverse needs.

Techniques

- **Storyboard First**
  Develop a storyboard to visualise how the script will align with visuals, interactions, and transitions.
- **Use the 3-Act Structure**
  Structure scripts with an introduction (hook), body (main content), and conclusion (call to action or summary).
- **Engage Emotionally**
  Use storytelling or relatable scenarios to evoke emotional connections and enhance retention.
- **Write for the Ear**
  Ensure scripts sound natural when spoken aloud; use shorter sentences and conversational language.
- **Include Pauses**
  Plan pauses for emphasis, reflection, or to synchronise with visual or auditory elements.

Content Development
Write Content Scripts

Examples

Scenario 1: Safety Training Video Script

- **Introduction:**
  "Start your day with safety top of mind. In this module, we'll walk through essential practices that help prevent workplace incidents before they happen."
- **Main Content:**
  "Begin every task with a checklist. It's your first line of defence, ensuring nothing critical is overlooked."
- **Conclusion:**
  "Safety isn't just compliance, it's culture. Let's commit to making every action a safe one for ourselves and our team."

Scenario 2: Software Tutorial Voiceover

- **Introduction:**
  "Hi there! In this short tutorial, we'll show you how to get started using the Project Manager tool like a pro."
- **Main Content:**
  "To begin a new project, simply click the 'Add' button at the top-right. Enter the required details in the form that appears. Like project name, deadlines, and team members, and hit 'Create'."
- **Conclusion:**
  "You're now ready to manage tasks more efficiently. Explore our other tutorials to unlock advanced features and boost your productivity."

How it's done

1. **Research and Select AI Tools**
   Identify and evaluate AI tools suited for content creation and optimisation. Select tools that meet organisational requirements and align with the desired learning outcomes.

2. **Establish Workflows**
   Develop workflows that integrate AI-driven content creation with manual review processes. Ensure human oversight is incorporated to maintain quality and relevance.

3. **Train Staff in AI Use**
   Provide comprehensive training to team members on using AI tools effectively. Emphasise ethical considerations, best practices, and the importance of monitoring outputs for inclusivity and accuracy.

4. **Monitor AI Outputs**
   Regularly review AI-generated content to ensure alignment with learning objectives, quality standards, and organisational goals. Make adjustments as needed to maintain consistency and relevance.

Core Elements

- **AI Tools Tested and Approved**
  AI tools are evaluated and selected for content development based on their suitability and effectiveness.

- **Workflows Established**
  Processes are in place to integrate AI-generated content with manual review for quality assurance.

- **Team Trained**
  Staff are trained in ethical AI use and best practices, ensuring responsible and effective implementation.

- **Outputs Reviewed**
  AI-generated content is consistently monitored for accuracy, inclusivity, and compliance with organisational standards.

- **Content Updated Regularly**
  Processes are established to ensure content is periodically reviewed and updated based on AI-driven insights.

Content Development
Write Content Scripts

Checklist

1. Align script content directly with learning objectives
2. Structure script to match delivery format (e.g. video, voiceover, animation)
3. Maintain clarity, tone, and flow suited to target learners
4. Incorporate prompts for visuals, interactivity, or narration cues
5. Apply plain language principles for readability
6. Include instructional hooks, transitions, and signposting
7. Review for technical accuracy and consistency
8. Validate with SMEs and adapt based on feedback

AI Considerations

- Use AI to draft or refine voiceover scripts based on learning points
- Generate alternate versions for tone, level, or length
- Auto-insert signposting, transitions, or rhetorical devices
- Compare drafts to objectives using LLM-based validation
- Translate scripts for localisation or multilingual deployment

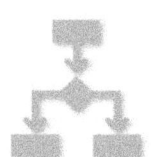
Key Takeaways

AI-driven content development in the Development Phase enables organisations to create engaging, accessible, and localised learning materials efficiently.

By combining AI capabilities with human oversight, instructional designers enhance content quality and inclusivity while ensuring alignment with organisational goals.

Regular monitoring and updates ensure learning materials remain relevant, effective, and compliant with quality standards. This balanced approach leverages AI's efficiency while preserving the nuance and contextual understanding provided by human expertise.

Content Development
Prepare Shot List

Prepare Shot List

Why this is important

A well-prepared shot list is essential for ensuring an efficient and effective video production process.

It provides a structured plan that aligns each shot with the instructional content and learning objectives, keeping the visual narrative focused and purposeful.

By clearly detailing camera angles, movements, and framing, the shot list guides the production team in capturing the right visuals the first time, minimising delays and reducing unnecessary resource use.

Most importantly, it supports a smooth integration of visuals with the accompanying script and voiceover, helping to create a cohesive and engaging learning experience.

Tips

- **Begin with the Script**
  Use the script as the foundation for determining the required shots, ensuring alignment with the instructional narrative.
- **Prioritise Key Shots**
  Focus on shots that are essential to achieving the learning objectives or conveying critical concepts.
- **Use Visual Storytelling**
  Plan shots that illustrate concepts visually, reducing the reliance on lengthy verbal explanations.
- **Consider Transitions**
  Include notes on how shots will transition to maintain a smooth visual flow.
- **Account for Accessibility**
  Plan for alternative visual formats or descriptive narration for learners with visual impairments.

Traps

- **Overcomplicating Shots**
  Complex camera movements or effects can distract from the content and increase production time.
- **Inconsistent Style**
  Variations in lighting, framing, or angles can create a disjointed viewing experience.
- **Ignoring the Audience**
  Shots that are too artistic or abstract may confuse learners rather than enhance understanding.
- **Skipping Rehearsals**
  Failing to test the feasibility of shots can lead to production delays or reshoots.
- **Neglecting B-Roll**
  Omitting secondary footage for transitions or context can limit editing flexibility.

Techniques

- **Storyboarding First**
  Use a storyboard to visualise each shot before creating the list, ensuring alignment with the script and learning objectives.
- **Group Shots by Location**
  Plan shots by location or setting to optimise the shooting schedule and reduce setup changes.
- **Include Technical Details**
  Note camera angles, lighting setups, equipment requirements, and any special effects for each shot.
- **Plan for Flexibility**
  Allow room for improvisation or adjustments during filming to accommodate unforeseen issues.
- **Integrate Multimedia**
  Identify points where graphics, animations, or text overlays will complement the video footage.

Content Development
Prepare Shot List

Examples

Scenario 1: Training Video on Workplace Safety

- **Shot 1:**
  Wide-angle shot of a worker donning personal protective equipment in a well-lit workshop setting, establishing context and compliance.
- **Shot 2:**
  Close-up of the worker inspecting safety gloves, with emphasis on checking for tears or contamination.
- **Shot 3:**
  Over-the-shoulder angle showing a printed safety checklist being marked off with a pen, reinforcing the procedural approach.

Scenario 2: Software Tutorial

- **Shot 1:**
  Screen capture of the software dashboard, with a smooth zoom-in on the top navigation menu as the user prepares to begin a task.
- **Shot 2:**
  Cut to a close-up of hands on a keyboard, entering project details, with a shallow depth of field to keep the viewer's focus.
- **Shot 3:**
  Screen recording with animated cursor movement, synchronised with voiceover, highlighting key tools and dropdown options in sequence.

How it's done

1. **Define Learning Objectives**
   Start by identifying the purpose of the script and the key messages learners need to understand and retain. Ensure these objectives align with the broader instructional goals.

2. **Understand the Audience**
   Gather insights into the demographics, preferences, and prior knowledge of the target audience. This understanding shapes the tone, language, and structure of the script.

3. **Draft a Storyboard**
   Plan the script in tandem with visuals and interactions. Create a storyboard to map out how the script will align with media elements and enhance engagement.

4. **Write the First Draft**
   Craft a clear and concise draft, focusing on the key points learners need to take away. Use conversational and accessible language to maintain engagement.

5. **Align with Visuals**
   Ensure the script complements and synchronises seamlessly with planned visuals, animations, or other media elements. Maintain consistency between content and delivery.

6. **Review and Revise**
   Edit the script for tone, clarity, and accuracy. Seek feedback from stakeholders or subject matter experts (SMEs) to refine the draft and address any gaps.

7. **Pilot the Script**
   Conduct a test-read to ensure the script flows naturally, sounds conversational, and aligns with the intended pacing and objectives.

8. **Finalise for Production**
   Prepare the script for production by including annotations for tone, pacing, and emphasis. Ensure accessibility considerations, such as captions or alternative formats, are addressed.

Content Development
Prepare Shot List

Core Elements

- **Alignment with Objectives**
  The script supports the learning objectives and emphasises key points.
- **Conversational Language**
  The script uses clear, engaging, and easy-to-understand language.
- **Visual Integration**
  The script complements and synchronises with visuals and media elements.
- **Engaging Tone**
  The tone is appropriate for the target audience and fosters engagement.
- **Optimised Length**
  The script is concise and suitable for the medium and audience's attention span.
- **Accessibility Ensured**
  Captions, alternative formats, and other accessibility features are included.
- **Reviewed for Accuracy**
  The script is thoroughly reviewed and refined for clarity and accuracy.
- **Pilot Tested**
  The script is tested to ensure natural delivery, appropriate pacing, and effectiveness.

Checklist

1. Identify all scenes or visual segments needed for production
2. Break down each screen or script line into corresponding shots
3. Specify camera angle, framing, duration, and motion cues
4. Include asset references (e.g., graphics, animations, props)
5. Confirm alignment with storyboard and script timing
6. Include notes on transitions, overlays, and captions
7. Review with production team or media vendor
8. Finalise and distribute shot list for scheduling

AI Considerations

- Use AI to convert scripts into shot list outlines
- Generate draft visual descriptions or camera cues from narration
- Optimise shot sequencing for editing efficiency
- Auto-tag shots with required assets (e.g., title cards, transitions)
- Simulate timing and pacing using AI-powered storyboard preview tools

Key Takeaways

Script writing in a learning and development context blends creativity with strategy. It requires aligning content with learning objectives, tailoring it to the audience, and crafting an engaging narrative that works seamlessly with visuals and media.

By focusing on clarity, engagement, and accessibility, instructional designers can create scripts that enhance the overall learning experience, improving knowledge retention and application.

Through thoughtful planning, iterative refinement, and a learner-centred approach, script writing becomes a powerful tool for delivering impactful educational content.

Content Development
Document Manual and Guides

Document Manual and Guides

Why this is important

Developing clear, structured manuals and guides is essential to support effective delivery across different formats, whether face-to-face, instructor-led, or online.

Well-designed manuals should align closely with the learning objectives, enhancing the experience for both learners and facilitators.

Consistency between learner and facilitator guides ensures smooth instruction and fosters better engagement.

These resources must provide practical instructions, tools, and references that aid in teaching and learning, while also being accessible and usable across diverse learner needs and instructional settings.

Tips

- **Understand the Audience**
  Tailor the tone, language, and content of manuals to suit the needs and preferences of learners and instructors
- **Maintain Alignment**
  Ensure manuals align with course content, learning objectives, and instructional strategies
- **Include Visuals**
  Use diagrams, tables, and images to break up text and enhance understanding of complex concepts
- **Provide Flexibility**
  Incorporate optional activities or supplementary resources to allow for customisation in delivery
- **Prioritise Accessibility**
  Design manuals to be accessible, including large print, braille, or digital formats where necessary

Traps

- **Overloading with Information**
  Avoid including unnecessary details that may overwhelm learners or instructors
- **Ignoring Feedback**
  Failing to incorporate feedback from pilot tests or stakeholders can lead to ineffective manuals
- **Lack of Consistency**
  Inconsistent formatting, language, or structure can confuse users
- **Missing Cross-References**
  Omitting links to related content (e.g., additional resources, glossary terms) can hinder understanding
- **Underestimating Usability**
  Manuals that are not user-friendly, with poor layout or unclear instructions, may frustrate learners and instructors.

Techniques

- **Use Templates**
  Develop standardised templates for learner and facilitator manuals to maintain consistency and reduce development time
- **Focus on Actionable Content**
  Prioritise instructions, exercises, and examples that actively engage learners and instructors
- **Incorporate Learning Aids**
  Add quick-reference sections like summaries, glossaries, or FAQs to enhance usability
- **Utilise Modular Design**
  Break content into logical sections or modules to improve navigation and facilitate understanding
- **Leverage Feedback Loops**
  Gather feedback from instructors and learners to refine manuals over time.

Content Development
Document Manual and Guides

Examples

- *Learner Guide*
  Includes course objectives, key content, exercises, and reflection prompts to guide individual learning
- *Facilitator Manual*
  Provides lesson plans, instructions for activities, suggested pacing, and troubleshooting tips for instructors
- *Journal Format*
  A structured learner journal includes spaces for notetaking, self-reflection, and documenting personal progress
- *Face-to-Face Example*
  A printed facilitator manual outlining group activities, time allocations, and discussion prompts
- *Online Example*
  A downloadable PDF learner guide integrated with hyperlinks to supplementary resources and videos.

How it's done

- **Analyse Course Needs**
  Begin by determining the type and purpose of manuals required, considering the course delivery format, such as face-to-face, instructor-led, or online learning.
- **Define Content Scope**
  Outline the key content areas, learning activities, and supplemental resources to be included in the manuals. Ensure alignment with the course's learning objectives and desired outcomes.
- **Develop Layout and Structure**
  Design a clear and logical structure for the manuals, incorporating sections such as objectives, instructional content, exercises, and additional resources. Use consistent headings and navigation aids for ease of use.
- **Write Content**
  Draft content that is tailored to the target audience, ensuring clarity and alignment with learning goals. Use concise, learner-friendly language to maximise engagement and understanding.
- **Design Visual Aids**
  Incorporate graphics, tables, and diagrams to enhance comprehension and engagement. Ensure visuals are clear, relevant, and supportive of the instructional material.
- **Incorporate Accessibility Features**
  Design manuals to meet accessibility standards, including alternative formats where necessary. Address diverse learner needs to ensure inclusivity.
- **Pilot Test**
  Test the manuals with representative learners and instructors to gather feedback on usability, content clarity, and overall effectiveness.
- **Revise and Finalise**
  Refine the manuals based on pilot test feedback. Ensure consistency, accuracy, and quality in the final versions, readying them for distribution in both digital and physical formats.

Content Development
Document Manual and Guides

Core Elements

- **Tailored Manuals**
  Manuals are designed to suit the specific course delivery format.
- **Content Alignment**
  Content is aligned with learning objectives and outcomes.
- **Logical Structure**
  Manuals are structured with clear sections, headings, and navigation aids.
- **Effective Visual Aids**
  Graphics, tables, and diagrams are used to enhance comprehension and engagement.
- **Accessibility Ensured**
  Manuals include features to meet accessibility standards and cater to diverse learners.
- **Facilitator Manuals**
  Include lesson plans, activity instructions, and troubleshooting tips.
- **Learner Guides**
  Provide exercises, reflection prompts, and supplemental resources.
- **Feedback Incorporated**
  Pilot test feedback is used to refine the final versions.
- **Quality Checked**
  Manuals are reviewed for consistency, accuracy, and usability.
- **Digital-Friendly**
  Manuals are formatted for easy distribution and use in digital formats.

Checklist

1. Identify manuals or guides required (facilitator, learner, technical, etc.)
2. Structure content into clear, navigable sections
3. Include visuals, examples, and step-by-step instructions
4. Apply consistent formatting and terminology
5. Ensure accessibility (e.g., readable fonts, alt text, captioned images)
6. Review with SMEs and technical reviewers
7. Store in central repository with version control
8. Prepare printable and digital-ready formats

AI Considerations

- Use AI to draft standard procedures or instructions from content modules
- Generate summary tables, checklists, and FAQs from narrative text
- Translate manuals into other languages or reading levels
- Auto-format guides using pre-trained style templates
- Suggest layout improvements or restructure content for clarity

Key Takeaways

Documenting manuals and guides is a critical step in bridging the gap between course design and implementation.

Well-designed manuals, whether for learners or facilitators, ensure instructional materials are accessible, engaging, and aligned with learning objectives.

By creating clear structures, incorporating engaging visuals, and ensuring accessibility, instructional designers produce tools that enhance the educational experience.

These manuals not only support diverse learner needs but also contribute to the overall success of instructional programmes, ensuring consistency and ease of use across varied delivery formats.

Translation and Localisation Prep

In a global learning ecosystem, instructional content must be built not just for clarity in its original form, but for adaptability across languages, cultures, and platforms.

The **Translation and Localisation Prep** phase ensures that every element, text, images, audio, video, and interactivity, is designed with foresight to enable smooth and meaningful localisation.

This is far more than converting words from one language to another. It's about making smart structural, visual, and technical decisions early in the development cycle that prevent downstream friction, reduce costly rework, and safeguard the learner experience in every market.

This phase brings together content creators, learning designers, technical teams, and localisation specialists to align on standards, define expectations, and optimise materials for multilingual delivery. It embeds scalability, inclusivity, and consistency into the DNA of the course.

Key Sub-Steps are:

- **Identify Target Languages and Regions**
  Pinpoint which markets and dialects require tailored content to meet cultural, regulatory, and linguistic needs.

- **Prepare Content for Translation Compatibility**
  Format source materials using localisation-friendly structures, tools, and markup that minimise disruption during translation.

- **Establish Localisation Standards and Style Guides**
  Define tone, terminology, and formatting conventions to ensure consistency across all language versions.

- **Coordinate with Translation and Localisation Vendors**
  Engage the right partners, set expectations, and streamline workflows to manage timelines, tools, and responsibilities.

- **Integrate QA Processes for Localised Versions**
  Build in review mechanisms, test plans, and feedback loops to maintain quality, usability, and instructional intent in all translated outputs.

By preparing with precision and planning for localisation from the outset, this phase helps organisations deliver culturally authentic, brand-consistent learning at scale.

Without delays, compromises, or lost meaning.

Overview

Translation and Localisation Prep
Document Manual and Guides

Outcomes

By the end of this phase, the instructional design team will have:

1. Identified the required target languages and geographic regions for localisation based on learner demographics and organisational needs.
2. Audited and prepared all source content to ensure compatibility with translation workflows, including avoidance of embedded text and idiomatic phrasing.
3. Established clear localisation standards and style guides per language or region, including approved glossaries and tone-of-voice guidelines.
4. Coordinated with translation and localisation vendors, setting clear expectations for workflows, QA procedures, file handling, and communication protocols.
5. Integrated structured, scalable QA processes for all localised versions, covering linguistic, functional, and visual quality criteria.
6. Ensured all content and assets are ready for seamless and culturally appropriate adaptation prior to pilot testing or global rollout.

Summary

Translation and localisation are no longer optional extras in large-scale learning deployments, they are mission-critical components that determine reach, effectiveness, and learner trust. This phase creates the foundation for a globally inclusive learning experience by preparing all assets for reliable, culturally nuanced adaptation.

The steps taken here reduce the cost, risk, and timeline of localisation efforts while ensuring consistency in learning outcomes across languages. When content is prepared and localisation workflows are tightly managed, the result is a high-quality, branded learning product that performs equally well in Tokyo, Johannesburg, São Paulo, and Toronto.

A well-executed **Translation and Localisation Prep** phase enables scale, compliance, and learner engagement across regions, supporting both enterprise growth and educational equity.

Identify Target Languages and Regions

Why this is important

Accurate identification of target languages and regions is foundational to the localisation process. Without this, translation efforts may miss key markets, introduce irrelevant cultural assumptions, or waste resources duplicating unnecessary work.

It's not just about language, it's about knowing which audiences matter, where they are, and what they expect from a learning experience.

Tips

- Align localisation efforts with business priorities and learner demographics.
- Differentiate between language and locale. Spanish in Spain ≠ Spanish in Mexico.
- Use historical analytics, user profiles, or regional partners to prioritise localisation tiers (must-have vs nice-to-have).
- Consider both external learners (clients) and internal audiences (employees).

Traps

- Assuming "one version fits all" in global rollouts.
- Neglecting dialect, tone, or legal terminology differences across regions.
- Overextending by selecting too many target languages without assessing ROI.
- Ignoring smaller markets with high cultural sensitivity needs.

Techniques

- **Region–Language Mapping Matrix**: Match languages to course modules and deployment plans.
- **Tiered Prioritisation**: Segment into high, medium, and low priority based on reach and impact.
- **Needs Analysis Interviews**: Engage regional teams or learners to identify true localisation gaps.

Examples

- A mining safety course translated into Brazilian Portuguese and Canadian French for compliance.
- A global sales onboarding adapted for APAC markets with variations for Japanese vs Mandarin.
- A leadership module rewritten to reflect collectivist vs individualist workplace norms.

How it's done

1. Review learner data, business goals, and regulatory requirements.
2. List all potential regions and assess training language needs.
3. Engage stakeholders to prioritise based on legal, cultural, or strategic relevance.
4. Document final list of target languages and delivery locales.
5. Communicate scope clearly to content, design, and vendor teams.

Translation and Localisation Prep
Identify Target Languages and Regions

Core Elements

- Primary and secondary languages
- Regional cultural profiles
- Legal and compliance drivers
- Local market sensitivity
- Business value alignment

Checklist

1. Define business and learning goals for localisation.
2. Identify core learner groups requiring translation.
3. Segment languages into priority tiers.
4. Differentiate between language and regional dialects.
5. Confirm compliance requirements by region.
6. Engage regional SMEs or managers to validate assumptions.
7. Finalise and circulate approved list of target languages/regions.

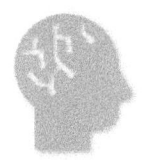
AI Considerations

- Use AI to analyse learner demographics and infer top localisation needs.
- Predict future localisation demand based on business expansion models.
- Generate comparison tables of dialect differences (e.g., Spanish–Spain vs Spanish–LatAm).
- Draft preliminary justification reports for each target region using AI synthesis.

Key Takeaways

- Define which languages and regions are essential based on learner demographics, regulatory requirements, and business priorities.
- Avoid blanket assumptions, Targeting should be data-informed and culturally relevant.
- Prioritise languages with large or strategic learner populations first.

Prepare Content for Translation Compatibility

Why this is important

Preparing content for translation compatibility is a proactive process that ensures your learning materials are structurally, visually, and linguistically ready for localisation into multiple languages. Without this preparatory step, content can become a translation nightmare, resulting in broken layouts, increased costs, cultural missteps, or learner confusion. Translation-ready content avoids idioms, slang, and unnecessary complexity, while also ensuring formatting elements like text boxes, tables, and animations are adaptable. Proper preparation reduces turnaround time for localisation, improves consistency across versions, and increases the success rate of multilingual rollouts. It also builds trust among global learners, who expect polished, culturally relevant experiences.

Tips

- Write source content in **clear, neutral English**. Avoid idioms, jargon, and humour that may not translate well.
- Use **standard formatting** styles in authoring tools to allow for seamless text expansion.
- Design layouts with **extra white space** to accommodate longer translations (German, for example, can expand 30% over English).
- Keep **sentences short and modular**, especially in audio and captioned content, to ease synchronisation across languages.
- Create a **master glossary** of key terms and brand-specific vocabulary before any translation begins.

Traps

- Embedding text in graphics or animations. This requires costly re-editing or redesign during translation.
- Using **voiceover timing** that's too tight. Non-English audio may not fit if scripts weren't prepared with pacing flexibility.
- Assuming a linear translation. Many languages require grammatical restructuring (e.g., subject-verb-object order shifts).
- Over-relying on AI translation without a human localisation pass can lead to culturally inappropriate phrasing or confusing tone.

Techniques

- **Internationalisation (i18n) Review**: Systematically examine all text, layout, media, and navigation for compatibility.
- **XML or XLIFF Export**: Use structured file formats from your authoring tools to manage translatable content efficiently.
- **Style Guides for Localisation**: Define tone, formatting rules, units of measure, and conventions for each locale.
- **Cultural Sensitivity Checks**: Assess all imagery, icons, metaphors, colours, and case examples for cultural resonance or taboos.
- **Pre-translation Pseudo-localisation**: Run a simulation that fills content with accented characters and longer placeholder text to check formatting durability.

Examples

- A video eLearning course originally created in Articulate Storyline is reviewed to remove embedded text from PNG graphics and convert them into dynamic text fields that can be swapped out per language.
- Source content written for American audiences ("hit the ground running") is rewritten as "start with confidence" for easier global localisation.
- Tables originally set to fixed column widths are adjusted to auto-fit content, avoiding overflow issues when translating into French or German.

Translation and Localisation Prep
Prepare Content for Translation Compatibility

233

How it's done

1. Review all course assets, documents, media, and interactions for text formatting, language complexity, and embedded elements.
2. Standardise layouts using paragraph styles and structured templates in authoring tools like Storyline, Rise, Captivate, or Word.
3. Remove all embedded text in graphics or create layered formats (e.g., SVGs) with editable captions.
4. Rewrite idiomatic phrases or culturally specific examples into universally understandable equivalents.
5. Prepare a terminology guide and style sheet for translators.
6. Run a pseudo-localisation test on the draft course to identify layout breakages or display issues.
7. Confirm with translation vendors or internal language leads that the content is compatible and structured to facilitate clean handoff.

Core Elements

- Language-neutral writing style
- Translation style guide
- Translatable content extraction (text, labels, alt tags, captions)
- Editable media assets (non-baked text)
- Localisation-ready layouts and white space design
- Pseudo-localisation pass for quality control
- Final compatibility validation checklist

Checklist

1. Standardise all text formatting across assets
2. Remove or convert embedded text from images, animations, and videos
3. Rewrite idiomatic or culturally biased language
4. Add padding and white space for text expansion
5. Prepare a centralised glossary and style guide
6. Run pseudo-localisation tests for layout and character rendering
7. Validate compatibility with LMS and eLearning authoring tools
8. Confirm readiness with language service provider or in-country reviewers

AI Considerations

- Use generative AI to detect idiomatic expressions and propose neutral rewordings.
- Auto-scan content for embedded text in media and flag non-translatable elements.
- Employ AI to run pseudo-localisation simulations, checking how text expands or contracts in different languages.
- Apply machine learning models to predict which screens or assets are at highest risk of layout breakage during localisation.
- Use AI to auto-generate style guides based on existing translated content for consistency.

Key Takeaways

- Strip out idioms, slang, and culturally bound references early in the process.
- Use plain language and consistent terminology to ease the translation load.
- Separate translatable content from interface or platform-specific elements where possible.

Establish Localisation Standards and Style Guides

Why this is important

Establishing localisation standards and style guides ensures that translated learning content is not only linguistically accurate but also consistent, culturally appropriate, and aligned with your brand's tone and instructional purpose.

Without defined standards, different translators or teams may introduce inconsistencies in terminology, tone, punctuation, visuals, or formatting, even within the same language variant.

Style guides act as a blueprint for translators and reviewers, reducing ambiguity and improving turnaround time.

This step is crucial for organisations deploying learning across multiple regions, where precision in legal phrasing, cultural sensitivity, and learner expectations can make or break effectiveness and credibility.

Tips

- Involve **native-speaking reviewers** or in-country leads in drafting the localisation style guide. They bring valuable cultural nuance.
- Maintain **separate guides per language or region**, even within the same language family (e.g., Brazilian Portuguese vs. European Portuguese).
- Include examples of **do's and don'ts**, preferred terms, and tone of voice guidelines for maximum clarity.
- Reference **terminology from corporate comms, HR, legal, and marketing**, to ensure alignment across departments.
- Treat your localisation style guide as a **living document**. Update it based on translator feedback and evolving business contexts.

Traps

- Copying and pasting a generic style guide from another department. Learning has specific needs (e.g., pedagogical clarity, assessment phrasing).
- Using machine-generated translation memory without human review or tone adjustment.
- Assuming that language equivalency equals cultural equivalency, which can result in confusing or even offensive content.
- Omitting date formats, units of measurement, and instructional voice direction (formal/informal, second-person, etc.) from the guide.

Techniques

- **Collaborative Development**: Co-create your localisation style guides with translators, reviewers, SMEs, and in-market leads to ensure ownership and usability.
- **Glossary Development**: Build a master list of technical terms, acronyms, proper nouns, and key instructional language with approved translations per locale.
- **Tone and Voice Definition**: Specify whether the learner should be addressed in formal or informal language, second or third person, active or passive voice.
- **Formatting Conventions**: Define how headings, lists, bolding, dates, numbers, and decimal separators should appear in each language.
- **Media and Visual Guidelines**: Specify acceptable icons, imagery, colours, and culturally appropriate graphics.

Examples

- In the **Japanese** localisation guide: use polite form ("-masu") rather than casual form, avoid idiomatic expressions, and ensure double-byte character spacing.
- In the **French (France)** guide: decimal commas instead of points, "vous" form instead of "tu", and exact localisation of compliance terminology.
- The **Arabic** localisation guide may specify right-to-left layout, mirrored interfaces, and culturally sensitive imagery substitutions (e.g., hand gestures, clothing).
- Brand-specific terms: Always translate "Learning Pathway" as "Parcours de formation" in French, never as "Chemin d'apprentissage".

Translation and Localisation Prep
Establish Localisation Standards and Style Guides

How it's done

1. Gather existing terminology used across your organisation, including training, HR, compliance, and marketing.
2. Meet with regional representatives or localisation partners to discuss known challenges and preferences.
3. Draft an initial style guide per language, including sections on tone, grammar, usage rules, formatting, and do/don't examples.
4. Create a separate **glossary** file per language, listing all key terms, approved translations, and contextual notes.
5. Conduct a review session with translators and in-country stakeholders to validate and finalise the guide.
6. Publish guides centrally (e.g., Confluence, Google Drive, SharePoint) with version control.
7. Provide access and training to anyone involved in content creation, translation, or QA.
8. Update guides after each major localisation cycle based on translator feedback or observed inconsistencies.

Core Elements

- Language-specific tone and register (e.g., formal/informal)
- Glossary of approved terminology
- Rules for grammar, punctuation, and instructional voice
- Formatting conventions (e.g., lists, decimals, date/time)
- Acceptable/unacceptable idioms, imagery, and cultural references
- Usage examples, preferred translations, and common pitfalls
- Version control and update protocol
- Ownership and escalation contact for each language

Checklist

1. Collect reference materials and past translations
2. Define tone, formality, and instructional voice per locale
3. Create a glossary of key terms, phrases, acronyms, and UI labels
4. Document formatting rules and style preferences
5. Include culturally sensitive guidance on imagery and icons
6. Validate guides with in-country reviewers or localisation experts
7. Publish and share style guides and glossaries centrally
8. Establish a feedback loop and update process post-project

AI Considerations

- Use AI to **extract terminology** from existing documents and flag inconsistencies across translated versions.
- Generate **draft localisation guides** from existing content, identifying tone, phrase patterns, and preferred language use.
- Use AI-based **translation memory tools** to build glossary suggestions and auto-validate them against past usage.
- Apply AI for **style enforcement** by scanning new translations against the established guide.
- AI co-pilots can highlight deviations, tone shifts, or incorrectly applied terms in real-time during translation reviews.

Key Takeaways

- Create or adapt a localisation guide that defines tone, terminology, formatting, and cultural sensitivities.
- Align guides with organisational voice and compliance requirements.
- Distribute these guides to all internal and external contributors to avoid rework.

Coordinate with Translation and Localisation Vendors

Why this is important

Coordinating effectively with translation and localisation vendors is critical to ensuring high-quality, on-time, and cost-effective delivery of multilingual learning content.

Vendors are not just passive service providers, they are key partners in preserving instructional intent, cultural nuance, regulatory accuracy, and learner engagement across languages.

Miscommunication, unclear scope, or lack of contextual guidance can lead to costly rework, inconsistencies, or brand misalignment. Establishing a structured relationship with your vendor, including workflows, file formats, escalation channels, and quality standards, ensures smoother collaboration, faster turnaround, and output that meets both linguistic and instructional expectations.

Tips

- Choose vendors with **experience in eLearning** or instructional design translation, not just general content translation.
- Provide **access to source files**, visual context, and a clear brief (including learner personas and instructional goals).
- Establish an upfront agreement on **rounds of revision**, file types, QA expectations, and versioning.
- Maintain a **single point of contact** on both sides to avoid miscommunication and project sprawl.
- Ask for **sample translations** and engage your internal reviewers to validate quality before full-scale rollout.

Traps

- Treating localisation as a last-minute handoff instead of a concurrent workflow.
- Failing to communicate the instructional purpose behind the content, leading to literal but pedagogically weak translations.
- Relying only on the vendor's in-house reviewers without involving local SMEs or in-market validation.
- Using inconsistent file formats or versions, resulting in lost edits or mismatched strings.
- Ignoring time zone differences or holiday calendars that affect delivery timing.

Techniques

- **Vendor Briefing Deck**: Create a standardised onboarding pack with sample modules, terminology guides, visual walkthroughs, and learner context.
- **Project Charter**: Include expectations around turnaround time, quality criteria, contact roles, and review protocols.
- **Translation Memory Integration**: Use tools like SDL Trados, MemoQ, or Smartling to ensure consistency and reduce cost across future projects.
- **Shared QA Scorecards**: Agree on a quality assurance rubric and review cycle in advance, so feedback can be structured and actionable.
- **Progress Dashboards**: Track status by language, module, and review stage using collaborative platforms like Monday.com, Trello, or Google Sheets.

Examples

- A vendor translating a digital safety course into five languages is given full access to Storyline source files, a glossary of approved terminology, and screenshots of each screen to understand context.
- The vendor agreement includes one draft round, one SME feedback cycle, and a final linguistic QA, all tracked via a shared Kanban board.
- The vendor sends test samples for a Spanish course to be reviewed by Argentinian and Mexican SMEs to validate regional terminology before bulk translation begins.

Translation and Localisation Prep
Coordinate with Translation and Localisation Vendors

How it's done

1. Select a vendor (or shortlist) based on experience, technology capability, and subject matter familiarity.
2. Schedule an initial onboarding meeting and share key assets: source content, style guides, glossaries, and technical specifications.
3. Establish a shared timeline with clear milestones for draft, review, revision, and delivery per language.
4. Define communication pathways. Who owns what, how feedback is handled, and when escalation is appropriate.
5. Provide a detailed brief with learning objectives, tone expectations, and any cultural sensitivities.
6. Confirm QA and validation workflows, including internal SMEs and in-country reviewers.
7. Use structured file formats (e.g., XLIFF, DOCX, XML) to ease handoffs and maintain formatting.
8. Monitor progress weekly, address blockers early, and document all changes for version control.

Core Elements

- Vendor selection and onboarding documentation
- Approved translation brief and delivery plan
- File handoff protocol and accepted formats
- Defined roles for reviewers, translators, and project leads
- Style guides and glossaries aligned to the learning content
- Milestone and QA checkpoints
- Escalation matrix and feedback channels
- Contractual terms (revisions, delivery timelines, confidentiality, etc.)

Checklist

1. Select experienced eLearning translation vendors
2. Share content brief, learning context, and sample materials
3. Provide localisation style guides and glossaries
4. Define delivery schedule and review cycles
5. Set up version control and file management system
6. Confirm communication channels and escalation paths
7. Establish shared QA process with scorecard or checklist
8. Monitor translation progress, validate feedback implementation
9. Archive finalised translations with documented approvals
10. Conduct post-project review for future optimisation

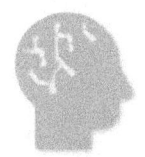

AI Considerations

- Use AI to **automate file prep** and content extraction into translation-ready formats (XLIFF, SRT, CSV).
- Apply machine learning to **predict vendor delivery risks** based on scope, complexity, and past vendor performance.
- Use AI chat agents to simulate translation briefs and ensure clarity before handoff.
- Deploy real-time AI tools to **evaluate linguistic quality** or tone consistency across translations.
- Integrate with vendor platforms that support AI-assisted memory matching and dynamic glossary updates.

Key Takeaways

- Select vendors with domain knowledge in learning content and familiarity with your LMS or authoring tools.
- Lock in timelines and file format requirements early to avoid costly delays.
- Maintain a shared glossary and asset library across all projects and providers.

Integrate QA Processes for Localised Versions

Why this is important

Integrating robust QA processes for localised versions ensures that translated content not only preserves the meaning and instructional intent of the source material but also functions technically, visually, and culturally across all delivery platforms. Even the most accurate translations can fall short if layout breaks, caption mismatches, truncation, or LMS compatibility issues go unspotted. QA is the critical safeguard that protects the learner experience, regulatory compliance, and brand integrity. It ensures that global learners receive the same quality of engagement, accuracy, and usability as the original audience. Without a structured localisation QA process, costly post-launch fixes, learner confusion, and reputation risks become almost inevitable.

Tips

- **Perform QA in the final delivery environment**, not just within authoring tools, this catches rendering and functionality issues.
- Always use a **multi-step QA process**: linguistic review, functional testing, and visual/layout QA.
- Engage **native-speaking in-market reviewers** for final sign-off. Especially for tone, phrasing, and cultural appropriateness.
- Build a **QA checklist tailored to each language**, as different scripts and writing systems (e.g., Arabic, Japanese) have unique display needs.
- Treat localisation QA as a **core project phase**, not a final task. Plan for revisions and sign-off cycles.

Traps

- Assuming that machine or vendor QA alone is sufficient, internal validation is still essential.
- Overlooking layout issues caused by text expansion or directionality changes (e.g., RTL languages).
- Rushing QA into tight timeframes, especially if translations arrive late.
- Failing to document issues or apply corrections across all learning assets consistently (e.g., duplicate screens, captions, transcripts).
- Ignoring interactive components like drag-and-drop, branching, or quiz feedback, may not translate cleanly.

Techniques

- **Linguistic QA**: Use trained reviewers or language leads to validate tone, clarity, terminology, and learner appropriateness.
- **Functional QA**: Test all media (audio, video, animations), interactions, links, SCORM tracking, and responsiveness.
- **Visual QA**: Check layout, text wrapping, image alignment, text-in-graphics, and readability across devices.
- **Cross-language Regression Testing**: Compare localised versions to the original to confirm instructional parity.
- **Defect Logging and Resolution Tracker**: Use a shared log (e.g., JIRA, Google Sheets, Trello) to manage issues and approvals.

Examples

- A course translated into German shows multiple cases of text overflow in buttons and callouts. Functional QA identifies these issues, and developers adjust layouts to accommodate the expanded strings.
- A video-based module in Spanish has subtitles that don't sync with the voiceover. The visual QA team flags timing discrepancies and re-exports corrected caption files.
- A Mandarin version of an eLearning module has issues with embedded fonts not displaying correctly in HTML5 export. Will be caught during functional QA testing on mobile devices.

Translation and Localisation Prep
Integrate QA Processes for Localised Versions

How it's done

1. Build a QA plan with defined steps, reviewers, and turnaround timelines per language.
2. Provide each reviewer access to the course in its final delivery format (LMS, app, or offline).
3. Use structured QA checklists covering linguistic, technical, and visual criteria.
4. Capture feedback with clear severity ratings, timestamps/screenshots, and proposed corrections.
5. Assign fixes to development teams and translators as needed.
6. Re-test fixed versions to confirm resolution.
7. Document sign-offs and store final assets and logs for audit/compliance.
8. Conduct a post-QA review to improve future localisation cycles.

Core Elements

- QA plan aligned to delivery platform and timeline
- Multilingual QA checklists (linguistic, functional, visual)
- Issue tracking tool and feedback templates
- Reviewer access to sandbox/test environment
- Escalation protocol for critical blockers
- Approval/sign-off documentation
- Master record of resolved defects
- Final validation criteria per language

Checklist

1. Define QA phases: linguistic, functional, visual
2. Select and brief in-country reviewers and QA testers
3. Provide final format files or LMS versions for testing
4. Use structured checklists to evaluate each course
5. Log all issues with screenshots and recommendations
6. Assign issues to appropriate translator or developer
7. Confirm all fixes and re-test where needed
8. Obtain formal approval from reviewers
9. Archive all QA assets and resolution logs
10. Capture lessons learned for future localisation projects

Translation and Localisation Prep
Integrate QA Processes for Localised Versions

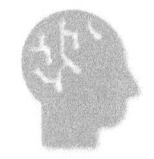

AI Considerations

- Use AI to **auto-detect layout issues**, text overflows, and truncations across screen sizes and languages.
- Apply natural language models to **spot inconsistencies** in translated phrasing or terminology compared to your glossary.
- Automate **caption timing validation** using AI to ensure subtitle sync across localised videos.
- Use visual recognition AI to detect alignment or font display issues post-translation.
- Employ AI-driven QA bots to run functional checks on SCORM/xAPI tracking and UI responsiveness across device types.

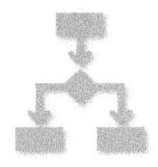

Key Takeaways

- Build in native-speaker review loops to validate context, tone, and clarity.
- Test localised versions within the actual platform to ensure layout, alignment, and functionality.
- Use AI tools to flag inconsistencies but never skip human review for high-stakes content.

Media Production

Overview

The **Media Production** step in the Development phase of the ADDIE model focuses on creating the multimedia elements that bring the course to life. This stage includes crafting voice-over narration, designing graphics, and managing all aspects of video and audio production. By integrating these components effectively, this step ensures a dynamic and engaging learning experience that supports the course's instructional goals.

High-quality media production not only enhances learner engagement but also reinforces key concepts, making the course more impactful and accessible. Each media element must align with the learning objectives to ensure that the final product is cohesive and effective.

Key Sub-Steps are:

- **Record Voice Narration**
  Write and record clear, engaging voice-over scripts that guide learners and highlight important content.
- **Graphic Production**
  Design and produce visual aids such as infographics, illustrations, and animations to complement and clarify the course material.
- **Video and Audio Production**
  Oversee casting, location scouting, filming, recording, and editing to produce polished, professional video and audio components.

Outcomes

The outcomes of the **Media Production** step are to develop multimedia elements that are professional, engaging, and aligned with learning outcomes.

Key outcomes include:

- **Record Voice Narration**
  Develop and record narration that is concise, aligned with course objectives, and maintains learner interest.
- **Graphic Production**
  Create graphics, animations, and other visual elements that reinforce the content, ensuring consistency in style and design.
- **Video and Audio Production**
  Ensure excellence in all aspects of media creation, from talent selection and filming to post-production.

Summary

The **Media Production** step is critical in transforming instructional plans into a rich, immersive learning experience.

By producing high-quality multimedia elements, including voice-overs, graphics, and video, this step ensures that the course engages learners while reinforcing the instructional goals.

Adhering to best practices, such as detailed planning, consistent design templates, and thorough quality assurance, helps avoid pitfalls like inconsistent visuals or unclear audio.

The result is a well-executed course that is visually appealing, accessible, and impactful, providing learners with a seamless and effective educational journey.

Record Voice Narration

 **Why this is important**	Recording voice narration is a critical step in transforming written scripts into high-quality audio assets that bring learning content to life. Choosing the right voice, whether a professional artist or an AI-generated voice, ensures the tone and style match the instructional intent. Clear, engaging, and well-paced delivery helps maintain learner attention and supports comprehension across the course. The narration should integrate smoothly with visuals, animations, and other multimedia components to create a cohesive learning experience. Planning for regular updates to voice-over recordings also helps keep the content accurate and relevant over time.
 **Tips**	• **Match Voice to Content** Choose a voice talent or AI-generated voice that aligns with the audience and the learning objectives. For example, use a professional yet approachable tone for corporate training or an enthusiastic tone for motivational content • **Prioritise Clarity** Ensure the recording is free from background noise and the voice-over is clear and easy to understand, especially for audiences where English may not be their first language • **Use Professional Tools** Record in a soundproof environment with high-quality microphones and audio editing software for the best results • **Plan for Maintenance** Store raw and edited audio files systematically, making it easy to update portions of the script without re-recording the entire audio • **Use AI Voices Wisely** AI-generated voices can save time and cost but choose options that sound natural and test their effectiveness with a sample audience.
 **Traps**	• **Inconsistent Tone** Using multiple voice talents or styles without continuity can confuse and disengage learners • **Ignoring Regional Nuances** Overlooking accents, pronunciations, or cultural references that resonate with the target audience can alienate learners • **Poor Audio Quality** Recording with subpar equipment or in an unsuitable environment can detract from the learning experience • **Overuse of AI Voices** While convenient, overusing AI-generated voices without quality checks can lead to a robotic or inauthentic feel • **Failure to Plan Updates** Not considering how changes to scripts or content will be integrated into existing voice-over materials can lead to costly re-recordings.

Media Production
Record Voice Narration

Techniques

- **Choose the Right Voice Talent**
  Look for professional voice-over artists with experience in e-learning. Review demos and conduct auditions to find the best fit
- **Leverage AI Voices**
  Tools like ElevenLabs or Amazon Polly can generate high-quality AI voices that mimic natural speech, reducing costs for minor projects
- **Script Segmentation**
  Record in segments or modules to simplify editing and future updates
- **Monitor Pacing**
  Use a metronome or pacing guide to ensure the voice-over matches the timing requirements of the visuals or animations
- **Post-Production Refinement**
  Use audio editing software like Adobe Audition or Audacity to remove background noise, adjust volume levels, and add effects if necessary
- **Pilot Test**
  Test recordings with a small group of the target audience to gather feedback on clarity, engagement, and relevance
- **Plan for Localisation**
  Record multiple versions or work with voice-over artists fluent in the required languages if localisation is part of the strategy.

Examples

- *Professional Voice Talent*
  A corporate compliance training module uses a deep, authoritative male voice to convey seriousness and importance
- *AI-Generated Voice*
  A quick onboarding video for a software tool uses a friendly, conversational AI voice for efficiency and cost-effectiveness
- *Interactive Module*
  A customer service e-learning course integrates an upbeat, empathetic female voice to guide learners through scenarios
- *Multilingual Project*
  A global sales training programme uses a mix of professional voice talent and AI for translations in French, Spanish, and Mandarin.

Media Production
Record Voice Narration

How it's done

- **Select Voice Talent or AI Tool**
  Choose either professional voice talent or an AI-generated voice based on the project's tone, style, and budget. Ensure the choice resonates with the target audience and aligns with the learning objectives.

- **Prepare the Recording Environment**
  Set up a soundproof recording space equipped with professional-grade microphones and audio interfaces. This ensures clear, high-quality audio recordings.

- **Conduct Voice-Over Sessions**
  Work closely with voice talent to record the script, focusing on proper pacing, emphasis, and tone. For AI-generated voices, input the script and fine-tune pronunciation and inflections for natural delivery.

- **Edit and Refine**
  Use audio editing software to clean up recordings, balance audio levels, and match the timing to visuals or multimedia elements.

- **Synchronise with Visuals**
  Align the audio with animations, slides, or videos to ensure a seamless and engaging learner experience.

- **Create Alternate Versions**
  Produce additional versions or variations if the course includes branching scenarios, localisation, or alternative pathways.

- **Document and Store Files**
  Organise all audio files systematically, labelling them clearly as raw recordings, edited versions, and final outputs. Maintain a logical folder structure for easy access.

- **Test and Iterate**
  Pilot the voice-over with a sample audience to assess clarity, engagement, and alignment with the learning objectives. Gather feedback to refine the final product.

- **Prepare for Maintenance**
  Store raw audio sessions securely to enable efficient updates or modifications in the future, reducing the need for complete re-recordings.

Core Elements

- **Alignment with Objectives**
  The voice-over tone, style, and content align with the learning objectives and audience needs.

- **Clear and Professional Audio**
  Recordings are free from background noise, with clear delivery and optimised audio quality.

- **Pacing and Timing**
  Audio pacing matches the timing requirements of visuals and multimedia elements.

- **Systematic File Management**
  Audio files are segmented, labelled, and stored for easy updates.

- **Pilot Testing Conducted**
  Sample audiences have evaluated the voice-over for clarity, engagement, and effectiveness.

- **Accessibility Ensured**
  Captions or transcripts are prepared to meet accessibility requirements.

- **Future Updates Planned**
  Raw audio sessions are retained for seamless updates and localisation efforts.

Media Production
Record Voice Narration

Checklist

1. Finalise approved script with clear VO cues and tone notes
2. Select narrator(s) matching learner audience and language preferences
3. Set up or book recording studio with appropriate acoustics
4. Conduct sound check and voice warm-up before session
5. Record narration in logical segments for easier editing
6. Review takes in-session for clarity, pronunciation, and pacing
7. Save and label audio files with version and content reference
8. Perform initial quality check and flag for re-record if needed

AI Considerations

- Use AI voices to prototype narration before committing to human VO
- Generate alternate tone or dialect versions for comparison
- Use AI to detect misreads, inconsistencies, or poor pacing
- Apply AI-enhanced audio cleanup (noise reduction, leveling)
- Auto-generate closed captions and transcripts from recordings

Key Takeaways

Recording voice narration is a critical component of e-learning media production, enhancing the learner experience and supporting engagement.

Whether using professional voice talent or AI-generated voices, it's essential to maintain clarity, alignment with learning objectives, and a professional tone.

By preparing a high-quality recording environment, implementing best practices for audio editing, and conducting pilot testing, instructional designers can produce effective and flexible audio assets.

These assets not only elevate the learning experience but also provide the scalability needed for updates and localisation.

Graphic Production

Why this is important

Creating high-quality graphics is essential for enhancing the learning experience and supporting instructional objectives.

Graphics such as images, infographics, charts, and diagrams help make complex ideas more accessible and engaging.

To be effective, visuals must be purposeful, visually appealing, and consistent with the overall course design.

They should also be tailored to the target audience's needs, preferences, and learning styles.

Using the right tools and techniques ensures the output is both professional and meaningful.

It's equally important to optimise graphics for seamless performance across various platforms and devices, maintaining both quality and accessibility for all learners.

Tips

- **Understand the Audience**
  Design graphics that resonate with the learners' cultural context, preferences, and learning styles.

- **Use Professional Tools**
  Employ tools such as Adobe Illustrator, Canva, Figma, or Visme for creating high-quality visuals. For basic needs, tools like PowerPoint or Google Slides can also be effective.

- **Consistency is Key**
  Maintain a consistent visual style, including colour schemes, typography, and design elements, throughout all graphics.

- **Simplify Complex Concepts**
  Use visual aids like flowcharts or infographics to break down complex information into digestible formats.

- **Optimize for Speed**
  Compress graphics without losing quality to ensure quick loading times in digital courses.

- **Iterate and Test**
  Gather feedback on initial designs and refine them based on input from stakeholders and pilot testing.

Traps

- **Overloading Visuals**
  Including too many details in a single graphic can overwhelm learners and hinder comprehension.

- **Ignoring Accessibility**
  Failing to add alt text, proper colour contrast, or scalable designs can exclude learners with disabilities.

- **Using Unlicensed Images**
  Always ensure graphics and visuals comply with copyright laws. Avoid using unlicensed stock images.

- **Poor Quality Control**
  Low-resolution graphics or inconsistent styles can reduce the professionalism of your learning materials.

- **Neglecting Cultural Sensitivity**
  Graphics that inadvertently include culturally inappropriate elements may alienate or offend learners.

Media Production
Graphic Production

Techniques

- **Layered Design**
  Use layered software like Photoshop or GIMP to edit images, ensuring flexibility for future revisions.
- **Colour Theory**
  Apply colour psychology to evoke specific emotions or focus learner attention. For instance, blue for trust, green for growth, or red for urgency.
- **Infographics**
  Tools like Piktochart or Canva are great for creating visually engaging infographics that summarise data or processes.
- **Data Visualisation**
  Use apps like Tableau or Excel for charts and graphs that clearly present numerical data.
- **Interactive Graphics**
  Leverage tools such as Adobe Animate or Articulate Storyline to create graphics with interactive elements.
- **SVG Formats**
  For scalable graphics that maintain quality across devices, save files in SVG (Scalable Vector Graphics) format.
- **Templates**
  Use pre-designed templates for common graphic types to save time while ensuring professional quality.

Examples

- *Infographic*
  A timeline infographic visually explains the history of a topic in an e-learning course.
- *Diagram*
  A labelled diagram illustrates the parts of a machine in a technical training module.
- *Flowchart*
  A flowchart helps learners understand a decision-making process in a leadership training session.
- *Interactive Map*
  An interactive map lets learners click on regions to learn more about a global supply chain in a business course.
- *Animated GIF*
  A looping GIF demonstrates how to use a tool or software feature step-by-step.

Media Production
Graphic Production

How it's done

- **Review Design Requirements**
  Start by reviewing earlier design documents to fully understand the instructional goals, audience, and objectives for the graphics. Ensure alignment with the overall course design.
- **Select Tools and Resources**
  Choose the most suitable graphic design tools based on the project's complexity and the team's expertise. Popular options include Adobe Creative Suite, Canva, or Affinity Designer.
- **Gather Raw Materials**
  Collect the necessary resources, such as images, data, and other materials, that will serve as the foundation for creating the graphics.
- **Sketch or Prototype**
  Develop rough drafts or wireframes to visualise the layout and key elements. This helps in refining the design direction before final production.
- **Develop Graphics**
  Create high-quality graphics using the selected tools, ensuring that they align with the instructional objectives and enhance the learning experience.
- **Test for Accessibility**
  Verify that all graphics meet accessibility standards, including features such as alt text, proper contrast, and scalable designs.
- **Refine and Finalise**
  Incorporate feedback from stakeholders or pilot testers to revise and improve the graphics. Finalise designs that meet quality and instructional standards.
- **Optimise for Deployment**
  Compress images and select appropriate file formats (e.g., PNG for transparency, SVG for scalability) to ensure fast loading and seamless integration across platforms.
- **Integrate into Courseware**
  Embed the final graphics into the e-learning platform or presentation materials, ensuring a smooth and cohesive user experience.
- **Archive Files**
  Store editable graphic files and associated documentation systematically to facilitate future updates or revisions.

Core Elements

- **Alignment with Objectives**
  Graphics are designed to support course objectives and adhere to design guidelines.
- **Engaging and Consistent**
  Visuals are clear, engaging, and maintain visual consistency throughout the materials.
- **Accessibility Ensured**
  Graphics include alt text, proper contrast, and scalable designs for inclusivity.
- **Optimised for Platforms**
  Images are high resolution but optimised for fast loading across various platforms.
- **Copyright Compliance**
  All visuals comply with copyright and licensing requirements.
- **Simplification of Complexity**
  Graphics effectively clarify complex information and support learner understanding.
- **Learner Feedback Incorporated**
  Feedback on graphic prototypes is used to refine designs.
- **Interactive Functionality Verified**
  Any interactive graphics are fully functional and tested.
- **Organised File Storage**
  Files are properly documented, organised, and backed up for future use.

Media Production
Graphic Production

Checklist

1. Confirm graphic asset list from storyboard or shot list
2. Apply brand guidelines and instructional style consistently
3. Use correct resolution and dimensions for delivery platform
4. Optimise file sizes for web or mobile delivery
5. Include alt text and accessibility metadata as needed
6. Review graphics for cultural appropriateness and clarity
7. Store assets in shared repository with version control
8. Validate final graphics with design lead or instructional designer

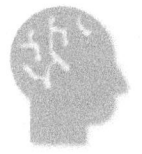
AI Considerations

- Use generative AI to create concept visuals or icons from prompts
- Auto-check for brand colour compliance and contrast accessibility
- Generate visual variants (e.g., character diversity, scenery)
- Optimise and compress images using AI tools without quality loss
- Flag graphics that may overwhelm or distract learners based on layout analysis

Key Takeaways

Graphic production is a vital step in the Development Phase of the ADDIE model, ensuring visual elements enhance learning materials.

By applying professional design principles, using advanced tools, and prioritising accessibility, instructional designers can create graphics that simplify complex ideas, engage learners, and reinforce learning objectives.

Effective graphics contribute significantly to learner retention and comprehension while enhancing the overall aesthetic and usability of the instructional materials.

With a structured approach, designers can produce visuals that align with educational goals and adapt seamlessly to future needs.

Video and Audio Production

Why this is important

Producing high-quality video and audio content is a vital part of creating immersive and effective learning experiences.

Every element, from selecting locations and scheduling shoots to coordinating talent and managing equipment, contributes to the quality and success of the final product.

Careful planning ensures the production process runs smoothly while staying within budget and timeline constraints.

A well-managed shoot results in polished, professional multimedia assets that align with instructional design goals.

Audio and video must be clear, engaging, and properly integrated to capture attention and aid understanding. Safety, compliance, and quality control are also key to delivering a professional result that meets learning objectives and enhances the learner journey.

Tips

- **Start with a Detailed Plan**
  Develop a comprehensive production plan that outlines roles, timelines, and deliverables.
- **Scout Locations Early**
  Evaluate locations for lighting, acoustics, and logistical feasibility before finalising.
- **Use a Shot List**
  Create a shot list for each scene to ensure that all necessary footage is captured efficiently.
- **Test Equipment**
  Run tests for cameras, microphones, and lighting setups to avoid technical issues during the shoot.
- **Prioritise Audio Quality**
  Poor audio can undermine even the best visuals. Invest in quality microphones and soundproofing.

Traps

- **Overlooking Acoustics**
  Failing to consider ambient noise and echoes can lead to poor audio quality.
- **Underestimating Lighting Needs**
  Inadequate lighting can result in unprofessional visuals that detract from the content.
- **Rushing the Schedule**
  A tight production schedule leaves little room for error or creativity.
- **Ignoring Talent Comfort**
  Neglecting the needs of actors or presenters can result in unconvincing performances.
- **Skipping Rehearsals**
  Failing to rehearse scenes can lead to mistakes, re-takes, and wasted time.

Techniques

- **Storyboard the Script**
  Visualise the script through detailed storyboards to guide shot composition and scene transitions.
- **Use Professional Tools**
  Invest in or rent high-quality cameras, audio recorders, and editing software.
- **Apply Three-Point Lighting**
  Use a key light, fill light, and backlight to achieve balanced, professional lighting for video shoots.
- **Conduct Sound Checks**
  Test and adjust audio levels before recording to ensure clarity and consistency.
- **Record Multiple Takes**
  Capture several takes of each scene to provide options during the editing process.

Media Production
Video and Audio Production

Examples

- **On-Site Video**
  A leadership training programme records scenes in a corporate office, using natural lighting and a professional presenter.
- **Green Screen Production**
  A software tutorial uses a green screen to overlay the instructor against animated visuals of the software interface.
- **Podcast-Style Audio**
  A module on ethics features a discussion between two subject matter experts recorded in a soundproof studio.
- **Role-Play Scenario**
  A customer service training course films actors demonstrating common scenarios and responses.
- **Interactive Video**
  A compliance course uses branching videos to simulate decision-making scenarios with embedded learner choices.

How it's done

- **Create a Production Schedule**
  Establish a detailed timeline covering pre-production, shooting, and post-production stages. Share this schedule with all team members to ensure alignment and adherence to deadlines.
- **Scout and Secure Locations**
  Visit potential locations to assess their suitability for the script and instructional goals. Book and prepare selected venues to ensure they meet the project's requirements.
- **Assemble a Production Crew**
  Hire or assign key roles such as director, cinematographer, sound engineer, and editor. Clearly define responsibilities to streamline the production process.
- **Cast Talent**
  Conduct auditions or recruit presenters and actors who match the project's tone and instructional objectives. Ensure they are comfortable with the material and target audience.
- **Prepare Equipment**
  Rent or purchase all necessary equipment, including cameras, microphones, and lighting. Test equipment prior to filming to ensure functionality.
- **Draft a Shot List**
  Develop a comprehensive shot list detailing scenes, angles, and transitions to capture during the shoot. This ensures an organised and efficient filming process.
- **Conduct Rehearsals**
  Run through scenes with the crew and talent to identify potential issues and make adjustments before filming begins.
- **Film and Record Audio**
  Execute the shoot according to the planned schedule and shot list, capturing high-quality video and audio that aligns with the instructional objectives.
- **Review Footage and Sound**
  Assess recorded materials for quality and completeness at the end of each day to ensure all required content is captured.
- **Backup Media Files**
  Securely store all raw footage and audio files to prevent data loss and facilitate smooth post-production workflows.

Media Production
Video and Audio Production

Core Elements

- **Production Schedule Finalised**
  The timeline is clear, realistic, and shared with all stakeholders.
- **Locations Prepared**
  Filming venues are scouted, booked, and fully equipped for production.
- **Crew and Talent Briefed**
  Roles and responsibilities are clearly defined, and everyone is aligned with the project's goals.
- **Equipment Tested**
  All gear is in working order, with backups available as needed.
- **Shot List Completed**
  A detailed plan for capturing scenes, angles, and transitions is available on set.
- **Audio Quality Ensured**
  Sound is tested and recorded at a professional standard, with contingencies in place.
- **Permits Secured**
  Necessary permissions and legal requirements are addressed.
- **Rehearsals Conducted**
  Crew and talent are prepared, and adjustments are made before filming begins.
- **Safety Measures in Place**
  Compliance with safety protocols is ensured throughout the production.
- **Media Files Backed Up**
  All recordings are reviewed and securely stored to prevent data loss.

Checklist

1. Confirm all raw footage and audio assets are available and approved
2. Align media edits with storyboard, shot list, and learning flow
3. Apply consistent transitions, effects, and lower-thirds
4. Sync voice narration, captions, and visuals precisely
5. Mix audio for clarity across devices (mobile, desktop, headphones)
6. Render in multiple formats for deployment needs (MP4, streaming, SCORM)
7. Conduct peer or SME review of final product
8. Store source and rendered files securely with metadata and version tags

AI Considerations

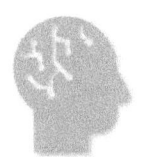

- Use AI tools for auto-editing rough cuts or stitching scenes
- Apply AI-driven audio balancing, denoising, and EQ
- Auto-generate subtitles in multiple languages
- Suggest pacing adjustments based on learner attention models
- Use AI to scan for visual inconsistencies or branding errors before final render

Key Takeaways

The Video and Audio Production step in the Development Phase of the ADDIE model transforms instructional plans into engaging multimedia assets.

By carefully managing logistics, coordinating talent and crew, and utilising professional-grade equipment, production teams can create high-quality videos and audio that align with learning objectives.

Attention to detail, thorough planning, and adherence to timelines and budgets are critical for ensuring a smooth and successful production process.

Well-executed video and audio content enhance the overall learning experience, making instructional materials more engaging and impactful.

Courseware Assembly

Overview

The **Courseware Assembly** step in the Development phase of the ADDIE model focuses on bringing together all multimedia, interactive, and textual elements to create a unified and engaging learning experience. This step ensures that all components are seamlessly integrated, professionally polished, and aligned with the learning objectives to deliver a cohesive final product.

By combining interactive modules, assessments, video and audio elements, and written content, instructional designers ensure that the course provides an engaging and smooth learner experience. This phase also involves quality checks to address inconsistencies and maintain high standards across all elements.

Key Sub-Steps are:

- **Courseware Development**
  Build interactive components, modules, and assessments that align with learning objectives and foster active engagement.

- **Video Editing, Audio Dubbing, and Text Integration**
  Refine video content for professional quality, ensuring alignment with course objectives and consistency in style.

- **Usability Testing**
  Conduct thorough testing of courseware to ensure seamless navigation, intuitive design, and compatibility across devices, while gathering feedback to refine content and improve learner experience.

Outcomes

The outcomes of the **Courseware Assembly** step are to produce a cohesive, high-quality course that effectively supports learning outcomes.

Key outcomes include:

- **Create Interactive Courseware**
  Develop modules and assessments that actively engage learners, reinforcing key concepts and promoting retention.

- **Ensure Professional Video and Audio Quality**
  Refine and edit multimedia elements to meet professional standards, enhancing learner immersion and engagement.

- **Integrate Multimedia Seamlessly**
  Combine video, audio, text, and interactive elements into a single, structured course that flows logically and aligns with instructional goals.

- **Enhance Accessibility**
  Add captions, subtitles, and other textual elements to ensure content is inclusive and easily understood by diverse audiences.

- **Maintain Consistency Across Components**
  Standardise styles, formats, and quality across all elements to create a cohesive and polished learner experience.

Summary

The **Courseware Assembly** step is a pivotal stage in creating a polished, learner-centred course.

By integrating multimedia elements, interactive content, and textual components, this step ensures the final product is engaging, accessible, and aligned with instructional goals.

Best practices such as detailed prototyping, iterative reviews, and maintaining consistent formatting help avoid common issues like disjointed content or mismatched media quality.

The result is a seamless, professional course that delivers a high-impact learning experience and sets the stage for successful implementation.

Courseware Development

Why this is important

Courseware development brings the instructional design to life by transforming storyboards, scripts, and media assets into a cohesive and functional learning experience.

This step integrates multimedia, assessments, navigation, and interactivity to create a seamless and engaging course that supports learner success.

Ensuring each element aligns with the defined learning objectives is vital for delivering purposeful instruction.

Rigorous testing of components helps identify and resolve usability and compatibility issues before deployment.

A well-developed course must be fully prepared for release through the designated platform, whether a learning management system or web-based delivery, ensuring smooth access and functionality for all users.

Tips

- **Follow the Storyboard**
  Use the storyboard as a blueprint to ensure consistency with the instructional design plan.
- **Utilise Templates**
  Leverage development templates to streamline formatting, navigation, and visual consistency.
- **Iterative Testing**
  Test each module or segment as it's developed to identify and fix issues early.
- **Maintain Communication**
  Regularly collaborate with instructional designers, media producers, and subject matter experts (SMEs) for feedback and clarification.
- **Ensure Accessibility**
  Build in accessibility features such as closed captions, screen reader compatibility, and keyboard navigation.
-

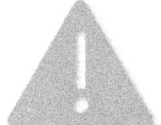

Traps

- **Ignoring the Plan**
  Deviating from the storyboard or design documentation can lead to inconsistencies and missed objectives.
- **Overloading Interactivity**
  Excessive or unnecessary interactive elements can overwhelm learners and detract from the content.
- **Poor Version Control**
  Failing to manage versions of files and updates can lead to lost progress or incorrect deployments.
- **Inconsistent Navigation**
  Non-intuitive or inconsistent navigation can frustrate learners and hinder engagement.
- **Neglecting Testing**
  Skipping thorough testing can result in bugs or user experience issues that disrupt learning.

Techniques

- **Modular Development**
  Build the course in modular chunks to simplify testing and allow for easy updates.
- **Layered Integration**
  Gradually integrate multimedia, text, and interactivity to ensure smooth transitions and compatibility.
- **Responsive Design**
  Use responsive development techniques to optimise the course for multiple devices and screen sizes.
- **Custom Coding When Necessary**
  Enhance functionality with custom code but rely on standard tools where feasible for easier updates.
- Regularly consult accessibility guidelines (e.g., WCAG) during development to ensure inclusivity.

Courseware Assembly
Courseware Development

Examples

- **Scenario-Based Learning**
  A healthcare training course includes interactive decision-making scenarios supported by animations and quizzes.
- **Gamified Content**
  A compliance module uses a points system and badges to encourage learner participation and completion.
- **Microlearning Modules**
  A software tutorial breaks lessons into short, focused videos paired with interactive simulations.
- **Branching Scenarios**
  A leadership course offers multiple paths based on learner decisions, showcasing consequences and outcomes.
- **Multimedia-Rich E-Learning**
  A product knowledge course integrates videos, infographics, and voiceover narration for diverse learning styles.

How it's done

- **Assemble Content**
  Organise and import all course materials, including text, images, videos, and audio, into the chosen authoring tool or course platform. Ensure that the content aligns with the storyboard and learning objectives.
- **Build Navigation**
  Design a user-friendly navigation structure with clear menus, progress indicators, and intuitive controls, making it easy for learners to move through the course.
- **Integrate Assessments**
  Incorporate quizzes, knowledge checks, and final assessments that align with the learning objectives and measure learner progress effectively.
- **Embed Media**
  Add multimedia elements such as videos, animations, and interactive simulations. Ensure that these elements enhance the learning experience and support the course content.
- **Test Functionality**
  Conduct functionality tests to verify that navigation, interactivity, and multimedia elements work seamlessly across different devices and browsers.
- **Apply Branding**
  Incorporate consistent branding elements such as logos, colours, and fonts to ensure alignment with organisational standards and create a professional appearance.
- **Ensure Compatibility**
  Verify that the course package is compatible with the designated Learning Management System (LMS) or web platform. Address any technical issues to ensure smooth deployment.
- **Review Accessibility**
  Ensure compliance with accessibility standards by including features such as captions, alternative text, and keyboard navigation, making the course inclusive for all learners.
- **Perform Quality Assurance**
  Conduct comprehensive quality assurance checks to identify and resolve any errors or inconsistencies. This includes testing content, interactivity, and technical functionality.
- **Prepare Deployment**
  Package the course for deployment, ensuring all files, configurations, and settings are optimised for the hosting platform. Back up all files to safeguard against data loss.

Courseware Assembly
Courseware Development

Core Elements

- **Content Assembled**
  All materials are organised and imported, aligning with the storyboard and objectives.
- **Intuitive Navigation**
  User-friendly menus, progress indicators, and controls are implemented for seamless navigation.
- **Multimedia Embedded**
  Videos, animations, and simulations are added and tested for compatibility and engagement.
- **Assessments Functional**
  Quizzes and knowledge checks are aligned with objectives and fully operational.
- **Accessibility Ensured**
  Features such as captions, alternative text, and keyboard navigation are included for inclusivity.
- **Consistent Branding**
  Logos, colours, and fonts are applied consistently across the course.
- **Quality Assurance Completed**
  Rigorous testing is conducted for functionality, usability, and device compatibility.
- **LMS Compatibility Confirmed**
  The course is tested and verified for compatibility with the intended LMS or platform.
- **Deployment Ready**
  Files are backed up and packaged for smooth deployment and implementation.

Checklist

1. Finalise lesson scripts, media, and assessments for import
2. Select authoring tool based on format (e.g., Storyline, Rise, Captivate)
3. Apply templates and standards for layout, navigation, and interaction
4. Integrate narration, graphics, activities, and quizzes into modules
5. Ensure consistent instructional flow across all lessons
6. Embed accessibility features (alt text, keyboard navigation, captions)
7. Test functionality of navigation, triggers, and feedback mechanisms
8. Version-control all builds and backup source files

AI Considerations

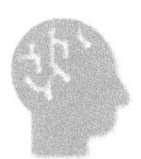

- Use AI to convert structured scripts into draft module layouts
- Auto-detect layout inconsistencies or missing elements
- Generate voiceover timing data for animation syncing
- Use AI checkers for compliance with accessibility and UX standards
- Suggest or prototype micro-interactions based on learning objectives

Key Takeaways

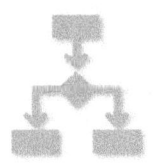

The Courseware Development step in the Development Phase is where the course transforms into a cohesive, interactive learning experience.

By adhering to the storyboard and leveraging effective tools and techniques, developers ensure the course achieves its instructional goals while maintaining accessibility, usability, and engagement.

Rigorous testing, attention to detail, and collaboration with the design team are critical for delivering polished, impactful courseware ready for deployment.

This structured approach ensures the course is well-prepared to meet the needs of both learners and organisational objectives.

Courseware Assembly
Video Editing, Audio Dubbing, and Text Integration

Video Editing, Audio Dubbing, and Text Integration

Why this is important

This step is where multimedia assets come together to form a polished and cohesive learning experience. Integrating video, audio, and on-screen text requires careful attention to timing, quality, and accessibility.

Audio narration must be synchronised with visual elements, while supporting text overlays should enhance, not distract from, the instructional message.

Ensuring consistency in branding, style, and accessibility features such as captions and transcripts helps maintain a professional finish and broadens inclusivity.

Preparing the final multimedia files correctly ensures they are ready for integration into the course platform without technical issues, enabling learners to engage effectively across different devices and environments.

Tips

- **Plan Before Editing**
  Review the storyboard and script to create a clear editing roadmap.
- **Use Professional Tools**
  Choose professional grade editing software for advanced functionality, such as Adobe Premiere Pro, Final Cut Pro, or DaVinci Resolve.
- **Maintain Consistency**
  Use consistent fonts, colours, and styles for on-screen text to enhance readability and visual appeal.
- **Optimise for Devices**
  Edit with mobile and desktop compatibility in mind, ensuring the output resolution fits various screen sizes.
- **Incorporate Feedback Loops**
  Allow time for review cycles with stakeholders, subject matter experts, and instructional designers.

Traps

- **Overcomplicating Visuals**
  Avoid overwhelming learners with excessive animations, transitions, or effects.
- **Poor Audio Quality**
  Background noise, uneven volume levels, or poorly mixed audio can detract from learner engagement.
- **Misaligned Text**
  On-screen text that does not match narration or video timing can confuse learners.
- **Neglecting Accessibility**
  Failing to include captions, transcripts, or alt text can exclude learners with disabilities.
- **Skipping File Optimisation**
  High-resolution files without compression may cause loading delays on slower devices or networks.

Techniques

- **Editing Workflow**
  Begin with rough cuts, followed by finer edits, colour correction, and audio syncing to streamline the editing process.
- **Audio Cleaning**
  Use tools like Audacity or Adobe Audition to remove background noise, equalise sound levels, and add professional effects.
- **Text Integration**
  Use dynamic text overlays to highlight key points, instructions, or terms, ensuring text timing matches spoken content.
- **Colour Grading**
  Apply consistent colour grading to improve video aesthetics and maintain visual cohesion.
- **Captioning Tools**
  Use platforms like Rev or built-in captioning in editing software to generate accurate and synchronised captions.

Courseware Assembly
Video Editing, Audio Dubbing, and Text Integration

Examples

- **Instructional Video**
  A software tutorial integrates screen recordings, voiceover narration, and captions explaining each step.
- **Scenario-Based Training**
  A safety training video includes role-play scenarios with dubbed instructions and on-screen tips.
- **Animated Explainer**
  A health module uses animation with synced voiceover and keyword text overlays for reinforcement.
- **Microlearning Video**
  A product demo uses short clips, crisp audio, and on-screen text to summarise features.
- **Interactive Video**
  A leadership training module integrates decision points with voiceovers and text prompts for learner interaction.

How it's done

- **Assemble Content**
  Organise and import all course materials, including text, images, videos, and audio, into the chosen authoring tool or course platform. Ensure that the content aligns with the storyboard and learning objectives.
- **Build Navigation**
  Design a user-friendly navigation structure with clear menus, progress indicators, and intuitive controls, making it easy for learners to move through the course.
- **Integrate Assessments**
  Incorporate quizzes, knowledge checks, and final assessments that align with the learning objectives and measure learner progress effectively.
- **Embed Media**
  Add multimedia elements such as videos, animations, and interactive simulations. Ensure that these elements enhance the learning experience and support the course content.
- **Test Functionality**
  Conduct functionality tests to verify that navigation, interactivity, and multimedia elements work seamlessly across different devices and browsers.
- **Apply Branding**
  Incorporate consistent branding elements such as logos, colours, and fonts to ensure alignment with organisational standards and create a professional appearance.
- **Ensure Compatibility**
  Verify that the course package is compatible with the designated Learning Management System (LMS) or web platform. Address any technical issues to ensure smooth deployment.
- **Review Accessibility**
  Ensure compliance with accessibility standards by including features such as captions, alternative text, and keyboard navigation, making the course inclusive for all learners.
- **Perform Quality Assurance**
  Conduct comprehensive quality assurance checks to identify and resolve any errors or inconsistencies. This includes testing content, interactivity, and technical functionality.
- **Prepare Deployment**
  Package the course for deployment, ensuring all files, configurations, and settings are optimised for the hosting platform. Back up all files to safeguard against data loss.

Courseware Assembly
Video Editing, Audio Dubbing, and Text Integration

Core Elements

- **Content Assembled**
  All materials are organised and imported, aligning with the storyboard and objectives.
- **Intuitive Navigation**
  User-friendly menus, progress indicators, and controls are implemented for seamless navigation.
- **Multimedia Embedded**
  Videos, animations, and simulations are added and tested for compatibility and engagement.
- **Assessments Functional**
  Quizzes and knowledge checks are aligned with objectives and fully operational.
- **Accessibility Ensured**
  Features such as captions, alternative text, and keyboard navigation are included for inclusivity.
- **Consistent Branding**
  Logos, colours, and fonts are applied consistently across the course.
- **Quality Assurance Completed**
  Rigorous testing is conducted for functionality, usability, and device compatibility.
- **LMS Compatibility Confirmed**
  The course is tested and verified for compatibility with the intended LMS or platform.
- **Deployment Ready**
  Files are backed up and packaged for smooth deployment and implementation.

Checklist

1. Import final audio, video, and text assets into editing platform
2. Sync voiceover with visuals, on-screen text, and animations
3. Add transitions, annotations, titles, and branded elements
4. Review all content for spelling, timing, and visual consistency
5. Ensure captions, subtitles, and transcripts are accurate and synced
6. Adjust audio levels for consistency and clarity
7. Render videos in formats compatible with LMS or distribution platform
8. Conduct quality assurance review before final export

AI Considerations

- Use AI tools to auto-sync dubbing with mouth movement or visuals
- Auto-detect awkward silences, speech overlaps, or pacing issues
- Apply smart trimming, transitions, and visual overlays
- AI can auto-generate subtitle tracks and time them to voiceovers
- Use LLMs to scan for text errors or mismatches with spoken content

Key Takeaways

The Courseware Development step in the Development Phase is where the course transforms into a cohesive, interactive learning experience.

By adhering to the storyboard and leveraging effective tools and techniques, developers ensure the course achieves its instructional goals while maintaining accessibility, usability, and engagement.

Rigorous testing, attention to detail, and collaboration with the design team are critical for delivering polished, impactful courseware ready for deployment.

This structured approach ensures the course is well-prepared to meet the needs of both learners and organisational objectives.

Usability Testing

Why this is important

Usability testing ensures that courseware is intuitive, accessible, and fully functional before launch.

It identifies potential user experience issues, allowing teams to address them early and avoid disruptions during delivery.

Testing with real users helps validate whether navigation, interactivity, and multimedia elements are working as intended and meet the needs of diverse learners.

Confirming accessibility compliance ensures that all learners, regardless of ability, have equal access to the material.

By streamlining the user experience and refining course design based on feedback, usability testing strengthens learner engagement and lays the groundwork for successful deployment.

Tips

- **Involve Real Users**
  Test the courseware with a representative group of learners to gather authentic feedback
- **Focus on Navigation**
  Ensure the interface is intuitive, with clear pathways for accessing content, activities, and assessments
- **Check Consistency**
  Maintain consistent design elements, such as fonts, colours, and button placements, throughout the courseware
- **Test in Real Environments**
  Use the same devices, browsers, and platforms learners will use to uncover potential technical issues
- **Encourage Feedback**
  Provide clear instructions on how testers can report usability issues or suggest improvements.

Traps

- **Neglecting Diverse User Needs**
  Failing to test with users of varying technical proficiency can overlook critical usability issues
- **Skipping Accessibility Testing**
  Ignoring accessibility standards can exclude learners with disabilities and result in compliance issues
- **Overlooking Device Compatibility**
  Not testing on different devices and browsers can lead to functionality issues for some users
- **Limited Feedback Collection**
  Restricting feedback channels may prevent testers from reporting critical usability problems
- **Delaying Usability Testing**
  Waiting until the final stages of development can make it difficult to address significant issues.

Techniques

- **User Testing Sessions**
  Conduct live testing sessions where participants navigate the courseware while providing real-time feedback
- **Surveys and Feedback Forms**
  Gather structured feedback from testers through targeted questions on usability and functionality
- **Task-Based Testing**
  Ask testers to complete specific tasks to identify navigation or interaction challenges
- **Screen Recording Tools**
  Use screen recording software to observe user behaviour and pinpoint problem areas
- **Accessibility Checkers**
  Utilise tools like WAVE or Axe to test for accessibility compliance and address issues
- **Performance Testing**
  Evaluate loading times and responsiveness on various devices and networks to ensure smooth delivery.

Courseware Assembly
Usability Testing

Examples

- *Interactive Element Testing*
  Assess usability of drag-and-drop activities, quizzes, and simulations to confirm they are intuitive and functional
- *Navigation Flow Test*
  Verify that learners can move seamlessly between modules, lessons, and assessments
- *Accessibility Validation*
  Test content with screen readers, keyboard navigation, and other assistive technologies
- *Cross-Browser Testing*
  Check compatibility on Chrome, Firefox, Safari, and Edge to ensure a consistent experience
- *Feedback Analysis*
  Review tester feedback to identify common issues, such as unclear instructions or confusing navigation.

How it's done

1. **Define Testing Objectives**
   Establish clear goals for usability testing, such as identifying navigation issues, assessing interactivity, and confirming accessibility compliance. These objectives guide the focus of the testing process.

2. **Recruit Testers**
   Select a diverse group of participants who represent the target audience. This ensures the feedback is relevant and considers a range of learner needs.

3. **Prepare Test Scenarios**
   Develop realistic scenarios that allow testers to navigate through course modules, interact with multimedia elements, and complete activities. Scenarios should mimic real-world usage to gather actionable insights.

4. **Conduct Usability Tests**
   Facilitate live testing sessions or distribute courseware for remote testing. Observe testers' interactions and note any challenges or areas of confusion.

5. **Collect Feedback**
   Gather detailed feedback from testers using surveys, forms, or interviews. Focus on usability, navigation, interactivity, and overall user experience.

6. **Analyse Test Results**
   Review and categorise feedback to identify patterns and prioritise issues. Use these insights to inform improvements to the courseware.

7. **Make Iterative Improvements**
   Address the identified issues and conduct re-tests to ensure that all resolutions are effective. This iterative approach ensures continuous refinement of the courseware.

8. **Document Findings**
   Compile a comprehensive report summarising the test results, identified issues, resolutions, and implemented changes. Share this with stakeholders for review and future reference.

Courseware Assembly
Usability Testing

Core Elements

- **Diverse Testing Group**
  Courseware is tested by a varied group of participants representing the target audience.
- **Functional Navigation**
  Navigation pathways are intuitive and free from technical issues.
- **Interactive Elements Tested**
  All interactive components operate as intended without glitches.
- **Accessibility Standards Met**
  Courseware accommodates diverse learner needs, meeting accessibility compliance requirements.
- **Multimedia Compatibility**
  Videos, audio, and other media elements function correctly across devices and browsers.
- **Feedback Analysed**
  Detailed feedback is reviewed and categorised for actionable improvements.
- **Issues Resolved**
  All identified issues are addressed, and solutions are validated through re-testing.
- **Cross-Platform Compatibility**
  The courseware is tested and confirmed to work seamlessly across devices, browsers, and platforms.
- **Ongoing Review Plan**
  A post-launch plan for regular usability reviews ensures continued performance and learner satisfaction.

Checklist

1. Define test objectives (navigation, clarity, accessibility, engagement)
2. Select test participants representative of the target audience
3. Prepare test scripts and observation checklists
4. Monitor learner interaction with courseware on target devices
5. Capture usability issues via observation and user feedback
6. Log functional bugs, UI/UX pain points, and access barriers
7. Debrief participants and summarise qualitative insights
8. Report findings and prioritise fixes for final release

AI Considerations

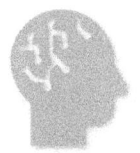

- Use AI heatmaps and session replays to observe learner behaviour
- Auto-summarise qualitative feedback from usability sessions
- Detect click patterns or navigation breakdowns
- Predict frustration or disengagement based on interaction metrics
- Generate prioritised bug lists or usability recommendations

Key Takeaways

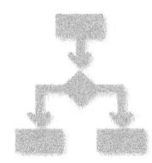

- Usability testing ensures that learners can navigate and interact with the courseware intuitively, without frustration or confusion.
- Real users should complete realistic tasks while observing where they stumble, hesitate, or drop off.
- Focus on accessibility, readability, responsiveness, and load performance across all devices and platforms.
- Gather both **quantitative data** (e.g. error rates, task completion times) and **qualitative feedback** (e.g. user impressions, perceived ease of use).
- Prioritise fixes that impact **comprehension, navigation, or learner flow** before cosmetic refinements.
- Don't rely solely on internal testers, include fresh eyes from your target audience segment.
- Use iterative testing: early low-fidelity prototypes, then fully integrated courseware.

Pilot Preparation and Readiness

Overview

The **Pilot Preparation and Readiness** step in the Development phase of the ADDIE model ensures that a course is thoroughly prepared for a controlled trial before its full launch. This step provides the foundation for gathering actionable feedback, refining the course, and addressing any potential issues. Pilot testing with a small, representative group of learners allows instructional designers to validate the course's content, delivery methods, and technical functionality.

Key Sub-Steps are:

- **Conduct Quality Review**
  Conduct a comprehensive review of all course materials, including content, multimedia elements, and interactive components, to ensure they meet design and quality standards.

- **Contact Test Learners & SMEs**
  Identify and confirm participation from a representative group of test learners and Subject Matter Experts (SMEs) to gather a range of perspectives.

- **Set Date for Pilot Testing**
  Establish a clear schedule and timeframe for the pilot test, ensuring all participants are informed and ready.

Outcomes

The outcomes of the **Pilot Testing Setup** step are to ensure the course is fully prepared for testing, engage suitable participants, and create a structured process for gathering feedback.

Key outcomes include:

- **Verify Course Readiness**
  Ensure that all instructional materials, media, and interactive elements are functional and adhere to design standards.

- **Engage Representative Participants**
  Select a group of test learners and SMEs that reflect the target audience to provide relevant and diverse feedback.

- **Establish a Defined Pilot Schedule**
  Set clear testing dates and provide participants with adequate preparation time to maximise their contributions.

- **Facilitate Feedback Collection**
  Prepare surveys, forms, or interview templates that guide participants to provide detailed, constructive feedback.

- **Minimise Technical Disruptions**
  Test technical aspects such as platform compatibility and accessibility to avoid issues during the pilot test.

Summary

The **Pilot Testing Setup** step is a critical phase in preparing a course for its initial trial.

By focusing on quality assurance, engaging representative participants, and setting a realistic schedule, instructional designers can ensure that the pilot test provides valuable insights for course refinement.

Best practices like pre-pilot testing of technology, clear communication with participants, and detailed feedback tools help streamline the process and minimise disruptions.

A well-prepared pilot testing setup supports a smooth testing experience, enabling instructional designers to deliver a polished, learner-centred course for the full launch.

Conduct Quality Review

Why this is important

A thorough quality review ensures that all instructional materials meet high standards before pilot testing begins.

This step validates alignment between the content and the intended learning objectives while identifying and resolving any errors, inconsistencies, or technical issues.

Multimedia elements such as videos, graphics, and audio must be fully functional and accessible across devices and platforms.

By reviewing flow, usability, and formatting, and addressing any issues early, instructional designers reduce the risk of setbacks during pilot testing.

This review creates confidence in the readiness of the courseware, laying the foundation for a smooth, effective pilot phase.

Tips

- **Collaborate with Experts**
  Involve SMEs, instructional designers, and quality assurance professionals for comprehensive reviews.
- **Test the Flow**
  Navigate through the materials from the learner's perspective to identify usability issues or confusing elements.
- **Consistency is Key**
  Verify consistent formatting, branding, and style across all content.
- **Documentation**
  Document identified issues and resolutions to streamline subsequent reviews and ensure transparency.

Traps

- **Rushing the Review**
  Skipping or rushing the quality review to meet deadlines can lead to critical errors being missed.
- **Overlooking Accessibility**
  Failing to test for accessibility compliance can exclude learners with disabilities.
- **Ignoring Feedback Loops**
  Not incorporating feedback from earlier stages may result in unresolved issues surfacing during pilot testing.
- **Unverified Media Elements**
  Neglecting to test multimedia components can result in glitches or missing files during testing.
- **Neglecting Technical Checks**
  Failing to verify technical compatibility across devices and platforms can lead to usability issues.

Techniques

- **Cross-Team Reviews**
  Organise cross-functional team reviews to ensure diverse perspectives on quality and usability.
- **Usability Testing**
  Conduct usability tests with a small internal group to simulate the learner experience.
- **Content Validation**
  Match every piece of content to its corresponding learning objective to confirm alignment.
- **Technical Testing**
  Use tools to test multimedia elements and course functionality across different devices and browsers.
- **Error Logs**
  Maintain a centralized error log to track issues and confirm their resolution.

Pilot Preparation and Readiness
Conduct Quality Review

Examples

- *Learning Module Check*
  A course module with interactive quizzes is reviewed to ensure all questions function correctly and feedback is clear.

- *Multimedia Verification*
  Videos are tested to ensure they play seamlessly, have synchronized captions, and meet accessibility standards.

- *Content Accuracy*
  A safety training module is reviewed by SMEs to ensure compliance with legal and regulatory requirements.

- *Platform Compatibility*
  The course is accessed on various devices (desktop, tablet, mobile) to confirm responsive design and functionality.

- *Simulation Testing*
  An interactive simulation for a software tutorial is tested to ensure user inputs yield correct outcomes.

How it's done

- **Review Learning Objectives**
  Begin by verifying that all content aligns with the defined learning objectives and instructional goals. Ensure every element supports the intended outcomes of the course.

- **Check Content Accuracy**
  Conduct a detailed review of the content for accuracy, relevance, and clarity. Identify and address any errors or outdated information.

- **Verify Multimedia Functionality**
  Test all videos, animations, graphics, and audio files to ensure they load and function as intended. Check for quality and smooth playback across devices.

- **Assess Navigation**
  Evaluate the navigation structure to confirm it is intuitive and follows a logical flow, providing a seamless user experience.

- **Validate Accessibility**
  Ensure the course complies with accessibility standards, incorporating features such as captions, alt text, and keyboard navigation to support diverse learner needs.

- **Test Interactive Features**
  Check the functionality of quizzes, simulations, and other interactive components. Ensure they align with learning objectives and function without glitches.

- **Evaluate Consistency**
  Review formatting, branding, and style to ensure consistency across all materials, including fonts, colour schemes, and design elements.

- **Perform Technical Testing**
  Test the course materials on various devices, browsers, and operating systems to ensure compatibility and functionality.

- **Document Findings**
  Record all identified issues and communicate them to the development team for resolution. Maintain clear documentation of findings and actions taken.

- **Sign Off**
  Obtain final approval from stakeholders after resolving identified issues. This ensures the materials are ready for pilot testing and deployment.

Pilot Preparation and Readiness
Conduct Quality Review

Core Elements

- **Alignment with Objectives**
  Content is verified to align with learning objectives and instructional goals.
- **Content Accuracy**
  Materials are reviewed for relevance, clarity, and correctness.
- **Multimedia Functionality**
  All media elements function as intended and meet quality standards.
- **Accessibility Compliance**
  Accessibility features such as captions and alt text are implemented and tested.
- **Navigation Usability**
  The user interface is intuitive, and navigation is logical and seamless.
- **Interactive Features**
  Quizzes, simulations, and other interactive elements are fully functional.
- **Consistency Maintained**
  Formatting, branding, and style are uniform across all materials.
- **Technical Compatibility**
  Materials are tested on multiple devices, browsers, and platforms.
- **Issues Resolved**
  All identified problems are addressed before stakeholder review.
- **Stakeholder Approval**
  Final sign-off is documented before proceeding to pilot testing.

Checklist

1. Assemble QA checklist covering content, navigation, media, and assessments
2. Review all course components against instructional design standards
3. Validate that all links, triggers, and branching paths function correctly
4. Verify narration, graphics, and text are in sync and error-free
5. Confirm accessibility compliance (e.g., captions, alt text, keyboard access)
6. Perform cross-device and cross-browser testing
7. Log and prioritise any issues or deviations for correction
8. Secure final approval from design lead or QA specialist

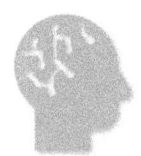

AI Considerations

- Use AI to scan courseware for broken links, missing assets, or logic errors
- Auto-check consistency in voiceover text, captions, and on-screen elements
- Apply AI-powered accessibility audits (e.g., WCAG compliance checks)
- Run automated UI/UX tests to simulate learner paths
- Use LLMs to flag unclear instructions, ambiguous questions, or tone inconsistencies

Key Takeaways

The Quality Review step is a critical phase in the Development Phase of the ADDIE model.

It ensures that all instructional materials are accurate, functional, and aligned with learning objectives before they reach learners or SMEs for pilot testing.

By systematically validating content, media, interactivity, and technical compatibility, instructional designers can identify and resolve potential issues early, saving time and resources while enhancing the overall learner experience.

A thorough quality review establishes a strong foundation for a smooth and effective pilot testing process, ultimately contributing to the success of the instructional programme.

Contact Test Learners & SMEs

Why this is important

Establishing early and clear communication with test learners and subject matter experts is essential for coordinating a successful pilot testing session.

This step ensures participants are informed about their roles, understand what is expected of them, and have access to the necessary materials in advance.

Confirming availability and setting clear expectations supports high engagement and quality feedback.

A collaborative relationship encourages openness and commitment, which is critical to gathering constructive insights that will improve the course before full rollout.

Tips

- **Be Clear and Concise**
  Clearly explain the purpose of the pilot test, their role, and what is expected of them.
- **Provide Flexibility**
  Offer multiple date and time options to accommodate their schedules.
- **Use Professional Tone**
  Communicate professionally to build trust and maintain credibility.
- **Leverage Technology**
  Use scheduling tools like Doodle or Calendly to streamline the scheduling process.
- **Follow Up**
  Send reminders leading up to the pilot test to ensure participants remain committed.

Traps

- **Overloading Participants**
  Avoid overwhelming test learners and SMEs with excessive information or unrealistic expectations.
- **Unclear Communication**
  Failing to explain roles and expectations can lead to confusion and ineffective feedback.
- **Scheduling Conflicts**
  Not considering participants' availability can result in low attendance or last-minute cancellations.
- **Neglecting Accessibility**
  Ensure all test learners and SMEs can access the necessary materials and platforms.
- **Ignoring Feedback Needs**
  Not explaining the importance of their feedback may result in minimal or unhelpful responses.

Techniques

- **Personalised Outreach**
  Tailor your communication to address each participant's specific role and expertise.
- **Centralized Communication**
  Use a project management tool or email thread to keep all participants informed and aligned.
- **Pre-Survey**
  Send a brief survey to gather availability and preferences for the testing session.
- **Role-Based Guidance**
  Share specific instructions for SMEs and learners based on their respective contributions to the pilot test.
- **Feedback Preparation**
  Provide a feedback form or rubric to help guide their evaluations during the pilot test.

Pilot Preparation and Readiness
Contact Test Learners & SMEs

Examples

- *Learner Outreach*
  "Dear [Learner Name], we're excited to have you participate in our upcoming pilot test. The session will allow us to refine the course and ensure it meets its objectives effectively. Please let us know your availability by completing this [survey link]."

- *SME Outreach*
  "Dear [SME Name], your expertise is invaluable in reviewing our course materials. We've outlined key areas for your input. Please select a convenient time for the pilot test using this [link]."

- *Coordination Message*
  "Hello Team, the proposed pilot test dates are [Date 1], [Date 2], and [Date 3]. Please confirm your availability by [response deadline]. We look forward to your participation!"

- *Reminder*
  "This is a friendly reminder for the upcoming pilot test on [Date/Time]. Please find the session details and materials attached. Let us know if you have any questions."

How it's done

- **Prepare Communication Materials**
  Draft email templates and instructions tailored for learners and SMEs, clearly outlining the purpose of the pilot test, their roles, and the objectives.

- **Determine Availability**
  Use scheduling tools or direct communication to identify dates and times that work for all participants, ensuring maximum attendance and engagement.

- **Send Invitations**
  Reach out to test learners and SMEs with detailed invitations that include session goals, instructions, and proposed schedules. Include any relevant background information to help them prepare.

- **Provide Access**
  Share necessary materials, login details, or links to the testing platforms well in advance. Ensure participants can access all required resources smoothly.

- **Confirm Participation**
  Follow up with participants to confirm their attendance and address any queries they may have. Provide additional clarity if needed to eliminate confusion.

- **Send Reminders**
  Send timely reminders, ideally one or two days before the scheduled session, to reinforce attendance and ensure participants are prepared.

- **Offer Support**
  Remain available to troubleshoot technical issues or address participant concerns leading up to the pilot test. Proactive support fosters a smooth and successful session.

Pilot Preparation and Readiness
Contact Test Learners & SMEs

Core Elements

- **Clear Objectives and Expectations**
  Communications clearly outline what is expected of participants during the pilot test.
- **Confirmed Availability**
  Availability of test learners and SMEs is confirmed to avoid last-minute scheduling conflicts.
- **Flexible Scheduling**
  Any conflicts are resolved with flexibility to accommodate as many participants as possible.
- **Advance Resource Sharing**
  All necessary materials, links, and access credentials are provided in advance.
- **Tailored Instructions**
  Guidance is customised to each participant's role to ensure clarity and effectiveness.
- **Reminder Notifications**
  Timely reminders reinforce attendance and readiness for the session.
- **Contingency Plans in Place**
  Backup strategies are prepared to handle no-shows or technical difficulties.
- **Guided Feedback**
  Feedback forms or rubrics are shared in advance to guide participant evaluations.

Checklist

1. Finalise and verify the pilot participant list (learners and SMEs)
2. Prepare and send briefing communications explaining the pilot's purpose
3. Include expectations, timelines, login instructions, and feedback process
4. Confirm receipt and understanding of the invitation
5. Provide contact points for support during the pilot
6. Collect participant consent or acknowledgment (if required)
7. Distribute any pre-reading, access credentials, or technical instructions
8. Document all communications for tracking and follow-up

AI Considerations

- Use AI to personalise mass communications based on participant roles
- Auto-generate onboarding guides or help documentation
- Schedule and manage communications using AI-enhanced email sequencing
- Analyse past response patterns to predict likely dropouts or delays
- Create smart reminders and automated follow-up messages

Key Takeaways

The **Contact Test Learners and SMEs** step is a crucial yet straightforward part of the pilot testing setup in the Development Phase of the ADDIE model.

This step ensures that participants are informed, prepared, and aligned with the goals of the session.

Clear communication, flexible scheduling, and proactive support create a seamless process, fostering collaboration and engagement.

By ensuring participant readiness and addressing potential issues in advance, this step sets the stage for a successful pilot testing phase and valuable feedback for improving the course.

Set Date for Pilot Testing

Why this is important

Selecting and confirming a suitable date for pilot testing is key to maximising participation and ensuring a well-coordinated session.

The timing must accommodate both test learners and SMEs, align with project milestones, and account for logistical details such as technology readiness or venue availability.

Effective scheduling also reduces the risk of conflicts, cancellations, or under-attendance.

Clear communication of the session details enables all stakeholders to prepare adequately, supporting a smooth and productive testing experience that yields meaningful feedback.

Tips

- **Consult Early**
  Begin scheduling discussions well in advance to identify potential conflicts.
- **Offer Options**
  Provide multiple date options to accommodate busy schedules.
- **Differentiate Formats**
  For in-person sessions, confirm logistics like venue availability, travel time, and resource setup. For online sessions, confirm technology readiness and time zone considerations.
- **Be Clear**
  Clearly outline the time commitment required for the session, including preparation time.
- **Time Zone Awareness**
  For virtual sessions with diverse participants, use tools like World Time Buddy to identify overlapping availability.

Traps

- **Overbooking**
  Trying to fit too many participants into a single session may lead to scheduling conflicts or rushed feedback.
- **Last-Minute Changes**
  Avoid making sudden changes to the schedule, as this can confuse or alienate participants.
- **Ignoring Time Zones**
  Overlooking time zone differences can lead to unintentional exclusions or absenteeism.
- **Venue Overlaps**
  For in-person sessions, failing to secure a venue in advance can lead to rescheduling or cancellations.
- **Vague Communication**
  Not specifying start times, durations, or session formats can create confusion.

Techniques

- **Doodle Polls or Scheduling Apps**
  Use tools like Doodle, Calendly, or When2Meet to simplify the process of gathering participant availability.
- **Batch Scheduling**
  If participants can't attend the same session, schedule multiple smaller sessions to cover all feedback needs.
- **Anchor Around SMEs**
  Prioritise SMEs' availability, as their time is often more constrained, and work learner scheduling around that.
- **Hybrid Solutions**
  For in-person ILT sessions with tight logistics, consider combining face-to-face participants with remote attendees via video conferencing tools.
- **Calendar Holds**
  Send out calendar invites immediately once the date is set to ensure everyone blocks their time.

Pilot Preparation and Readiness
Set Date for Pilot Testing

Examples

- **In-Person ILT Testing**
  "The pilot test for the 'Advanced Communication Skills' course is scheduled for March 10, 2024, at the Downtown Learning Centre. Please arrive by 00 AM for a session lasting approximately 4 hours."
- **Online Testing**
  "The online pilot test will take place on April 5, 2024, from 00 PM to 00 PM (AEST). A Zoom link and testing instructions will be shared in advance."
- **Hybrid Format**
  "We've arranged an in-person pilot test at the Sydney Office on May 15, 2026, with remote attendees joining via MS Teams. Please confirm your participation preference by May 1."

How it's done

- **Identify Participant Availability**
  Use scheduling tools or direct communication to gather participants' preferred dates and times. Ensure the process captures a wide range of availability for flexibility.
- **Prioritise SME Schedules**
  Since Subject Matter Experts (SMEs) often have limited time, prioritise their schedules when selecting a date. Their input is critical to the pilot testing process.
- **Confirm Logistics for ILT**
  For in-person Instructor-Led Training (ILT) sessions, secure the venue, confirm the availability of resources such as equipment and materials, and arrange travel or accommodation if required.
- **Verify Technology for Online Sessions**
  Test the chosen online platform to ensure it is accessible, functional, and easy for participants to use. Resolve any technical issues before the session.
- **Finalise the Date**
  Select a date that accommodates the majority of participants, aligns with project timelines, and avoids conflicts.
- **Send Invitations**
  Communicate the confirmed date, time, and detailed preparatory instructions to all participants. Include any relevant materials or access links.
- **Include Contingencies**
  Plan for an alternate date to account for unforeseen conflicts, low participation, or emergencies. This ensures the session can proceed smoothly if adjustments are needed.

Core Elements

- **Comprehensive Availability**
  Participant availability is collected and reviewed to find the best possible time.
- **SME Schedules Prioritised**
  SME availability is given precedence due to their critical role and limited time.
- **In-Person Logistics**
  Venues, equipment, and travel arrangements are confirmed for ILT sessions.
- **Online Platform Readiness**
  Technology platforms are tested and functional for seamless online testing.
- **Clear Communication**
  Final dates, session details, and expectations are shared via calendar invites and follow-up emails.
- **Backup Plan Prepared**
  An alternate date is established for rescheduling if necessary.
- **Session Expectations Defined**
  Duration, format, and participant roles are clearly communicated to all involved.

Pilot Preparation and Readiness
Set Date for Pilot Testing

Checklist

1. Select a date range that accommodates learner schedules and project timelines
2. Coordinate availability with SMEs, facilitators, and IT support
3. Ensure all courseware is finalised and deployed in the LMS
4. Account for holidays, shifts, or operational blackout periods
5. Communicate test window and expectations clearly to all parties
6. Build in time buffers before and after for prep and debrief
7. Align pilot timing with any business reporting or launch deadlines
8. Lock dates in project timeline and notify stakeholders

AI Considerations

- Use AI to recommend optimal scheduling windows based on participant calendars
- Generate calendar invites and timezone-aware reminders
- Predict scheduling conflicts using organisational data
- Use natural language agents to coordinate date options across stakeholders
- Simulate impact of date changes on downstream deliverables

Key Takeaways

The **Set Date for Pilot Testing** step ensures that all participants, including test learners and SMEs, are aligned and prepared to engage in the evaluation process.

While in-person sessions require additional logistical coordination, online sessions demand robust platform testing and scheduling flexibility.

With clear communication, collaborative tools, and careful planning, this step lays the groundwork for a successful pilot testing phase.

By maximising participation and anticipating potential issues, instructional designers can ensure meaningful and actionable feedback is obtained.

Personalisation Tag Planning

Today's digital learners expect more than static, linear experiences.

They expect content that responds to who they are, what they know, and what they need next. **Personalisation Tag Planning** is the phase where this expectation is transformed into intentional design infrastructure. It is the architectural blueprint for delivering content that dynamically adapts based on each learner's context, role, region, preferences, or progress.

It involves not just deciding what to personalise, but building the logic, tagging systems, and platform alignment to make it scalable and seamless.

All of this happens without compromising the integrity of the learning path.

Personalisation becomes a measurable design principle, not a marketing buzzword, and allows the experience to feel human, relevant, and responsive at every step.

Key Sub-Steps are:

- **Define Personalisation Goals and Use Cases**
  Clarify what types of personalisation will deliver the most value. This could be based on role, region, performance, or preference. Link these decisions to business or learning outcomes.

- **Map Learner Variables and Triggers**
  Identify the data points, behaviours, or profile fields that will act as triggers for personalised experiences within your delivery platform.

- **Design Conditional Logic and Branching Structure**
  Build rules-based decision flows that determine what content a learner sees based on their individual inputs or progress through the course.

- **Establish Tagging and Metadata Framework**
  Create a structured system of tags and metadata to classify, group, and retrieve personalised content efficiently using your LMS, LXP, or CMS.

- **Validate Platform Capabilities and Technical Constraints**
  Ensure your delivery systems support dynamic personalisation logic, tagging protocols, and reporting requirements.

- **Test Personalisation Flow Scenarios**
  Prototype, simulate, and refine various learner paths to confirm that personalisation functions as intended and enhances the overall experience.

By planning personalisation from the ground up, this phase ensures your course can adapt to each learner intelligently, without becoming fragmented or unmanageable. It enables flexibility with discipline and scalability with substance.

Overview

Personalisation Tag Planning
Set Date for Pilot Testing

Outcomes

By the end of this phase, the instructional design team will have:

1. Defined and documented the learning and business goals for personalisation.
2. Mapped out all learner variables and trigger conditions that will drive content differentiation.
3. Designed logic pathways and branching flows that ensure each learner receives a coherent, outcome-aligned experience.
4. Created a structured tagging and metadata system that enables content filtering, adaptive delivery, and reuse.
5. Validated the delivery platform's capabilities and limitations to ensure technical feasibility of planned logic.
6. Developed and executed a scenario-based testing plan that confirms all personalisation paths function as intended.
7. Documented all personalisation structures, tags, and logic flows for QA, maintenance, and potential reuse.

Summary

Personalisation Tag Planning transforms abstract learner differences into precise, dynamic learning paths. It enables the design team to build modular content structures that adapt to each learner's profile, behaviour, or performance, all while maintaining instructional integrity.

This phase ensures that adaptive features are grounded in clear logic, compatible with delivery platforms, and scalable across languages, roles, and regions.

It bridges strategy and execution, allowing technology to support pedagogy, not complicate it.

When executed with foresight and discipline, this phase results in a more engaging, relevant, and effective learning experience, one that respects learner diversity and aligns with business goals. It also lays a reusable foundation for future adaptive learning initiatives across the organisation.

Define Personalisation Goals and Use Cases

Why this is important

Personalisation isn't just a buzzword. It's a strategy that enhances learner relevance, motivation, and engagement by tailoring experiences to individual needs.

But to do this well, the goals must be intentionally defined up front. Without clear personalisation goals, efforts risk becoming cosmetic, leading to superficial branching or wasted development. This step is essential to link personalisation to learning outcomes, ensuring it's pedagogically justified and adds value.

Whether it's role-based paths, knowledge-level adaptation, or contextual reinforcement, having defined goals ensures personalisation is measurable, scalable, and purposeful, not just gimmicky.

Tips

- Start by identifying **clear instructional gaps** or learner variations that personalisation should address (e.g., job roles, prior knowledge, region).
- Prioritise **use cases that are scalable** across cohorts or can be reused in future projects.
- Document the **business drivers** behind personalisation, compliance, productivity, learner retention, or risk reduction.
- Involve **stakeholders and SMEs** early to validate that proposed use cases are practical and valuable.

Traps

- Jumping into technical design before defining the why, leading to over-engineering without ROI.
- Mistaking personalisation for mere "cosmetic changes" (like name tags or colour swaps).
- Defining too many niche branches that fragment the course and become unmanageable.
- Ignoring **data availability.** Personalisation goals must be matched to data you can realistically collect or infer.

Techniques

- **Use Case Mapping**: Create a table linking each personalisation scenario to a learner need, business value, and delivery strategy.
- **Personas + Pathways**: Map hypothetical learner personas to content pathways to visualise adaptive opportunities.
- **Scoping Matrix**: Rate each personalisation idea for instructional value, scalability, technical feasibility, and effort required.
- **Impact Forecasting**: Estimate learner outcome improvement or business benefit per personalisation goal.

Examples

- In a sales enablement program, new hires receive foundational product training, while experienced reps skip straight to objection handling and competitive differentiation.
- A compliance module delivers different risk examples depending on whether the learner is in mining, construction, or healthcare.
- An onboarding course personalises the messaging and support resources based on geographic region and language preference.

How it's done

1. Gather learner data and business requirements that support a need for differentiated learning experiences.
2. Interview SMEs and review past learning performance to identify key variables (e.g., region, experience, prior scores).
3. Define specific learner segments and what variations in content, sequence, or support each should receive.
4. Prioritise personalisation cases using a benefit-effort matrix.
5. Draft a short brief for each personalisation path explaining its purpose, learner trigger, and expected outcome.
6. Review these goals with stakeholders and development leads to align expectations.

Personalisation Tag Planning
Define Personalisation Goals and Use Cases

Core Elements

- Defined learner segments
- Clear instructional triggers or use cases
- Mapped business outcomes or learning metrics
- Personalisation ROI rationale
- Prioritisation/effort mapping
- Stakeholder alignment
- Documentation of all accepted goals

Checklist

1. Identify learner groups that vary significantly in need
2. Define why personalisation would improve engagement or outcomes
3. Link each use case to a measurable business or learning goal
4. Draft use cases and learner paths in plain language
5. Assess technical feasibility and scalability of each case
6. Prioritise top 1–3 personalisation goals
7. Document these in a brief and review with stakeholders
8. Validate readiness for next-step development

AI Considerations

- Use AI to **cluster learner data** and uncover logical personalisation groups.
- Apply AI to scan historic course feedback for signals about where personalisation would have improved experience.
- Use large language models to generate sample use cases, tone adjustments, or role-specific phrasing per learner group.
- Train AI agents to detect whether a learning object supports reuse across different personalisation paths.

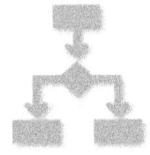

Key Takeaways

- Personalisation must serve a **clear learning purpose**, not just aesthetic appeal.
- Define and prioritise goals before building anything, strategy first, execution second.
- Keep it scalable, measurable, and tightly linked to learner or business value.
- Document everything to avoid drift once development begins.

Personalisation Tag Planning
Map Learner Variables and Triggers

Map Learner Variables and Triggers

Why this is important

Mapping learner variables and triggers is the foundation of adaptive content delivery. Without clearly defined input data, such as role, geography, performance, or preferences, the logic behind personalisation collapses.

This step translates the intent of personalisation into actionable mechanics by specifying what learner attributes will be used to trigger which content, paths, or interactions.

It also determines how and when those variables are collected, whether pre-loaded from HRIS systems, captured via pre-assessments, or selected manually by the learner.

Clarity here enables the development of effective branching logic, accurate reporting, and seamless platform integration.

Tips

- Use **variables that already exist** in enterprise systems (e.g., department codes, location, previous completions) to reduce complexity.
- Choose **a manageable number of variables.** Start small and build.
- Consider **how data will be collected** (e.g., from LMS profiles, pre-tests, dropdown selections, cookies).
- Document **when** each trigger will activate and what its default fallback will be if no value exists.
- Always plan for a **universal path** for learners who don't meet any specific triggers.

Traps

- Defining triggers for data that isn't accessible at runtime (e.g., CRM tags not exposed to LMS).
- Forgetting to test **null states** or what happens if a variable is empty or unrecognised.
- Overcomplicating logic with too many conditions, which creates unnecessary production and QA overhead.
- Allowing learners to select complex profiles without guardrails, leading to logic errors or incorrect content.

Techniques

- **Variable Mapping Grid**: Create a table listing each variable, its source, value type (e.g. boolean, string), and what it controls.
- **Trigger-Path Flowchart**: Map how each variable feeds into branching decisions.
- **Data Source Audit**: Review what learner data your LMS or LXP can provide automatically vs. what needs to be collected in-course.
- **Fallback Design**: For each condition, define what happens if no trigger is detected.

Examples

- A learner selects "Project Manager" during onboarding → triggers a content path that includes scheduling, stakeholder communication, and risk analysis modules.
- Learners from the APAC region automatically receive a version of the case study that references local compliance laws and currency formats.
- A pre-test score below 60% triggers a remedial module and disables final assessment until remediation is complete.

How it's done

1. Review personalisation goals and identify what variables are required to differentiate paths.
2. Document each variable: name, format, data source, and where it is used.
3. For each trigger, define what content, module, or logic it activates.
4. Validate with your platform team which variables are technically available and how to access them.
5. Create a flow diagram showing the sequence of decisions based on these variables.
6. Assign default values or fallback logic where applicable.
7. Conduct a dry run using test profiles to confirm triggers behave as expected.

Personalisation Tag Planning
Map Learner Variables and Triggers

Core Elements

- Variable map (name, type, source, usage)
- Defined trigger events and content links
- Platform data capability checklist
- Fallback and default behaviours
- Visual logic flow or decision tree
- Documentation of when/where triggers are activated

Checklist

1. Identify all learner attributes needed to trigger content
2. Verify availability of each variable in LMS/LXP/HRIS
3. Document trigger values and corresponding content outcomes
4. Create fallback logic for undefined or null states
5. Map each trigger to specific screens, paths, or content sections
6. Test triggers in staging environment with sample learner data
7. Validate with dev and QA teams for technical feasibility
8. Archive all mappings and update as logic evolves

AI Considerations

- Use AI to analyse historical learner data and recommend meaningful segmentation variables.
- Apply AI models to predict learner behaviours and auto-trigger content dynamically (e.g. AI sees low engagement and adjusts path).
- AI can validate logic models by simulating learner profiles across variable combinations and checking for conflicts or dead ends.
- Natural language AI can generate readable logic documentation for stakeholder review.

Key Takeaways

- Clearly defined learner variables are essential for executing personalisation logic.
- Triggers must be feasible, tested, and mapped to concrete outcomes.
- Plan for what happens when data is missing or ambiguous.
- Simplicity and clarity in trigger logic ensures scalability and stability.

Design Conditional Logic and Branching Structure

Why this is important

Conditional logic and branching structures are what make personalisation operational. While learner variables define who gets personalisation, branching defines how it unfolds.

This step determines the rules, sequences, and flows that adapt the learning experience in real-time based on learner input, role, prior performance, or selections.

Without clear logic, courses can become confusing, dysfunctional, or fail to meet learning goals. Designing this structure ensures that each learner journey is purposeful, pedagogically sound, and free of logic gaps or contradictions.

It also creates a blueprint for developers and reviewers, ensuring the course behaves as expected across all paths.

Tips

- Start with **simple if/then conditions** and visualise them as flow diagrams before moving into authoring tools.
- **Label every branch clearly**, both in your design docs and inside your authoring platform, for ease of QA and maintenance.
- Use **consistent logic patterns** (e.g. always show "intro" before "case study") across branches to reduce production errors.
- Include **progression parity** across paths. Ensure no group receives significantly more or less content unless justified.
- Consider accessibility and usability for learners re-entering the course from different points.

Traps

- Overcomplicating with too many nested branches, this creates QA nightmares and breaks SCORM tracking.
- Creating unbalanced branches that result in inequitable learning or assessment opportunities.
- Forgetting to define **exit and rejoin points**. Some learners may need to move between paths or return to main content.
- Not documenting conditions and flows, making debugging or localisation extremely difficult.

Techniques

- **Branching Flowcharts**: Use tools like Lucidchart, Miro, or even PowerPoint to map logic before building.
- **Decision Trees**: Model outcomes using structured conditional diagrams ("IF X, THEN Y").
- **Path Testing Scripts**: Write simple test cases for each branch with inputs, expected screens, and outcomes.
- **Layered Logic Grids**: Create a matrix showing how combinations of variables affect branching options.

Examples

- Learners selecting "new manager" are routed to a foundational module set, while "experienced leader" bypasses those and begins with performance coaching techniques.
- Learners failing a scenario receive a feedback loop and retry opportunity, while those succeeding proceed directly to the next challenge.
- In a multi-region course, choosing "Asia" as a region shows different compliance case studies than "North America."

Personalisation Tag Planning
Design Conditional Logic and Branching Structure

How it's done

1. Gather defined personalisation triggers and map them to content segments.
2. Use visual mapping tools to sketch flow diagrams representing all branches and conditional points.
3. Define clear entry and exit points for each branch.
4. Write logic conditions in plain language before encoding them in authoring tools (e.g. "If score < 80%, show remediation module").
5. Validate each branch with SMEs to ensure pedagogical integrity.
6. Annotate each branching node with metadata, content references, and fallback paths.
7. Conduct a logic dry run using hypothetical learner profiles.
8. Review structure with development and QA teams to identify conflicts or inefficiencies.

Core Elements

- Conditional triggers tied to learner variables
- Visual flowcharts or logic trees
- Entry, progression, and exit points for each branch
- Balanced content distribution across all learner types
- Developer-ready logic statements
- Clear fallback logic for ambiguous or multi-trigger conditions
- QA testing plan per branch

Checklist

1. Identify all branching decision points
2. Map out visual logic flow for each path
3. Define entry, progression, and exit logic clearly
4. Document all conditional logic using plain English and variable references
5. Validate that all branches lead to the same learning outcome unless otherwise intended
6. Write test cases for each path
7. Annotate all branching nodes with fallback scenarios
8. Share diagrams and logic maps with all stakeholders and developers
9. Perform walkthroughs with test users to confirm expected outcomes
10. Archive logic documentation for future reference and versioning

Personalisation Tag Planning
Design Conditional Logic and Branching Structure

AI Considerations

- Use AI to **simulate learner journeys** across all branches to detect dead ends or logical inconsistencies.
- Generate logic trees or conditional statements from written descriptions using natural language AI.
- Use AI to highlight inefficient or duplicated branches that could be merged or optimised.
- Apply machine learning to predict which paths produce the best outcomes and refine branching accordingly.
- Employ generative AI to convert complex logic flows into human-readable walkthrough documents.

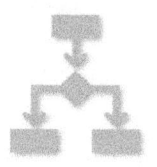

Key Takeaways

- Branching logic turns personalisation theory into lived learner experience.
- Simplicity and clarity in logic design reduce risk and enhance maintainability.
- Always visualise and document logic before building to ensure alignment across teams.
- Balanced, accessible branching is key to delivering equitable outcomes for all learner profiles.

Establish Tagging and Metadata Framework

Why this is important

A robust tagging and metadata framework is the backbone of scalable, adaptable, and trackable personalisation. Without it, content targeting becomes inconsistent, adaptive logic breaks, and analytics lose clarity.

Tagging enables content objects to be filtered, sequenced, triggered, and reused based on learner variables, behaviours, and platform conditions.

Metadata, including language, region, role, and skill level, ensures that each learning object can be dynamically pulled or presented with precision.

This step ensures your personalisation system is not only functional but maintainable over time, especially in multi-path, multi-region, or evergreen courses.

Tips

- Define tags early, **before course assembly begins**, so content creators use them consistently.
- Use **taxonomy structures** for role, topic, complexity, or region (e.g., "Role:Manager", "Level:Advanced").
- Store tags and metadata in a **centralised, version-controlled glossary** that all authors and devs use.
- If using a CMS or LXP, map your tags to platform-specific filters or delivery engines.
- Apply **multi-tagging only when necessary**. Keep tag sets lean to avoid confusion or performance issues.

Traps

- Creating too many tags without governance, leads to redundancy or conflicting logic.
- Tagging inconsistently between teams or modules, causing personalisation mismatches.
- Not updating tags when content is revised, deleted, or relocated, creating orphaned conditions.
- Applying ambiguous tags like "general" or "other", which dilute utility and reporting.

Techniques

- **Tagging Matrix**: Create a spreadsheet mapping each tag to its function, content area, and related learner variable.
- **Controlled Vocabulary**: Use predefined tag sets with naming rules to avoid confusion.
- **Metadata Schema**: Apply structured fields for each content object (e.g., title, ID, tag, version, path).
- **Tag Application Workflows**: Assign specific tagging responsibilities during content upload or publishing to ensure consistency.

Examples

- A Rise course includes modules tagged "Role: Sales", "Region: APAC", and "Skill: Intermediate", so that learners in sales roles from Asia receive content filtered to their context.
- Storyline interactions are tagged "Remedial:Yes" and linked to triggers activated by pre-assessment scores.
- An LMS rule pulls all objects tagged "Path:Compliance" and "Level:Mandatory" for auto-enrolment.

Personalisation Tag Planning
Establish Tagging and Metadata Framework

How it's done

1. Define personalisation goals and identify what tags are needed to support conditional logic.
2. Build a master tagging schema with tag categories (e.g., Role, Level, Path, Language, Region).
3. Establish naming conventions for each tag (e.g., use title case, no spaces, prefix categories if needed).
4. Train content developers, SMEs, and media teams on correct tag usage.
5. Store all tags in a central glossary or CMS metadata table.
6. Apply tags consistently during content development or import into LMS/LXP.
7. Regularly audit tags for redundancy, usage frequency, and relevance.
8. Archive unused tags and update linked content as needed.

Core Elements

- Master tag glossary
- Controlled vocabulary and naming conventions
- Metadata schema (fields and values)
- Tagging workflow and ownership protocol
- Platform tag-to-variable mapping
- Audit and update process
- Documentation of tag logic and purpose

Checklist

1. Identify all required tag categories (e.g., Role, Region, Level)
2. Build and publish a controlled vocabulary for tags
3. Define naming rules and versioning for tags
4. Map each tag to a learner variable, use case, or logic rule
5. Tag all content objects during creation or upload
6. Validate tags through preview and QA scenarios
7. Train all stakeholders in tagging protocols
8. Regularly audit tag consistency and utility
9. Update or retire obsolete tags with version control
10. Document tagging logic and include in technical specs

AI Considerations
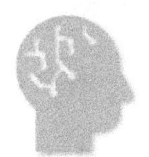

- Use AI to **auto-suggest tags** for content objects based on analysis of titles, objectives, and copy.
- Apply AI to detect **inconsistent tagging patterns** or unused/duplicate tags across your library.
- Employ natural language processing to **auto-classify new content** into existing taxonomies.
- AI can generate **metadata summaries** or tag clouds for admin dashboards.
- Smart agents can maintain a **living glossary** and flag deviations or conflicts in real time.

Key Takeaways
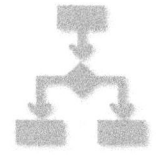

- Tagging is critical for precision personalisation, adaptive logic, and scalable content reuse.
- Clarity, consistency, and governance are more important than volume.
- Tags should align tightly with learner variables and platform capabilities.
- Metadata strategy is an ongoing asset, not a one-time task.

Validate Platform Capabilities and Technical Constraints

 **Why this is important**	Even the most sophisticated personalisation logic and tagging plans can fail if your delivery platform doesn't support them. This step is about **aligning your adaptive strategy with the real capabilities and limitations** of the LMS, LXP, or delivery engine you're working with. Many instructional design failures occur not due to bad content, but because teams assume the platform will "just handle it." Verifying constraints early prevents disappointment, rework, and wasted development time. It also helps you design within feasible boundaries. Choosing the right conditional triggers, file types, and tracking mechanisms your platform can reliably support.
 **Tips**	• Engage your **LMS/LXP administrator** early to understand system permissions, limitations, and configuration options. • Test personalisation logic in a **sandbox environment**. Don't rely on theoretical specs. • Document what types of logic the system supports (e.g., branching, role-based visibility, dynamic content injection). • Always ask: "Can this be tracked, triggered, and reported at scale?" • Clarify whether **third-party authoring tools** (Storyline, Rise, etc.) interact seamlessly with your platform's logic and reporting.
 **Traps**	• Designing for features your LMS doesn't support (e.g. xAPI analytics, dynamic content swapping, nested branching). • Assuming a feature works at scale. Some logic works fine with 10 users, but fails with 10,000. • Overloading your SCORM/XLIFF files with logic beyond what the wrapper or player can handle. • Ignoring **data privacy laws** when triggering personalisation based on location or performance history. • Failing to document constraints for future maintainers, can cause long-term platform fragility.
 **Techniques**	• **Capability Matrix**: List all personalisation requirements (e.g., "branching based on role") and mark whether each is supported by your platform. • **Logic Prototyping**: Build a mini-course or interaction that uses your most complex planned logic to see how the system handles it. • **Platform Compatibility Checklist**: Create a table of supported file types, data types, variables, and user attributes. • **Integration Testing**: Check whether third-party authoring tools maintain their logic post-export into your LMS or LXP.
 **Examples**	• Your LXP supports learner segmentation by role and region, but not dynamic sequencing, so you adapt your branching model to use visibility toggles instead. • An xAPI-based course offers fine-grained event tracking, but your LMS only supports SCORM 1.2, so you scale back your reporting plan. • You discover that custom JavaScript used in your Storyline file gets stripped out during upload to the LMS, forcing you to rebuild logic natively.

Personalisation Tag Planning
Validate Platform Capabilities and Technical Constraints

How it's done
1. List all personalisation features you intend to use (e.g., branching logic, pre-test gating, content swapping).
2. Conduct a platform capability audit. Talk to your LMS/LXP team or vendor and gather documentation.
3. Test edge-case logic in a sandbox (e.g., 3-branch scenario with conditional triggers).
4. Identify which learner variables are supported natively (e.g., role, department) and which must be custom-built.
5. Review compatibility between authoring tools and delivery platforms.
6. Document all platform constraints, quirks, and technical workarounds.
7. Adjust your personalisation strategy to fit within confirmed boundaries.
8. Share this validation document with all content developers and QA staff.

Core Elements
- Platform capability matrix
- Supported logic types (branching, toggles, gating, sequencing)
- Compatible content formats and export settings
- Known limitations or failure modes
- Documentation of validated variables and integrations
- Sandbox testing results
- Escalation or support contacts for tech issues

Checklist
1. Define all desired personalisation features
2. Audit LMS/LXP documentation and confirm feature availability
3. Identify which learner variables are supported natively
4. Build and test logic prototypes using real platform conditions
5. Confirm compatibility of authoring tool exports with your platform
6. Note and document technical constraints and limitations
7. Share findings with all development stakeholders
8. Adjust logic and tags based on platform readiness
9. Record support paths for platform escalation or vendor queries
10. Finalise validation documentation as a shared resource

AI Considerations
- Use AI to analyse platform documentation and extract feature availability or limitations automatically.
- Deploy AI agents to run compatibility tests between exported content packages and LMS upload environments.
- AI can simulate large-scale logic activation across learner profiles to stress test personalisation flows.
- Predict platform bottlenecks or failure points based on historical usage patterns.
- Use AI to match personalisation requirements to the most compatible tool or platform configuration.

Key Takeaways
- Never assume your platform can support your logic, validate everything.
- Design for real-world constraints, not ideal scenarios.
- Keep documentation transparent and centralised so all stakeholders stay aligned.
- Early testing prevents rework, course failure, and frustration.

Test Personalisation Flow Scenarios

Why this is important

Even the best-designed personalisation logic can break down in real-world execution. Testing flow scenarios ensures that each learner receives the correct content, interactions, and assessment path, based on the variables, tags, and logic you've established.

This step validates that all paths behave as intended, that learners aren't trapped in loops or dead ends, and that content loads properly under each condition

. It also identifies invisible errors, such as trigger misfires, skipped segments, or incorrect scoring, before they impact thousands of learners. Rigorous testing safeguards instructional integrity and user trust.

Tips

- Create **test personas or profiles** representing each learner path. Document what each should experience.
- Use **QA checklists per scenario**, not just per screen, verify progression logic, content visibility, scoring, and feedback.
- Include edge cases (e.g., unknown role, empty variable) and confirm default logic works as intended.
- Test using the **actual deployment platform**, not just preview modes from authoring tools.
- Conduct **walkthroughs with SMEs** to validate that each flow still supports intended outcomes.

Traps

- Only testing the "happy path", ignoring what happens if learners don't trigger any logic.
- Skipping mobile or cross-device tests, which can cause visual issues or logic failures.
- Failing to track which content blocks are reused across paths, leading to unintended duplication or overwrite errors.
- Overlooking non-obvious bugs, like variables not resetting between sessions or hidden screens not reporting completion.

Techniques

- **Scenario Testing Matrix**: List each learner persona, expected path, key checkpoints, and success indicators.
- **Trigger Simulation**: Manually or automatically simulate each variable condition and observe outcomes.
- **QA Scripting**: Write detailed walkthroughs for testers with required inputs, expected screens, and pass/fail notes.
- **SME Playback Reviews**: Record test runs and play back for SME validation of logic and learning flow.

Examples

- Test User A (Role: Supervisor, Region: ANZ) receives a compliance module with local law examples and completes an extra audit assessment.
- Test User B (no role or region assigned) defaults to a generalised learning path with standard scenarios.
- Test User C (scored 40% on pre-assessment) triggers the remedial path, is locked out of final quiz, and directed to revision content.

Personalisation Tag Planning
Test Personalisation Flow Scenarios

How it's done	1. Identify each personalisation path defined by your variables and tags. 2. Create representative learner profiles for each path (real or simulated). 3. Build a flow matrix or spreadsheet listing what each profile should experience. 4. Run the course for each persona on the actual LMS/LXP or platform. 5. Track whether the correct screens, content blocks, quizzes, and scores appear as expected. 6. Record all issues, misfires, broken links, incorrect logic, or mismatched content. 7. Fix issues and re-test until all paths are confirmed stable. 8. Retain documentation for QA, audit, or future updates.
Core Elements	• Test persona definitions • Flow expectations and triggers per persona • Visual test tracking (matrix or flow chart) • QA script with clear pass/fail indicators • Feedback logging and issue resolution trail • Cross-device and cross-role testing • Final validation sign-off
Checklist	1. List all personalisation paths and learner conditions 2. Create test personas or learner profiles for each 3. Define expected screen flow and content blocks per persona 4. Build a tracking matrix to log test outcomes 5. Test each scenario in the final delivery platform 6. Log bugs, logic misfires, and deviations 7. Re-test and confirm issue resolution 8. Validate outputs with SMEs and stakeholders 9. Run tests across devices and screen sizes 10. Archive test results and flow diagrams
AI Considerations	• Use AI to **simulate user journeys** across hundreds of possible learner variables to find gaps, logic overlaps, or missed triggers. • Automatically flag anomalies in flow sequencing or unexpected screen patterns. • AI-powered screen recording tools can document flow for stakeholder playback and validation. • AI can also review completion data and identify inconsistencies in scoring or progress that hint at unseen logic bugs. • Machine learning can be applied post-launch to refine logic based on real learner behaviour.
Key Takeaways	• Scenario testing is the only way to guarantee personalisation works in the real world. • Don't just test screens, test logic, flow, and outcomes. • Validate every path, including defaults and fallbacks. • Rigorous QA up front prevents cascading errors in deployment.

Part 4: The **IMPLEMENTATION** phase

The Implementation phase is a critical turning point in the ADDIE process. It is the moment when everything built, refined, and tested is released into the real world. This is where learning becomes a lived experience. Every assumption is validated or challenged. Every design decision is put to the test. The impact of your instructional product starts to appear in the behaviour of real learners.

While often seen as a simple deployment step, Implementation goes far beyond delivering content. It involves coordinating people, platforms, communications, logistics, and systems. Each part must work in harmony and be closely managed. This phase ensures that delivery is not only timely and technically sound but also aligned with strategy, centred on the learner, and ready for change.

A well-executed implementation begins with a controlled pilot. This allows facilitators and learners to interact with the course in real conditions. It offers insights into what works, what needs improvement, and what must change immediately. Data from observation, digital tracking, feedback forms, and interviews feeds into a fast revision cycle before the full rollout.

Facilitators and line managers are key players at this stage. They act as on-the-ground amplifiers who bring the content to life. That is why facilitator training and manager alignment are essential. These briefings should go beyond logistics and messaging. They must equip stakeholders to lead learning outcomes, answer questions, and reinforce the course in the workplace. Job aids, support materials, escalation paths, and FAQs should be shared before the course launches, not after.

Just as important is the change enablement strategy that supports the rollout. Implementation does not happen in isolation. Learners are busy professionals juggling competing demands. Change communications, leadership messaging, and reinforcement tools must be part of the plan. These include scheduled communications, visible leadership support, and follow-up nudges to help learners retain and apply knowledge.

Real-time monitoring and fast response are essential. Implementation is a live setting. Any issues with access, performance, comprehension, or engagement must be addressed quickly. This is where your course support strategy becomes active. It should include helpdesks, communities of practice, or assigned internal champions.

The Implementation phase is where you earn credibility. It reflects your design strategy, creativity, technical build, and delivery quality. When done well, it builds trust and momentum. When neglected, even a great course can lose its impact. Implementation is not the end. It is the link between delivery and long-term learning success, leading directly into the Evaluation phase.

Pilot Test Execution

Overview

The **Pilot Testing Execution** step in the Implementation phase of the ADDIE model involves running the pilot test with a selected group of learners to assess the course's real-world effectiveness. This step allows instructional designers to evaluate course design, content, and delivery, ensuring it aligns with learning objectives and meets the needs of the target audience.

By systematically monitoring and collecting data during this phase, instructional designers can pinpoint areas for refinement and make informed adjustments. A well-executed pilot testing process ensures a smoother and more successful full-scale launch.

Key Sub-Steps are:

- **Execute Pilot Test sessions**
  Facilitate the pilot in a controlled setting, allowing learners to engage with the course and providing opportunities to observe its functionality and impact.

- **Collect and Manage Data**
  Systematically gather and organise feedback, including both quantitative metrics (e.g., time on task, completion rates) and qualitative insights (e.g., learner satisfaction, usability observations).

Outcomes

The outcomes of the **Execute Pilot Test Sessions** step are focused on evaluating course performance, collecting actionable data, and identifying areas for improvement.

Key outcomes include:

- **Evaluate Course Effectiveness**
  Assess whether the course meets learning outcomes, is engaging, and provides a seamless user experience.

- **Gather Constructive Feedback**
  Use structured tools like surveys, focus groups, or interviews to collect detailed feedback from learners and stakeholders.

- **Identify Specific Refinements**
  Analyse collected data to highlight content, design, or technical elements that require adjustments for improved outcomes.

- **Ensure Feedback Accuracy**
  Validate that the feedback collected is representative and relevant, ensuring it can reliably guide post-pilot improvements.

- **Prepare for Course Optimisation**
  Leverage insights gained from the pilot to fine-tune the course, optimising it for the full launch.

Summary

The **Pilot Testing Execution** step is a pivotal moment in the course development process, providing a real-world trial that highlights strengths and areas for improvement.

By running the course with a representative learner group, instructional designers can assess its performance and gather valuable feedback.

Effective methods such as participant observation, structured surveys, and data analytics tools ensure that feedback is reliable and actionable.

Avoiding common issues like unstructured data collection or insufficient learner representation ensures the pilot delivers meaningful insights.

This step lays the groundwork for refining the course, ensuring it is engaging, functional, and aligned with learning objectives before the final launch.

Execute Pilot Test Sessions

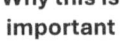

Why this is important

Executing pilot test sessions is essential for validating the instructional design, content, and delivery methods in a controlled, low-risk environment.

It enables the project team to conduct a real-world trial with selected learners and subject matter experts (SMEs) to confirm that the course meets its intended learning outcomes.

This step helps identify and address content gaps, delivery issues, or unintended user friction before full deployment.

Meaningful feedback is collected directly from participants, providing actionable insights that inform revisions and refinements.

It also tests the logistical and technical setup for both instructor-led (ILT) and online delivery formats, ensuring that the course runs smoothly and as intended across all channels.

By simulating actual delivery conditions, this step significantly reduces implementation risk and boosts confidence in the final product.

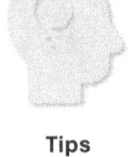

Tips

- **Prepare Thoroughly**
  Ensure all materials, tools, and logistics are ready before the session. For ILT, confirm venue setup; for online sessions, test platforms and ensure access links work.

- **Set Expectations**
  Brief learners and SMEs on the objectives of the pilot test and their role in providing constructive feedback.

- **Use a Moderator**
  Assign a moderator or facilitator to manage the session, especially for online tests, to ensure smooth transitions and address technical issues.

- **Engage Participants**
  Actively encourage learners to participate and interact as they would during the actual course to simulate realistic conditions.

- **Document Observations**
  Record the session (with consent) and take detailed notes on learner behaviours, questions, and feedback.

Traps

- **Overloading Participants**
  Avoid overwhelming participants with too much content or feedback requests during the session.

- **Ignoring Logistics**
  Neglecting venue arrangements for ILT or technology setup for online sessions can cause delays or disruptions.

- **Lack of Clarity**
  Failing to provide clear instructions or objectives to participants may result in vague or unhelpful feedback.

- **Content Bias**
  focusing too heavily on content accuracy while neglecting delivery dynamics or learner experience.

- **Missed Follow-Ups**
  Failing to follow up with learners and SMEs after the session can lead to missed insights or unresolved issues.

Pilot Test Execution
Execute Pilot Test Sessions

Techniques

- **Simulate Real Scenarios**
  Conduct the pilot test under conditions as close as possible to the intended implementation environment (e.g., live classroom, virtual setting).

- **Incorporate Interactive Elements**
  Use quizzes, group discussions, and practical exercises to evaluate learner engagement and material effectiveness.

- **Gather Immediate Feedback**
  Provide short surveys or questionnaires immediately after the session to capture participants' first impressions.

- **Observation and Recording**
  Observe learner interactions and behaviours during the session and record the proceedings for detailed analysis.

Examples

- **ILT Pilot Test:**
  For the ILT course on 'Project Management Basics,' the pilot test included 12 learners and an SME facilitator in a conference room. The learners completed a hands-on activity, and feedback was collected through group discussion and individual surveys.

- **Online Pilot Test:**
  The online training for 'Data Analytics Essentials' was tested with 20 learners. Participants navigated through the LMS, completed a self-paced module, and attended a live Q&A session via Zoom. Post-session feedback was gathered using Google Forms.

How it's done

- **Prepare Materials**
  Ensure all instructional materials, handouts, and resources are complete, accurate, and easily accessible to participants. This step ensures a smooth learning experience.

- **Confirm Logistics**
  For instructor-led training (ILT), verify the venue setup, seating arrangements, and availability of necessary materials. For online sessions, test all digital platforms and tools to confirm functionality.

- **Set Up Technology**
  Check audio, video, and internet connectivity for online sessions to avoid disruptions. For ILT, ensure classroom AV equipment is fully operational and ready for use.

- **Provide Orientation**
  Brief learners and SMEs on session objectives, expectations for participation, and any preparatory activities. Clear communication sets the stage for a productive session.

- **Facilitate the Session**
  Deliver the course content as planned, engaging participants through discussions, activities, and interactive components. Actively guide learners to maximise understanding and retention.

- **Observe and Note**
  Monitor participant engagement, questions, and challenges during the session. Take detailed notes or recordings for later analysis and refinement.

- **Collect Feedback**
  Distribute surveys or questionnaires immediately after the session to gather feedback from learners and SMEs. Conduct debriefs with SMEs to capture additional insights.

- **Review Outcomes**
  Compile and analyse feedback to evaluate the session's strengths and areas for improvement. Use these insights to inform final adjustments and optimise the course.

Pilot Test Execution
Execute Pilot Test Sessions

Core Elements

- **Materials Ready**
  All course materials, handouts, and resources are prepared and accessible.
- **Logistics Confirmed**
  ILT venues are set up, or online platforms and tools are tested and functional.
- **Technology Functional**
  AV equipment, internet, and other technological tools are operational.
- **Participants Oriented**
  Learners and SMEs are briefed on session objectives and expectations.
- **Session Facilitated**
  Content delivery and participant engagement are carried out effectively.
- **Observations Conducted**
  Engagement and challenges are monitored, and notes are taken for review.
- **Feedback Collected**
  Surveys and debriefs capture actionable feedback from learners and SMEs.
- **Outcomes Reviewed**
  Feedback is analysed to identify strengths and areas for improvement.
- **Contingency Plans Ready**
  Backup plans are in place to address technical or logistical issues.

Checklist

1. Confirm all content, platforms, and support channels are live and functional
2. Notify pilot participants with reminders and access instructions
3. Monitor learner progress and engagement in real time (where possible)
4. Provide technical and instructional support during sessions
5. Capture usability observations or learner feedback during live sessions
6. Maintain logs of any errors, delays, or confusion points
7. Communicate session wrap-up instructions and feedback mechanisms
8. Debrief facilitators and support staff post-session

AI Considerations

- Use AI dashboards to monitor learner behaviour, pacing, and click paths
- Trigger alerts for inactivity, login issues, or unusual navigation patterns
- Deploy AI chatbots for real-time learner assistance and data capture
- Auto-log performance metrics during session playback
- Record and transcribe pilot sessions for later review using AI tools

Key Takeaways

Conducting a pilot test is a critical step in validating the instructional design and delivery of your course.

Whether delivered through ILT or online, this process identifies gaps, refines content, and tests logistical setups under realistic conditions.

By engaging learners and SMEs, instructional designers collect actionable feedback to fine-tune the course before full implementation.

Proper planning, facilitation, and follow-up ensure the pilot test is a valuable part of the ADDIE process, paving the way for a successful course launch.

Pilot Test Execution
Collect and Manage Data

Collect and Manage Data

Why this is important

Collecting and managing data during pilot testing is a foundational step in transforming isolated learner experiences into meaningful insights.

A well-designed data collection and management plan enables the instructional team to gather accurate, reliable, and actionable information for evaluating the effectiveness of the course materials, delivery methods, and learner engagement. This ensures that feedback is not anecdotal but grounded in evidence.

By synthesising both quantitative and qualitative findings, instructional designers can pinpoint areas of strength, diagnose issues, and apply focused refinements.

Moreover, structured data analysis supports iterative evaluation and continuous improvement, ensuring the course aligns with learning objectives and delivers measurable impact during final rollout.

Tips

- **Plan Ahead**
  Define clear objectives and criteria for data collection before the pilot test begins.
- **Use Multiple Methods**
  Employ diverse methods such as surveys, interviews, observations, and analytics to capture a holistic view.
- **Train Collectors**
  Ensure those collecting data (facilitators or moderators) understand the data requirements and methods.
- **Anonymity**
  Guarantee anonymity in feedback forms to encourage honest and constructive input from participants.
- **Centralise Data**
  Use a centralized system for managing and storing data securely, such as an LMS or data analytics platform.

Traps

- **Lack of Clarity**
  Ambiguously defined data objectives or collection criteria can lead to irrelevant or incomplete data.
- **Overwhelming Participants**
  Overloading learners with surveys or excessive requests for feedback can result in low-quality responses.
- **Feedback Homogeneity**
  Collecting data from a homogeneous group may lead to insights that are not generalisable.
- **Ignoring Data Quality**
  Failing to clean or validate data can lead to errors in analysis.
- **Over-reliance on One Source**
  Relying solely on one data collection method may give a skewed perspective.

Techniques

- **Structured Questionnaires**
  Use well-designed surveys with a mix of quantitative (Likert scales) and qualitative (open-ended) questions.
- **Observation Grids**
  Develop grids to systematically record learner behaviours and interactions during the pilot.
- **Focus Groups**
  Conduct focus groups with learners and SMEs to delve deeper into specific feedback areas.
- **Digital Analytics Tools**
  Use LMS reporting, data dashboards, or tools like Google Forms and SurveyMonkey to streamline and visualise data collection and learner performance patterns.
- **Data Triangulation**
  Cross-reference data from multiple sources (e.g., surveys, interviews, performance metrics) to validate findings.

Pilot Test Execution
Collect and Manage Data

Examples

- **Survey Feedback**:
  "After a pilot test for an online coding course, learners completed a survey rating the clarity of instructions and difficulty of exercises. Responses highlighted a need for clearer examples in Module 3."

- **Performance Metrics**:
  "For an ILT course on financial modelling, assessment scores were tracked to identify weak areas. The data showed consistent struggles with the scenario analysis section."

- **Qualitative Insights**:
  "Interviews with SMEs revealed that while content was comprehensive, learners needed more real-world examples to relate to."

How it's done

- **Define Data Objectives**
  Clarify the specific aspects you aim to measure, such as content effectiveness, learner engagement, or platform usability. Establish clear goals to guide the data collection process.

- **Choose Collection Methods**
  Select suitable tools and techniques for data collection, such as surveys, interviews, observations, or performance metrics. Match methods to the objectives for reliable results.

- **Prepare Instruments**
  Develop the necessary instruments, including surveys, interview guides, and observation templates. Ensure these tools are aligned with the defined objectives and easy to use.

- **Train Data Collectors**
  Provide facilitators with clear guidelines on how to collect consistent and unbiased data. Include training on using data collection tools and handling participant interactions effectively.

- **Collect Feedback**
  Distribute surveys, conduct interviews, and monitor performance metrics during and after the pilot test. Capture both quantitative and qualitative data for a comprehensive evaluation.

- **Clean Data**
  Validate responses, remove duplicates, and address inconsistencies in the collected data. This step ensures the quality and accuracy of the dataset.

- **Analyse Data**
  Apply statistical methods to quantitative data and thematic analysis to qualitative data. Extract actionable insights that highlight strengths, gaps, and areas for improvement.

- **Synthesise Findings**
  Combine insights from all data sources to identify trends, recurring themes, and actionable recommendations. Create a unified overview to inform decision-making.

- **Document Results**
  Compile findings into a detailed report. Include summaries of the data analysis, proposed refinements, and supporting evidence to guide stakeholders.

- **Share Insights**
  Present the results to stakeholders through reports or presentations. Seek their feedback and incorporate it into the course refinement process.

Pilot Test Execution
Collect and Manage Data

Core Elements

- **Data Objectives Defined**
  Clear objectives for data collection are established.
- **Collection Methods Selected**
  Appropriate tools and techniques are chosen to gather data effectively.
- **Instruments Prepared**
  Surveys, interview guides, and observation templates are ready for deployment.
- **Participants Briefed**
  Pilot participants are informed about the data collection process and its purpose.
- **Data Collected**
  Surveys, interviews, and other tools are distributed and monitored during the pilot.
- **Data Cleaned**
  Validation processes ensure responses are accurate and duplicates are removed.
- **Analysis Tools Ready**
  Software tools like Excel, SPSS, or NVivo are set up for analysis.
- **Findings Documented**
  Data insights are compiled into a cohesive report.
- **Recommendations Shared**
  Actionable insights and proposed refinements are presented to stakeholders.

Checklist

1. Gather data from multiple sources: LMS, surveys, feedback forms, observation notes
2. Ensure data privacy compliance (e.g., anonymise learner identifiers if required)
3. Consolidate all quantitative and qualitative pilot data in a central repository
4. Review data for completeness, validity, and anomalies
5. Tag and categorise open-ended responses or issue logs
6. Prepare visual summaries and heatmaps of learner interaction
7. Share structured datasets with evaluation and design teams
8. Back up data securely and maintain access protocols

AI Considerations

- Use AI to auto-clean, structure, and summarise large pilot datasets
- Apply sentiment analysis to qualitative feedback
- Generate usage heatmaps, quiz analytics, and learner path visualisations
- Cluster learner responses to detect trends, confusion points, or outliers
- Auto-generate executive summaries or dashboards for stakeholders

Key Takeaways

The Collect and Manage Data sub-step is essential for transforming pilot testing into actionable improvements.

By gathering comprehensive quantitative and qualitative data through surveys, observations, interviews, and performance metrics, instructional designers can evaluate the effectiveness of their materials thoroughly.

A structured approach to analysis and synthesis ensures insights are accurate and impactful, guiding refinements that align with learning objectives and user needs.

A well-executed data collection and management process sets the foundation for continuous improvement, paving the way for a successful final implementation.

Pilot Feedback Evaluation

Overview

The **Pilot Feedback Evaluation** step in the Implementation phase of the ADDIE model is critical for refining the course before its full deployment.

This step focuses on evaluating the pilot test results by analysing both quantitative data (e.g., test scores, completion rates) and qualitative feedback (e.g., learner comments, SME insights).

By conducting structured interviews and focus groups, instructional designers gain a deeper understanding of learner and stakeholder experiences.

The insights gathered in this phase guide targeted revisions, ensuring the course aligns with learning objectives and delivers a high-quality learning experience.

Key Sub-Steps are:

- **Analyse Data**
  Review and interpret quantitative metrics and qualitative responses to evaluate the course's effectiveness.
- **Conduct Interviews**
  Engage learners and SMEs in discussions to explore their experiences, challenges, and suggestions for improvement.
- **Implement Revisions based on Feedback**
  Use feedback and data insights to refine course content, design, or delivery methods, ensuring alignment with objectives and learner needs.

Outcomes

The outcomes of the **Pilot Feedback Evaluation** step are to assess course performance, gather actionable insights, and refine the course for its full launch.

Key outcomes include:

- **Evaluate Pilot Performance**
  Assess how well the course met learning objectives using pilot testing metrics, combining both quantitative and qualitative data.
- **Gather Comprehensive Feedback**
  Obtain detailed insights from learners and SMEs through interviews, surveys, or focus groups to understand strengths, weaknesses, and areas needing improvement.
- **Identify Areas for Improvement**
  Pinpoint specific content, design, or delivery elements that require adjustments to enhance the learner experience.
- **Optimise the Course for Launch**
  Implement targeted revisions based on feedback and data analysis to ensure the course meets quality and effectiveness standards.
- **Avoid Overcorrection**
  Use structured methods, such as data visualisation and feedback loops, to ensure revisions are evidence-based and avoid unnecessary or excessive changes.

Summary

The **Pilot Feedback Evaluation** step is a vital part of the ADDIE model, ensuring that the course is polished and aligned with both learner needs and organisational goals.

By systematically evaluating pilot test results and incorporating feedback from learners and SMEs, instructional designers can identify areas for improvement and implement targeted refinements.

This step serves as the final quality checkpoint before the course is launched. Leveraging structured methods like data visualisation and clear feedback loops prevents over-adjustment or misinterpretation of results.

The outcome is a well-optimised course that delivers a relevant, engaging, and impactful learning experience to its target audience.

Pilot Feedback Evaluation
Analyse Data

Analyse Data

Why this is important

Analysing pilot test data is essential for evaluating how effectively the course achieves its learning objectives.

This process enables instructional designers to identify both strengths and weaknesses in content, activities, and assessments.

Through careful examination of trends and feedback, designers can refine materials based on solid evidence rather than assumptions.

It also validates the instructional design by determining whether it aligns with the learners' needs and the organisation's goals.

By transforming raw data into actionable insights, this step ensures that final course delivery is not only accurate and effective but also learner-centred and strategically informed.

Tips

- **Establish Clear Metrics**
  Define specific success metrics (e.g., minimum pass rates, completion times) to benchmark performance.
- **Use a Mixed-Methods Approach**
  Combine quantitative data (e.g., test scores) with qualitative feedback (e.g., learner comments) for a comprehensive analysis.
- **Segment Data**
  Analyse data by learner demographics or roles to identify patterns or trends within subgroups.
- **Use Tools**
  Employ tools like Excel, Tableau, or SPSS for quantitative analysis and NVivo or thematic coding for qualitative feedback.
- **Focus on Key Questions**
  Structure your analysis around critical questions, such as "Did learners achieve the intended outcomes?"

Traps

- **Overlooking Qualitative Insights**
  Ignoring open-ended feedback may lead to missing critical user experience issues.
- **Bias in Interpretation**
  Allowing preconceived notions about the course to influence data analysis.
- **Insufficient Data Cleaning**
  Failing to clean or validate data can result in errors or misleading findings.
- **Analysing Data in Isolation**
  Neglecting to cross-reference findings from multiple sources may give an incomplete picture.
- **Overcomplicating Analysis**
  Using overly complex methods when simpler ones could yield actionable insights.

Techniques

- **Descriptive Statistics**
  Calculate averages, medians, and percentages for quantitative data to summarise key trends.
- **Cross-Tabulation**
  Compare results across different learner groups to identify patterns or disparities.
- **Thematic Analysis**
  Code qualitative data to group similar feedback themes and identify recurring issues or strengths.
- **Correlation Analysis**
  Explore possible relationships between variables, such as the link between learner engagement and performance outcomes.
  Note that correlation does not imply causation."
- **Gap Analysis**
  Compare pilot test results against desired learning objectives to identify areas of misalignment.

Pilot Feedback Evaluation
Analyse Data

Examples

- ***Quantitative Analysis Example***
  Pilot results showed a 75% average on post-course assessments, with Module 4 scoring consistently lower than others. This suggests the need for additional clarity in that module.

- ***Qualitative Analysis Example***
  Learners frequently mentioned that the navigation menu was unclear, leading to confusion. This feedback highlights the need for a more intuitive design.

- ***Cross-Tabulation Example***
  Experienced learners completed the course 30% faster than novices, suggesting the potential for adaptive pacing options.

How it's done

- **Compile Data**
  Collect all relevant data from various sources, including test scores, survey responses, and interview transcripts. Organise this data to ensure it is ready for analysis.

- **Clean Data**
  Prepare the dataset by removing duplicates, addressing missing values, and validating the accuracy of the data. This step ensures reliability in subsequent analysis.

- **Analyse Quantitative Data**
  Apply statistical methods to assess numerical data, focusing on trends, averages, and performance metrics. This helps identify measurable outcomes and gaps.

- **Analyse Qualitative Data**
  Examine open-ended feedback, interview transcripts, and observations to identify themes and insights. Use coding techniques to categorise recurring patterns.

- **Segment Results**
  Group data by learner demographics, roles, or other relevant variables to generate targeted insights. This segmentation ensures analysis is tailored and meaningful.

- **Compare to Objectives**
  Assess how well the pilot course results align with the stated learning objectives and benchmarks. This step validates the course's effectiveness in meeting its goals.

- **Identify Patterns**
  Look for consistent feedback, trends, and discrepancies across data sources. Highlighting patterns helps pinpoint areas of success and improvement.

- **Synthesise Findings**
  Combine insights from quantitative and qualitative analyses into a unified summary. This cohesive overview captures the full scope of the data.

- **Validate Insights**
  Share preliminary findings with stakeholders or SMEs for review and confirmation. Incorporate their feedback to ensure interpretations are accurate and actionable.
  This step adds rigour to the analysis and helps secure stakeholder buy-in for recommended refinements.

Pilot Feedback Evaluation
Analyse Data

Core Elements

- **Data Compiled**
  All data from surveys, tests, and interviews is gathered and organised.
- **Data Cleaned**
  Duplicates are removed, missing values addressed, and data accuracy validated.
- **Quantitative Data Analysed**
  Statistical methods reveal trends, averages, and performance metrics.
- **Qualitative Data Analysed**
  Recurring themes and patterns are identified through coding and categorisation.
- **Results Segmented**
  Data is grouped by relevant variables for targeted analysis.
- **Alignment Checked**
  Findings are cross-referenced with learning objectives to ensure alignment.
- **Insights Validated**
  Results are reviewed with stakeholders or SMEs for accuracy.
- **Findings Synthesised**
  A cohesive summary or report consolidates all insights.
- **Recommendations Outlined**
  Actionable recommendations for course refinements are developed.

Checklist

1. Consolidate all pilot data sources (LMS logs, surveys, feedback, observations)
2. Organise data by category: engagement, performance, usability, satisfaction
3. Validate data completeness and remove duplicates or corrupt entries
4. Identify patterns, anomalies, and high-frequency issues
5. Quantify learner success rates, time on task, and assessment performance
6. Summarise qualitative feedback into themes or sentiment buckets
7. Cross-reference findings with learning objectives and design intent
8. Document key insights, metrics, and supporting evidence in a formal report

AI Considerations

- Use AI tools to clean and structure large datasets automatically
- Apply sentiment analysis to open-ended responses or transcripts
- Cluster related issues across learners to detect systemic problems
- Visualise engagement patterns through AI-generated heatmaps or timelines
- Use LLMs to summarise findings into plain-language reports or dashboards

Key Takeaways

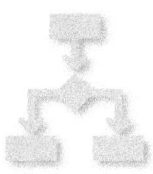

The Analyse Data sub-step is a critical component of the Data Analysis and Feedback step in the Implementation phase.

By thoroughly examining quantitative and qualitative data, instructional designers can evaluate the pilot course's performance and identify areas for improvement.

This step ensures that the course is not only effective but also responsive to learners' needs.

Using a structured approach to data analysis and synthesising findings into actionable recommendations, instructional designers lay the groundwork for a polished and impactful final course.

Conduct Interviews

Why this is important

Conducting interviews provides an essential opportunity to gather rich, qualitative insights that often go beyond what can be captured through surveys or analytics alone.

Speaking directly with learners and subject matter experts (SMEs) allows instructional designers to explore specific challenges, confusion points, and moments of success from the participants' perspectives.

These conversations can validate or challenge findings from quantitative data, adding depth and nuance to the overall evaluation.

Interviews are also valuable for identifying what worked well, reinforcing effective design strategies, and surfacing suggestions that might not emerge through other methods.

Beyond data collection, interviews foster a collaborative atmosphere, giving stakeholders a voice in the refinement process and promoting a sense of ownership in the learning experience.

Tips

- **Prepare Questions**
  Develop a semi-structured interview guide with open-ended questions focused on key learning objectives, content, and user experience.
- **Create a Comfortable Atmosphere**
  Ensure participants feel at ease by explaining the purpose of the interview and encouraging honest feedback.
- **Record Sessions**
  Use audio or video recordings (with consent) to capture all details accurately for later review.
- **Probe for Details**
  Ask follow-up questions to clarify or expand on points raised by participants.
- **Balance Perspectives**
  Include a mix of learners and SMEs to gather diverse viewpoints.

Traps

- **Leading Questions**
  Avoid phrasing questions in a way that biases participants toward a particular response.
- **Ignoring Nonverbal Cues**
  Pay attention to tone, hesitation, and body language for additional context.
- **Overloading Participants**
  Avoid asking too many questions or making the interview too long, which can lead to fatigue.
- **Failing to Follow Up**
  Skipping follow-up questions can result in missed opportunities for deeper insights.
- **Assuming Representativeness**
  Avoid assuming that one participant's feedback applies to all learners or SMEs.

Pilot Feedback Evaluation
Conduct Interviews

Techniques

- **Semi-Structured Interviews**
  Use a mix of prepared questions and spontaneous follow-ups to guide the conversation while allowing flexibility.
- **Focus Groups**
  Facilitate discussions with small groups of participants to encourage interaction and diverse perspectives.
- **Thematic Analysis**
  Identify recurring themes or patterns in participant responses for a structured interpretation of feedback.
- **Active Listening**
  Use reflective techniques such as paraphrasing or summarising to ensure accurate understanding of responses.
- **Triangulation**
  Compare and cross-validate interview insights with findings from surveys, performance data, and observational feedback to ensure consistency and depth.

Examples

- *Question Example*
  How well did the course meet your expectations, and what could have improved your experience?
- *Follow-Up Example*
  You mentioned difficulty navigating the module. Can you elaborate on which sections were confusing?
- *Success Identification*
  Several learners mentioned that the simulations were engaging and realistic. What specific aspects made them effective?
- *SME Perspective*
  Do you feel the course content aligns with real-world applications? If not, what changes would you recommend?

How it's done

- **Prepare an Interview Guide**
  Develop a set of open-ended and follow-up questions tailored to learners and SMEs. Ensure the questions are designed to elicit honest, constructive, and actionable feedback.
- **Recruit Participants**
  Identify and invite a diverse group of learners and SMEs to participate in interviews or focus groups. Select participants who can provide varied perspectives to enhance the richness of the insights.
- **Schedule Interviews**
  Arrange interview sessions at times convenient for participants. Confirm all logistics, such as locations, online meeting links, or required materials, to ensure smooth execution.
- **Obtain Consent**
  Secure informed consent from participants for recording their responses and using their feedback in the evaluation process. This step respects participants' rights and ensures ethical practices.
- **Conduct Interviews**
  Facilitate structured yet conversational discussions, encouraging participants to share their thoughts openly. Use the interview guide to stay focused while allowing for natural flow.
- **Record Responses**
  Take detailed notes or use recording devices (with participants' consent) to ensure the accuracy of captured responses. This helps preserve the integrity of the feedback for later analysis.
- **Analyse Feedback**
  Review and analyse interview responses to identify recurring themes, key insights, and actionable recommendations. Focus on patterns that highlight both strengths and areas for improvement.
- **Share Findings**
  Present key findings to stakeholders in an accessible format, highlighting implications for course improvement and strategic alignment.

Pilot Feedback Evaluation
Conduct Interviews

Core Elements

- **Interview Guide Prepared**
  Well-crafted, open-ended questions are ready to guide discussions.
- **Participants Recruited**
  A diverse mix of learners and SMEs is selected for interviews or focus groups.
- **Schedules Finalised**
  Interview timings and logistics are arranged and confirmed.
- **Consent Obtained**
  Participants' permission for recording and feedback use is secured.
- **Interviews Conducted**
  Sessions are carried out in a structured yet flexible manner to encourage openness.
- **Responses Recorded**
  Detailed notes or recordings are captured to preserve accuracy.
- **Themes Identified**
  Recurring patterns and actionable insights are analysed from feedback.
- **Findings Shared**
  Results are synthesised into a report or presentation for stakeholders.

Checklist

1. Identify target groups for interviews (learners, SMEs, facilitators, sponsors)
2. Prepare interview guides tailored to each role and purpose
3. Schedule and confirm availability for interviews
4. Conduct interviews using consistent questioning approach
5. Record sessions (with consent) and take structured notes
6. Transcribe and categorise responses into themes or priorities
7. Identify design issues, successes, and improvement suggestions
8. Store transcripts securely and reference findings in revision plan

AI Considerations

- Use AI tools to transcribe audio interviews quickly and accurately
- Apply NLP to extract themes, keywords, or recurring issues
- Summarise long transcripts into key points or visual mind maps
- Detect emotional tone or hesitancy via AI-powered voice analysis
- Auto-generate comparison reports across interview groups

Key Takeaways

The **Conduct Interviews** sub-step in the Data Analysis and Feedback stage of the Implementation Phase is critical for gathering qualitative insights into the pilot course's effectiveness.

By engaging learners and SMEs in structured discussions, instructional designers can uncover nuanced feedback, validate quantitative findings, and identify actionable improvements.

This collaborative process ensures the course meets both learner and organisational needs before full deployment.

Structured interviews provide a platform for deeper understanding and thoughtful course refinement, ensuring a polished and impactful learning experience.

Implement Revisions Based on Feedback

Why this is important

Implementing revisions based on feedback is essential for transforming evaluation insights into tangible course improvements.

By identifying specific weaknesses, gaps, or usability issues revealed during pilot testing, instructional designers can refine the learning experience to better meet the needs of the target audience.

This step ensures that changes are purposeful and aligned with the intended learning outcomes.

It allows both qualitative and quantitative feedback from learners and subject matter experts (SMEs) to inform content updates, media enhancements, and assessment refinements. Improving areas such as clarity, accessibility, and navigation not only enhances usability but also increases learner satisfaction and engagement.

Ultimately, this step ensures that the final version of the course is polished, effective, and ready for full deployment.

Tips

- **Prioritise Changes**
  Focus on revisions that have the most significant impact on learning outcomes or user experience.
- **Collaborate with SMEs**
  Involve Subject Matter Experts to ensure the accuracy and relevance of content updates.
- **Iterate Incrementally**
  Make changes incrementally, testing revisions as you go to validate improvements.
- **Document Changes**
  Maintain a record of all revisions for reference and future updates.
- **Communicate Updates**
  Inform stakeholders and team members about the changes to ensure alignment and understanding.

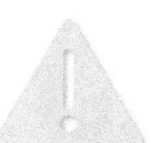

Traps

- **Unjustified Overhauls**
  Avoid making major changes without a clear basis from the data or feedback.
- **Ignoring Minor Issues**
  Small issues, such as typos or confusing navigation, can detract from the learner experience if left unresolved.
- **Focusing Solely on Negative Feedback**
  Balance revisions by reinforcing what worked well, not just addressing criticisms.
- **Underestimating Time Requirements**
  Revising content, media, and assessments can be time-intensive, plan accordingly.
- **Neglecting User Testing Post-Revisions**
  Ensure that changes are tested again to confirm their effectiveness.

Techniques

- **Gap Analysis**
  Compare current course performance against learning objectives to identify misalignments or deficiencies.
- **Feedback Categorisation**
  Organise feedback into themes, such as content accuracy, engagement, accessibility, and usability, to streamline the revision process.
- **Content Chunking**
  Break content into manageable sections during revisions to improve clarity and learner retention.
- **Iterative Prototyping**
  Apply small changes and test them with a subset of users before implementing them across the course.
- **Accessibility Checklist**
  Use accessibility standards (e.g., WCAG) to ensure revisions enhance inclusivity.

Pilot Feedback Evaluation
Implement Revisions Based on Feedback

Examples

- **Content Revision**
  A pilot test reveals that learners struggled with complex technical terms. Revisions simplify language and include glossaries or examples.
- **Assessment Update**
  Data shows that quiz questions are misaligned with learning objectives. Revisions ensure questions test the intended knowledge or skills.
- **Navigation Improvement**
  Learner feedback highlights confusing navigation. Adjustments add clearer menus and progress indicators.
- **Media Enhancement**
  SMEs recommend replacing outdated graphics with modern visuals to maintain relevance
- **Engagement Boost**
  Learners suggest adding gamification elements. The revised course includes badges and progress bars to enhance motivation.

How it's done

- **Analyse Feedback**
  Review results from pilot testing and participant interviews to identify key areas for improvement. Focus on both content and usability issues to ensure a comprehensive analysis.
- **Prioritise Revisions**
  Rank identified issues based on their potential impact on learning outcomes and user experience. Address high-priority areas first to maximise the effectiveness of revisions.
- **Consult Stakeholders**
  Collaborate with SMEs, instructional designers, and technical teams to validate proposed changes and ensure revisions align with organisational and learner goals.
- **Revise Content**
  Update course materials, including text, visuals, and multimedia, to close gaps and address issues highlighted during feedback analysis.
- **Adjust Assessments**
  Ensure quizzes, tests, and activities reflect revised learning objectives and content. This step ensures alignment between assessments and the updated course material.
- **Enhance Accessibility**
  Incorporate accessibility improvements, such as adding captions for videos, alternative text for images, and ensuring navigation is user-friendly for all learners.
- **Conduct Usability Testing**
  Test the revised course with a small group of users to validate changes and confirm that updates enhance the learning experience.
- **Document Changes**
  Maintain a detailed record of all revisions made, including updates to content, assessments, and usability features. This documentation supports transparency and serves as a reference for future improvements.
- **Prepare for Final Implementation**
  Ensure all revisions are thoroughly tested and seamlessly integrated into the final course version, ready for full deployment.

Pilot Feedback Evaluation
Implement Revisions Based on Feedback

Core Elements

- **Feedback Analysed**
  Data from pilot testing and participant interviews has been reviewed and categorised.
- **Revisions Prioritised**
  Changes are ranked based on their impact on learning objectives and user experience.
- **Stakeholders Consulted**
  SMEs and stakeholders validate proposed changes for alignment and feasibility.
- **Content Updated**
  Text, visuals, and multimedia are revised to address identified gaps and improve clarity.
- **Assessments Adjusted**
  Quizzes and tests are updated to align with revised learning objectives and course material.
- **Accessibility Enhanced**
  Improvements, such as captions and alternative text, are implemented to support inclusivity.
- **Usability Tested**
  Revised course materials are tested with a subset of users to validate updates.
- **Changes Documented**
  All updates are recorded for transparency and as a future reference.

Checklist

1. Prioritise feedback items based on learner impact and feasibility
2. Log all issues, decisions, and status in a version-controlled change log
3. Collaborate with SMEs and designers to revise content, media, or flow
4. Update instructional materials, assessments, or interactions as needed
5. Re-test critical fixes or rework for integrity and function
6. Ensure alignment with original objectives is preserved post-revision
7. Communicate updates to stakeholders and document rationale
8. Prepare revised courseware for full deployment

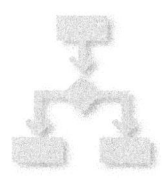
AI Considerations

- Use AI to match feedback to specific course elements needing revision
- Suggest rewritten scripts, new quiz questions, or alternate layouts
- Detect if new versions introduce inconsistencies or errors
- Generate change logs and revision summaries automatically
- Predict which changes will have the most positive learner impact

Key Takeaways

Implementing revisions based on feedback is a critical component of the Evaluation Phase in the ADDIE model.

By thoroughly analysing pilot test results and prioritising impactful changes, instructional designers can refine the course for maximum effectiveness and engagement.

Collaboration with SMEs and stakeholders ensures that revisions align with learning objectives, while usability testing validates the success of changes.

Attention to detail in areas such as accessibility, content clarity, and navigation ensures a polished and inclusive learning experience.

Documenting changes supports transparency and lays the groundwork for ongoing improvements, paving the way for a successful course launch.

Facilitator and Manager Briefing

The **Facilitator and Manager Briefing** step in the Implementation phase of the ADDIE model prepares those responsible for delivering and supporting the learning experience.

This step ensures facilitators are confident in the course content, delivery expectations, and technical setup, while line managers are informed and ready to reinforce learning outcomes on the job.

The goal is to align both groups with the course objectives, learning approach, and support mechanisms to promote consistency and maximise learner engagement.

Through structured training sessions, targeted briefings, and support resource distribution, this step builds internal capability and helps anticipate implementation risks.

It also creates a two-way communication channel that captures valuable pre-launch feedback, clarifies responsibilities, and strengthens organisational readiness for course deployment.

Key Sub-Steps are:

- **Conduct Facilitator Training Sessions**
  Deliver structured training to prepare facilitators for confident and consistent course delivery.

- **Provide Manager Awareness Briefings**
  Equip managers with key messages, expectations, and reinforcement strategies to support learners effectively.

- **Distribute Support Materials**
  Provide quick-reference guides, delivery checklists, FAQs, and escalation contacts to enable seamless facilitation.

- **Clarify Roles and Expectations**
  Ensure all stakeholders understand their responsibilities in the learning rollout, including follow-up and feedback mechanisms.

- **Capture Pre-launch Feedback from Facilitators**
  Engage facilitators in reviewing logistics, materials, and delivery plans to surface concerns or improvements before full deployment.

Overview

Facilitator and Manager Briefing
Implement Revisions Based on Feedback

Outcomes

The outcomes of the *Facilitator and Manager Briefing* step are to ensure all key personnel are prepared, aligned, and equipped to support the course effectively.

Key outcomes include:

- **Facilitator Readiness Confirmed**
  Facilitators are confident in course structure, content, timing, tools, and expected delivery standards.
- **Manager Support Activated**
  Managers understand their role in reinforcing learning outcomes and supporting behavioural change post-course.
- **Support Materials Distributed**
  All facilitators and managers receive relevant resources to aid in delivery, troubleshooting, and post-training actions.
- **Roles and Responsibilities Clarified**
  Each stakeholder group has clarity on their tasks and points of coordination, reducing ambiguity or role overlap.
- **Feedback Integrated Before Launch**
  Practical concerns and suggestions from facilitators are reviewed and resolved to prevent disruption during deployment.

Summary

The *Facilitator and Manager Briefing* step serves as the operational launchpad for a successful course deployment.

It ensures the people responsible for delivery and reinforcement are not only informed but truly prepared.

Through structured training sessions, briefing materials, and active engagement, this step reduces last-minute confusion, boosts facilitator confidence, and ensures managers are equipped to extend learning into the workplace.

By clarifying responsibilities, addressing potential challenges early, and gathering pre-launch insights, this step safeguards the quality of implementation.

A well-prepared delivery team becomes a powerful force in ensuring a smooth and impactful learning experience for every participant.

Conduct Facilitator Training Sessions

Why this is important

Facilitator training is essential to ensure that those delivering the course can do so with clarity, consistency, and confidence.

Even the best-designed instructional materials can fail if the facilitator is unfamiliar with the content or unclear about expectations.

A well-prepared facilitator understands how to use the learning materials, manage session timing, handle participant questions, and troubleshoot issues as they arise.

Effective training also enables facilitators to model the tone, style, and level of interactivity expected from learners.

Importantly, facilitator sessions provide a forum to rehearse delivery, align on messaging, and reinforce the reporting and feedback mechanisms required for quality assurance.

When facilitators are trained properly, they become confident ambassadors for the learning experience, equipped to uphold quality and respond dynamically in real time.

Tips

- Tailor the session to facilitator experience and technical ability
- Include hands-on practice using all course materials and delivery tools
- Simulate common learner questions and group dynamics for realism
- Reinforce the importance of consistent delivery across facilitators
- Provide an easy-to-use facilitator guide or session checklist
- Cover both the content flow and the logistical aspects of delivery
- Clarify escalation paths for content or technical issues
- • Allocate time for facilitator Q&A and peer knowledge exchange

Traps

- Assuming facilitators will "figure it out" on their own
- Overloading the session with theory and skipping practical rehearsal
- Failing to address technology requirements or setup steps
- Not explaining how to manage timing across different modules
- Ignoring the importance of tone, pacing, and engagement strategies
- Providing inconsistent or outdated versions of training materials
- Not preparing facilitators for challenging questions or objections

Techniques

- Facilitation walkthroughs with commentary from the instructional designer
- Mock delivery or "teach-backs" where facilitators practice sections live
- Live demos of platform navigation and interactive elements
- Q&A simulation with scripted difficult learner scenarios
- Use of a facilitator discussion board or shared document for ongoing tips
- Structured debriefing to review what worked well and where support is needed

Facilitator and Manager Briefing
Conduct Facilitator Training Sessions

Examples

- **Instructor-Led Training (ILT) Dry Run:**
  Facilitators rehearse delivery of a 90-minute ILT workshop using slides, facilitator guides, and physical props. Peer feedback is collected and adjustments are made.
- **eLearning Facilitation Training:**
  Facilitators practise navigating the LMS, using chat moderation tools, launching polls, and managing breakout rooms in Zoom.
- **Q&A Scenario Rehearsal:**
  Facilitators are presented with common learner objections and must respond while maintaining tone, clarity, and message consistency.
- **Reporting Protocol Review:**
  Facilitators are walked through the post-session reporting templates and shown how to document attendance, issues, and learner feedback.

How it's done

- Prepare a facilitator training agenda covering delivery structure, tools, and key responsibilities
- Schedule sessions in advance to allow for rehearsal and adjustment
- Provide all supporting materials, including facilitator guides, handouts, and platform access
- Conduct live walkthroughs of each module, including timing, transitions, and key messages
- Allocate time for mock delivery and peer or SME feedback
- Clarify how to handle technical issues, participant challenges, and deviations from plan
- Review post-delivery expectations, such as feedback collection and reporting protocols
- Capture questions and suggestions from facilitators and integrate into final deployment plan

Core Elements

- Facilitator guide prepared and distributed
- Delivery walkthrough conducted
- Course platform demo completed
- Key Q&A rehearsed
- Escalation and support procedures clarified
- Mock delivery completed
- Feedback mechanisms explained
- Reporting process reviewed

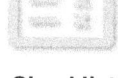
Checklist

1. Prepare facilitator training agenda and confirm all resources
2. Schedule training and invite all delivery personnel
3. Provide access to all learning materials and platforms
4. Conduct structured walkthrough of course content and flow
5. Include practical delivery rehearsals and peer feedback
6. Clarify delivery protocols and timing guidelines
7. Rehearse handling of learner questions and engagement techniques
8. Review post-session tasks such as reporting and learner follow-up
9. Capture facilitator feedback and address concerns
10. Confirm facilitator readiness for launch

Facilitator and Manager Briefing
Conduct Facilitator Training Sessions

AI Considerations

- Use AI-powered video rehearsal tools to give facilitators feedback on tone, pace, and clarity
- Provide AI-generated transcripts and summaries of training sessions for future reference
- Use AI chatbots to answer common facilitator questions post-training
- Track facilitator interaction during training and flag low engagement for follow-up
- Analyse facilitator feedback using sentiment analysis to spot concerns early

Key Takeaways

- Facilitator training ensures the course is delivered as intended, with energy, clarity, and consistency. It equips facilitators with the knowledge and tools to handle the material confidently and respond to learner needs in real time.
- A structured, hands-on training session builds familiarity with content, tools, and expectations, while also allowing for rehearsal and refinement.
- This preparation step reduces variability across delivery sessions, boosts facilitator confidence, and strengthens the overall learner experience.
- It is an essential bridge between development and deployment, ensuring that facilitators are not just informed, but fully empowered to succeed.

Provide Manager Awareness Briefings

Why this is important

Managers play a pivotal role in reinforcing learning outcomes and driving behavioural change once the course is complete.

Yet they are often the most under-briefed group in the implementation process. Manager awareness briefings ensure leaders understand what their teams are learning, why it matters, and how to support application of new skills or behaviours in the workplace.

When managers are aligned with the course objectives, they can reinforce key messages, create accountability, and integrate learning into daily workflows.

These briefings also help managers anticipate learner questions, plan for performance follow-up, and advocate for the initiative with credibility.

A well-briefed manager becomes a catalyst for learning transfer and a bridge between training and on-the-job impact.

Tips

- Focus on high-level learning outcomes and real-world implications
- Provide managers with summaries or "manager cheat sheets"
- Highlight the business case for the training to secure buy-in
- Explain how they can model and reinforce target behaviours
- Offer suggested post-course conversations or coaching prompts
- Include a clear call to action for their role post-training
- Keep the briefing short, sharp, and relevant to their priorities
- Allow time for questions and surface any concerns

Traps

- Treating managers as passive recipients rather than key enablers
- Overloading briefings with course design detail rather than practical impact
- Assuming managers already understand the purpose of the training
- Failing to explain their role in follow-up and reinforcement
- Ignoring their time constraints by scheduling overly long sessions
- Not tailoring messaging to their department or operational reality

Techniques

- Executive-style slide briefings with visual overviews of course goals
- Recorded videos summarising what the team will experience and why it matters
- Manager toolkits with talking points, timelines, and follow-up actions
- Pre-written email templates they can send to their teams
- Intranet posts or leadership memos aligned with course rollout
- Live Q&A forums or webinars to engage senior leaders

Facilitator and Manager Briefing
Provide Manager Awareness Briefings

Examples

- **Manager Briefing Pack:**
  A two-page summary includes key learning objectives, expected behaviour changes, support resources, and FAQs for managers to use in team meetings.
- **Video Message from the Sponsor:**
  A senior leader explains the course's importance and invites managers to champion the rollout.
- **Team Reinforcement Guide:**
  Managers receive a checklist of follow-up actions such as one-on-one conversations, workflow alignment tips, and encouragement strategies.
- **Live Manager Q&A:**
  Learning and Development runs a 30-minute briefing session with department heads to answer questions about the training and address concerns.

How it's done

- Identify key manager groups involved in post-training reinforcement
- Develop a concise briefing format that aligns with their role and priorities
- Create visual or video summaries to explain the course at a glance
- Share specific examples of how managers can support learning transfer
- Include tools such as post-course check-ins, coaching templates, or observation guides
- Provide access to facilitator guides or learner materials for context
- Deliver briefings live, via video, or through team leads depending on availability
- Capture questions, gather input, and reinforce their importance in the learning process

Core Elements

- Briefing content tailored to manager level and team context
- Summary of course purpose, duration, and expected learner outcomes
- Explanation of how learning links to performance goals
- Tools or templates to support post-course reinforcement
- Timeline or rollout calendar for reference
- Contact details for support or escalation
- Messaging aligned with internal change or capability priorities
- Documentation of participation or acknowledgement

Facilitator and Manager Briefing
Provide Manager Awareness Briefings

Checklist

1. Identify which managers require briefings and their role in learning transfer
2. Develop briefing materials: slides, summaries, videos, or talking points
3. Schedule briefing sessions or share recordings as appropriate
4. Align messaging with organisational goals and manager priorities
5. Include reinforcement strategies and post-training expectations
6. Provide access to relevant learning materials or guides
7. Capture manager questions and clarify support structures
8. Confirm understanding and follow up as needed

AI Considerations

- Use AI to summarise course materials into manager-ready briefing documents
- Generate tailored coaching prompts or action plans for each department
- Track manager engagement with video briefings and follow-up materials
- Analyse manager feedback through sentiment detection
- Automate delivery of post-course reinforcement reminders to managers

Key Takeaways

Providing manager awareness briefings is essential for bridging the gap between training and workplace performance.

These sessions ensure that managers understand the course objectives, support expected behaviour changes and reinforce learning in daily operations.

When managers are well-briefed, they become advocates for the learning program, helping their teams apply new skills and maintain momentum long after the training session ends.

Their involvement drives accountability, supports culture change, and turns learning into sustained impact across the organisation.

Distribute Support Materials

Why this is important

Support materials are essential tools that empower facilitators and managers to deliver and reinforce the course with confidence, precision, and consistency.

Even experienced facilitators can benefit from having key information at their fingertips during live sessions.

Quick-reference guides, job aids, and escalation protocols reduce reliance on memory and help standardise delivery across different locations or teams.

These resources also act as a safety net, allowing facilitators to troubleshoot issues on the spot and respond to learner questions accurately.

For managers, support materials serve as follow-up aids, helping them integrate learning into daily work practices.

Distributing these materials in advance builds readiness, reduces implementation errors, and supports a smoother rollout overall.

Tips

- Keep materials short, clear, and easy to navigate under pressure
- Use visuals and step-by-step formatting where possible
- Include both print-ready and digital versions for accessibility
- Version-control all documents to avoid outdated information
- Share access links in multiple formats (email, LMS, shared drive)
- Highlight escalation contacts clearly and keep them up to date
- Include a one-page "At a Glance" summary for quick orientation
- Pilot the materials with a small group and refine before full release

Traps

- Overloading users with too many documents or excessive detail
- Burying key instructions in dense or overly formal language
- Failing to update materials as the course evolves
- Not clarifying how and when to use each support item
- Forgetting to address online and offline use cases
- Distributing materials too late for proper review or practice
- Missing the opportunity to collect improvement suggestions

Techniques

- Create laminated job aids for classroom or field use
- Use iconography and colour-coding for quick scanning
- Build FAQs into cheat sheets based on pilot feedback
- Embed QR codes in facilitator guides linking to troubleshooting videos
- Develop role-specific support packs (e.g., one for facilitators, another for managers)
- Include hyperlinks in digital PDFs for fast navigation and cross-referencing

Facilitator and Manager Briefing
Distribute Support Materials

Examples

- ***Facilitator Quick-Reference Guide***:
  One-page overview of session timing, key transitions, and reminders on how to handle common learner questions.
- ***Job Aid for LMS Navigation***:
  Step-by-step screenshots showing how to launch modules, mark attendance, and access learner progress reports.
- ***Cheat Sheet for Virtual Delivery***:
  Tips for using breakout rooms, polls, and chat moderation in Zoom or MS Teams.
- ***Escalation Protocol Card***:
  Contact flow for reporting content issues, platform failures, or learner incidents, including after-hours support options.
- ***Manager Follow-Up Guide***:
  Brief checklist for reinforcing learning through coaching questions and workflow reminders.

How it's done

- Identify what materials are needed by facilitators and managers for successful delivery and follow-up
- Draft concise, user-friendly documents using plain language and clear formatting
- Use a consistent template and naming convention across all materials
- Test the materials with a small group and incorporate their feedback
- Finalise version control and ensure all documents are current and accessible
- Share materials via multiple channels, such as email, shared drives, or LMS portals
- Provide brief orientation on how and when to use each item
- Set up a feedback loop for ongoing improvements to support resources

Core Elements

- Quick-reference materials prepared and clearly formatted
- Separate guides for facilitators and managers
- Key delivery and troubleshooting tips included
- Escalation protocols documented and accessible
- Delivery tools aligned with course delivery mode (ILT or online)
- Version-controlled documents stored centrally
- Support materials distributed in advance of deployment
- Usage guidelines or walkthrough provided

Facilitator and Manager Briefing
Distribute Support Materials

Checklist

1. List all roles requiring support resources (e.g., facilitator, manager, admin)
2. Create or update job aids, guides, cheat sheets, and escalation protocols
3. Apply version control and document owner details
4. Format materials for ease of use in real-time scenarios
5. Review for clarity, accuracy, and alignment with the course
6. Test usability with a sample group and gather feedback
7. Upload materials to accessible, centralised storage (LMS, intranet, shared drive)
8. Communicate where to find materials and how to use them
9. Set up feedback collection mechanism for future iterations
10. Confirm distribution to all required personnel before launch

AI Considerations

- Auto-generate facilitator guides or cheat sheets using AI templates
- Translate materials into multiple languages using AI localisation tools
- Use AI to suggest content summaries or icons for visual guides
- Analyse facilitator queries to improve or expand support materials
- Tag common issues during delivery for automated future updates

Key Takeaways

Distributing well-designed support materials ensures that facilitators and managers can deliver and reinforce the course with consistency and confidence.

These resources help bridge the gap between training intent and practical execution, allowing for better real-time decision-making and reduced cognitive load.

From checklists to escalation contacts, support materials create a safety net and standardise quality across delivery environments.

Providing them in advance and in usable formats strengthens implementation readiness and improves both facilitator and learner outcomes.

Clarify Roles and Expectations

 **Why this is important**	Clarity of roles and expectations is essential for ensuring that everyone involved in the learning rollout knows their responsibilities and understands how their actions contribute to the success of the course. Without clear role definitions, confusion, delays, duplicated effort, or missed tasks can easily occur. This is especially true in cascading delivery models or train-the-trainer scenarios, where responsibilities multiply across layers. Clearly defining who is accountable for delivery, facilitation, learner support, performance follow-up, and reporting helps streamline operations and build trust across the team. When expectations are clear, people feel more confident, prepared, and aligned with the intended learning outcomes. This clarity also promotes consistency in delivery and enables faster issue resolution throughout implementation.
 **Tips**	• Use role matrices or RACI charts to document responsibilities • Communicate expectations both verbally and in writing • Align roles with the course delivery timeline and milestones • Involve stakeholders in defining their own expectations for buy-in • Make space for Q&A to clarify any grey areas or overlaps • Reinforce responsibilities during briefings and check-ins • Provide "who to contact" lists for each course element • Ensure clarity on pre-course, during-course, and post-course responsibilities
 **Traps**	• Assuming roles are already understood based on job titles • Providing vague or overly general instructions • Not addressing role expectations for post-course support and follow-up • Allowing overlapping responsibilities without ownership • Neglecting to define who manages feedback loops or reporting • Omitting escalation protocols for breakdowns in accountability
 **Techniques**	• Develop a simple one-page role and responsibility summary for each stakeholder group • Use briefing sessions to walk through the implementation workflow and assignments • Introduce RACI models (Responsible, Accountable, Consulted, Informed) to clarify who does what • Create scenario-based role discussions to pre-empt confusion • Assign a point of contact or course coordinator to manage queries and role clarification • Share real-world examples of what success looks like for each role

Facilitator and Manager Briefing
Clarify Roles and Expectations

Examples

- ***Facilitator Role Summary***:
  Deliver course sessions, encourage participation, manage technical delivery, report attendance, and log learner issues.
- ***Manager Role Summary***:
  Brief team before the course, reinforce key messages afterwards, and monitor behavioural change.
- ***L&D Coordinator Role***:
  Ensure facilitator readiness, manage material distribution, gather feedback, and escalate technical issues.
- ***SME Role***:
  Review content for accuracy pre-launch, support facilitators during delivery, and assist with learner Q&A if required.
- ***Learner Role Expectations***:
  Complete pre-work, engage actively during sessions, and apply learning in the workplace with follow-up check-ins.

How it's done

- Identify all individuals and groups involved in course delivery and support
- Map out the full implementation workflow, including handoffs and dependencies
- Define tasks and expectations clearly for each role, using plain language
- Create documentation such as a role matrix, one-pagers, or flowcharts
- Review responsibilities with each group during briefings or training
- Reinforce accountability by connecting roles to course success metrics
- Clarify escalation procedures and who is responsible for what at each stage
- Gather feedback to identify and address any ambiguity before launch

Core Elements

- All roles involved in delivery and support are identified
- Expectations documented for each role in clear, practical terms
- Responsibilities mapped across pre-, during-, and post-course stages
- Accountability structures defined (e.g., RACI or lead contact lists)
- Briefings conducted to explain and confirm role understanding
- Support tools provided, such as responsibility summaries or flowcharts
- Escalation and feedback protocols outlined
- Role clarity validated through feedback or sign-off

Facilitator and Manager Briefing
Clarify Roles and Expectations

Checklist

1. List all roles involved in the implementation (facilitators, managers, SMEs, coordinators)
2. Define responsibilities for each phase: before, during, and after delivery
3. Draft a clear responsibilities summary or RACI model
4. Validate with stakeholders that responsibilities are accurate and feasible
5. Review role expectations during briefings or onboarding
6. Distribute responsibility documents via shared platform or email
7. Clarify escalation paths for issues or role confusion
8. Confirm role clarity with a short survey, sign-off, or verbal confirmation
9. Document any suggested refinements for future rollouts

AI Considerations

- Auto-generate role summaries from project plans or delivery schedules
- Use AI to suggest role assignments based on workload or experience
- Analyse historical delivery data to flag role ambiguity or task overlap
- Set up AI chatbots to answer role-related queries in real time
- Use AI to monitor task completion and notify owners of pending responsibilities

Key Takeaways

Clarifying roles and expectations ensures that every stakeholder knows what to do, when to do it, and how to do it well.

This reduces ambiguity, boosts efficiency, and ensures consistency across course delivery.

Whether using a centralised or cascading model, role clarity is a critical success factor in avoiding breakdowns and bottlenecks.

When everyone understands their part in the process, the entire implementation becomes smoother, more collaborative, and more impactful.

Capture Pre-launch Feedback from Facilitators

Why this is important

Capturing pre-launch feedback from facilitators is a vital quality checkpoint before course deployment.

Facilitators are uniquely positioned to identify potential issues that others may overlook, such as unclear instructions, technical glitches, inconsistent content, or unrealistic delivery expectations.

Because they engage directly with the materials and platforms during training, their perspective often highlights risks, misunderstandings, or improvement opportunities that need attention before rollout.

This feedback loop also empowers facilitators by giving them a voice in the implementation process, increasing ownership and engagement.

Addressing issues proactively at this stage can prevent disruption during live sessions, reduce support burden, and enhance the overall learner experience.

Tips

- Schedule feedback sessions shortly after facilitator training while details are still fresh
- Use structured forms or checklists to guide input and keep it actionable
- Encourage facilitators to speak candidly without fear of judgement
- Provide both group and one-on-one feedback opportunities
- Focus feedback on readiness, usability, and clarity, not personal preference
- Capture both what works well and what could be improved
- Document all feedback and responses transparently
- Close the loop by informing facilitators which suggestions were actioned

Traps

- Collecting feedback too late to implement meaningful changes
- Ignoring facilitator feedback because of time constraints or rollout pressure
- Failing to distinguish between critical issues and nice-to-haves
- Allowing unstructured or vague feedback that lacks actionability
- Not validating whether feedback applies across all sessions or just isolated cases
- Overcorrecting based on a single facilitator's experience or style

Techniques

- Use digital surveys with scaled questions and open-text fields
- Host facilitated debrief sessions with key delivery staff
- Create a shared comment log or collaborative feedback document
- Review common feedback themes using affinity grouping
- Conduct informal "readiness check-ins" post-training
- Ask facilitators to rate their confidence on delivery elements to flag weak areas

Facilitator and Manager Briefing
Capture Pre-launch Feedback from Facilitators

Examples

- ***Readiness Survey***:
  After training, facilitators complete a short survey rating their confidence in content mastery, platform navigation, and learner engagement strategies.
- ***Live Debrief Workshop***:
  A 30-minute session is held where facilitators share what felt smooth and what could cause confusion. Responses are clustered into themes.
- ***Feedback Log with Tags***:
  Facilitators submit observations into a shared spreadsheet, using tags like "content," "technical," or "timing" for easy sorting.
- ***Escalation Flag***:
  A facilitator raises a concern about a quiz question that contradicts content in the previous module, prompting a last-minute fix.
- ***Suggestion Loop***:
  A facilitator recommends an alternative intro activity, which is adopted into the standard delivery format.

How it's done

- Schedule feedback capture immediately following facilitator training sessions
- Develop a structured feedback form or digital survey to collect consistent data
- Invite facilitators to flag concerns, suggestions, or uncertainties they encountered
- Organise live or virtual group debrief sessions for verbal feedback and discussion
- Aggregate feedback and identify recurring issues or high-impact themes
- Prioritise changes based on feasibility, urgency, and alignment with learning goals
- Action critical updates and confirm resolution with facilitators
- Communicate final rollout decisions and clarify what changes were made or deferred

Core Elements

- Feedback process scheduled and communicated in advance
- Structured tools developed to collect focused facilitator input
- Live debriefs or survey sessions conducted
- Common themes analysed for urgency and impact
- Key updates implemented based on facilitator insights
- Non-actioned suggestions documented with rationale
- Final rollout version adjusted accordingly
- Feedback loop closed with communication to all facilitators

Facilitator and Manager Briefing
Capture Pre-launch Feedback from Facilitators

Checklist

1. Schedule post-training facilitator feedback collection sessions
2. Prepare structured tools for gathering input (surveys, logs, forms)
3. Provide clear guidance on what kind of feedback is helpful
4. Collect both strengths and challenges noted by facilitators
5. Identify patterns across responses using thematic analysis
6. Prioritise urgent issues requiring pre-launch attention
7. Make final adjustments to materials, instructions, or delivery flow
8. Communicate what changes were made in response to feedback
9. Thank facilitators for their contributions and confirm readiness
10. Document unresolved items for post-launch review

AI Considerations

- Use AI to summarise open-text responses and detect recurring issues
- Tag feedback by topic automatically (e.g., navigation, timing, clarity)
- Prioritise high-impact suggestions using sentiment analysis or frequency counts
- Cluster similar concerns to streamline action planning
- Track resolution status of each piece of feedback with AI-powered dashboards

Key Takeaways

Capturing pre-launch feedback from facilitators helps surface risks, confusion points, and enhancement opportunities while there's still time to act.

Their hands-on interaction with the course content and delivery environment gives them a unique perspective that can prevent small issues from becoming major rollout problems.

This step not only improves course quality and delivery confidence but also reinforces a culture of collaboration and shared ownership.

When facilitators feel heard and supported, they are more likely to engage fully and deliver the learning experience with clarity, energy, and precision.

Change Management Enablement

The **Change Management Enablement** step in the Implementation phase of the ADDIE model ensures that the learning initiative is not only delivered but adopted and sustained within the organisation. This step addresses the human side of implementation by preparing, equipping, and supporting individuals and teams to embrace behavioural and performance changes that the course is designed to produce. Without effective change enablement, even the most well-crafted learning experiences risk being forgotten, ignored, or undermined by competing priorities.

This step begins by engaging key stakeholders in strategic communication planning to promote understanding and buy-in. A tailored communication toolkit is developed to support consistent messaging across leadership and operational levels. The learning initiative is then aligned with broader organisational goals, ongoing projects, and success metrics to ensure relevance and support. Post-deployment, a reinforcement strategy is activated to embed learning into day-to-day practices. Finally, feedback loops are established to monitor uptake, gather insight, and drive continuous engagement well beyond launch.

Key Sub-Steps are:

- **Engage Key Stakeholders in Communication Planning**
  Collaborate with leaders and influencers to develop messaging strategies that promote alignment and readiness.

- **Develop and Share Change Communication Toolkit**
  Create practical tools such as email templates, briefing notes, posters, and talking points to support consistent and widespread communication.

- **Align with Existing Initiatives and Metrics**
  Position the learning within the context of current organisational priorities to increase visibility and perceived value.

- **Reinforce Strategy Post-Deployment**
  Maintain momentum through nudges, reminders, and manager-led follow-up to strengthen application and retention.

- **Create Feedback Loops for Ongoing Engagement**
  Capture learner sentiment, monitor behavioural outcomes, and adjust communications and support strategies based on real-time feedback.

Overview

Change Management Enablement
Capture Pre-launch Feedback from Facilitators

Outcomes

The outcomes of the *Change Management Enablement* step are to increase learner adoption, reduce resistance, and foster long-term behavioural change.

Key outcomes include:

- **Stakeholder Alignment**
  Senior leaders and managers are actively engaged in supporting and communicating the learning initiative.
- **Message Consistency**
  Learners receive clear, timely, and aligned communications that clarify the value and purpose of the training.
- **Strategic Integration**
  The learning is positioned alongside existing organisational priorities, increasing its relevance and likelihood of uptake.
- **Post-Launch Reinforcement**
  Follow-up communications and engagement tactics help sustain learner motivation and support knowledge transfer.
- **Dynamic Feedback Loops**
  Mechanisms are in place to gather ongoing feedback, monitor progress, and adapt support strategies as needed.

Summary

The **Change Management Enablement** step ensures that learning does not stop at delivery but is carried through into practice. It shifts the focus from "training as an event" to "learning as transformation."

Through strategic communications, stakeholder engagement, and sustained reinforcement, this step builds the organisational commitment needed for meaningful change.

By integrating the course with broader initiatives and metrics, and by capturing real-time feedback from the field, instructional designers can proactively support learners and adapt to emerging needs.

The result is increased engagement, improved performance, and a stronger return on investment for the learning initiative.

Change Management Enablement
Engage Key Stakeholders in Communication Planning

Engage Key Stakeholders in Communication Planning

Why this is important

Engaging key stakeholders in communication planning ensures that learning initiatives are visibly championed, strategically aligned, and well-supported from the top down.

When leaders, sponsors, and influencers are actively involved in shaping how the course is positioned and discussed, it builds credibility and accelerates adoption.

Their input helps tailor messaging to resonate with different audiences, anticipate potential resistance, and coordinate timing with other organisational priorities.

This step also promotes a unified voice across all communication channels, reducing mixed messages and confusion.

By co-designing the communication plan with those who hold influence, you embed ownership and secure the leadership advocacy essential to successful change.

Tips

- Identify both formal and informal influencers across departments
- Brief stakeholders early on the course objectives and change rationale
- Involve them in crafting key messages to ensure authenticity
- Align communication with current business priorities or concerns
- Use simple visual frameworks to show how learning supports performance goals
- Ask leaders to record short videos or quotes to personalise the message
- Reinforce their role as champions, not just approvers
- Document and share the agreed communication cadence and channels

Traps

- Treating communication as an afterthought instead of a strategic enabler
- Assuming stakeholders will automatically support the initiative
- Relying too heavily on email without personal engagement
- Using overly generic language that lacks relevance for specific audiences
- Allowing siloed messaging across departments
- Failing to confirm leadership availability for key communication touchpoints

Techniques

- Stakeholder mapping to identify influence and communication roles
- Communication planning workshops or huddles to align messaging
- Joint drafting of emails, launch announcements, or video scripts
- Message testing with small groups to check for clarity and resonance
- Use of briefing packs with talking points and rollout timelines
- Storyboarding a sample communication cascade across levels and channels

Change Management Enablement
Engage Key Stakeholders in Communication Planning

Examples

- **Executive Briefing Session**:
  A one-hour meeting with senior leaders where the L&D team presents course outcomes and co-develops key talking points for launch.
- **Department Champion Strategy**:
  Mid-level managers and influencers are assigned as internal champions and consulted on communication preferences and timing.
- **Stakeholder Input Roundtable**:
  SMEs and operational leads meet to identify potential barriers and fine-tune the tone and timing of internal messaging.
- **Shared Communication Calendar**:
  All stakeholder contributors work from a centralised plan showing message dates, channels, and responsibilities.
- **Leadership Endorsement Video**:
  A senior executive records a 90-second video explaining the importance of the training and encouraging team participation.

How it's done

- Identify stakeholders with influence over course success, including executives, sponsors, and line managers
- Schedule early engagement sessions to explain the purpose and potential impact of the training
- Collaboratively develop communication goals, target audiences, and messaging pillars
- Draft communication assets such as talking points, briefing notes, or introductory videos with stakeholder input
- Validate messaging tone and alignment with current organisational priorities
- Assign communication roles and responsibilities across the stakeholder group
- Consolidate all inputs into a formalised communication plan
- Share the plan with relevant teams and integrate it into the broader implementation timeline

Core Elements

- Stakeholder engagement sessions scheduled and conducted
- Key audiences and influencers mapped
- Communication goals and strategies agreed
- Messaging reviewed and endorsed by stakeholders
- Launch talking points, emails, and templates drafted
- Communication roles defined and assigned
- Communication plan documented and distributed
- Timeline integrated with implementation milestones

Change Management Enablement
Engage Key Stakeholders in Communication Planning

Checklist

1. Identify all key stakeholders across business units, support teams, and leadership
2. Map their influence level and preferred communication role
3. Schedule and conduct stakeholder briefings and planning workshops
4. Co-create key messages, tone, and delivery approach
5. Develop communication artefacts (scripts, emails, toolkits)
6. Validate messaging alignment with strategic objectives
7. Assign roles for who communicates what and when
8. Finalise and distribute the communication plan
9. Coordinate with other departments for timing and visibility
10. Monitor initial engagement and adjust the plan if needed

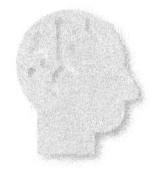

AI Considerations

- Use AI to generate draft stakeholder messages tailored to different audiences
- Analyse past stakeholder communication patterns to optimise channel and timing
- Automate stakeholder mapping and influence scoring
- Use AI to summarise stakeholder feedback or objections for planning purposes
- Apply predictive analytics to identify where stakeholder buy-in may be weak

Key Takeaways

Engaging key stakeholders in communication planning is foundational to successful learning adoption.

It builds shared ownership, strengthens leadership advocacy, and ensures communication is timely, relevant, and aligned with business priorities.

When stakeholders contribute to shaping the message, they become active champions rather than passive bystanders.

This collaborative planning process enables better anticipation of resistance, promotes transparency, and ensures that the right messages reach the right people in the right way.

Develop and Share Change Communication Toolkit

Why this is important

A well-designed change communication toolkit empowers stakeholders to deliver consistent, accurate, and engaging messages that support the learning initiative.

It removes the burden of creating communications from scratch and ensures that all materials align with the course's goals, tone, and branding.

By supplying tools such as email templates, intranet blurbs, posters, and talking points, the toolkit enables leaders, managers, and internal communicators to promote the course confidently and efficiently.

It also standardises how the training is presented across the organisation, increasing clarity and reinforcing the course's relevance.

When these materials are shared in advance and tailored to audience needs, they strengthen buy-in, reduce resistance, and enhance learner engagement at every touchpoint.

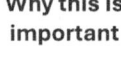

Tips

- Keep messaging clear, action-oriented, and jargon-free
- Create short, medium, and long versions of key messages for different formats
- Use visual elements and branding consistent with course materials
- Include a "plug-and-play" section with editable templates
- Provide guidance on when and how to use each item in the toolkit
- Include contact information for queries or troubleshooting
- Make the toolkit available in multiple formats (PDF, editable Word, intranet page)
- Co-brand with leadership quotes or departmental logos for added credibility

Traps

- Assuming one-size-fits-all messaging will resonate across all departments
- Overloading the toolkit with too many options or overly complex materials
- Providing materials without guidance on timing or distribution
- Forgetting to align tone with organisational culture or current priorities
- Not updating the toolkit if course details evolve pre-launch
- Limiting access to only a few roles or locations

Techniques

- Develop a messaging framework that outlines key themes and desired actions
- Design visual assets like banners, posters, or digital slides for internal displays
- Include pre-written launch emails, calendar blurbs, and newsletter snippets
- Draft FAQs that anticipate learner concerns or questions
- Create a short internal comms guide explaining when and how to deploy each resource
- Localise toolkit assets for different regions or business units where needed

Change Management Enablement
Develop and Share Change Communication Toolkit

Examples

- **Launch Email Template**:
  A ready-to-send message for line managers to introduce the course, highlight relevance, and encourage participation.
- **Intranet Blurb**:
  A 150-word announcement summarising what the course is, who it's for, and where to access it, accompanied by a hero image.
- **Poster Design**:
  Visually engaging printable posters featuring course benefits, deadlines, and a QR code linking to the LMS.
- **Leadership Talking Points**:
  Short scripts for executives or sponsors to speak confidently about the initiative at team meetings or town halls.
- **Change Announcement Kit**:
  A zip folder with editable assets for different platforms and user roles, complete with instructions for use.

How it's done

- Collaborate with internal communications or branding teams to define tone and voice
- Draft core messages that explain the course purpose, timing, and benefits
- Build a structured toolkit with templates and assets for different channels
- Include editable formats and usage guidelines for each component
- Design visual materials in line with organisational branding standards
- Test key materials with a pilot audience for clarity and impact
- Upload the toolkit to a shared location with clear instructions for access
- Notify stakeholders and champions of availability and walk them through the contents

Core Elements

- Messaging framework aligned with course goals and learner needs
- Email and meeting templates for leaders, managers, and L&D teams
- Digital assets for intranet, newsletters, and screensavers
- Printable materials such as posters, tent cards, or flyers
- FAQ and talking point documents for consistency in language
- Guidelines for when and how to use each communication item
- Toolkit version-controlled and centrally stored
- Distribution plan in place for stakeholder access

Change Management Enablement
Develop and Share Change Communication Toolkit

Checklist

1. Define core course messages and align with business tone
2. Draft communication templates for different channels and audiences
3. Design visual assets with consistent branding and formatting
4. Include editable versions for customisation by teams or regions
5. Write usage instructions for each item in the toolkit
6. Review with internal comms or key stakeholders for feedback
7. Test toolkit clarity and relevance with a small group
8. Upload final version to shared platform with clear navigation
9. Notify stakeholders and champions of availability
10. Update toolkit if course scope or details change before launch

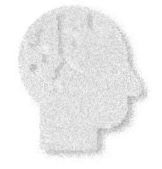
AI Considerations

- Use AI to generate draft communication templates tailored to different roles
- Translate toolkit content for multilingual audiences with AI localisation tools
- Analyse engagement with toolkit items (e.g., email opens, poster downloads)
- Generate visual content options using AI image tools for digital assets
- Summarise toolkit materials into short reminders or leadership talking points

Key Takeaways

Developing and sharing a change communication toolkit ensures that every stakeholder can confidently and consistently promote the learning initiative.

These materials bridge the gap between strategy and execution, allowing leaders, managers, and support teams to communicate with clarity and credibility.

By aligning messaging with course goals and organisational culture, and by offering user-friendly formats for various channels, the toolkit boosts visibility, reinforces purpose, and reduces communication fatigue.

It becomes a practical lever for accelerating adoption and embedding learning in the flow of work.

Align with Existing Initiatives and Metrics

Why this is important

Aligning the course with existing organisational initiatives and metrics ensures that it is not seen as a stand-alone effort but as a strategic contributor to broader business goals.

This alignment increases relevance for both learners and leaders, helping them understand how the training fits into priorities such as safety, diversity and inclusion, digital transformation, or performance optimisation.

By mapping course outcomes to current initiatives, you build momentum, reduce resistance, and leverage existing communication and reporting frameworks.

Additionally, linking the training to measurable success criteria reinforces accountability and allows the impact of learning to be tracked and demonstrated over time.

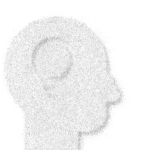

Tips

- Identify key organisational initiatives already underway that align with the course objectives
- Use familiar language and metrics from other projects to frame course outcomes
- Consult business leaders to understand what success looks like in their context
- Integrate course metrics into existing dashboards or reporting structures where possible
- Highlight how the training fills known capability or compliance gaps
- Show connections to other recent learning, change, or performance programs
- Reinforce this alignment in communications and course materials
- Ensure metrics track both engagement (e.g. participation) and outcomes (e.g. behaviour change)

Traps

- Designing training in isolation from broader business strategies
- Using generic or abstract metrics that are hard to measure or relate to
- Failing to tailor alignment messaging to specific departments or functions
- Treating alignment as a communications afterthought rather than a design input
- Over-promising impact without follow-through or measurement capability
- Ignoring cultural or regional variations in how initiatives are received

Techniques

- Use a goal mapping tool to visually align course objectives with strategic priorities
- Include a section in the course overview that links each module to business initiatives
- Interview initiative leads to understand where the training can support their goals
- Create a metrics matrix showing what will be measured, how, and when
- Use pilot data or SME input to select realistic indicators of behavioural change
- Include success stories from similar initiatives to build credibility

Change Management Enablement
Align with Existing Initiatives and Metrics

Examples

- **Safety Alignment**:
  A frontline safety training program is explicitly mapped to the company's "Zero Harm" initiative, with reporting integrated into monthly safety briefings.
- **Inclusion Focus**:
  A leadership development course embeds inclusive language and cultural awareness content that supports the broader Diversity, Equity, and Inclusion strategy.
- **Agile Transformation**:
  A change-readiness course is aligned with the rollout of agile work practices and measured through feedback on sprint planning participation.
- **Digital Uplift**:
  Training on a new software tool is tied to the digital transformation roadmap and evaluated using digital adoption metrics.
- **Customer Centricity**:
  A course on empathetic communication links directly to NPS (Net Promoter Score) improvement goals and customer service KPIs.

How it's done

- Review the organisation's strategic plan and key current initiatives
- Identify where the course objectives overlap with business goals or capability frameworks
- Consult initiative owners to confirm alignment opportunities and shared success criteria
- Develop a messaging map that explicitly connects learning outcomes with known priorities
- Integrate relevant language, goals, or metrics into course content and support materials
- Determine which existing dashboards or scorecards can include training metrics
- Share alignment visuals or infographics with stakeholders and learners
- Build alignment into post-course reporting and evaluation discussions

Core Elements

- Course objectives mapped to strategic initiatives and cultural drivers
- Initiative owners consulted and alignment confirmed
- Shared success metrics identified and documented
- Messaging aligned with current organisational language and themes
- Course materials updated to reflect alignment
- Reporting pathways established for shared metrics
- Stakeholders informed of alignment and measurement plans
- Impact tracking embedded into evaluation strategy

Change Management Enablement
Align with Existing Initiatives and Metrics

Checklist

1. Identify active organisational initiatives relevant to the course
2. Consult leaders or initiative owners for strategic alignment opportunities
3. Map course goals to existing business outcomes or transformation plans
4. Align course terminology with business language and culture
5. Define what success looks like for each area of alignment
6. Select measurable indicators to track course impact
7. Integrate metrics into reporting dashboards or post-course evaluations
8. Communicate the alignment clearly to both stakeholders and learners
9. Capture anecdotal evidence or success stories post-deployment
10. Review alignment impact periodically and update as initiatives evolve

AI Considerations

- Use AI to scan company initiatives, annual reports, or intranet content for alignment themes
- Automatically generate a mapping matrix between course outcomes and strategic priorities
- Suggest relevant metrics based on historical course performance and business KPIs
- Analyse post-course data for alignment impact across departments or roles
- Track language usage and sentiment in learner feedback to assess alignment effectiveness

Key Takeaways

Aligning the course with existing initiatives and success metrics helps it gain traction, visibility, and value across the organisation.

It signals that the training is not just a compliance task but a meaningful contribution to broader strategic goals.

When learners and leaders see the connection between training and outcomes that matter to them, whether safety, digital adoption, inclusion, or performance, engagement improves, and resistance drops.

This alignment also makes it easier to track impact, prove value, and sustain learning over time as part of an integrated transformation effort.

Reinforcement Strategy Post-Deployment

 **Why this is important**	Reinforcement after deployment is essential for embedding learning into daily habits and sustaining behaviour change over time. While initial training builds awareness and capability, it is the post-course nudges, prompts, and engagement activities that help learners retain and apply what they've learnt. Without reinforcement, knowledge fades, momentum slows, and the training risks becoming a forgotten event rather than a catalyst for change. This sub-step ensures that learning is not only retained but translated into consistent action. Through micro-interventions like refreshers, gamified challenges, and just-in-time reminders, the strategy keeps the learning alive, relevant, and part of the workflow, long after the course concludes.
 **Tips**	• Plan reinforcement activities at the time of course design, not as an afterthought • Use multiple channels (email, intranet, SMS, chat) to sustain visibility • Keep reinforcement short, engaging, and closely tied to real work scenarios • Involve line managers in follow-up conversations or coaching • Introduce spaced repetition and application prompts to aid retention • Use friendly, informal tone in nudges to avoid "training fatigue" • Track which reinforcement methods are most effective • Refresh content regularly to maintain interest and relevance
 **Traps**	• Assuming a single training session is enough to change long-term behaviour • Failing to include reinforcement in the project scope or budget • Over-relying on generic email reminders without personalisation • Launching too many reinforcement messages at once, causing overload • Ignoring the importance of social recognition or peer engagement • Not measuring the impact of reinforcement on behaviour or performance
 **Techniques**	• Schedule automated nudges through LMS or internal messaging tools • Create short refresher quizzes or microlearning modules • Send weekly "Did You Know?" tips or reminders tied to course content • Launch mini-challenges or scenario-based tasks with leaderboards • Use digital badges or reward systems to encourage engagement • Develop quick team activities for use in stand-ups or toolbox talks • Encourage peer sharing of success stories or application wins

Change Management Enablement
Reinforcement Strategy Post-Deployment

Examples

- **Weekly Micro-Tips**:
  Learners receive a short reminder with a tip or reflection question aligned to the course theme every Monday for four weeks.
- **Gamified Challenges**:
  Learners complete a scenario-based task and earn points or badges that appear on a leaderboard visible to their team.
- **Manager-Led Check-In**:
  One week post-course, managers receive a prompt with discussion questions to ask during team meetings.
- **"One Thing" Tracker**:
  Learners are asked to commit to one behavioural change and receive follow-up messages to check progress.
- **Video Refreshers**:
  Short 2-minute video clips recap key points from the training and suggest practical applications.

How it's done

- Define reinforcement goals based on the behaviours or knowledge you want to sustain
- Select delivery channels suited to your audience's preferences and work environment
- Develop a reinforcement calendar outlining timing and format of each activity
- Create lightweight, engaging content such as tips, quizzes, challenges, or video clips
- Involve managers by providing them with coaching prompts or follow-up templates
- Schedule automated or recurring delivery of reinforcement elements
- Monitor participation and collect feedback to adjust future reinforcement
- Recognise learners who engage with follow-ups to build momentum and visibility

Core Elements

- Reinforcement strategy mapped to learning objectives
- Content created for microlearning, nudges, or gamified engagement
- Delivery methods selected and tested (email, LMS, chat, in-person)
- Calendar of post-deployment activities established
- Manager engagement prompts or support packs developed
- Participation tracked and reviewed for optimisation
- Feedback mechanisms in place for learner input
- Recognition or rewards aligned with engagement milestones

Checklist

1. Define reinforcement goals tied to course outcomes or behaviours
2. Choose formats that suit your learners (e.g. videos, nudges, quizzes)
3. Build a content calendar for at least 4–6 weeks post-course
4. Develop or source reinforcement materials and tools
5. Automate delivery where possible to ensure consistency
6. Involve managers in planned follow-up conversations or actions
7. Track learner participation, responses, and engagement
8. Refresh or rotate content periodically to maintain interest
9. Recognise or reward participation where appropriate
10. Evaluate the impact of reinforcement on retention and behaviour change

Change Management Enablement
Reinforcement Strategy Post-Deployment

AI Considerations

- Use AI to personalise nudges based on learner performance or role
- Schedule reinforcement touchpoints automatically across multiple channels
- Generate adaptive quizzes or content based on previous learner responses
- Analyse engagement data to identify patterns or drop-off points
- Apply natural language generation to write friendly, on-brand nudges at scale

Key Takeaways

Reinforcement is what turns learning from an isolated event into lasting behaviour change.

It ensures that the course stays top-of-mind and that learners are supported as they apply new skills in the workplace.

Through timely nudges, practical refreshers, and engaging micro-challenges, this step extends the value of training and strengthens retention.

By building reinforcement into the learning plan from the outset and aligning it with the learner's real-world context, you create a supportive ecosystem that sustains change and drives impact.

Create Feedback Loops for Ongoing Engagement

Why this is important

Creating feedback loops for ongoing engagement ensures that the learning initiative remains dynamic, responsive, and connected to real outcomes.

After deployment, it is easy for momentum to fade and for learners to move on without reflecting on what they've gained or applied.

Feedback loops keep the conversation alive by inviting learners, managers, and stakeholders to share their experiences, challenges, and success stories.

These mechanisms not only uncover valuable insights for continuous improvement but also build a sense of community and reinforce the learning culture.

Whether through town halls, manager debriefs, social threads, or feedback forms, consistent and visible engagement shows learners that their input matters and that learning is part of a broader organisational dialogue.

Tips

- Choose feedback channels that suit your audience's preferences and workflows
- Use structured prompts to help learners and managers share useful insights
- Keep it informal and conversational to encourage honest participation
- Showcase stories of impact to inspire others and reinforce outcomes
- Close the loop by acknowledging feedback and communicating actions taken
- Balance synchronous (e.g. town halls) and asynchronous (e.g. online posts) methods
- Involve sponsors or leaders in feedback discussions to boost visibility
- Schedule regular touchpoints post-rollout to sustain engagement

Traps

- Treating feedback as a one-off survey instead of an ongoing process
- Asking vague or overly broad questions that generate unusable input
- Ignoring feedback or failing to respond with meaningful follow-up
- Overcomplicating the feedback process with too many platforms or forms
- Focusing only on issues instead of capturing positive stories and outcomes
- Assuming all feedback must be formal or quantified to be useful

Techniques

- Host monthly town halls or online forums to share wins and challenges
- Set up team-level debriefs where managers ask structured post-training questions
- Use social platforms (e.g. Yammer, Teams) to encourage sharing and discussion
- Launch a "Share Your Impact" campaign with recognition for stories submitted
- Rotate short pulse surveys to measure evolving attitudes and learning application
- Establish a feedback mailbox or form that learners can use at any time

Change Management Enablement
Create Feedback Loops for Ongoing Engagement

Examples

- *Manager Debrief Pack*:
  Managers receive a guide with reflection questions to ask their teams during routine check-ins, focusing on learning application.
- *Yammer Discussion Thread*:
  A dedicated channel is created for learners to post how they've applied what they learnt, with likes and comments to build momentum.
- *Quarterly Learning Town Hall*:
  The L&D team hosts a session where learners share their stories and business leaders discuss how the training supports performance.
- *Impact Storyboard*:
  Learners submit brief case studies of changes they've made or results they've seen, which are displayed on the intranet or shared in newsletters.
- *Ongoing Pulse Survey*:
  A three-question survey is sent two months post-training to capture usage, challenges, and suggested improvements.

How it's done

- Identify appropriate feedback mechanisms for each audience segment (e.g. learners, facilitators, managers)
- Schedule ongoing feedback collection points well beyond course completion
- Develop toolkits or templates to help managers and teams share their experiences
- Use social or internal communication platforms to surface and celebrate stories of success
- Rotate discussion topics or prompts to keep engagement fresh
- Analyse feedback regularly and identify trends, gaps, or emerging needs
- Communicate what has been learnt from the feedback and any changes made
- Recognise contributions to encourage continued participation

Core Elements

- Feedback methods selected and implemented (town halls, debriefs, threads, surveys)
- Structured prompts or templates provided to guide discussions
- Channels of participation made visible and easy to access
- Schedule of engagement activities created and communicated
- Feedback analysed and shared with stakeholders
- Celebratory content published showcasing learner stories and impact
- Feedback response loop closed with visible action or acknowledgement
- Learner input integrated into future course iterations or support strategies

Change Management Enablement
Create Feedback Loops for Ongoing Engagement

Checklist

1. Choose 2–3 primary feedback mechanisms that suit your context
2. Design templates or guides to structure useful input (e.g. debrief packs, question sets)
3. Launch the first round of post-deployment engagement (town hall, post, survey)
4. Promote participation through leadership and internal communications
5. Monitor input and identify recurring themes or standout stories
6. Share feedback summaries with relevant teams or sponsors
7. Recognise contributors publicly to build momentum
8. Close the loop by showing how feedback informed changes
9. Refresh prompts or formats periodically to sustain interest
10. Document lessons learned for future learning projects

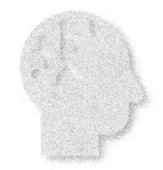
AI Considerations

- Use AI to analyse free-text feedback and identify themes or sentiment trends
- Auto-generate summaries of discussions from social platforms or debrief transcripts
- Recommend follow-up actions or content based on learner engagement patterns
- Use chatbots to gather quick feedback at scale in real time
- Cluster learner stories or suggestions into topic areas for targeted response

Key Takeaways

Creating feedback loops for ongoing engagement helps maintain energy and visibility around a learning initiative long after the initial deployment.

These mechanisms give learners and managers a voice, promote reflection, and reinforce the application of skills in the real world.

More than just a way to identify issues, feedback loops uncover success stories, reveal emerging needs, and contribute to a living, breathing learning culture.

When organisations listen, respond, and celebrate input, they send a clear message that learning is continuous, valued, and worth investing in.

Course Deployment

Overview

The **Course Deployment** step in the Implementation phase of the ADDIE model marks the culmination of all previous efforts, where the course is officially made available to the full learner audience. This step ensures that every component, content, media, assessments, and interactive elements, is functional, accessible, and aligned with quality standards.

Successful implementation involves careful coordination, thorough readiness checks, and proactive support to minimise issues and optimise the learner experience. Early monitoring post-launch allows instructional designers to address any immediate concerns and fine-tune the course for long-term success.

Key Sub-Steps are:

- **Go Live**
  Verify that all course elements meet quality, technical, and accessibility standards.

- **Establish Support Channels**
  Set up clear channels for technical and content-related support to assist learners and stakeholders during the launch phase.

Outcomes

The outcomes of the Final Launch step focus on ensuring a smooth deployment, maximising accessibility, and establishing ongoing support.

Key outcomes include:

- **Ensure Readiness for Deployment**
  Confirm that all course components are functional, aligned with objectives, and meet quality standards, including accessibility requirements.

- **Execute a Smooth Launch**
  Deploy the course with minimal technical or logistical disruptions, ensuring learners have immediate and seamless access.

- **Maximise Accessibility**
  Verify that the course complies with accessibility standards (e.g., WCAG), ensuring it accommodates diverse learner needs.

- **Monitor Early Engagement**
  Use analytics tools to collect initial feedback and performance data, enabling quick responses to any issues or trends.

- **Establish Support Systems**
  Provide well-defined support channels to resolve technical or content-related queries efficiently, ensuring a positive learner experience.

Summary

The **Final Launch** step is a critical phase where the instructional design project transitions from development to full-scale implementation. By thoroughly preparing for deployment, instructional designers can ensure a smooth rollout that meets quality and accessibility standards.

Proactive strategies, such as conducting a soft launch, using detailed Checklists, and setting up monitoring systems, help mitigate risks and ensure learners have a seamless experience. By addressing any immediate issues identified through early feedback and performance tracking, this step lays the foundation for a successful, impactful course.

Through careful planning, robust support systems, and ongoing monitoring, the Final Launch ensures that learners receive an engaging and effective educational experience, aligned with both instructional goals and organisational objectives.

Course Deployment
Go Live

Go Live

Why this is important

The Go Live moment is the transition point from course preparation to delivery, and it is critical that the learning experience is fully accessible to the intended audience.

This means ensuring all technical, media, and content components are functional, compatible, and inclusive.

A smooth launch requires meticulous attention to logistical, technical, and instructional details well before the go-live date, reducing the risk of disruptions or learner frustration.

First impressions matter, the course must engage learners from the outset with compelling content, intuitive navigation, and clear onboarding instructions.

Early feedback plays a crucial role in identifying issues quickly, so systems must be in place to monitor learner behaviour, satisfaction, and technical performance in real time.

Just as importantly, a robust support system must be activated to handle learner questions and resolve problems efficiently, ensuring confidence in the course and reducing resistance to engagement.

Tips

- **Conduct a Final System Check**
  Double-check all course elements, including links, media, assessments, and navigation, to ensure everything is functioning as intended.

- **Test Across Devices**
  Verify that the course performs well on all platforms and devices (desktop, tablet, mobile).

- **Communicate Clearly**
  Send clear instructions to learners about accessing the course, including login credentials, platform details, and support contact information.

- **Soft Launch First**
  Consider rolling out the course to a small, representative group of learners before full deployment to identify and fix any last-minute issues.

- **Prepare for High Traffic**
  Ensure the LMS or delivery platform can handle the expected number of concurrent users, especially for large audiences.

Traps

- **Neglecting Last-Minute Checks**
  Skipping a final review of course components can lead to errors that disrupt the learner experience.

- **Underestimating Support Needs**
  Not preparing adequately for learner questions or technical issues can result in frustration and disengagement.

- **Ignoring Scalability**
  Failing to ensure the platform's scalability for larger audiences can lead to performance issues, such as slow load times or crashes.

- **Assuming All Users Are Tech-Savvy**
  Overlooking the need for simple instructions or troubleshooting resources can alienate learners unfamiliar with the technology.

- **Failing to Monitor the Launch**
  Not actively monitoring the launch can cause delays in identifying and addressing potential issues.

Course Deployment
Go Live

Techniques

- **Soft Launch Testing**
  Deploy the course to a small group of users before the official launch to ensure readiness.
- **Live Monitoring**
  Use analytics tools to monitor user activity, system performance, and engagement metrics in real time during the launch.
- **Issue Escalation Plan**
  Have a clear escalation path for addressing critical issues, such as platform outages or content errors.
- **Support Hub**
  Create a dedicated online hub with FAQs, troubleshooting guides, and a direct support contact form for learners.
- **Clear Onboarding Materials**
  Provide an onboarding guide or video to help learners navigate the course effectively.

Examples

- *Example 1*
  A university launching an online course schedule a soft launch to a test group, identifying and fixing a compatibility issue with mobile devices before the full rollout.
- *Example 2*
  A corporate training programme for sales professionals includes a welcome email with step-by-step access instructions and a support hotline, reducing learner frustration.
- *Example 3*
  A compliance training programme for healthcare workers uses a soft launch to validate the functionality of assessments and address any errors in scoring mechanisms.
- *Example 4*
  A multinational company ensures its LMS can handle a high number of users simultaneously during the launch of a global leadership training programme.
- *Example 5*
  A nonprofit provides a walkthrough video to help participants navigate an interactive simulation course, boosting initial engagement rates.

Course Deployment
Go Live

How it's done

- **Perform Final Quality Checks**
  Verify that all course content, media, and assessments are functional and error-free. Ensure that navigation paths, links, and multimedia components operate seamlessly.

- **Prepare Communication Materials**
  Develop learner support materials, such as emails, onboarding guides, or instructional videos, to assist users in accessing the course and navigating its features.

- **Test Accessibility**
  Confirm compliance with accessibility standards (e.g., WCAG) and ensure the course is fully functional across all devices, providing an inclusive learning experience.

- **Conduct a Soft Launch**
  Release the course to a small group of users to test functionality in a real-world setting. Identify and resolve any unforeseen issues before the full launch.

- **Ensure Scalability**
  Test the platform's ability to handle high traffic, particularly for large-scale deployments. Verify that infrastructure can support increased usage without performance issues.

- **Activate Support Systems**
  Ensure help desks, live chat, or email support are ready to assist learners during the launch phase. Provide clear contact details for troubleshooting.

- **Monitor Performance**
  Set up analytics tools to track learner engagement, technical performance, and content usage. Use this data to identify any issues quickly.

- **Launch the Course**
  Officially release the course to the target audience, ensuring all systems and support mechanisms are active and ready to handle the rollout.

- **Address Issues Promptly**
  Monitor feedback and analytics during the launch period. Resolve any technical or content-related issues reported by learners or identified through live monitoring.

Core Elements

- **Quality Checks Completed**
  All course content, media, and assessments are functional and error-free.

- **Navigation and Links Tested**
  All navigation paths, links, and multimedia components are operational.

- **Platform Scalability Tested**
  The LMS or delivery platform has been validated for performance under high traffic.

- **Communication Materials Prepared**
  Login instructions, onboarding guides, and support contact information are distributed to learners.

- **Accessibility Compliance Verified**
  The course meets accessibility standards for all learners.

- **Support Systems Activated**
  Help desks and other support mechanisms are ready to assist learners.

- **Soft Launch Conducted**
  The course is tested with a small group of users, and issues are resolved before the full launch.

- **Performance Monitored**
  Analytics tools are set up to track learner engagement and technical performance.

- **Contingency Plan in Place**
  A plan is ready to address any technical or logistical issues during the launch.

Course Deployment
Go Live

Checklist

1. Confirm all final course content is reviewed, approved, and version-locked
2. Upload and test course on the live LMS or platform
3. Validate SCORM/xAPI tracking, completion criteria, and assessment logic
4. Ensure all accessibility and compatibility checks are passed
5. Confirm integration with HRIS or reporting systems is functioning
6. Schedule official launch communications to target learners
7. Monitor first-wave access to ensure no login or access issues
8. Document go-live checklist completion and notify stakeholders

AI Considerations

- Use AI tools to monitor real-time learner engagement and flag unusual patterns, such as drop-offs or navigation issues
- Apply AI-based load testing to simulate peak traffic and validate platform scalability before launch
- Deploy AI-powered chatbots to handle learner queries and provide 24/7 support during the initial rollout
- Analyse early learner behaviour using AI dashboards to identify technical issues, content friction points, or unmet expectations
- Auto-generate alerts when learners encounter repeated errors, slow-loading content, or platform downtime
- Use AI to transcribe and summarise learner feedback collected through helpdesk tickets or open-text surveys during launch
- Apply predictive analytics to forecast potential issues based on historical launch data
- Segment learner data using AI to identify groups needing targeted support or intervention in real time

Key Takeaways

The Go Live sub-step marks the transition from course development to delivery, making the instructional materials accessible to the intended audience.

A successful launch relies on thorough preparation, including final quality checks, effective communication with learners, and active monitoring of the launch process.

By conducting a soft launch and resolving pre-launch issues, instructional designers can ensure a seamless and engaging learner experience.

This step lays the groundwork for achieving the course's learning objectives while minimising disruptions and maximising impact.

Proactive monitoring and support during the launch phase set the stage for success and learner satisfaction.

Course Deployment
Establish Support Channels

Establish Support Channels

Why this is important

Establishing effective support channels is essential for learner success, ensuring that help is readily available when technical, content-related, or logistical issues arise.

Prompt, accessible support contributes directly to maintaining learner engagement by reducing frustration and keeping participants focused on the learning experience.

In addition to supporting learners, these channels also assist facilitators and key stakeholders in managing smooth and reliable course delivery.

Well-prepared resources such as FAQs, troubleshooting guides, and helpdesk instructions empower both learners and instructors to resolve common problems independently, promoting self-sufficiency and reducing support load.

Importantly, support interactions also serve as a valuable source of feedback, revealing patterns or recurring issues that can inform future improvements to the course and its delivery.

Tips

- **Offer Multiple Channels**
  Provide a mix of email, live chat, forums, and phone support to cater to diverse learner preferences.
- **Create Self-Service Options**
  Develop an FAQ section or knowledge base for common issues to reduce reliance on live support.
- **Train Support Teams**
  Ensure support staff are well-versed in course content and technical tools.
- **Monitor Response Times**
  Set response time goals to address queries efficiently and maintain learner satisfaction.
- **Use Feedback Proactively**
  Track the types of issues reported to continuously improve content, tools, and processes

Traps

- **Overcomplicated Channels**
  Providing too many options without clear guidance can confuse learners and reduce support effectiveness.
- **Neglecting Availability**
  Limited support hours or unresponsive teams can frustrate learners and disrupt their progress.
- **Ignoring Technical Support**
  Overlooking platform-related issues may lead to learner dissatisfaction.
- **Lack of Documentation**
  Failing to document resolved issues can result in repetitive problems and inefficient resolutions.
- **Delaying Escalations**
  Not having a clear process for escalating complex issues can lead to unresolved learner concerns.

Techniques

- **Centralise Support Information**
  Use a dedicated support portal to house all resources, contact details, and troubleshooting guides.
- **Automate FAQs**
  Implement chatbots to provide instant answers to common questions.
- **Conduct Regular Training**
  Hold workshops for support staff to stay updated on course content and tools.
- **Feedback Integration**
  Set up a system for logging and categorising support tickets to identify trends and inform course improvements.
- **Test Support Channels**
  Pilot test support processes with a small group to ensure functionality and responsiveness before the full launch.

Course Deployment
Establish Support Channels

Examples

- **Live Chat Support**
  An LMS course provides 24/7 live chat assistance for technical issues, such as login problems or navigation queries.
- **Knowledge Base**
  A corporate training programme includes a searchable FAQ with step-by-step guides and video tutorials.
- **Instructor Hotline**
  Instructors have access to a direct phone line for urgent issues during live sessions.
- **Discussion Forums**
  An online learning programme includes forums for peer-to-peer support, moderated by facilitators.
- **Feedback Surveys**
  Post-support surveys collect data on learner satisfaction with the assistance provided.

How it's done

- **Identify Support Needs**
  Analyse common challenges that learners and facilitators may encounter during the course. Consider technical difficulties, content comprehension issues, and platform navigation challenges.
- **Develop Resources**
  Create support materials such as FAQs, step-by-step guides, and video tutorials to address frequently encountered issues. Ensure resources are clear, concise, and easily accessible.
- **Set Up Support Channels**
  Establish multiple support options, including email, live chat, phone assistance, and self-service portals. Provide learners and facilitators with clear instructions on how to access these channels.
- **Train Support Teams**
  Equip support teams with in-depth knowledge of the course content, tools, and troubleshooting procedures. Ensure they are well-prepared to handle learner and facilitator queries effectively.
- **Test Support Processes**
  Pilot the support channels with a small group to identify any gaps or inefficiencies. Use feedback to refine the processes before the full launch.
- **Monitor and Evaluate**
  Track key metrics such as response times, resolution rates, and user satisfaction to assess the effectiveness of the support system. Use analytics tools and feedback mechanisms to gather insights.
- **Refine Processes**
  Continuously update and improve support resources and procedures based on feedback, user trends, and evolving course requirements. Ensure support remains responsive and relevant.

Course Deployment
Establish Support Channels

Core Elements

- **Support Channels Established**
  Functional and accessible support channels, including live chat, email, and self-service portals, are in place.
- **Support Teams Trained**
  Teams are trained in course content, tools, and troubleshooting methods.
- **Resources Developed**
  FAQs, guides, and tutorials are comprehensive and easy to navigate.
- **Response Goals Defined**
  Support availability and response time expectations are clearly communicated.
- **Processes Pilot Tested**
  Support processes have been tested and refined based on pilot feedback.
- **Feedback Mechanisms Implemented**
  Surveys and other tools are in place to collect insights from learners and facilitators.
- **Escalation Procedures Ready**
  Protocols for handling complex issues are established.
- **Ongoing Monitoring**
  Support channels are regularly monitored and updated to ensure continued effectiveness.

Checklist

1. Identify types of support needed (technical, instructional, admin)
2. Set up help desk email, chatbot, or hotline for learner inquiries
3. Prepare FAQ documents, video walk-throughs, and quick-start guides
4. Train support team or facilitators on course content and platform
5. Establish response time expectations and escalation procedures
6. Provide support availability details within the course interface
7. Monitor support requests to identify common issues or gaps
8. Regularly update support resources based on learner feedback

AI Considerations

- Deploy AI chatbots to handle common support queries 24/7
- Use AI to analyse support tickets and cluster frequent issues
- Generate and update FAQs automatically from learner questions
- Predict learner confusion points and proactively offer help triggers
- Use AI-driven sentiment analysis to gauge learner frustration in support logs

Key Takeaways

Establishing support channels is a vital component of the Final Launch step in the Implementation Phase of the ADDIE model.

By providing accessible and effective support for both learners and facilitators, instructional designers can enhance the overall learning experience and ensure the course runs smoothly.

A mix of live assistance, self-service resources, and feedback mechanisms helps address a wide range of challenges while informing future improvements.

Proper training, thorough testing, and ongoing refinement of support processes ensure that issues are resolved promptly, empowering learners and facilitators to focus on achieving their goals.

Part 5: The **EVALUATION** phase

The Evaluation phase is the critical final step of the ADDIE model and the gateway to perpetual improvement. Far more than a post-mortem review, this phase serves as the feedback engine that powers the entire learning lifecycle. Its purpose is to systematically assess whether learning objectives were achieved, determine the effectiveness of instructional strategies and content, and measure the broader organisational impact of the solution.

This phase draws from a wide range of inputs, including quantitative results, qualitative feedback, behavioural observations, and performance outcomes. It actively involves learners, facilitators, business stakeholders, compliance teams, and increasingly, AI-powered analytics.

At its core, evaluation seeks to answer five powerful questions:

1. Did the learning intervention deliver what it promised?
2. Were the learners engaged, supported, and changed by the experience?
3. Has behaviour shifted in the workplace as a result?
4. Can the organisation see measurable return on its investment?
5. What must be improved before this program runs again?

The Evaluation phase typically unfolds in four integrated steps:

- Measuring Learning Impact, where we assess effectiveness, retention, learner sentiment, and stakeholder satisfaction
- ROI and Business Impact Reporting, which translates learning outcomes into bottom-line performance gains
- Compliance and Audit Readiness, ensuring all records, completions, and standards are documented and defensible
- Continuous Improvement Cycle, where feedback loops, lessons learned, and incremental refinements keep the solution evolving

By anchoring evaluation as a strategic activity, not just a tick-box afterthought, learning teams demonstrate value, build trust, and secure future investment.

This phase loops back on itself. What we learn here not only refines the current program, but directly influences how future needs are analysed, designed, and implemented. It reinforces the commitment to quality, relevance, and results, and ensures that learning never becomes stale, disconnected, or unaccountable.

In an AI-powered world of rapid change, rigorous evaluation is no longer optional. It is the compass that keeps learning aligned with business priorities and human growth.

Measure Learning Impact

The **Measure Learning Impact** step within the Evaluation phase focuses on determining how effectively a course achieves its learning objectives and whether it supports long-term knowledge retention and application. This step provides essential insights into the course's strengths, weaknesses, and areas requiring updates to maintain relevance.

Evaluation draws on both quantitative metrics, such as assessment results, participation levels, and completion rates, and qualitative feedback that explores learner satisfaction, engagement, and overall experience. Together, these insights enable instructional designers to refine the course and enhance its ongoing impact.

Key sub-steps include:

- **Assess Overall Effectiveness**
  Analyse test scores, engagement data, completion rates, and feedback to measure the extent to which learning objectives were achieved.

- **Gather Learner Feedback**
  Collect input through surveys, interviews, or focus groups to understand the learner experience, including clarity, relevance, and engagement levels.

- **Assess Learner Retention Metrics**
  Evaluate long-term knowledge retention and application using follow-up assessments, performance data, or observational metrics.

- **Stakeholder Review**
  Involve key stakeholders, such as SMEs and business leaders, to validate course effectiveness and ensure alignment with organisational goals.

- **Identify Ongoing Maintenance Needs**
  Determine any areas requiring content updates, technical fixes, or usability improvements to ensure sustainability and ongoing effectiveness.

Overview

Measure Learning Impact
Establish Support Channels

Outcomes

The **Measure Learning Impact** step aims to confirm the success of the course and set a foundation for continuous improvement. Key outcomes include:

- **Confirm Learning Objectives Are Met**
  Use evaluation data to verify whether learners achieved the intended outcomes.
- **Evaluate Engagement and Satisfaction**
  Assess learner perceptions and participation levels, including interaction with course components.
- **Identify Areas for Enhancement**
  Pinpoint content or delivery elements that require refinement for better effectiveness and learner experience.
- **Establish a Sustainability Plan**
  Develop a plan for ongoing updates, ensuring the course remains aligned with organisational needs and technological standards.
- **Implement Comprehensive Evaluation Models**
  Apply models such as Kirkpatrick's Four Levels to evaluate outcomes across reaction, learning, behaviour, and results.

Summary

Measure Learning Impact is a vital step in ensuring that learning solutions deliver meaningful and lasting outcomes.

By integrating both qualitative and quantitative data, instructional designers can validate success while identifying practical opportunities for improvement.

Avoiding a narrow focus on surface-level metrics, like completion rates, is key. Instead, a comprehensive approach that includes frameworks such as Kirkpatrick's Four Levels and a well-managed revision strategy will keep content effective and engaging.

This step ensures that each course remains relevant and valuable, not just for today's learners, but as part of a broader organisational learning strategy that evolves over time.

Assess Overall Effectiveness

Why this is important

Assessing overall effectiveness is vital to determine whether the course has successfully achieved its intended learning objectives.

It enables instructional designers to evaluate learner performance through measures such as knowledge retention, skill application, and outcome-based performance metrics.

This step also involves analysing engagement levels to understand how well learners interacted with the content, tools, and activities.

By identifying strengths and pinpointing gaps or weaknesses in the instructional design, this sub-step helps drive informed decisions about potential improvements.

Importantly, it supports the long-term sustainability of the course by ensuring that content remains relevant, adaptable, and aligned with organisational needs and evolving learner expectations.

Tips

- **Use a Balanced Approach**
  Combine quantitative data (e.g., test scores, completion rates) with qualitative feedback (e.g., surveys, interviews) to gain a comprehensive understanding of course effectiveness.

- **Align Metrics with Objectives**
  Ensure the metrics you evaluate directly relate to the course's intended outcomes and instructional goals.

- **Engage Stakeholders**
  Collaborate with SMEs, learners, and instructors to gather diverse perspectives on the course's impact.

- **Leverage Technology**
  Use learning analytics tools to track engagement, completion rates, and performance trends effectively.

- **Focus on Transferability**
  Evaluate whether learners are able to apply the knowledge or skills gained to real-world situations.

Traps

- **Over-reliance on Completion Rates**
  High completion rates do not always indicate learning success; focus on deeper metrics like retention and application.

- **Neglecting Long-Term Relevance**
  Failing to consider how the course will remain relevant over time can result in diminished value.

- **Ignoring Qualitative Feedback**
  Overlooking learner comments and feedback can lead to missed insights about the course experience.

- **Inadequate Sample Size**
  Drawing conclusions from insufficient or unrepresentative data can lead to inaccurate evaluations.

- **Biased Evaluations**
  Allowing personal or team biases to influence the assessment process can skew results.

Measure Learning Impact
Assess Overall Effectiveness

Techniques

- **Kirkpatrick's Model**
  Use the four levels of evaluation, reaction, learning, behaviour, and results, to assess the course's effectiveness comprehensively.
- **Surveys and Focus Groups**
  Gather direct feedback from learners and instructors about their experiences and perceived value of the course.
- **Analytics Tools**
  Leverage LMS analytics or other data platforms to monitor performance trends, engagement metrics, and completion rates.
- **Benchmarking**
  Compare the course outcomes to industry standards or similar programmes to gauge its relative success.
- **Case Studies**
  Analyse individual learner experiences to identify patterns and specific areas for improvement.

Examples

- *Example 1*
  A sales training programme achieves its objectives by showing a 30% increase in monthly sales figures among participants after completing the course.
- *Example 2*
  Learners in a compliance course report through surveys that interactive elements made the material more engaging and easier to retain.
- *Example 3*
  Analytics from an LMS reveal a drop in engagement halfway through a course, prompting revisions to the mid-point activities.
- *Example 4*
  A healthcare training programme is revised after feedback highlights outdated medical terminology, ensuring the course remains current.
- *Example 5*
  A technical certification course receives high marks for clarity but mixed reviews on the difficulty level, leading to an adjustment of assessment rigor.

Measure Learning Impact
Assess Overall Effectiveness

The **Assess Overall Effectiveness** sub-step in the Evaluate phase ensures the instructional programme achieves its intended goals while providing meaningful value to learners and stakeholders. This involves a structured process to review performance, engagement, and feedback comprehensively.

1. **Review Course Objectives**
   Start by verifying that all learning objectives have measurable success metrics and align seamlessly with the evaluation framework. This ensures the course's outcomes can be effectively assessed.

2. **Analyse Learner Performance**
   Gather and examine test scores, project outcomes, and skill assessments to measure knowledge retention and skill acquisition against predefined objectives.

3. **Monitor Engagement Metrics**
   Leverage Learning Management System (LMS) analytics to study engagement metrics such as time spent on activities, number of quiz attempts, and course completion rates. Look for trends or anomalies that indicate learner behaviour.

4. **Gather Feedback**
   Conduct surveys, interviews, and focus groups with learners, subject matter experts (SMEs), and instructors to collect qualitative insights. Feedback sheds light on the learner experience and identifies potential barriers or enhancements.

5. **Assess Application**
   Evaluate how effectively learners apply the acquired knowledge or skills in real-world contexts, such as workplace tasks or job performance. Collaborate with stakeholders to gather these insights.

6. **Compare to Benchmarks**
   Measure course performance against industry standards, organisational benchmarks, or comparable training programmes. This helps position the course competitively and identifies areas for improvement.

7. **Compile Insights**
   Summarise findings from data analysis, feedback, and engagement metrics into a cohesive evaluation report. Highlight strengths, weaknesses, and any notable trends.

8. **Develop Recommendations**
   Based on the insights gathered, create actionable recommendations for refining and improving the course. Include specific strategies to address weaknesses and leverage strengths.

9. **Plan Revisions**
   Establish a clear plan for implementing course revisions, ensuring the next iteration addresses identified gaps while maintaining alignment with learning objectives.

How it's done

Measure Learning Impact
Assess Overall Effectiveness

Core Elements

- **Alignment with Learning Objectives**
  Every evaluation metric is directly mapped to a stated learning objective, ensuring a clear link between what was taught and what was assessed.
- **Holistic Data Collection**
  Both quantitative data (e.g., test scores, completion rates) and qualitative input (e.g., learner feedback, interviews) are systematically gathered and analysed.
- **Engagement Analysis**
  Learner interaction rates, progress tracking, and time-on-task data are reviewed for patterns, inconsistencies, and drop-off points.
- **Real-World Applicability**
  Evidence is collected to confirm that learners can apply acquired knowledge and skills in workplace scenarios or job-specific tasks.
- **Stakeholder Feedback Integration**
  Input from learners, SMEs, and instructors is thoroughly assessed to capture diverse perspectives on course effectiveness.
- **Actionable Recommendations**
  A clear set of improvement strategies is documented, based on findings from data analysis and stakeholder input.
- **Planned Revision Path**
  A detailed, version-controlled plan is prepared for implementing updates, ensuring the course remains current and relevant.
- **Application of Kirkpatrick's Four Levels of Evaluation**
  The course is assessed across multiple dimensions:
    - **Reaction** – Learner satisfaction and initial impressions
    - **Learning** – Knowledge or skill acquisition outcomes
    - **Behaviour** – Evidence of learning transfer on the job
    - **Results** – Measurable impact on organisational goals

Checklist

1. Align evaluation with original objectives and success criteria
2. Collect data from LMS reports, assessments, surveys, and observations
3. Measure completion rates, learner satisfaction, and performance gains
4. Compare actual outcomes against targeted KPIs or benchmarks
5. Identify high-performing and low performing modules or segments
6. Validate effectiveness through triangulation (quant + qual data + SME review)
7. Prepare a formal evaluation report for stakeholders
8. Recommend improvements or next steps based on findings

Measure Learning Impact
Assess Overall Effectiveness

AI Considerations

- Use AI to summarise large volumes of feedback and test data
- Auto-generate comparison charts between projected vs. actual performance
- Identify learning modules correlated with lower scores or dropout
- Predict ROI or business impact from training outcomes
- Generate executive summaries or dashboards from evaluation data

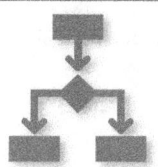

Key Takeaways

By integrating robust evaluation methods, instructional designers ensure that courses remain effective, relevant, and learner centred.

This approach not only fosters continuous improvement but also builds credibility and trust with stakeholders by demonstrating a commitment to quality and measurable outcomes.

Gather Learner Feedback

 **Why this is important**	Gathering learner feedback is essential to understanding the experience from the learner's point of view. It provides insight into how the course is perceived in terms of clarity, engagement, usability, pacing, workload, and real-world relevance. Unlike performance metrics, which measure outcomes, learner feedback surfaces the *why* behind those outcomes, what helped, what hindered, and what could be improved. This sub-step gives learners a voice in shaping future iterations of the course, fostering a sense of ownership and inclusivity. Feedback can highlight overlooked friction points, accessibility barriers, or content that may feel outdated, irrelevant, or confusing. It also enables continuous improvement by translating human experience into actionable insights.
 **Tips**	• **Use Multiple Feedback Channels** Combine surveys, open-ended forms, interviews, and informal check-ins to accommodate different communication styles. • **Ask the Right Questions** Go beyond "Did you enjoy it?" and ask about clarity, usefulness, relevance, pace, and confidence gained. • **Close the Loop** Let learners know how their feedback influenced changes. This builds trust and encourages future participation. • **Create Safe Spaces for Honesty** Offer anonymous feedback options or conduct sessions through neutral facilitators to reduce social pressure. • **Segment Feedback by Role or Persona** Different learner types (e.g., new hires vs. experienced staff) may experience the same course very differently.
Traps	• **Treating Feedback as a Formality** Asking for feedback with no intention of acting on it leads to learner disengagement and cynicism. • **Vague or Biased Questions** Poorly worded surveys can bias responses or fail to surface meaningful insights. • **Over-reliance on Satisfaction Scores** "Happy sheets" don't always correlate with actual learning or performance. • **Ignoring Minority Voices** Outlier feedback may reflect real barriers experienced by small but important learner groups. • **Timing Feedback Poorly** Asking for input too early or too late can result in vague or unhelpful responses.

Measure Learning Impact
Gather Learner Feedback

Techniques

- **Post-Course Surveys**
  Use Likert scales and open text boxes to collect immediate impressions of course elements.
- **Focus Groups and Interviews**
  Conduct small group sessions to explore themes like content clarity, perceived value, or usability in depth.
- **Pulse Checks During Delivery**
  Use mid-course feedback forms or in-module polls to capture reactions before the course ends.
- **Sentiment Analysis Tools**
  Automatically analyse open-text feedback to identify common themes or pain points.
- **Feedback Journals or Logs**
  Ask learners to document moments of confusion or "aha" moments as they move through the course.

Examples

- *Example 1*
  Learners report confusion with assessment instructions. The feedback prompts clearer guidance and formatting updates.
- *Example 2*
  Several learners mention that videos load too slowly on mobile. The team optimises file formats and hosting.
- *Example 3*
  Feedback reveals that a compliance course feels overly repetitive. Designers streamline the narrative and remove redundancy.
- *Example 4*
  New employees say the course uses jargon they don't understand. A glossary and language simplification strategy are introduced.
- *Example 5*
  Anonymous feedback highlights cultural references not understood by international learners. The content is updated for broader inclusivity.

How it's done

- **Design a Feedback Framework**
  Define what you want to know (e.g., usability, emotional tone, relevance) and select appropriate tools and methods.
- **Deploy Surveys and Collection Tools**
  Use a blend of structured and open-ended items, ideally embedded directly into the LMS or learning platform.
- **Facilitate Qualitative Interviews or Focus Groups**
  Organise sessions with diverse learner cohorts to explore experiences in depth.
- **Conduct Thematic Analysis**
  Categorise feedback into key themes, clarity, engagement, motivation, friction points, to spot trends.
- **Synthesize Insights**
  Combine qualitative findings with performance data to uncover root causes of issues or unexpected successes.
- **Validate with Stakeholders**
  Present key insights to SMEs, instructors, and business reps to check alignment with course intent.
- **Report and Close the Loop**
  Share back with learners what was learned and what will change, reinforcing their contribution.

Measure Learning Impact
Gather Learner Feedback

Core Elements

- **Learner Voice is Central**
  The course is evaluated not only by outcomes but by the learner's experience and perception.
- **Feedback is Multi-Modal**
  Surveys, discussions, and observational feedback are all used to paint a complete picture.
- **Themes Are Mapped to Design**
  Feedback is categorised into content, structure, delivery, and user experience to guide improvements.
- **Inclusivity is Prioritised**
  Feedback tools account for language barriers, accessibility, and cultural nuance.
- **Insights Translate into Change**
  All feedback is actioned or archived with clear rationale, and relevant updates are planned or implemented.

Checklist

1. Define feedback goals (e.g., clarity, engagement, accessibility)
2. Select collection tools (surveys, interviews, in-course polls)
3. Craft unbiased, specific questions aligned with objectives
4. Encourage honest input, with anonymity where appropriate
5. Analyse feedback by themes, frequency, and learner segment
6. Validate insights through stakeholder review
7. Prioritise and document actionable improvements
8. Communicate changes made in response to feedback

AI Considerations

- **Sentiment Analysis on Open-Text Comments**
  Identify emotional tone, satisfaction, and key friction points automatically.
- **Feedback Clustering**
  Group similar comments or issues across cohorts using machine learning.
- **Bias Detection**
  Use AI tools to detect systemic bias in feedback (e.g., overrepresentation of one group's views).
- **Predictive Modelling**
  Forecast future dropout risk or satisfaction trends based on current feedback patterns.
- **Auto-Generate Thematic Summaries**
  Use AI to summarise open-ended responses into clear, executive-ready bullet points.

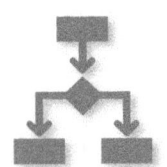

Key Takeaways

Gathering learner feedback is not a checkbox, it is a strategic listening practice.

When implemented thoughtfully, it provides powerful insight into the learner's reality, helping designers improve clarity, engagement, accessibility, and relevance.

By combining human empathy with structured analysis, and layering in AI tools where appropriate, this sub-step transforms passive feedback into fuel for innovation. It reinforces the principle that meaningful learning begins with understanding the learner and continues by listening to them.

Measure Learning Impact
Assess Learner Retention Metrics

Assess Learner Retention Metrics

Why this is important

Assessing learner retention metrics is essential for understanding the long-term effectiveness of training.

It evaluates how well learners retain knowledge and skills over time, providing insight into whether learning objectives are being met in a durable, practical way.

Retention analysis helps instructional designers identify knowledge gaps, measure how learning is applied in the workplace, and determine if refresher or reinforcement strategies are needed.

This feedback loop is critical for continuous improvement, allowing course materials and delivery methods to evolve based on real-world outcomes.

By focusing on long-term retention, not just short-term performance, learning programs can ensure meaningful, lasting impact.

Tips

- **Use Diverse Assessment Methods**
  Incorporate quizzes, practical tasks, and surveys to measure retention from multiple perspectives.
- **Measure Retention at Multiple Intervals**
  Evaluate retention at intervals (e.g., immediately post-course, one month later, and three months later) to observe trends.
- **Focus on Application**
  Design assessments that require learners to apply knowledge in realistic scenarios to validate understanding.
- **Leverage Analytics Tools**
  Use LMS or other platforms to track learner performance over time and generate retention reports.
- **Engage Stakeholders**
  Involve instructors, SMEs, and managers in analysing retention data to ensure a well-rounded understanding.

Traps

- **Overemphasis on Short-Term Metrics**
  Focusing solely on immediate post-course results may overlook long-term retention challenges.
- **Neglecting Practical Application**
  Failing to assess whether learners can apply retained knowledge in their roles diminishes the relevance of retention metrics.
- **Inconsistent Data Collection**
  Lack of standardised methods for measuring retention can lead to unreliable or incomplete results.
- **Ignoring Feedback from Learners**
  Overlooking learner perspectives on what helped or hindered retention may miss valuable insights.
- **Neglecting to Act on Insights**
  Gathering data without applying findings to improve the course undermines the value of retention assessments.

Measure Learning Impact
Assess Learner Retention Metrics

Techniques

- **Spaced Retrieval Practice**
  Incorporate activities that require learners to recall information at spaced intervals, reinforcing retention.
- **Scenario-Based Assessments**
  Design realistic scenarios where learners must apply retained knowledge to solve problems or make decisions.
- **Knowledge Checkpoints**
  Establish periodic assessments to track retention over time and identify trends.
- **Heatmap Analysis**
  Use analytics tools to create heatmaps showing areas of high and low retention within the course content.
- **Feedback Loops**
  Provide learners with immediate feedback during retention assessments to reinforce correct understanding and address misconceptions.

Examples

- *Post-Course Quiz*
  A safety training programme includes a follow-up quiz one month after course completion to measure knowledge retention on safety protocols.
- *Scenario Application*
  In a leadership course, learners are asked three months later to resolve a simulated conflict using course concepts.
- *Skill Demonstration*
  A technical course requires learners to complete a practical task, such as assembling a device, six weeks after training.
- *Reflection Survey*
  Participants in a compliance course complete a survey three months post-course to assess their ability to recall and apply regulations in their roles.
- *Job Performance Metrics*
  Retention is measured by tracking job performance improvements attributed to training outcomes over a six-month period.

Measure Learning Impact
Assess Learner Retention Metrics

Assessing Learner Retention Metrics in the Evaluate phase of the ADDIE model focuses on measuring the long-term impact of training by evaluating how well learners retain and apply knowledge and skills over time. This process involves defining clear metrics, designing effective assessments, and using data-driven insights to improve course content and learning strategies.

1. **Define Retention Metrics**
   Establish clear metrics to measure retention, such as quiz scores, practical task performance, and survey results. Ensure these align with the learning objectives and intended outcomes of the course.

2. **Design Assessments**
   Create assessments that evaluate both knowledge recall and the practical application of learned skills. Use varied formats, such as multiple-choice quizzes, scenario-based tasks, or real-world performance evaluations.

3. **Schedule Follow-Ups**
   Plan assessment intervals post-course to monitor retention trends over time. Typical intervals might include one week, one month, and three months after course completion.

4. **Collect Data**
   Use tools like LMS tracking, surveys, quizzes, and performance reviews to gather quantitative and qualitative data on learner retention.

5. **Analyse Results**
   Review data to identify retention rates, gaps, and trends. Look for patterns that indicate areas where learners struggle to retain or apply knowledge.

6. **Consult Stakeholders**
   Collaborate with subject matter experts (SMEs) and instructors to interpret findings, identify root causes of retention gaps, and brainstorm solutions.

7. **Refine Content**
   Update course materials and instructional strategies based on insights from retention data. Address areas where learners demonstrate lower retention or struggle with practical application.

8. **Report Insights**
   Compile a detailed report of findings, including trends, gaps, and actionable recommendations. Share this with stakeholders to inform the design of future training programs.

Core Elements

- Retention metrics are clearly defined and aligned with learning objectives.
- Post-course assessments are designed and scheduled at appropriate intervals.
- Assessment methods evaluate both recall and the practical application of knowledge.
- Data collection tools, such as LMS, surveys, and quizzes, are ready and tested.
- Retention results are thoroughly analysed for trends and gaps.
- Stakeholders, including SMEs and instructors, are consulted to validate findings.
- Course content and instructional strategies are refined based on retention data.
- Insights and recommendations are documented and shared with relevant teams.

Measure Learning Impact
Assess Learner Retention Metrics

Checklist

1. Define what constitutes retention (knowledge, application, behaviour change)
2. Schedule follow-up assessments at defined intervals (e.g., 30, 60, 90 days)
3. Compare retention scores with initial post-training assessments
4. Track application of learning on the job where feasible
5. Use manager input or workplace observations to validate retention
6. Identify skills or knowledge areas with high drop-off
7. Collate retention data for specific learner groups or regions
8. Document implications for reinforcement or refresher strategies

AI Considerations

- Use AI to detect retention decay trends from assessment comparisons
- Predict which learners are most at risk of forgetting based on engagement data
- Recommend microlearning or reinforcement content targeting weak areas
- Analyse behavioural data from job systems or performance logs
- Auto-generate longitudinal retention dashboards

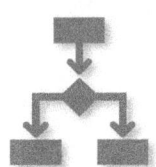
Key Takeaways

Retention evaluation is a vital step in assessing the long-term effectiveness of training programs.

By measuring knowledge recall and real-world application over time, instructional designers can refine course content to better meet learner needs and bridge the gap between learning and implementation.

Engaging stakeholders and using diverse assessment methods ensures a comprehensive approach to evaluation.

This process bridges the gap between learning and practical implementation, supporting sustained success for both learners and organisations.

Stakeholder Review

 **Why this is important**	Stakeholder review is essential for ensuring that learning initiatives remain aligned with broader organisational goals and expectations. By engaging stakeholders such as business leaders, subject matter experts, HR, compliance officers, and frontline managers, instructional designers gain diverse insights into the perceived value, effectiveness, and applicability of the learning experience. These perspectives help validate the learning outcomes, uncover blind spots, and identify emerging priorities. This collaborative process not only improves the quality and strategic relevance of the training but also builds trust and buy-in across the organisation. When stakeholders feel heard and involved, they are far more likely to champion the learning solution and support its ongoing evolution.
 **Tips**	• Engage a diverse group of stakeholders to gather a broad spectrum of insights. • Use structured review sessions with clear objectives and timelines. • Pre-brief stakeholders with a concise summary of learning goals and impact metrics • Encourage honest feedback by fostering a safe, non-judgemental review environment.
 **Traps**	• Neglecting to include key stakeholders, leading to gaps in feedback. • Overloading stakeholders with unnecessary details, causing disengagement. • Failing to document or act on stakeholder recommendations. • Allowing dominant voices to overshadow diverse perspectives, resulting in incomplete or biased conclusions
 **Techniques**	• Conduct surveys and interviews to gather individual stakeholder insights. • Use facilitated workshops to encourage collaborative discussion and alignment. • Employ visual aids like progress charts or dashboards to communicate outcomes effectively. • Develop a stakeholder feedback matrix to categorise and prioritise feedback. • Map stakeholders by function, interest, and influence to tailor communication and better anticipate concerns or expectations.
 **Examples**	• Hosting a stakeholder workshop to identify gaps in learning outcomes and brainstorm solutions. • Using a digital feedback platform to collect anonymous input from stakeholders. • Presenting a comparative analysis of learning outcomes against organisational benchmarks during review sessions. • Sharing a side-by-side comparison of course outcomes and organisational benchmarks to anchor stakeholder discussion in evidence

Measure Learning Impact
Stakeholder Review

Stakeholder Reviews in the Evaluate phase of the ADDIE model ensure learning outcomes align with organisational needs and expectations. This collaborative process fosters trust, enhances relevance, and drives continuous improvement in learning initiatives.

1. **Identify and Engage Stakeholders**
   Determine relevant stakeholders, including managers, SMEs, and learners, and invite them to participate in the review process.
2. **Develop a Structured Agenda**
   Prepare a detailed agenda and supporting materials to guide discussions during stakeholder review sessions, ensuring a focused and productive process.
3. **Collect and Analyse Feedback**
   Gather stakeholder input during review sessions, document the feedback, and categorise it into actionable insights.
4. **Close the Feedback Loop**
   Summarise findings, propose action plans, and share these with stakeholders to ensure transparency and foster collaboration.
5. **. Establish Ongoing Review Cadence**
   Schedule periodic check-ins or follow-up sessions with key stakeholders to ensure continued alignment and surface new priorities.

How it's done

Core Elements

- Relevant stakeholders are identified and engaged in the review process.
- Review sessions are scheduled and guided by a structured agenda.
- Stakeholder feedback is systematically documented and categorised.
- Findings and proposed actions are communicated to all stakeholders.
- Ongoing channels for stakeholder feedback are maintained to support continuous alignment

Checklist

1. Identify key stakeholders (e.g., HR, L&D, business leaders, sponsors)
2. Prepare evaluation summary with highlights, risks, and recommendations
3. Schedule and facilitate structured review sessions
4. Present findings clearly using visuals and evidence-based insights
5. Gather stakeholder feedback on alignment, value, and future needs
6. Document endorsements, concerns, or change requests
7. Incorporate review insights into the program improvement plan
8. Close the loop with stakeholders by outlining next steps

AI Considerations

- Generate visual summaries tailored to each stakeholder's focus
- Use AI to tailor data presentations (e.g., HR vs. operations vs. execs)
- Apply NLP to extract key stakeholder feedback themes from meeting transcripts
- Simulate impact of suggested changes based on feedback trends
- Track sentiment shifts across stakeholder groups over time

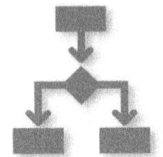

Key Takeaways

Stakeholder reviews are a vital component of the Evaluate phase, offering strategic insights that go beyond learner data.

By involving key decision-makers in structured, evidence-based discussions, instructional designers enhance trust, validate program direction, and strengthen alignment with business needs.

This collaborative process becomes a driver of continuous improvement, ensuring learning remains purposeful, responsive, and supported at all levels.

Identify Ongoing Maintenance Needs

Why this is important

Ongoing maintenance is essential to ensure that a course remains relevant, functional, and effective long after its initial rollout.

As industry standards, organisational goals, and learner expectations evolve, course content must be reviewed and updated to stay aligned.

Regular maintenance also helps identify and resolve technical issues, platform compatibility problems, and usability concerns that may impact learner access or engagement.

By planning structured update cycles and tracking performance metrics, instructional designers can enhance the user experience, maintain content accuracy, and optimise learning outcomes.

This proactive approach ensures that courses remain not only current, but also continuously improving over time.

Tips

- **Create a Maintenance Schedule**
  Define clear intervals for reviewing and updating the course, such as quarterly or annually, based on the nature of the content.
- **Use Analytics**
  Leverage LMS analytics to monitor engagement, completion rates, and technical issues that may indicate the need for updates.
- **Engage SMEs**
  Regularly collaborate with Subject Matter Experts to ensure content accuracy and relevance.
- **Document Changes**
  Maintain a log of all updates and revisions for accountability and future reference.
- **Automate Where Possible**
  Use automated tools for version control, error detection, and system compatibility checks.

Traps

- **Neglecting Feedback**
  Failing to act on learner or instructor feedback can lead to outdated or ineffective materials.
- **Ignoring Technology Updates**
  Overlooking advancements in technology or platform updates may result in compatibility issues or reduced course efficiency.
- **Overcomplicating Updates**
  Making frequent, unnecessary changes can lead to confusion and increased workload.
- **Inconsistent Standards**
  Allowing formatting, tone, or structural inconsistencies to creep into updates can degrade the course quality.
- **Delaying Maintenance**
  Procrastinating on needed updates can result in larger, more expensive overhauls later.

Measure Learning Impact
Identify Ongoing Maintenance Needs

Techniques

- **Feedback Loop Integration**
  Establish an ongoing mechanism for collecting learner and instructor feedback post-launch to identify maintenance needs.
- **Content Audits**
  Regularly review course content for accuracy, relevance, and alignment with learning objectives.
- **Technical Testing**
  Periodically test multimedia elements, interactive components, and platform compatibility to ensure seamless functionality.
- **Trend Analysis**
  Monitor trends in your industry or educational sector to proactively update course content with the latest information.
- **Version Control**
  Implement a version control system to manage and track changes to course materials.

Examples

- *Example 1*
  A compliance training course is updated annually to reflect changes in regulatory requirements.
- *Example 2*
  A leadership development programme incorporates feedback from managers to add real-world case studies every six months.
- *Example 3*
  A technical skills course includes quarterly updates to maintain compatibility with the latest software versions.
- *Example 4*
  An onboarding module adds subtitles and alternative text for images after accessibility feedback from learners.
- *Example 5*
  An eLearning course redesigns its quiz interface to align with new company branding guidelines.

How it's done

Identify Ongoing Maintenance Needs in the Evaluate phase of the ADDIE model focuses on ensuring courses remain accurate, functional, and aligned with both learner needs and organisational goals over time.

1. **Monitor Feedback Channels**
   Establish mechanisms to regularly gather feedback from learners, instructors, and SMEs, and review this feedback to identify improvement opportunities.
2. **Review Analytics**
   Analyse engagement metrics, completion rates, and error reports to pinpoint areas requiring attention or refinement.
3. **Schedule Content Audits**
   Plan periodic evaluations of course materials to ensure their accuracy, relevance, and overall quality.
4. **Update Content**
   Revise outdated information, integrate current case studies, and adjust assessments to reflect evolving needs and industry standards.
5. **Perform Technical Maintenance**
   Check course compatibility with the latest LMS updates, browser versions, and device formats to ensure a seamless user experience.
6. **Enhance Accessibility**
   Implement or refine accessibility features such as captions, transcripts, and responsive design elements to support diverse learner needs.
7. **Document Changes**
   Maintain a detailed record of all revisions, updates, and maintenance activities for transparency and future reference.
8. **Plan for Future Needs**
   Anticipate industry trends or organisational changes that may necessitate updates and prepare accordingly.

Measure Learning Impact
Identify Ongoing Maintenance Needs

Core Elements

- A feedback mechanism is in place for learners and instructors.
- Course content is regularly reviewed for accuracy and relevance.
- Technical components are tested for functionality and compatibility.
- Accessibility standards are reviewed and updated as needed.
- A maintenance schedule for periodic reviews and updates is established.
- SME feedback and industry updates are incorporated into the course.
- All changes and updates are documented for future reference.
- Future trends or organisational needs are identified and planned for.

Checklist

1. Review content for time-sensitive or regulatory dependencies
2. Identify modules likely to require frequent updates (e.g., software, policy)
3. Document asset ownership and update responsibility
4. Set review cadence for content audits (quarterly, annually, etc.)
5. Monitor learner feedback for emerging content gaps or outdated items
6. Prepare a maintenance log or tracker for version control
7. Confirm resource allocation for ongoing updates
8. Share maintenance plan with delivery and operations teams

AI Considerations

- Review content for time-sensitive or regulatory dependencies
- Identify modules likely to require frequent updates (e.g., software, policy)
- Document asset ownership and update responsibility
- Set review cadence for content audits (quarterly, annually, etc.)
- Monitor learner feedback for emerging content gaps or outdated items
- Prepare a maintenance log or tracker for version control
- Confirm resource allocation for ongoing updates
- Share maintenance plan with delivery and operations teams

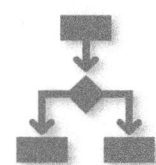

Key Takeaways

The ongoing maintenance of a course is essential for ensuring its long-term success and effectiveness.

By actively monitoring feedback, updating content, and performing technical checks, instructional designers can sustain the course's relevance and functionality.

Proactive planning and regular audits minimise disruptions while supporting the adaptability of instructional materials in dynamic learning environments.

Structured maintenance ensures courses continue to meet both learner expectations and organisational goals, fostering a sustainable and impactful learning experience.

ROI and Business Impact Reporting

Overview

The **ROI and Business Impact Reporting** step shifts the focus from learner outcomes to organisational value. It asks the pivotal question: *"Did this learning intervention create measurable impact for the business?"* This step is essential for demonstrating the return on investment (ROI) of training programs and translating learning results into business-relevant language that resonates with executives.

Instructional designers and learning leaders must align learning outcomes with strategic business objectives, gather performance data, and clearly communicate the tangible benefits realised from the learning initiative. This includes increased productivity, improved employee performance, reduced error rates, faster onboarding, or other cost-efficiency gains.

The goal is not just to justify past efforts, but to build a compelling case for future investment. By telling a meaningful "impact story" supported by credible metrics, this step positions the learning function as a strategic business partner rather than a cost centre.

Key sub-steps include:

- **Align Metrics with Business KPIs**
  Collaborate with business leaders to ensure learning evaluation criteria match broader organisational performance goals.

- **Capture Cost–Benefit and Productivity Shifts**
  Quantify savings, efficiencies, or revenue gains attributable to the learning intervention.

- **Evaluate Behavioural Change and Application on the Job**
  Assess how well learners have applied new skills or behaviours, and the resulting operational improvements.

- **Translate Learning into Business Impact Stories**
  Craft narratives that connect learning outcomes to real-world improvements, making the data meaningful and actionable.

- **Generate Reports for Executives**
  Present findings in clear, strategic formats suited to senior decision-makers, focusing on outcomes, ROI, and future recommendations.

ROI and Business Impact Reporting
Identify Ongoing Maintenance Needs

Outcomes

The **ROI and Business Impact Reporting** step helps the learning team demonstrate accountability, strategic alignment, and value creation. Key outcomes include:

- **Demonstrate Learning's Contribution to Business Results**
  Show measurable links between learning and key business metrics, such as productivity, quality, revenue, or safety.
- **Enhance Stakeholder Confidence in L&D**
  Build credibility with leadership by using data to validate the impact of learning interventions.
- **Identify High-Value Programs and Gaps**
  Use reporting insights to determine which programs yield the greatest impact and where improvements or resource reallocations are needed.
- **Support Budget Requests and Future Planning**
  Provide strong justification for future investment in L&D through evidence-based reporting.
- **Strengthen Cross-Functional Collaboration**
  Promote dialogue between L&D and business units, aligning training priorities with enterprise needs.

Summary

ROI and Business Impact Reporting elevates the learning conversation from participation and satisfaction to strategic contribution. It closes the loop between instructional effort and organisational performance, using real data to demonstrate that learning drives results.

By aligning measurement with business priorities, capturing cost savings and productivity gains, and communicating outcomes in ways that matter to executives, learning teams move from "training providers" to "value creators."

This step is critical not only for accountability, but for sustainability. When L&D proves its worth through credible, impactful reporting, it secures a seat at the strategic table and the resources needed to keep learning at the heart of organisational success.

Align Metrics with Business KPIs

Why this is important

Aligning learning metrics with business Key Performance Indicators (KPIs) ensures that training programs contribute directly to organisational objectives. Rather than measuring learning in isolation, such as course completion rates or quiz scores, this sub-step focuses on demonstrating how learning improves performance, productivity, compliance, safety, customer satisfaction, or profitability.

When learning outcomes are tied to business KPIs, stakeholders see clear value in the investment, enabling stronger executive buy-in and more strategic decision-making. This alignment also helps prioritise learning initiatives based on real business needs, rather than instructional preferences or assumptions. In short, this is the bridge between "what was learned" and "why it matters."

Tips

- **Start with Business Strategy**
  Understand the organisation's strategic goals before defining what to measure in the learning program.
- **Co-Design Metrics with Stakeholders**
  Collaborate with department heads, HR, operations, and finance to identify KPIs most relevant to the learning objectives.
- **Use Leading and Lagging Indicators**
  Combine immediate indicators (e.g. test results, satisfaction) with longer-term measures (e.g. reduced error rates, improved sales) for a fuller picture.
- **Create a Metrics Map**
  Build a visual alignment grid showing which learning outcomes influence which business KPIs.
- **Translate Learning into Operational Language**
  Frame learning outcomes using the terms and priorities familiar to business leaders.

Traps

- **Focusing Only on Learning Data**
  Tracking test scores without linking them to job performance or organisational priorities misses the point of ROI.
- **One-Size-Fits-All Metrics**
  Using the same KPIs across different business units can result in irrelevant or misleading conclusions.
- **Failing to Define Success Upfront**
  Waiting until the end to decide what to measure can lead to weak, retrofitted analysis.
- **Misinterpreting Correlation as Causation**
  Be cautious when attributing KPI movement solely to learning without controlling for other influencing factors.
- **Overloading with Data**
  Too many metrics dilute focus, choose those with the highest business relevance.

Techniques

- **KPI Mapping Workshop**
  Facilitate a session with key stakeholders to map course outcomes to relevant KPIs across business units.
- **Logic Models or Impact Chains**
  Use a visual framework to show how learning activities contribute to individual behaviour change and, ultimately, business results.
- **Balanced Scorecard Integration**
  Connect learning metrics to broader performance scorecards already in use within the organisation.
- **Pre-Post Comparison**
  Measure relevant KPIs before and after training to identify shifts attributable to learning interventions.
- **Stakeholder Interviews**
  Capture insights on which KPIs matter most to business leaders and how they track them.

ROI and Business Impact Reporting
Align Metrics with Business KPIs

Examples

- *Example 1*
  A customer service training program is mapped to KPIs like Net Promoter Score (NPS) and first-call resolution. Post-training, improvements in these areas validate the program's business impact.
- *Example 2*
  A warehouse safety course is aligned with a KPI of "incident rate per 100 employees." Post-training metrics show a 25% reduction, providing clear ROI.
- *Example 3*
  A leadership course focuses on team productivity and staff retention, both tracked quarterly. Department-level data shows improvements after rollout.
- *Example 4*
  A retail sales training program targets average basket size and upsell frequency. Both KPIs improve within 6 weeks of implementation.
- *Example 5*
  An onboarding program is linked to "time to productivity" for new hires. HR data reveals a 20% reduction compared to previous cohorts.

How it's done

1. **Review Strategic Business Goals**
   Start by understanding key business priorities from documents like the strategic plan, board reports, or business unit roadmaps.
2. **Engage Stakeholders Early**
   Identify KPIs used by each department that the training impacts, and hold discovery sessions to surface their performance concerns.
3. **Map Learning Outcomes to KPIs**
   Align each course objective with a business KPI using a simple matrix or logic chain.
4. **Define Success Criteria**
   Establish what constitutes improvement, e.g., "10% increase in sales," "15% reduction in complaints", and over what time frame.
5. **Build Baseline Measurements**
   Capture pre-training KPI data to establish a starting point for comparison.
6. **Integrate Tracking Mechanisms**
   Set up data pipelines from systems such as HRIS, CRM, or finance tools to pull relevant KPI data.
7. **Evaluate and Report**
   Post-training, analyse KPI trends and contextualise findings for stakeholders through dashboards, stories, and visual reports.

Core Elements

- **Business Goals are Clearly Understood**
  Learning is positioned in the context of organisational priorities and outcomes.
- **KPIs are Defined Collaboratively**
  Input from business stakeholders informs which metrics matter most.
- **Learning Outcomes are Mapped to KPIs**
  Each outcome has a direct or indirect line to a business result.
- **Baseline and Post-Training Data are Collected**
  Metrics are measured consistently before and after learning.
- **Metrics are Meaningful and Interpretable**
  Selected KPIs resonate with stakeholders and drive decision-making.
- **Data is Contextualised, Not Just Reported**
  Stories and commentary accompany the numbers to give them meaning.

ROI and Business Impact Reporting
Align Metrics with Business KPIs

Checklist

1. Identify key business objectives that the course supports
2. Engage stakeholders to select relevant KPIs
3. Develop a KPI-to-learning outcome mapping matrix
4. Define what success looks like for each KPI
5. Collect baseline data before training begins
6. Set up post-training data collection mechanisms
7. Validate data accuracy and relevance with stakeholders
8. Report on results using both visuals and narrative
9. Document insights and recommendations for future alignment
10. Archive metric alignment templates for reuse across programs

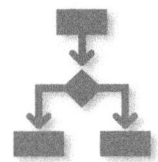
AI Considerations

- **Auto-Map Learning Outcomes to Business KPIs**
  Use AI to suggest linkages between training objectives and likely business impact areas based on past programs.
- **Predict KPI Movement Based on Historical Data**
  Leverage machine learning to estimate impact before rollout.
- **Generate Executive Reports**
  Use AI to create tailored reports and dashboards for different stakeholder groups.
- **Detect KPI Lag and Learning Gaps**
  Identify when KPIs plateau or dip post-training, prompting review of content or delivery.
- **Sentiment Analysis on Stakeholder Interviews**
  Use NLP to identify recurring business concerns or perceived training value.

Key Takeaways

Aligning learning metrics with business KPIs ensures that training is not only effective, but also strategic. It transforms learning from an isolated activity into a business tool for measurable performance improvement.

When KPIs are built into the evaluation process from the beginning, learning leaders gain the credibility and influence needed to secure executive support and ongoing investment.

This sub-step strengthens the case for ROI, tightens cross-functional alignment, and ultimately ensures learning drives the outcomes that matter most.

ROI and Business Impact Reporting
Capture Cost-Benefit and Productivity Shifts

Capture Cost-Benefit and Productivity Shifts

Why this is important

Understanding the return on learning investment requires more than measuring learning outcomes, it demands a clear picture of the costs involved and the benefits delivered. Capturing cost–benefit and productivity shifts enables instructional designers to show how training initiatives save time, reduce waste, increase output, or enhance efficiency in measurable terms.

This sub-step translates learning results into operational and financial impact, allowing organisations to quantify the value generated against the resources spent.

By comparing the cost of training delivery to the productivity gains, error reduction, or time savings achieved, L&D teams can demonstrate tangible value, prioritise high-impact programs, and make informed resourcing decisions.

Tips

- **Include Hidden and Indirect Costs**
  Consider time away from work, facilitator prep time, technology licensing, and opportunity costs, not just development budgets.
- **Establish Pre-Training Baselines**
  Document productivity or error metrics before training to serve as a comparison point.
- **Use Time-Saved as a Proxy**
  Quantify reduced time to complete tasks, fewer rework cycles, or decreased onboarding time.
- **Collaborate with Finance and Ops**
  Work with those managing the numbers to ensure accuracy and credibility in your calculations.
- **Convert Qualitative Gains Where Possible**
  Translate feedback like "faster resolution" or "easier collaboration" into estimated hours or cost savings.

Traps

- **Only Focusing on Cost**
  Obsessing over training expense without showing benefit undermines the ROI story.
- **Underestimating Indirect Benefits**
  Improved morale, retention, or collaboration may have major impact even if they don't immediately show up in financial statements.
- **Using Arbitrary Multipliers**
  Applying generic ROI formulas without context can lead to misleading results.
- **Failing to Segment Results**
  Different departments or learner cohorts may experience varied levels of benefit, averaging them can obscure value.
- **Overcomplicating the Model**
  Keep it simple and defensible, focus on key drivers of cost and value, not every decimal point.

Techniques

- **Cost–Benefit Analysis (CBA)**
  List all costs and benefits (tangible and intangible), quantify where possible, and calculate net value.
- **Productivity Delta Tracking**
  Measure change in output per person/hour before and after training (e.g. units handled, tickets resolved, transactions processed).
- **Time-to-Competency Comparison**
  Evaluate how quickly learners reach job readiness pre- and post-training improvements.
- **Error Rate Reduction**
  Track decrease in mistakes, quality issues, or compliance breaches that carry cost implications.
- **Opportunity Cost Modelling**
  Compare the benefit of delivering training versus what would be lost if the training were not implemented.

ROI and Business Impact Reporting
Capture Cost-Benefit and Productivity Shifts

Examples

- **Example 1**
  A software onboarding course reduces time-to-competency from 6 weeks to 4. Calculated savings: $50,000 in billable hours per cohort.
- **Example 2**
  A manufacturing skills course leads to a 40% drop in errors, cutting scrap and rework costs by $120,000 per quarter.
- **Example 3**
  Customer support training improves average call handling time by 1.2 minutes, equating to 10% more calls handled per agent daily.
- **Example 4**
  Leadership training reduces voluntary turnover in a sales team by 15%, saving an estimated $200,000 in recruitment and onboarding costs.
- **Example 5**
  A compliance refresher course leads to zero audit flags in the following quarter, avoiding potential penalties.

How it's done

1. **List All Training Costs**
   Include content development, facilitator time, platform costs, lost productivity during training, and any equipment or licensing fees.
2. **Establish Pre-Training Benchmarks**
   Capture key performance metrics like output per person, error rates, customer satisfaction, or resolution time before the training rollout.
3. **Measure Post-Training Shifts**
   Track the same KPIs after training to identify quantifiable improvements.
4. **Convert Improvements into Financial Value**
   Estimate the dollar value of time saved, errors avoided, or increased output using agreed assumptions with finance or operations.
5. **Calculate Net Gain or ROI**
   Subtract total costs from total estimated benefit. Optionally, express as an ROI percentage.
6. **Validate with Stakeholders**
   Share assumptions and findings with finance, business leaders, and HR to ensure credibility.
7. **Document Methodology for Repeat Use**
   Build a reusable framework or calculator template to apply in future evaluations.

Core Elements

- **Full Cost Visibility**
  All direct, indirect, and opportunity costs are accounted for in the analysis.
- **Benefits are Quantified and Credible**
  Measurable outcomes are linked to specific productivity or cost-saving results.
- **Baseline Data is Captured**
  Performance metrics before training are used as a reference point for comparison.
- **Post-Training Shifts are Measured**
  Consistent data collection allows identification of meaningful improvement.
- **Stakeholders Validate Assumptions**
  Finance and business units agree on calculations and methodology.
- **Results are Interpreted for Impact**
  Financial and operational outcomes are framed in stakeholder-relevant language.

ROI and Business Impact Reporting
Capture Cost-Benefit and Productivity Shifts

Checklist

1. Catalogue all direct and indirect training costs
2. Capture pre-training productivity, error, or performance metrics
3. Track post-training outcomes using the same KPIs
4. Quantify improvements in time, output, or quality
5. Convert gains into cost savings or value-added
6. Subtract training costs to calculate net benefit
7. Express as ROI % if applicable
8. Validate with relevant departments (Finance, Ops, HR)
9. Present findings using clear, visual summaries
10. Store the model for future evaluations

AI Considerations

- **Forecast ROI Based on Similar Programs**
  Use AI to analyse historical project data and predict expected ROI or time savings.
- **Identify Productivity Trends**
  Automatically surface performance shifts across departments post-training.
- **Estimate Cost Avoidance**
  Model the cost impact of reduced errors, rework, or staff turnover using historical cost patterns.
- **Flag Low-Impact Learning Areas**
  Detect training initiatives with weak performance correlation to target improvements.
- **Auto-Generate ROI Reports**
  Create ready-to-share summaries for executives, tailored to financial or operational priorities.

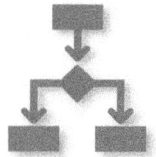

Key Takeaways

Capturing cost–benefit and productivity shifts is central to proving that learning delivers tangible organisational value. It moves beyond learning theory into business reality, quantifying time saved, errors reduced, and outcomes improved.

When done with integrity and stakeholder collaboration, this sub-step turns L&D from a perceived cost centre into a proven performance driver.

Clear ROI helps secure budgets, prioritise initiatives, and focus energy on what makes the biggest impact.

Evaluate Behavioural Change and Application on the Job

Why this is important

The ultimate goal of most training isn't just knowledge transfer, it's behavioural change.

Evaluating how well learners apply their new skills, processes, or mindsets on the job provides a direct link between learning and performance improvement.

This sub-step focuses on identifying observable changes in behaviour that reflect the course's real-world impact.

By assessing behavioural change, instructional designers can validate whether the training has moved beyond theory into workplace practice. It also reveals whether organisational culture, systems, or leadership support the application of learning.

Without this insight, even high knowledge scores may mask a failure to drive genuine improvement.

Tips

- **Use Observation-Based Methods**
  Leverage peer reviews, manager assessments, or self-assessments over time to capture behavioural changes.
- **Define What Change Looks Like**
  Collaborate with stakeholders to identify what "successful application" means for each role or competency.
- **Ensure Support Systems are in Place**
  Behavioural change often requires job aids, coaching, reinforcement, and manager encouragement, training alone is rarely enough.
- **Track Change Over Time**
  Immediate post-training improvements may fade without follow-up measurement.
- **Focus on Transfer Conditions**
  Evaluate whether the workplace environment supports or hinders behaviour change (e.g. resources, time, leadership).

Traps

- **Measuring Too Soon**
  Behavioural change takes time, evaluating it immediately after training is often premature.
- **Confusing Confidence with Competence**
  Just because a learner *says* they're applying new behaviours doesn't mean they're doing it correctly.
- **Ignoring External Influences**
  Behavioural outcomes may be affected by team dynamics, system constraints, or leadership, not just the training.
- **Over-Reliance on Self-Reporting**
  Self-assessments are prone to bias, balance them with peer or supervisor input.
- **Lack of Follow-Up**
  Failing to monitor ongoing application undermines the long-term impact of learning initiatives.

ROI and Business Impact Reporting
Evaluate Behavioural Change and Application on the Job

Techniques

- **360-Degree Feedback**
  Use structured feedback from peers, managers, and direct reports to identify changes in behaviour.
- **Behaviour Observation Checklists**
  Equip supervisors or mentors with simple checklists to record specific post-training behaviours.
- **Before-and-After Task Assessment**
  Evaluate work samples or observed tasks pre- and post-training to detect improvement.
- **Job Performance Dashboards**
  Use operational data (e.g. call handling metrics, sales numbers, compliance scores) to infer behavioural change.
- **Coaching Logs and Supervisor Notes**
  Capture manager insights on whether learners are applying new behaviours in team settings.

Examples

- *Example 1*
  After customer service training, managers report a 30% increase in agents using empathetic phrasing and de-escalation techniques during calls.
- *Example 2*
  A leadership program tracks how many team members have adopted regular 1:1 coaching sessions, usage rises from 20% to 75% within 3 months.
- *Example 3*
  A compliance training program reduces policy violations by 40%, with supervisors noting improved documentation practices.
- *Example 4*
  Sales staff demonstrate higher usage of the CRM's value-based selling prompts, as tracked by system logins and deal notes.
- *Example 5*
  A technical team shows marked improvement in adherence to new QA protocols following training, confirmed through audit logs.

How it's done

1. **Define Behavioural Objectives**
   Translate course outcomes into observable actions or decisions expected from learners on the job.
2. **Select Behaviour Indicators**
   Identify what evidence (quantitative or qualitative) would indicate that the behaviour is being demonstrated.
3. **Engage Managers and Supervisors**
   Involve team leaders in monitoring and validating whether learners are applying new behaviours.
4. **Capture Observations and Feedback**
   Use surveys, interviews, observation checklists, or system logs to gather data on post-training behaviour.
5. **Compare to Pre-Training Benchmarks**
   Where possible, compare new behaviours to baseline data collected before training.
6. **Identify Barriers to Transfer**
   Ask learners and managers what is helping or preventing behaviour change, tools, time, culture, etc.
7. **Summarise and Report Findings**
   Present clear insights on whether behaviour change occurred, and what supported or blocked its success.

ROI and Business Impact Reporting
Evaluate Behavioural Change and Application on the Job

Core Elements

- **Behavioural Expectations are Clearly Defined**
  Post-training behaviours are explicitly outlined and aligned with course objectives.
- **Baseline and Follow-Up Data is Collected**
  Observations are made before and after training for comparison.
- **Multiple Perspectives are Captured**
  Feedback includes input from learners, managers, and peers.
- **Transfer Conditions are Evaluated**
  Organisational enablers or barriers to behaviour change are identified.
- **Behaviour is Tracked Over Time**
  Short- and long-term behavioural shifts are measured for sustainability.
- **Findings are Actionable**
  Reports highlight what's working, what's not, and what support is needed to embed behaviour change.

Checklist

1. Translate learning objectives into observable workplace behaviours
2. Define indicators of successful application
3. Capture pre-training behaviour data (if possible)
4. Choose methods for observing or measuring change (360°, checklists, dashboards)
5. Train managers to identify and reinforce target behaviours
6. Collect and validate observations over time
7. Analyse behaviour change by team, role, or region
8. Identify what supports or hinders application
9. Present findings in clear business language
10. Recommend follow-up support (coaching, refreshers, job aids)

AI Considerations

- **Detect Behavioural Signals from System Logs**
  Use AI to analyse user actions in platforms (e.g. CRM, LMS, QA systems) to infer behaviour change.
- **Identify Transfer Gaps**
  Predict which learners are struggling to apply training based on post-training patterns.
- **Cluster Similar Behavioural Profiles**
  Group learners by behaviour change profiles to personalise follow-up support.
- **Analyse Feedback Transcripts**
  Use natural language processing (NLP) to extract patterns from manager or peer comments.
- **Visualise Behaviour Trends**
  Auto-generate dashboards tracking behaviour change over time, segmented by role or business unit.

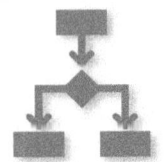
Key Takeaways

Evaluating behavioural change and application on the job is where learning proves its worth. It shows whether learners have moved from knowing to doing, and whether the organisation has supported that shift. By capturing observable behaviours, engaging with supervisors, and identifying enablers or barriers to application, this sub-step connects training to real-world performance. Done right, it confirms learning as a catalyst for transformation, not just information.

Translate Learning into Business Impact Stories

Why this is important

Data can inform, but stories persuade. Translating learning results into business impact stories turns raw metrics into meaningful narratives that resonate with decision-makers.

While graphs and dashboards show what happened, a well-told story explains *why it mattered*, linking a learning intervention to tangible changes in behaviour, outcomes, and business success.

Stories bring the learning journey to life by showing how a specific problem was addressed through training, what changed in the learner or team, and how that change improved operations, culture, or performance.

When paired with credible data, stories help stakeholders connect emotionally and intellectually, strengthening buy-in and demonstrating that L&D is not just a support function, but a strategic driver of growth and transformation.

Tips

- **Use a Clear Story Arc**
  Follow a structure: *Context → Challenge → Learning Intervention → Behavioural Change → Outcome*.
- **Feature Real People and Teams**
  Showcase named individuals or business units when possible, this adds authenticity and relatability.
- **Back Stories with Data**
  Complement the narrative with relevant KPIs, charts, or quotes to reinforce credibility.
- **Tailor Stories to the Audience**
  Executives care about cost, risk, and impact. Managers want to see operational results. Adapt accordingly.
- **Keep it Concise and Strategic**
  Focus on high-impact results, don't overwhelm with unnecessary detail or training jargon.

Traps

- **Focusing on the Training, Not the Outcome**
  A story about course content isn't compelling, focus on the problem solved or change achieved.
- **Making it Too Generic**
  Stories that could apply to "any course, anywhere" don't build credibility, specificity matters.
- **Lacking Proof**
  Anecdotes without supporting data may be dismissed as marketing spin.
- **Missing the Business Relevance**
  If the impact isn't tied to a business goal or KPI, the story will fall flat with senior stakeholders.
- **Telling Stories Too Late**
  Capture anecdotes and quotes during or soon after training, while experiences are fresh.

Techniques

- **Impact Story Template**
  Create a standard format that includes context, intervention, outcomes, and stakeholder testimonials.
- **Quote Collection Process**
  Build a repository of learner, manager, and SME quotes during training rollout for future story use.
- **Storyboards or Infographics**
  Visualise impact stories to make them digestible in presentations or reports.
- **Video Testimonials**
  Record brief interviews with learners or stakeholders describing their transformation and results.
- **Mini Case Studies**
  Use short-form case studies that blend narrative and metrics to spotlight learning success.

ROI and Business Impact Reporting
Translate Learning into Business Impact Stories

Examples

- **Example 1**
  "Before the training, our field engineers were making configuration errors weekly. After the new simulation-based course, error rates dropped 80%, and we saved over $200,000 in warranty claims in Q2."

- **Example 2**
  "Thanks to the new onboarding program, new hires in our contact centre are resolving issues two weeks faster than before, and our CSAT score jumped 15 points in just 90 days."

- **Example 3**
  "After the leadership program, one manager turned around a disengaged team with a 40% attrition rate. Six months later, her team's engagement score is the highest in the business unit."

- **Example 4**
  "We introduced accessibility training for our product designers. Within a month, two product teams delivered updates that reduced user complaints from customers with disabilities by 50%."

- **Example 5**
  "Following our fraud prevention eLearning module, we saw a 70% drop in policy violations and prevented two six-figure financial losses within three months."

How it's done

1. **Identify High-Impact Training Programs**
   Focus on programs with strong data and clear alignment to business goals.

2. **Collect Anecdotes and Observations**
   Ask learners, managers, and SMEs for real examples of behavioural or performance change post-training.

3. **Document the Journey**
   Use a consistent format: what was the issue, what training was delivered, what changed, and what improved.

4. **Link to KPIs or Metrics**
   Where possible, anchor the story with before-and-after data tied to business indicators.

5. **Obtain Permissions**
   Ensure you have consent to use names, photos, or quotes, especially in public-facing or executive reports.

6. **Tailor the Story to the Audience**
   Select the right level of detail and tone depending on whether your reader is an executive, manager, or practitioner.

7. **Share and Repurpose**
   Integrate stories into evaluation reports, dashboards, presentations, and learning showcases.

Core Elements

- **Clear Business Context**
  The story starts with a business challenge or performance gap.

- **Learning Intervention is Described Simply**
  The training solution is explained in plain terms, without excessive detail.

- **Behavioural or Performance Change is Evident**
  The outcome is observable and relevant to business stakeholders.

- **Quantified Results or KPIs are Included**
  The story is supported by credible data wherever possible.

- **Human Perspective is Present**
  The story includes the voice or experience of a real learner, manager, or team.

- **Message is Aligned to Audience Priorities**
  The framing reflects what matters most to the target audience (e.g. cost savings, culture change, compliance).

ROI and Business Impact Reporting
Translate Learning into Business Impact Stories

381

Checklist

1. Select a course or program with strong business impact
2. Identify a learner or team with a clear transformation story
3. Capture quotes, observations, or stakeholder feedback
4. Document what changed and how it was supported by the training
5. Link the outcome to a business KPI or strategic goal
6. Create a visual or narrative format for the story
7. Secure permissions and approvals where required
8. Customise the story to suit the intended audience
9. Include the story in reports, presentations, or dashboards
10. Archive for reuse in future communications or strategy sessions

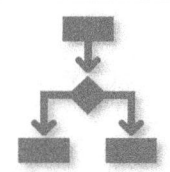

AI Considerations

- **Generate Draft Stories from LMS and Feedback Data**
  Use AI to scan learner feedback, course completions, and performance data to suggest potential impact stories.
- **Auto-Summarise Case Studies for Executives**
  Turn long-form evaluations into snappy summaries tailored to leadership.
- **Analyse Themes Across Programs**
  Use machine learning to detect recurring success patterns and narrative elements.
- **Convert Transcripts into Quotes**
  Extract and clean up quotes from interviews or video testimonials using natural language processing (NLP).
- **Match Stories to Strategic Goals**
  Classify stories based on strategic relevance (e.g. safety, sales, compliance) for targeted reporting.

Key Takeaways

Translating learning into business impact stories is where numbers meet narrative. It's how instructional designers move from reporting data to inspiring change.

A well-crafted story brings learning to life, showing the human and organisational benefit in a way that charts never could.

These stories win hearts, minds, and budgets, and ensure the learning function is seen as a strategic, value-driving partner.

Generate Reports for Executives

Why this is important

Executives don't need to see every learning metric; they need to see what matters.

Generating reports for executives means distilling complex evaluation data into strategic, actionable insights that speak the language of business performance, risk, cost, and opportunity.

This sub-step ensures that learning outcomes are communicated in a format and tone that aligns with executive expectations.

These reports must be credible, concise, and visually engaging, providing clarity around return on investment, alignment with business goals, and future recommendations.

When done well, executive reporting elevates L&D from a service function to a strategic partner, strengthening influence and securing future investment.

Tips

- **Lead with Business Impact**
  Highlight outcomes that connect directly to strategic priorities, productivity, risk, cost reduction, innovation, compliance.
- **Use Visual Storytelling**
  Charts, dashboards, and infographics are more effective than data tables. Executives scan, make insights pop.
- **Tailor by Role and Function**
  CFOs care about financial efficiency. COOs care about process and productivity. Align content to each stakeholder.
- **Include a One-Page Summary**
  Provide an executive snapshot that summarises key takeaways, metrics, and next steps.
- **Frame Recommendations Clearly**
  End with a strong call to action: continue funding, scale the program, or refine the model.

Traps

- **Overloading with Detail**
  Too much data can dilute your message. Be selective and focused.
- **Using Learning Jargon**
  Terms like "instructional scaffolding" or "formative assessment" can alienate non-L&D stakeholders.
- **Failing to Contextualise**
  Raw metrics without benchmarks, comparisons, or stories lack meaning.
- **Neglecting Risks or Gaps**
  Executives respect transparency, don't hide weaknesses. Frame them as opportunities for improvement.
- **Reporting Without Relevance**
  If the outcomes aren't clearly tied to business goals, the report becomes background noise.

Techniques

- **Executive Dashboards**
  Build high-level dashboards with drill-down options. Focus on KPIs, ROI, and trend visuals.
- **Impact Snapshots**
  Use templated one-pagers with a visual summary, strategic highlights, and key recommendations.
- **Traffic Light Reporting**
  Show what's on track, what needs attention, and what's underperforming with a simple colour-coded system.
- **Narrative-Driven Presentations**
  Present findings as part of a story arc, problem, intervention, outcome, future plan.
- **Tiered Reporting**
  Provide summaries up front, with supporting detail in appendices for those who want to go deeper.

ROI and Business Impact Reporting
Generate Reports for Executives

Examples

- **Example 1**
  A slide deck for the executive team shows that a digital transformation training program yielded a 23% improvement in system adoption and saved 1,200 labour hours in Q1.
- **Example 2**
  A one-pager summarises ROI from leadership development across three divisions, highlighting engagement improvements, retention gains, and productivity boosts.
- **Example 3**
  A dashboard presents real-time data on compliance training completions, linking them to audit readiness and risk mitigation across departments.
- **Example 4**
  A "learning health" infographic maps training programs to the top five business priorities, showing coverage, completion, and reported impact.
- **Example 5**
  A visual story report tracks how a critical onboarding redesign shortened time-to-productivity by 25%, aligned with HR's quarterly targets.

How it's done

1. **Clarify Executive Priorities**
   Meet with stakeholders or review strategic plans to understand what matters to the executive audience.
2. **Select High-Impact Data Points**
   Choose 4–6 key metrics that demonstrate business relevance, financial, operational, compliance, or cultural.
3. **Create a Strategic Narrative**
   Structure the report to show the problem, what was done, what changed, and what the business gained.
4. **Design Visual Elements**
   Use charts, icons, dashboards, or infographics to present insights quickly and clearly.
5. **Prepare Executive Summaries**
   Lead with a one-page overview, headlines, metrics, and a clear recommendation.
6. **Tailor by Role Where Necessary**
   Produce alternate versions for HR, Finance, Operations, or other key departments with relevant emphasis.
7. **Review and Validate**
   Check all figures, visuals, and claims for accuracy. Ensure consistency across slides or pages.
8. **Present, Don't Just Send**
   Where possible, present reports in person or via video briefing to engage discussion and clarify insights.

Core Elements

- **Alignment with Strategic Goals**
  The report connects training outcomes to key business drivers.
- **Visual Clarity and Brevity**
  The format is concise, attractive, and easy to scan.
- **Executive Summary is Included**
  A one-pager captures the essence of the report for time-poor leaders.
- **Data is Valid and Contextualised**
  Metrics are accurate, benchmarked, and framed for impact.
- **Recommendations are Clear and Actionable**
  The report concludes with a specific proposal or next step.
- **Customisation is Considered**
  Report content is adapted to the needs and concerns of different executive roles.

ROI and Business Impact Reporting
Generate Reports for Executives

Checklist

1. Identify executive audience and their key interests
2. Choose data that reflects impact on business outcomes
3. Draft a story-driven structure for the report
4. Build clear, visually appealing slides or pages
5. Create a concise one-page executive summary
6. Validate all data and source attribution
7. Include strategic recommendations tied to outcomes
8. Customise versions for HR, Finance, or Ops as needed
9. Schedule a review or presentation where possible
10. Save reporting templates for future evaluations

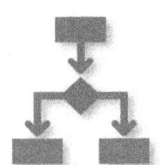
AI Considerations

- **Auto-Summarise Evaluation Data**
  Use AI to distil long-form analysis into key executive highlights.
- **Generate Role-Specific Dashboards**
  Create tailored reports for HR, Finance, or Operations based on shared base data.
- **Design Visuals with AI Tools**
  Use generative AI to create branded infographics, summary visuals, and dashboard layouts.
- **Natural Language Summary of Metrics**
  Turn raw data sets into narrative explanations for slide decks.
- **Scan Executive Feedback Trends**
  Use sentiment analysis to adapt tone and emphasis based on previous executive feedback.

Key Takeaways

Executive reporting is where learning results get turned into decisions.

When done well, it captures the attention of senior leaders, validates the value of L&D, and influences strategic direction.

It's not about reporting everything, it's about reporting the right things, in the right way, to the right people. Clear, data-backed, and action-oriented executive reports are a key differentiator for learning teams that want a seat at the decision-making table.

Compliance and Audit Readiness

The **Compliance and Audit Readiness** step ensures that learning programs meet legal, regulatory, and organisational standards. It provides the necessary structure and documentation to withstand both internal reviews and external audits. In regulated industries, this step is not optional, it is mission critical.

More than just ticking boxes, compliance requires robust version control, clear traceability of learning interventions, and thorough documentation of learner participation, assessment results, and policy alignment. Accessibility and inclusion are also becoming core components of compliance frameworks, especially in government and large enterprises.

This step safeguards the organisation from risk, ensures accountability, and strengthens the credibility of learning programs. Whether preparing for a formal audit or simply ensuring internal policies are met, this is the phase where compliance meets instructional design.

Key sub-steps include:

- **Review and Document Learning Records**
  Verify that enrolments, completions, assessments, and certifications are accurately captured and securely stored.

- **Ensure Version Control and Policy Mapping**
  Maintain records of learning content versions, update logs, and how each module maps to internal policies or regulatory frameworks.

- **Prepare for Internal and External Audits**
  Organise artefacts, reports, and evidence in formats that meet audit requirements, ensuring easy retrieval and traceability.

- **Validate Completion Against Compliance Mandates**
  Confirm that all required learners have completed mandatory training and that exceptions are documented and explained.

- **Store Evidence of Learning Accessibility and Inclusion**
  Maintain proof that training was accessible to all employees, including those with disabilities or language needs, to meet equity requirements.

Overview

Compliance and Audit Readiness
Generate Reports for Executives

Outcomes

The **Compliance and Audit Readiness** step ensures that learning solutions meet the highest standards of transparency, traceability, and regulatory alignment. Key outcomes include:

- **Mitigate Legal and Operational Risk**
  Reduce exposure to compliance breaches by ensuring training obligations are met and well-documented.
- **Demonstrate Due Diligence and Governance**
  Provide concrete evidence of training implementation, learner participation, and policy coverage.
- **Ensure Audit Preparedness**
  Maintain audit-ready records that meet internal quality checks and withstand external scrutiny.
- **Support Inclusion and Accessibility Mandates**
  Validate that learning offerings meet accessibility standards and reflect diversity, equity, and inclusion goals.
- **Streamline Reporting and Document Management**
  Organise learning records, policy references, and audit trails in ways that support operational efficiency and accountability.

Summary

Compliance and Audit Readiness is the assurance layer of the Evaluation phase. It protects the organisation by proving that learning programs are not only effective but also compliant, traceable, and equitable.

By establishing strong documentation practices, version control mechanisms, and accessible content design, this step prepares the organisation for audits and validates its commitment to governance and accountability.

In an era where regulators are placing increased scrutiny on corporate training, and where ESG reporting is rising in importance, this step ensures L&D holds up to legal, ethical, and operational standards.

Review and Document Learning Records

Why this is important

Reviewing and documenting learning records is foundational to audit readiness and regulatory compliance.

Accurate, up-to-date records serve as proof that training occurred, learners participated, and requirements were met. These records form the evidence trail that supports legal, safety, quality, and policy standards across the organisation.

Beyond compliance, well-maintained learning records allow for performance tracking, enable version control of content, and support certification or professional development requirements.

When records are incomplete, inconsistent, or inaccessible, it creates audit risk and undermines trust in the training process. This sub-step ensures that all learning activities are verifiable, traceable, and aligned with organisational and external standards.

Tips

- **Standardise Record Formats**
  Use consistent templates or data structures across systems and teams to ensure uniformity and clarity.
- **Define What Must Be Tracked**
  Clarify required data fields, e.g. enrolment, completion status, assessment scores, feedback, timestamps, facilitator notes.
- **Audit for Gaps and Inconsistencies**
  Conduct periodic reviews of learning records to identify missing data, duplicates, or discrepancies.
- **Integrate with HR and Compliance Systems**
  Sync learning data with HRIS or GRC platforms where possible to support broader compliance reporting.
- **Ensure Accessibility**
  Records should be easy to retrieve on demand for audits, incident reviews, or stakeholder queries.

Traps

- **Assuming LMS Data is Always Complete**
  Not all learning happens inside the LMS, offline or informal training may go undocumented.
- **Inconsistent Naming Conventions**
  Variations in course titles, codes, or user IDs can lead to confusion and missed reporting.
- **Relying Solely on Manual Tracking**
  Manual entry increases the risk of error. Where possible, automate data capture.
- **Lack of Version Control**
  Failing to document which version of a course a learner completed may cause issues during audits or re-certification.
- **Ignoring Legal Retention Requirements**
  Some industries mandate how long learning records must be stored. Don't purge data prematurely.

Techniques

- **LMS Configuration Audits**
  Review LMS settings to ensure all required data points are being captured and timestamped.
- **Learning Record Stores (LRS)**
  Use xAPI-compatible LRS tools to track learning across platforms and environments.
- **Course Completion Reports**
  Regularly generate and archive detailed reports showing enrolments, completions, scores, and feedback.
- **Data Validation Routines**
  Apply automated scripts or queries to check for blank fields, duplicates, or inconsistencies.
- **Metadata Tagging**
  Tag learning content and completions with relevant compliance categories for easier retrieval.

Compliance and Audit Readiness
Review and Document Learning Records

Examples

- *Example 1*
  A pharmaceutical company stores all GMP-related training records in a validated LMS, enabling instant recall during FDA inspections.
- *Example 2*
  An airline uses version-controlled logs to track which safety procedures were trained and when, ensuring traceability during incident investigations.
- *Example 3*
  A mining company conducts quarterly audits of their LMS to confirm that all high-risk job roles have completed mandatory environmental safety training.
- *Example 4*
  An HR team integrates the LMS with SAP SuccessFactors, allowing automatic updates of employee learning records across systems.
- *Example 5*
  A financial services firm maintains encrypted backups of compliance training logs to meet five-year data retention requirements.

How it's done

1. **Define Required Learning Data**
   Clarify what data must be captured for compliance, enrolment, completion, scores, facilitator comments, etc.
2. **Review Current Records**
   Audit the LMS and any supplementary systems for completeness, accuracy, and formatting consistency.
3. **Standardise Record-Keeping Practices**
   Implement naming conventions, course codes, and tracking protocols across all teams.
4. **Establish Version Control Protocols**
   Document course versions and ensure completions are linked to the specific version delivered.
5. **Store Records Securely and Accessibly**
   Ensure records are backed up, permission-controlled, and easy to retrieve during an audit or investigation.
6. **Schedule Routine Audits**
   Set recurring review points (e.g. quarterly) to validate data and update records as needed.
7. **Align with Retention Policies**
   Verify how long records need to be kept based on legal or organisational requirements.
8. **Train Administrators and Facilitators**
   Ensure those inputting or managing records understand compliance expectations and system procedures.

Compliance and Audit Readiness
Review and Document Learning Records

Core Elements

- **Required Data Points are Defined**
  Each course and learner record contains consistent, pre-agreed data fields.
- **All Learning Activities are Captured**
  Both formal (LMS-based) and informal or blended learning are recorded.
- **Versioning is Traceable**
  Records link learners to specific versions of training materials or modules.
- **Record Integrity is Ensured**
  Data is validated, backed up, and protected against unauthorised access or tampering.
- **Audit Readiness is Built-In**
  Records can be retrieved quickly and presented in compliant formats when requested.
- **Retention Rules are Applied**
  Records are kept for the appropriate length of time based on industry or regulatory standards.

Checklist

1. Define required learning data fields and metadata
2. Audit current records for completeness, accuracy, and consistency
3. Implement or update naming and version control standards
4. Ensure non-LMS activities are also documented (e.g. workshops, coaching)
5. Back up learning records and apply access controls
6. Align storage and purge policies with legal retention requirements
7. Train record-keepers on compliance expectations
8. Establish a regular review cycle for record maintenance
9. Prepare standard export formats for audits or reports
10. Link learning records to employee performance or certification data when relevant

AI Considerations

- **Auto-Detect Incomplete or Inconsistent Records**
  Use AI to flag missing fields, duplicate entries, or unusual timestamp patterns.
- **Smart Record Tagging**
  Apply AI-driven classification to group learning records by risk category, compliance area, or learner cohort.
- **Predict Record Retention Risks**
  Forecast when data may expire or become non-compliant based on retention policies.
- **Generate Audit-Ready Summaries**
  Auto-create exportable summaries of learning records formatted for auditors or regulators.
- **Voice-Activated Record Search (Optional Integration)**
  Use AI-powered search tools to retrieve records using natural language queries (e.g. "Show me all forklift training completions in the last 12 months").

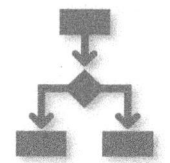
Key Takeaways

Reviewing and documenting learning records is the foundation of audit readiness. It ensures that every training activity is traceable, version-controlled, and aligned with regulatory or organisational expectations.

Clear, consistent records protect the business, support performance tracking, and instil confidence in the learning function's rigour.

In a compliance-focused world, if it's not recorded, it didn't happen, and that makes this sub-step a non-negotiable.

Ensure Version Control and Policy Mapping

Why this is important

Maintaining version control and mapping learning content to relevant policies are essential for demonstrating that training is accurate, up to date, and aligned with current regulatory, legal, or organisational standards. This sub-step ensures that any learner's completion record can be traced back to the exact version of the content they received, and that the content they received was aligned with an active policy or requirement at the time.

Without clear version control, organisations risk using outdated or unapproved materials, which can lead to compliance breaches, legal exposure, and audit failure.

Policy mapping provides the "why" behind the training, showing that the learning intervention was designed in direct response to formal business rules or external mandates. Together, version control and policy alignment ensure the integrity, relevance, and defensibility of your training programs.

Tips

- **Use Unique Version IDs**
  Assign distinct codes (e.g. v1.3, 2025Q2) to each update or major revision of a course.
- **Document Change Logs**
  Record what was changed, why, when, and by whom, this creates a transparent audit trail.
- **Link Each Course to Specific Policies or Standards**
  Tag or reference internal policies, legislation, or ISO standards within course metadata.
- **Coordinate with Compliance and Legal**
  Engage relevant departments during content updates to validate accuracy and relevance.
- **Include Version Details in Completion Records**
  Ensure each learner record shows which version of the course was completed and when.

Traps

- **Silent Updates Without Record**
  Updating content without documenting changes or incrementing the version number creates confusion and audit risk.
- **Misalignment with Outdated Policies**
  Linking a course to a superseded policy undermines compliance and may cause learners to apply incorrect practices.
- **Lack of Communication Across Teams**
  Designers, administrators, and compliance teams must be in sync, otherwise, version control can break down.
- **Overcomplicating the Process**
  Excessively complex naming or tagging schemes can reduce adoption and introduce errors.
- **Policy Mapping as an Afterthought**
  Mapping should be done during course design, not just before a compliance review.

Techniques

- **Content Version Register**
  Maintain a central log or register of all course versions, dates of release, and change summaries.
- **Policy-to-Course Mapping Matrix**
  Create a table showing which courses fulfil which compliance obligations, regulations, or business rules.
- **Automated Version Tracking in LMS**
  Use LMS features to track revisions, attach metadata, and lock prior versions to preserve audit trails.
- **Update Notification Workflows**
  Automatically notify SMEs, legal, and compliance when content updates are due or complete.
- **Embedded Version Stamps**
  Include version numbers and dates visibly within courseware (e.g. on the first slide or footer) for transparency.

Compliance and Audit Readiness
Ensure Version Control and Policy Mapping

Examples

- **Example 1**
  A banking compliance course linked to AML legislation includes version stamps and a change log showing updates aligned with regulatory amendments in March 2024.

- **Example 2**
  A mining site safety module tracks each release using a version register, ensuring that any incident investigation can trace back to the exact training content delivered to the worker involved.

- **Example 3**
  A healthcare organisation maintains a policy-to-course matrix showing how each clinical training module maps to internal procedures and external accreditation requirements.

- **Example 4**
  During an ISO audit, the L&D team presents version control logs and policy cross-references, demonstrating that all quality-related training is up to date.

- **Example 5**
  An aged care provider integrates LMS course metadata with their risk and compliance system, enabling real-time alignment tracking across policy updates.

How it's done

1. **Establish Version Control Standards**
   Define how course versions will be numbered, labelled, and updated across all platforms.

2. **Create a Central Version Register**
   Maintain a document or database logging all content updates, dates, responsible authors, and rationale for change.

3. **Map Courses to Policies**
   For each training module, list the internal or external policies it supports, referencing document numbers and clauses where applicable.

4. **Embed Metadata in Course Files**
   Add version numbers, last updated dates, and policy references within SCORM packages, PDFs, or slides.

5. **Ensure Version Info is Stored in the LMS**
   Configure the LMS to store and display version details in course settings and learner completion records.

6. **Engage SMEs and Compliance in the Review Cycle**
   Schedule regular reviews (e.g. annually or post-policy change) and document sign-off processes.

7. **Archive Superseded Versions**
   Retain prior versions securely with clear access controls to support retrospective audits if needed.

8. **Train Admins and Designers**
   Ensure those maintaining content understand versioning protocols and policy alignment procedures.

Core Elements

- **Unique Version Numbers are Applied Consistently**
  Every course version is labelled and tracked systematically.

- **Change History is Transparent**
  A documented summary exists for every update made to course materials.

- **Courses are Mapped to Policies**
  Each course shows which policies, regulations, or standards it supports.

- **LMS and Completion Records Reflect Version Info**
  Learner records indicate exactly which version of a course was completed.

- **Review and Update Cycles are Defined**
  A maintenance calendar or trigger-based review system is in place.

- **Prior Versions are Archived and Accessible**
  Superseded content is retained and protected for audit purposes.

Compliance and Audit Readiness
Ensure Version Control and Policy Mapping

Checklist

1. Define and document version control naming conventions
2. Maintain a version register or change log for all learning content
3. Create a policy-to-course mapping matrix
4. Embed version and policy metadata into course files
5. Store version info in LMS course settings and learner records
6. Review content regularly or when policies change
7. Involve compliance, legal, and SMEs in review and sign-off
8. Archive previous versions in a secure location
9. Train all content creators and admins on versioning standards
10. Prepare version history reports for audit readiness

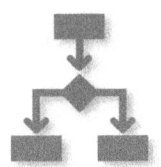

AI Considerations

- **Detect Content Out-of-Sync with Current Policies**
  Use AI to flag training materials linked to expired or superseded policies.
- **Auto-Generate Version Comparison Reports**
  Highlight differences between current and previous versions for audit purposes.
- **Map Policies to Courses Automatically**
  Use NLP to scan policy documents and suggest relevant course alignment.
- **Recommend Content Reviews Based on Policy Change Alerts**
  Trigger review workflows when associated policies or legislation are updated.
- **Tag and Categorise Content at Scale**
  Automatically apply metadata to large volumes of content using AI-driven tagging.

Key Takeaways

Version control and policy mapping are compliance essentials.

They ensure that learning content is traceable, up to date, and defensible in the face of audit or investigation.

Without clear documentation of what was taught, when, and why, even the best training programs may fail regulatory scrutiny.

This sub-step establishes confidence that your learning solutions are not just effective, but legally and procedurally sound.

Compliance and Audit Readiness
Prepare for Internal and External Audits

Prepare for Internal and External Audits

Why this is important

Audits are not just a test of record-keeping, they're a litmus test for your organisation's credibility, accountability, and compliance culture.

Preparing for both internal and external audits ensures that all learning activities, records, and processes can withstand formal scrutiny, whether from internal quality teams, regulatory bodies, government agencies, or industry auditors.

A successful audit hinges on readiness: the ability to produce complete, accurate, and timely evidence of training alignment, completion, and effectiveness.

This sub-step helps instructional designers and learning administrators identify what auditors will look for, ensure that documentation is easily retrievable, and present training data in a format that matches audit requirements. Being audit-ready not only reduces risk, it builds trust and strengthens organisational resilience.

Tips

- **Understand the Audit Scope Early**
  Clarify which regulations, departments, or learning programs are in scope to avoid last-minute scrambles.

- **Create a Central Audit Folder**
  Prepare a secure, central repository with all relevant evidence, documents, reports, and sign-offs.

- **Map Evidence to Requirements**
  Use a checklist or matrix to show how each audit criterion is supported by your learning documentation.

- **Conduct a Mock Audit or Pre-Review**
  Simulate the audit process internally to uncover gaps and test your team's readiness.

- **Be Transparent and Professional**
  Auditors value clarity and cooperation, be prepared to explain your processes clearly and factually.

Traps

- **Scrambling to Find Evidence**
  Disorganised records or reliance on individual staff knowledge can result in audit delays or failures.

- **Assuming LMS Output is Enough**
  Auditors may require additional evidence, such as policy mappings, facilitator credentials, or signed attendance sheets.

- **Presenting Incomplete Data**
  Missing completion dates, scores, or version information can invalidate compliance claims.

- **Failing to Rehearse the Process**
  Unprepared presenters or unclear documentation workflows often increase audit risk.

- **Ignoring Industry-Specific Requirements**
  Standards vary, what satisfies ISO may not satisfy a safety regulator or government department.

Compliance and Audit Readiness
Prepare for Internal and External Audits

Techniques

- **Audit Preparation Matrix**
  Build a table showing each requirement, the supporting documentation, its location, and responsible person.
- **Audit-Ready Reporting Templates**
  Use standard formats to export data directly from your LMS or LRS in audit-friendly formats.
- **Policy Crosswalks**
  Create visual diagrams showing how each training program links to policy or regulatory clauses.
- **Access-Controlled Document Repository**
  Store audit materials securely with clear version control and access logs.
- **Facilitated Walkthroughs**
  Brief stakeholders or facilitators on how to discuss the program structure, delivery, and outcomes during the audit.

Examples

- *Example 1*
  A healthcare organisation compiles a complete audit binder with learner records, facilitator qualifications, and version-controlled content linked to national health standards.
- *Example 2*
  A transport company prepares for a safety compliance audit by generating detailed reports on high-risk role training completions and policy alignment.
- *Example 3*
  An internal ISO 9001 audit is supported by a policy-to-course matrix, quarterly completion reports, and documented update cycles.
- *Example 4*
  A mining company builds a shared audit folder containing records of learner assessments, incident follow-up training logs, and audit checklists.
- *Example 5*
  A financial services provider includes screenshots of LMS dashboards and policy approval workflows in their external compliance audit report.

How it's done

1. **Clarify the Audit Requirements**
   Understand the scope, standards, timeframe, and documentation required for the audit.
2. **Identify Evidence Sources**
   Determine where training records, policies, facilitator credentials, and other documents are stored.
3. **Compile Supporting Documentation**
   Gather course completion data, change logs, mapping documents, evaluation reports, and attendance evidence.
4. **Use a Mapping or Checklist Framework**
   Create a matrix showing how each audit requirement is met and where supporting evidence is located.
5. **Format Documents for Audit Use**
   Ensure exports are clean, standardised, and labelled. Include version numbers and dates where appropriate.
6. **Conduct an Internal Pre-Audit**
   Review all materials and walk through the audit process with key stakeholders to identify gaps or inconsistencies.
7. **Assign Roles for Audit Day**
   Designate a primary contact, a document manager, and subject matter representatives.
8. **Prepare a Summary Document**
   Include an overview of your compliance framework, training strategy, and supporting materials.

Compliance and Audit Readiness
Prepare for Internal and External Audits

Core Elements

- **Audit Requirements are Clearly Understood**
  All team members are aware of what's in scope and how it will be evaluated.
- **Evidence is Mapped and Organised**
  Documentation is linked to audit criteria and stored in an accessible, structured way.
- **Data Accuracy and Completeness are Verified**
  All reports are reviewed for missing, incorrect, or inconsistent data points.
- **Stakeholders are Briefed**
  All relevant parties understand their role in the audit and are prepared to answer questions.
- **Documentation is Formatted for Audit Use**
  Materials are labelled, timestamped, version-controlled, and aligned with audit expectations.
- **A Backup Plan Exists**
  Contingency steps are in place in case of system outages or missing evidence during audit proceedings.

Checklist

1. Confirm audit scope and standards
2. Identify required learning programs and record types
3. Locate or export all relevant documents (reports, policies, logs)
4. Build an audit checklist or mapping matrix
5. Conduct an internal review or mock audit
6. Organise documents in a central, access-controlled folder
7. Format exports for clarity and consistency
8. Prepare a summary report or audit overview
9. Brief all stakeholders involved in the audit
10. Confirm roles, responsibilities, and access on audit day

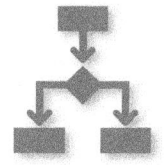
AI Considerations

- **Auto-Generate Audit Checklists**
  Use AI to interpret audit requirements and build a checklist of required evidence.
- **Identify Documentation Gaps**
  AI can scan your learning ecosystem and flag missing files, inconsistencies, or outdated materials.
- **Tag Audit-Relevant Materials**
  Apply smart tagging across documents and reports to simplify evidence retrieval.
- **Predict Audit Readiness Scores**
  Based on completeness and accuracy of data, AI can rate your audit readiness and highlight weak spots.
- **Generate Role-Specific Evidence Packs**
  Automatically compile targeted documentation by department, function, or audit focus area.

Key Takeaways

Audit readiness isn't about scrambling to gather records, it's about being consistently prepared.

This sub-step ensures that your training programs can stand up to scrutiny from regulators, executives, and quality teams alike.

When evidence is complete, structured, and defensible, your organisation is protected, and your learning team earns credibility as a strategic, compliance-aligned partner.

Validate Completion Against Compliance Mandates

Why this is important

Validating course completion against compliance mandates ensures that all required training has been delivered, completed, and recorded for the right people, at the right time.

This step directly supports regulatory, legal, and organisational obligations by verifying that no critical gaps exist in compliance coverage.

Many regulations specify which roles must complete specific training, how often, and by what date. This sub-step confirms that those requirements have been met and that completion data is defensible in the event of an audit, incident, or investigation.

Failure to validate completions can expose the organisation to legal penalties, operational risk, and reputational damage.

Getting this right means knowing exactly *who* needed to complete training, *what* they completed, and *when*.

Tips

- **Define Role-Based Requirements Up Front**
  Work with HR and compliance to establish a matrix of who needs to complete what and by when.
- **Use Completion Thresholds**
  Set minimum required completion rates by department, site, or job function for mandated programs.
- **Automate Reporting**
  Configure your LMS to generate regular reports showing completion status against each compliance area.
- **Reconcile Against Workforce Data**
  Cross-reference training records with HRIS or payroll data to ensure no learners are missing from the report.
- **Flag Exceptions Proactively**
  Identify and follow up with overdue, non-compliant, or at-risk learners before audits occur.

Traps

- **Assuming 100% LMS Visibility**
  Not all training is tracked digitally; external or informal learning may be missed.
- **Overlooking Role Changes**
  Learners who change positions or departments may require different training, ensure the system tracks this.
- **Incomplete Record Transfers**
  Onboarding new employees or contractors without transferring past training records can create compliance gaps.
- **Manual Reconciliation Errors**
  Matching completions to roles or policies manually is error prone. Automate where possible.
- **Not Accounting for Re-Certification**
  Some compliance training must be renewed periodically; ensure recurrence schedules are enforced.

Compliance and Audit Readiness
Validate Completion Against Compliance Mandates

Techniques

- **Compliance Completion Matrix**
  Build a spreadsheet or dashboard showing which learners have completed which mandated training, colour-coded for visibility.
- **Automated Role Mapping**
  Use LMS-HRIS integration to automatically assign required training based on job role, location, or department.
- **Exception Reporting**
  Set up automated alerts or reports showing overdue or missing completions.
- **Certification Expiry Monitoring**
  Track re-certification timelines and notify learners in advance of expiration.
- **Completion Validation Logs**
  Maintain audit logs showing when training was assigned, started, completed, and by whom.

Examples

- *Example 1*
  A financial institution validates that all AML training completions are logged, mapped to specific employee IDs, and completed within the annual compliance window.
- *Example 2*
  A logistics company automates assignment of driver safety training based on role codes from SAP, and flags any overdue completions weekly.
- *Example 3*
  A healthcare provider uses a dashboard to track completion of infection control training by role and location, ensuring mandatory compliance by quarter-end.
- *Example 4*
  A construction firm audits their subcontractor training register to confirm all site workers have completed site-specific safety induction.
- *Example 5*
  An aged care organisation tracks CPR certification expiry dates and sends automated reminders to staff 30 days prior to renewal due dates.

How it's done

1. **Define Mandatory Training by Role**
   Work with compliance, HR, and legal teams to determine who must complete what, and how often.
2. **Assign Training Automatically**
   Configure your LMS or LXP to assign required training based on roles, job codes, and locations.
3. **Track Completion Status Regularly**
   Generate reports that show progress toward full compliance, flag any incomplete, late, or expired completions.
4. **Cross-Check Against Active Workforce**
   Match LMS data to current HRIS records to confirm that all employees (and relevant contractors) are covered.
5. **Validate Data Quality**
   Confirm that completion records include names, dates, scores (if applicable), and version of training completed.
6. **Escalate Exceptions**
   Develop a formal process to notify managers or compliance teams when staff are non-compliant or overdue.
7. **Log Completion Verification Activities**
   Keep records of when reports were reviewed, by whom, and what action was taken for audit defensibility.

Compliance and Audit Readiness
Validate Completion Against Compliance Mandates

Core Elements

- **Role-to-Training Mapping is Clear**
  Every learner has a defined list of required training based on their current job role and work context.
- **Completion Data is Verified**
  Training records are accurate, complete, and time stamped.
- **Reports are Current and Accessible**
  Real-time or scheduled completion reports are readily available to managers and auditors.
- **Exceptions are Managed Proactively**
  Late, missed, or incomplete training is flagged and followed up in a structured way.
- **Re-Certification is Enforced**
  Time-limited training is tracked with expiry alerts and re-enrolment mechanisms.
- **Audit Trail is Maintained**
  Evidence of validation and exception handling is documented and retained.

Checklist

1. Identify mandatory training by role, location, and business unit
2. Assign training automatically based on mapped roles
3. Reconcile completions with HRIS or payroll data
4. Validate that records include learner name, date, and course version
5. Run scheduled reports showing compliance status by group or business area
6. Track overdue, missed, or upcoming expirations
7. Notify managers or compliance leads of at-risk learners
8. Document review and validation of reports
9. Track certification expiry and re-assign training as needed
10. Maintain an audit-ready history of completions and exception handling

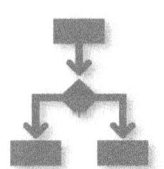
AI Considerations

- **Auto-Match Roles to Mandates**
  Use AI to suggest required training for new job roles based on compliance patterns.
- **Predict Non-Compliance Risk**
  Identify learners at risk of non-completion based on past behaviour or system activity.
- **Generate Real-Time Compliance Dashboards**
  Visualise completion data and highlight gaps across departments or regions.
- **Auto-Alert Learners and Managers**
  Trigger reminders or escalation workflows when training is due or overdue.
- **Smart Re-Certification Scheduling**
  Predict when learners will need refreshers and adjust training calendars dynamically.

Key Takeaways

Validating training completion against compliance mandates is a non-negotiable requirement for audit-readiness and operational safety.

It ensures that no employee falls through the cracks and that all training obligations are met on time, every time.

By automating checks, reconciling with workforce data, and proactively managing exceptions, this sub-step reduces risk, protects the business, and ensures that learning supports the regulatory framework, rather than scrambling to catch up with it.

Store Evidence of Learning Accessibility and Inclusion

Why this is important

Accessibility and inclusion are not just best practice; they're legal and ethical imperatives. This sub-step ensures that your organisation can demonstrate, with evidence, that all learners, including those with disabilities, language barriers, or unique learning needs, had equitable access to training.

Documenting accessibility and inclusion efforts protects the organisation from discrimination claims, regulatory breaches, or exclusionary practices. More importantly, it signals a commitment to fairness, diversity, and equal opportunity.

Storing evidence of these efforts, such as alt-text, transcripts, language options, interface customisation, and learner support, ensures that your compliance claims extend beyond what was taught to how it was delivered and who could access it.

Tips

- **Track Accessibility Compliance by Design**
  Store checklists or QA results that show how each course meets WCAG or local accessibility standards.
- **Capture Inclusion Enhancements**
  Record how learning was adapted to accommodate different literacy levels, languages, cultures, or abilities.
- **Log Accommodation Requests and Resolutions**
  Document learner requests for adjustments and how they were addressed.
- **Store Assistive Content Versions**
  Maintain copies of alternate formats (e.g. transcripts, audio-described videos, screen reader-optimised files).
- **Align with Broader Inclusion Policies**
  Ensure your documentation reflects enterprise DEI (Diversity, Equity, Inclusion) strategy and commitments.

Traps

- **Assuming Default LMS Settings Are Enough**
  Accessibility tools must be tested, verified, and documented, built-in doesn't mean compliant.
- **Only Focusing on Disability Access**
  Inclusion extends beyond disability, language, culture, neurodiversity, and socioeconomic background all matter.
- **Not Saving the Evidence**
  If accessibility features were implemented but not recorded, you can't prove compliance in an audit.
- **Inconsistent Documentation**
  Failing to standardise what "counts" as inclusion or accessibility evidence can lead to confusion or audit gaps.
- **Relying Solely on Vendor Claims**
  Don't assume third-party content meets standards, test and verify independently.

Compliance and Audit Readiness
Store Evidence of Learning Accessibility and Inclusion

Techniques

- **Accessibility Audit Logs**
  Keep internal checklists or reports showing how each learning product was reviewed for accessibility.
- **Inclusive Design Documentation**
  Capture course design decisions intended to serve a wide range of learners (e.g. flexible pacing, plain English, inclusive visuals).
- **Learner Support Logs**
  Store records of learner support provided, language interpreters, captions, tech troubleshooting, etc.
- **Feedback Capture on Inclusion**
  Use learner surveys to assess the perceived inclusiveness and accessibility of the course.
- **Language and Format Versions Registry**
  Maintain a record of available translations, simplified versions, or alternate delivery formats.

Examples

- *Example 1*
  A government agency stores WCAG compliance reports for all eLearning modules, ensuring they meet accessibility legislation.
- *Example 2*
  A mining company logs all requests for extended test time due to learning disabilities, along with actions taken.
- *Example 3*
  A healthcare provider maintains a master file of all translated course versions, including proof of linguistic QA checks.
- *Example 4*
  A bank includes inclusion checklists as part of their instructional design review process, archived with each project file.
- *Example 5*
  A university stores student survey results on accessibility, confirming whether learners could access content using screen readers or preferred fonts.

How it's done

1. **Define What Evidence Must Be Stored**
   Work with compliance, legal, and DEI teams to clarify what counts as proof of accessibility and inclusion.
2. **Audit and Document Accessibility Features**
   Use a checklist or tool to verify that each learning product meets relevant accessibility standards (e.g. WCAG 2.1 AA).
3. **Capture Alternate Format Versions**
   Save copies of screen-reader-friendly formats, captioned videos, transcripts, and translated content.
4. **Log Learner Accommodation Activities**
   Maintain records of requests and actions related to learning adjustments or support.
5. **Store Survey or Feedback Data on Inclusion**
   Archive learner responses related to access, fairness, or usability across different learner groups.
6. **Tag Learning Materials with Accessibility Metadata**
   Use tags to label content with its accessibility features (e.g. "captioned," "keyboard-navigable," "available in Spanish").
7. **Review Periodically and Archive Securely**
   Regularly review evidence files for completeness and keep them organised, secure, and accessible for audits.

Compliance and Audit Readiness
Store Evidence of Learning Accessibility and Inclusion

Core Elements

- **Standards are Defined and Followed**
  Accessibility and inclusion expectations are based on internal policy and/or legal frameworks.
- **Evidence is Stored and Organised**
  All relevant files, audits, transcripts, alternate formats, feedback, are securely archived and easy to retrieve.
- **Support and Adjustments are Tracked**
  Records exist showing how learners were supported when issues arose.
- **Inclusion is Broadly Considered**
  Evidence reflects efforts to support diverse learning styles, cultural backgrounds, and access needs.
- **Learner Voice is Captured**
  Surveys or comments that reflect learner experience of inclusion are part of the documentation.
- **Content is Versioned and Timestamped**
  Each piece of evidence is traceable to a point in time, training version, and learner group.

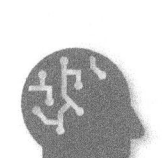

Checklist

1. Define evidence types required for accessibility and inclusion
2. Store audit reports or compliance checklists for each training product
3. Archive alternate content formats (captions, transcripts, translated versions)
4. Track and log learner accommodation requests and outcomes
5. Capture inclusion-related survey or feedback data
6. Tag content with accessibility metadata (e.g. visual contrast, alt text, captioned)
7. Verify accessibility of third-party content
8. Align evidence with internal DEI or accessibility policy
9. Ensure stored files are organised, secure, and retrievable
10. Review and update documentation practices regularly

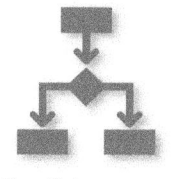

AI Considerations

- **Detect Missing Accessibility Elements**
  Use AI to scan learning content for missing alt-text, transcripts, or captioning.
- **Auto-Tag Accessibility Metadata**
  Apply smart labels to content based on format and accessibility features.
- **Summarise Inclusion Feedback**
  Use sentiment analysis on open-ended survey comments to detect access barriers.
- **Recommend Accessibility Enhancements**
  AI tools can suggest adjustments for colour contrast, reading level, or navigation based on user patterns.
- **Monitor Equity in Course Completion Rates**
  Identify disparities in participation or success across learner demographics using AI analytics.

Key Takeaways

Storing evidence of accessibility and inclusion is more than just an ethical safeguard, it's an operational necessity.

It protects learners, supports equity, and proves that your training programs are built for everyone.

With increasing regulatory focus on inclusion, documenting these efforts shows that your organisation walks the talk, and that your learning strategy is both compliant and compassionate.

AI-Enhanced Evaluation Practices

The AI-Enhanced Evaluation Practices step integrates artificial intelligence into the evaluation process to deliver faster, more accurate, and more actionable insights.
Rather than relying solely on manual analysis of quantitative and qualitative data, AI tools can process vast volumes of learner information, detect emerging patterns, and generate insights that inform strategic decisions.

These practices go beyond efficiency. They enhance the ability to analyse open-ended feedback, predict skill decay and retraining windows, generate real-time learning health dashboards, and evaluate bias within feedback algorithms. This not only accelerates decision-making but also supports fairer, more inclusive evaluation outcomes.

By embedding AI into evaluation frameworks, learning teams can shift from reactive assessments to proactive strategies that prevent problems, amplify successful practices, and optimise resources. AI does not replace human judgment, it enhances it, providing precision and scale that were previously unattainable.

Overview

Key sub-steps include:

- **Use AI to Analyse Qualitative Feedback**
  Leverage natural language processing to quickly interpret open-ended learner responses, identify emerging themes, and detect sentiment shifts across cohorts.
- **Predict Skill Decay and Retraining Windows**
  Apply predictive analytics to anticipate when critical skills are likely to decline, enabling proactive scheduling of refresher training and support resources.
- **Auto-Generate Learning Health Dashboards**
  Use AI-powered data visualisation tools to create real-time dashboards that track learner progress, engagement, and performance metrics for faster decision-making.
- **Evaluate Model Bias in Feedback Algorithms**
  Continuously test AI models for unintended bias to ensure fair and equitable evaluation of learner feedback and performance across all demographic groups.

AI-Enhanced Evaluation Practices
Store Evidence of Learning Accessibility and Inclusion

Outcomes

The **AI-Enhanced Evaluation Practices** step aims to elevate the quality and efficiency of learning evaluation by embedding intelligence throughout the process.

Key outcomes include:

- **Accelerated Insight Generation**
  Reduce the time required to process and analyse learner data, especially open-ended feedback and behavioural patterns.

- **Improved Decision-Making Accuracy**
  Enable more data-driven, evidence-based instructional decisions by identifying trends and outliers early.

- **Enhanced Learner Retention and Engagement**
  Use predictive insights to support timely interventions that boost learning reinforcement and knowledge application.

- **Bias Detection and Ethical Evaluation**
  Assess fairness and objectivity in feedback analysis and decision-support systems to promote inclusive learning practices.

- **Real-Time Visualisation of Learning Health**
  Generate dynamic dashboards that provide stakeholders with a snapshot of course impact, engagement, and risk areas.

Summary

AI-Enhanced Evaluation Practices represent the future-ready evolution of the ADDIE model. This step introduces a layer of intelligence that transforms how we understand learning performance, adapt instruction, and demonstrate impact.

By using AI to analyse feedback, anticipate skill decay, visualise learning trends, and surface bias, instructional designers gain a sharper, broader, and more equitable view of what's working, and what's not. These tools enable learning teams to respond quickly, iterate confidently, and align more closely with business outcomes.

But the power of AI comes with responsibility. Ethical implementation, transparency, and human oversight remain essential. When paired with sound instructional practice, AI doesn't just make evaluation faster, it makes it smarter, fairer, and far more strategic.

Use AI to analyse qualitative feedback

Why this is important

Qualitative feedback offers rich, nuanced insights that go beyond test scores or completion rates. It reveals learner perceptions, frustrations, moments of confusion, and unmet needs, often in their own words.

However, manually analysing open-ended comments, interview transcripts, or survey narratives is time-consuming and error prone.

AI enables instructional designers to process vast amounts of unstructured feedback quickly and consistently.

Natural language processing (NLP) can identify recurring themes, sentiment patterns, emotional tone, and emerging issues that might otherwise be missed. This not only saves time, it transforms anecdotal data into strategic insight, enabling faster, more responsive course improvements.

When used responsibly, AI does not replace the human interpretation of feedback, it enhances it by revealing what's under the surface.

Tips

- **Use AI Tools with Transparent Logic**
  Choose NLP tools that offer explainable outputs (e.g. keyword mapping, sentiment scoring) so findings are easy to interpret and defend.

- **Clean the Data First**
  Remove duplicates, irrelevant comments, or corrupted text before feeding data into the AI engine.

- **Segment by Learner Group**
  Analyse feedback by role, department, region, or cohort to surface group-specific insights.

- **Combine with Quantitative Data**
  Correlate themes from qualitative feedback with assessment scores or completion rates for richer context.

- **Refine Models with Human Oversight**
  Periodically review AI outputs manually to calibrate accuracy and spot false positives.

Traps

- **Over-Reliance on Sentiment Scores**
  Sentiment alone doesn't explain why learners feel a certain way, context matters.

- **Ignoring Minority Voices**
  Low-frequency themes can be important, don't let AI models filter them out just because they're rare.

- **Treating AI Output as Truth**
  AI identifies patterns, it doesn't validate meaning. Human interpretation is still essential.

- **Skipping Language Review**
  Cultural nuances, idioms, or sarcasm can confuse AI models, ensure linguistic alignment with your audience.

- **Failing to Close the Loop**
  Analysing feedback without action creates frustration. Feed insights back into course improvements.

AI-Enhanced Evaluation Practices
Use AI to analyse qualitative feedback

Techniques

- **Topic Modelling**
  Use AI to group comments into topic clusters (e.g. navigation issues, pacing concerns, content clarity).
- **Sentiment Analysis**
  Analyse positive, negative, or neutral tone in learner feedback to gauge satisfaction levels.
- **Theme Frequency Visualisation**
  Generate word clouds or bar charts to visualise the most common topics or phrases.
- **Text Classification**
  Automatically categorise feedback into predefined buckets (e.g. design, assessment, technology, facilitator).
- **Quote Highlighting**
  Extract representative comments for each theme to humanise the analysis in reports.

Examples

- *Example 1*
  AI analysis of post-course survey comments reveals frequent negative sentiment around the user interface, prompting a redesign of navigation flow.
- *Example 2*
  Feedback clustering identifies recurring confusion around assessment instructions, leading to a rewrite and video walk-through.
- *Example 3*
  Sentiment mapping across regional offices shows strong positive feedback in Europe but mixed satisfaction in APAC, prompting targeted review.
- *Example 4*
  A leadership program surfaces dozens of comments related to unrealistic scenarios. Designers revise case studies for cultural and operational relevance.
- *Example 5*
  Learner comments in Spanish are translated and analysed using multilingual NLP tools, ensuring feedback equity for non-English speakers.

How it's done

1. **Gather Qualitative Feedback**
   Collect data from surveys, interviews, discussion boards, comments, or helpdesk transcripts.
2. **Clean and Pre-Process the Text**
   Remove irrelevant entries, duplicates, and formatting noise. Translate if required.
3. **Select an AI Analysis Tool**
   Use an NLP engine or built-in LMS feedback analytics feature to process the data.
4. **Run Topic and Sentiment Analysis**
   Generate clusters, sentiment scores, and keyword maps to surface dominant themes.
5. **Segment by Learner Group or Region**
   Break results down by department, geography, or role to spot localised insights.
6. **Review and Interpret Themes**
   Use human judgement to validate patterns, prioritise issues, and extract illustrative quotes.
7. **Document and Report Findings**
   Create a summary showing top themes, sentiment trends, and recommended actions.
8. **Feed Back Into Course Improvement**
   Share results with content designers, SMEs, and facilitators to inform revisions.

AI-Enhanced Evaluation Practices
Use AI to analyse qualitative feedback

Core Elements

- **Unstructured Feedback is Collected and Centralised**
  All relevant comments and qualitative data are pooled and prepared for analysis.
- **AI Tools are Used to Detect Patterns**
  NLP or feedback analytics engines process data at scale for speed and consistency.
- **Themes and Sentiment are Interpreted, Not Just Listed**
  Results are contextualised to explain *why* certain feedback patterns exist.
- **Insights are Segmented for Relevance**
  Analysis includes breakout views by learner type, region, or team.
- **Illustrative Quotes are Used to Humanise Data**
  Real comments bring clarity and emotional resonance to the themes identified.
- **Findings Inform Action**
  Recommendations are passed to design teams or SMEs for targeted course improvements.

Checklist

1. Collect qualitative feedback from multiple sources
2. Clean and normalise the data set for analysis
3. Choose a suitable AI/NLP tool or module
4. Run sentiment and topic analysis
5. Segment insights by learner cohort or region
6. Extract and tag representative quotes
7. Interpret results and summarise themes
8. Link insights to course evaluation or revision cycles
9. Share findings with relevant stakeholders
10. Track changes implemented because of feedback analysis

AI Considerations

- **Use Multilingual NLP Engines**
  Analyse feedback from diverse audiences in their native languages.
- **Apply Weighted Scoring**
  Assign significance to sentiment strength, keyword frequency, or source credibility.
- **Flag Unusual Patterns**
  Detect sudden spikes in complaints or praise related to specific modules or features.
- **Generate Visual Summaries Automatically**
  Create graphs, dashboards, or theme maps from the data with minimal manual effort.
- **Detect Emotional Tone and Urgency**
  Use advanced sentiment analysis to surface frustration, confusion, or enthusiasm in feedback.

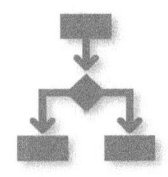

Key Takeaways

AI transforms feedback from a slow, manual chore into a powerful driver of learning improvement.

By automating the analysis of qualitative data, L&D teams can respond faster, spot hidden trends, and improve courses more strategically.

But the power of AI lies not just in detection, it lies in interpretation.

When human judgement is combined with machine precision, qualitative feedback becomes a roadmap for building smarter, more responsive learning experiences.

Predict skill decay and retraining windows

Why this is important

Even the most effective training fades over time. Skills that aren't reinforced or applied regularly begin to erode, a phenomenon known as skill decay. This sub-step focuses on using AI to detect when retention starts to drop and to predict the optimal timing for reinforcement or refresher training.

Traditionally, retraining schedules have been set arbitrarily (e.g. annually or bi-annually), often resulting in wasted effort or missed windows of vulnerability.

AI allows for a more dynamic and personalised approach. By analysing patterns in assessment results, job performance, system usage, or learner activity, instructional designers can forecast when a particular skill or knowledge area is likely to weaken, and schedule retraining accordingly.

This enables a more targeted, efficient, and proactive learning strategy that protects performance while avoiding overtraining fatigue.

Tips

- **Integrate Post-Training Performance Data**
  Use KPIs or behavioural indicators (e.g. system errors, task completion time) to monitor real-world application over time.
- **Baseline Skill Retention Early**
  Capture post-course performance metrics at regular intervals to establish a decay curve.
- **Segment by Role or Risk Level**
  Some roles decay faster than others, use business impact to prioritise monitoring.
- **Set Thresholds for Retraining Triggers**
  Define performance drop-offs or confidence dips that indicate when a refresher is needed.
- **Use Microlearning for Reinforcement**
  Target predicted weak spots with short, timely refreshers instead of full re-certification.

Traps

- **Assuming All Skills Decay Equally**
  High-frequency tasks decay more slowly than rarely used procedures, don't use a one-size-fits-all timeline.
- **Ignoring Informal Learning or Practice**
  On-the-job reinforcement may delay decay, make sure your AI model factors this in.
- **Relying Only on Self-Assessment**
  Learners often overestimate their competence, objective data is more reliable.
- **Failing to Validate the Model**
  Predictive accuracy should be reviewed periodically to adjust assumptions and inputs.
- **Delaying Intervention**
  If retraining is only reactive (after errors or incidents), you've waited too long, prediction should guide pre-emptive action.

Techniques

- **AI-Based Performance Monitoring**
  Use learning analytics and job system data to track performance trends over time.
- **Decay Curve Modelling**
  Apply predictive modelling to forecast when proficiency begins to drop post-training.
- **Trigger-Based Retraining Alerts**
  Automatically flag learners or cohorts for review when performance dips below defined benchmarks.
- **Knowledge Retention Checkpoints**
  Schedule mini assessments at set intervals to measure ongoing retention and reinforce learning.
- **Competency Heat Maps**
  Visualise retention across skill areas to identify which competencies are declining fastest.

AI-Enhanced Evaluation Practices
Predict skill decay and retraining windows

Examples

- *Example 1*
  A safety-critical role (e.g. confined space entry) is monitored using periodic assessment data. AI forecasts that most learners begin to forget key procedures after 10 weeks, prompting targeted refreshers.
- *Example 2*
  A customer service team's call quality metrics start declining 3 months after initial onboarding. The AI model triggers microlearning modules to reinforce call handling best practices.
- *Example 3*
  A sales organisation uses CRM usage data to detect declining product knowledge based on reduced feature mentions, learners are prompted with short scenario-based quizzes to retain fluency.
- *Example 4*
  A hospital tracks post-training checklist compliance and uses AI to predict when retraining on infection control is required, based on observed behaviour.
- *Example 5*
  A logistics firm's forklift operators receive spaced learning refreshers automatically when their safety audit scores begin to dip after 6 months.

How it's done

1. **Define Critical Skills or Knowledge Areas**
   Identify what must be retained over time for safe, effective job performance.
2. **Collect Longitudinal Data**
   Track learner performance and behaviour over weeks or months following training.
3. **Feed Data into Predictive Models**
   Use AI tools or LMS analytics to detect drop-off patterns in retention, usage, or performance.
4. **Establish Decay Thresholds**
   Define what level of decline indicates skill erosion (e.g. 20% score drop, 3 missed compliance steps, etc.).
5. **Segment by Learner Profile**
   Analyse decay patterns by role, region, frequency of skill use, or tenure.
6. **Schedule Proactive Reinforcement**
   Deliver microlearning, coaching, or refresher content before performance drops below acceptable thresholds.
7. **Continuously Refine the Model**
   Validate predictions against real-world outcomes and update parameters as needed.

Core Elements

- **Skill Retention Metrics are Defined**
  Clear indicators are in place to track whether learning is being maintained over time.
- **AI Models are Used to Forecast Decay**
  Predictive analytics identify when knowledge or performance begins to erode.
- **Risk-Based Segmentation is Applied**
  Learners are prioritised based on risk, role criticality, and observed decay patterns.
- **Retraining is Scheduled Proactively**
  Reinforcement occurs *before* skills drop below threshold, not in response to failure.
- **Models are Continuously Validated**
  Predictive accuracy is checked against real outcomes and adjusted regularly.
- **Human Oversight is Maintained**
  Final decisions about retraining are reviewed by instructional leaders or performance managers.

AI-Enhanced Evaluation Practices
Predict skill decay and retraining windows

Checklist

1. Identify key skills or competencies where decay is a risk
2. Define metrics that indicate performance or retention levels
3. Track learner data over time (e.g. scores, audits, system usage)
4. Apply AI or analytics tools to model decay patterns
5. Set decay thresholds or trigger conditions for intervention
6. Schedule proactive reinforcement based on predicted drop-offs
7. Segment insights by learner role, team, or task frequency
8. Validate predictions against observed outcomes
9. Adjust models based on new data or course changes
10. Document decay timelines and reinforcement strategies for audit and optimisation

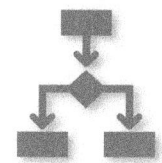

AI Considerations

- **Forecast Retention Drop-Off Timelines**
  Use historical data to predict how long specific skills remain sharp post-training.
- **Identify At-Risk Learners or Teams**
  Flag individuals or groups with declining performance before issues occur.
- **Recommend Reinforcement Interventions**
  Suggest specific refresher content based on observed decay profiles.
- **Optimise Spaced Learning Cadence**
  Tailor microlearning delivery intervals based on predicted knowledge decay curves.
- **Correlate Decay with Business Impact**
  Link skill loss to operational risk, safety incidents, or productivity metrics.

Key Takeaways

Using AI to predict skill decay transforms retraining from guesswork to precision.

Instead of relying on calendar-based refreshers, organisations can act based on actual learner behaviour and performance trends.

This ensures the right people receive the right support at the right time, reducing risk, optimising resource use, and protecting the integrity of learning outcomes.

Auto-generate learning health dashboards

Why this is important

In fast-paced organisations, static reports quickly go stale. Learning health dashboards provide real-time, interactive visualisations of the effectiveness, engagement, and reach of learning programs.

When powered by AI, these dashboards can be automatically generated and continuously updated, turning raw data into timely, actionable insight.

Dashboards provide instructional designers, managers, and executives with a bird's-eye view of learner progress, completion rates, knowledge retention, content performance, and skills gaps.

They highlight what's working, what's stalling, and where intervention is needed. By automating this process with AI, L&D teams reduce manual workload and dramatically increase visibility and responsiveness across the learning ecosystem.

These dashboards don't just report, they inform decision-making at every level.

Tips

- **Design for Stakeholder Relevance**
  Customise dashboard views by audience, executives need strategic KPIs, while designers need module-level data.
- **Use Visual Hierarchy**
  Prioritise the most critical insights using charts, gauges, heat maps, and alerts, not raw data tables.
- **Automate Data Feeds**
  Connect dashboards to your LMS, LRS, or HRIS to ensure real-time updates without manual intervention.
- **Track More Than Completion**
  Include metrics on engagement, sentiment, retention, and knowledge transfer to tell the full story.
- **Highlight Risk Areas Visually**
  Use colour-coded flags, drop-down trends, or comparison bars to draw attention to potential problem zones.

Traps

- **Overloading the Dashboard**
  Too many metrics lead to confusion, focus on 5–10 key indicators per audience.
- **Ignoring Data Context**
  Without baseline comparisons or benchmarks, charts may mislead rather than inform.
- **Focusing Only on Quantitative Data**
  Blend in summaries of qualitative themes, especially if sourced from AI feedback analysis.
- **No Call to Action**
  Dashboards that don't guide next steps fail to close the loop, interpretive notes are critical.
- **Data Gaps Undermine Confidence**
  Missing or inconsistent data feeds erode trust, validate sources regularly.

Techniques

- **Learning Performance Dashboards**
  Show metrics like course completions, assessment scores, drop-offs, and time spent.
- **Engagement Heat Maps**
  Visualise learner interaction levels across modules, topics, or user types.
- **Skill Gap Dashboards**
  Display competencies across teams and flag where proficiency is below target.
- **Sentiment and Feedback Layers**
  Add real-time feedback analysis to dashboards using AI-driven NLP.
- **Custom View Templates**
  Offer different views for executives, managers, L&D staff, and compliance officers.

AI-Enhanced Evaluation Practices
Auto-generate learning health dashboards

Examples

- **Example 1**
  An enterprise-wide learning health dashboard updates daily to show leadership which business units are on track with mandated training, and which are falling behind.
- **Example 2**
  A university uses skill heat maps to show which disciplines are struggling with retention, prompting a redesign of assessment formats.
- **Example 3**
  A retail organisation displays a dashboard combining sales data with recent product training completions, revealing a direct correlation in two regions.
- **Example 4**
  A compliance team monitors real-time dashboard metrics showing training completions versus audit deadlines, helping to prioritise follow-up.
- **Example 5**
  An L&D team uses an AI-powered dashboard to highlight which learning modules have the highest dropout rates and which cohorts are most affected.

How it's done

1. **Define Dashboard Objectives by Stakeholder Group**
   Clarify what insights each group needs, strategic, operational, or instructional.
2. **Select Key Metrics to Track**
   Choose high-impact indicators such as completion rates, engagement trends, skills gaps, and feedback sentiment.
3. **Connect to Data Sources**
   Integrate your LMS, LXP, HRIS, survey tools, and LRS to create live or regularly updated feeds.
4. **Build Custom Views and Filters**
   Tailor dashboards by learner group, region, role, business unit, or program.
5. **Apply AI-Powered Insights**
   Enable trend detection, sentiment analysis, or predictive alerts to surface deeper meaning.
6. **Validate Data Accuracy and Visual Logic**
   Test all widgets and metrics for reliability and use a clean layout that supports fast interpretation.
7. **Train Stakeholders to Use the Dashboards**
   Provide guides or walkthroughs so users understand how to interpret and act on what they see.
8. **Review and Evolve Regularly**
   Update metric relevance and dashboard layout based on user feedback and business needs.

Core Elements

- **Metrics Are Relevant and Role-Specific**
  The dashboard content reflects what matters most to its intended audience.
- **Visual Design Supports Fast Insight**
  Data is organised for clarity, with strong use of colour, charts, and indicators.
- **Automated Data Feeds Ensure Freshness**
  Data is updated regularly without manual effort or risk of error.
- **AI Adds Interpretive Value**
  Trends, sentiment, and predictive risk indicators are layered into the visualisation.
- **Insights Support Decision-Making**
  Dashboards not only show data, but they also guide action and prioritisation.
- **Accessibility is Ensured**
  Dashboards are easy to access and understand, with optional export or sharing capabilities.

AI-Enhanced Evaluation Practices
Auto-generate learning health dashboards

Checklist

1. Identify key dashboard users and their insight needs
2. Define success metrics aligned to strategic goals
3. Connect to LMS, HRIS, LRS, and feedback tools
4. Design visual elements (charts, heat maps, status indicators)
5. Automate regular data updates and alerts
6. Include AI-driven trend or sentiment insights
7. Enable filters and views for drill-down by role or region
8. Validate dashboard accuracy and visual clarity
9. Provide stakeholder training and usage documentation
10. Schedule periodic dashboard reviews for optimisation

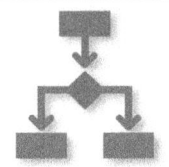

AI Considerations

- **Auto-Generate Dashboard Views**
  Let AI create role-specific visualisations based on usage patterns and access behaviour.
- **Detect Learning Health Trends**
  Highlight declining engagement, growing skill gaps, or overdue completions in real time.
- **Natural Language Summary of Dashboard Data**
  Offer AI-generated written summaries that explain key metrics in plain English.
- **Predict At-Risk Learner Groups**
  Use dashboards to flag potential dropouts or non-compliance based on past behaviours.
- **Visualise Impact by Business Unit**
  Link learning data to business performance metrics for integrated storytelling.

Key Takeaways

Auto-generated learning health dashboards shift evaluation from reactive reporting to real-time, data-driven strategy.

By combining automation, AI, and smart design, these dashboards keep stakeholders informed, highlight emerging risks, and reinforce the value of learning.

They don't just show what's happening, they guide what to do next.

Evaluate model bias in feedback algorithms

Why this is important

As AI becomes more integrated into learning evaluation, the risk of reinforcing bias grows. Feedback algorithms, used to analyse sentiment, categorise themes, or prioritise insights, can unintentionally amplify existing inequities if they're trained on unbalanced data or lack appropriate oversight.

This sub-step ensures that the AI tools used in evaluation are fair, inclusive, and representative. It involves testing whether AI models interpret feedback consistently across different learner demographics, cultures, and communication styles.

By auditing for bias, organisations protect the integrity of their evaluation practices and uphold their commitment to ethical, inclusive learning design.

Ignoring bias in AI feedback systems doesn't just skew results, it undermines trust, limits impact and can reinforce structural inequality. Addressing it directly elevates both credibility and effectiveness.

Tips

- **Test Across Diverse Data Sets**
  Run feedback samples from different regions, cultures, and learner profiles through your AI models to compare outcomes.

- **Use Human Review Panels**
  Validate AI outputs with diverse human reviewers to detect unintended bias or blind spots.

- **Check Language Sensitivity**
  Ensure your NLP model correctly interprets non-standard grammar, idioms, or cultural expressions.

- **Regularly Retrain and Recalibrate Models**
  Keep algorithms updated with diverse, current data to reduce drift and overfitting.

- **Document Model Assumptions**
  Be transparent about how the model was built, what it's optimised for, and what limitations exist.

Traps

- **Assuming Model Neutrality**
  No AI model is bias-free. All are shaped by their training data and assumptions.

- **Over-Trusting Sentiment Scores**
  Emotion detection is culturally contextual, "blunt" feedback may not equal negative intent.

- **Lack of Representation in Training Data**
  If certain learner groups are underrepresented, the AI will underperform or misinterpret their input.

- **Ignoring Feedback Outliers**
  Dismissing unusual responses may silence important minority voices.

- **Using Black-Box Models Without Oversight**
  Tools that can't be audited or explained pose a serious compliance and equity risk.

AI-Enhanced Evaluation Practices
Evaluate model bias in feedback algorithms

Techniques

- **Bias Detection Frameworks**
  Use AI ethics toolkits (e.g. Google's PAIR, IBM AI Fairness 360) to assess for demographic or cultural skew in results.
- **Confusion Matrix Reviews**
  Evaluate how often the model misclassifies neutral or positive comments as negative (or vice versa), broken down by group.
- **Diversity Audits on Input Samples**
  Analyse whether all key learner demographics are represented in the data set used to train or test the model.
- **Cross-Cultural Sentiment Testing**
  Submit identical feedback in different dialects, tones, or languages to test model interpretation consistency.
- **Shadow Testing with Human Review**
  Compare AI categorisation with diverse human raters to expose bias blind spots.

Examples

- *Example 1*
  A multinational company discovers that their feedback AI consistently misinterprets short, direct comments from Asian learners as "negative" due to tone bias.
- *Example 2*
  A mining company runs a gender bias test and finds the AI underrepresents themes raised predominantly by female employees. The model is retrained with balanced input.
- *Example 3*
  An L&D team uses shadow review, comparing AI-generated themes against those identified by human reviewers across multiple regions. Discrepancies lead to a recalibration of the algorithm.
- *Example 4*
  A university identifies that learner sentiment from ESL students is under-represented due to misunderstood grammar structures, resulting in AI tagging neutral comments as "unclear."
- *Example 5*
  A feedback system for a leadership course is tested across generational cohorts. Boomer learners' direct phrasing is flagged as "negative," prompting a tone analysis model update.

How it's done

1. **Identify Bias Risk Points**
   Determine where bias might appear, in language interpretation, sentiment scoring, theme clustering, or prioritisation.
2. **Segment Feedback Samples by Demographic**
   Group feedback by region, age, gender, language, or other relevant learner variables.
3. **Run Comparative Analysis Through the AI Tool**
   Process the segments and compare outputs, note differences in interpretation, classification, or sentiment scoring.
4. **Conduct Human Validation**
   Have diverse reviewers manually assess AI outcomes for accuracy, fairness, and unintended distortion.
5. **Measure and Document Disparities**
   Quantify any bias patterns or anomalies using audit metrics or confusion matrices.
6. **Adjust the Model or Retrain as Needed**
   Use fresh, balanced data sets or adjust weightings and sensitivity parameters.
7. **Establish Ongoing Monitoring Protocols**
   Schedule regular reviews of model performance to ensure continued fairness as feedback evolves.

AI-Enhanced Evaluation Practices
Evaluate model bias in feedback algorithms

Core Elements

- **Bias Risk is Acknowledged and Assessed**
  Evaluation teams actively seek out and address possible bias in AI-powered systems.
- **Feedback is Analysed by Segment**
  Insights are validated across different learner profiles and demographic groups.
- **Human Oversight is Applied**
  Machine-generated themes and sentiment scores are reviewed for contextual and cultural accuracy.
- **Audit Tools or Frameworks are Used**
  Fairness, interpretability, and transparency are assessed using dedicated bias detection methods.
- **Corrective Action is Documented**
  Bias mitigation steps (e.g. model retraining, threshold adjustments) are recorded and traceable.
- **Feedback Quality is Protected**
  The evaluation process respects and amplifies diverse learner voices, not just dominant ones.

Checklist

1. Define potential areas for algorithmic bias in your evaluation process
2. Segment learner feedback by demographic, language, and region
3. Run comparative analysis on how AI interprets different groups' feedback
4. Perform manual validation to assess fairness and accuracy
5. Use bias detection tools to visualise disparities
6. Adjust AI model parameters or retrain with diverse data sets
7. Document all assumptions, changes, and audit results
8. Share findings with compliance or DEI teams
9. Monitor model behaviour regularly as data evolves
10. Ensure transparency in reporting, note bias risk and mitigation in executive summaries

AI Considerations

- **Use Fairness Metrics in Model Evaluation**
  Leverage AI fairness tools to measure disparate impact, false positives/negatives, and representation gaps.
- **Apply Multilingual and Cultural Sensitivity Models**
  Choose NLP engines designed to handle linguistic diversity and cultural variation.
- **Retrain Models with Diverse Data**
  Incorporate underrepresented groups to improve recognition accuracy and reduce systemic bias.
- **Highlight Uncertainty or Confidence Scores**
  Where AI is unsure, flag results for human review instead of guessing.
- **Auto-Generate Bias Detection Reports**
  Use AI to produce dashboards or summaries showing how different learner groups are represented and interpreted.

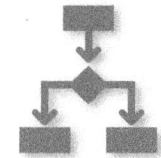
Key Takeaways

Bias in feedback algorithms doesn't just distort data, it distorts reality.

Evaluating and mitigating that bias ensures that your learning ecosystem remains fair, inclusive, and credible.

With AI now shaping how feedback is prioritised and interpreted, it's essential that systems treat all learners equally, regardless of voice, background, or communication style.

Responsible AI starts with visibility and ends with action.

Continuous Improvement Cycle

Evaluate model bias in feedback algorithms

The Continuous Improvement Cycle step ensures that learning solutions remain relevant, effective, and engaging over time. It reinforces the iterative nature of the ADDIE model by embedding ongoing review and refinement into the lifecycle of the course.

This step focuses on collecting meaningful feedback, analysing learner and performance data, and implementing thoughtful updates that align with both current learner needs and evolving industry standards. Rather than treating evaluation as a final checkpoint, this phase builds a continuous loop of learning, feedback, and optimisation.

Instructional designers use insights from learners, instructors, and stakeholders to enhance content, structure, and delivery methods. The aim is to preserve alignment with learning objectives while continually improving the learner experience.

Overview

Key sub-steps include:

- **Regular Updates Based on Feedback**
  Use feedback from multiple sources, including learners, facilitators, and performance analytics, to make targeted updates that improve course quality, engagement, and effectiveness.

- **Identify Trends Across Projects**
  Analyse data from multiple courses to uncover patterns in learner behaviour, content effectiveness, and delivery methods, enabling scalable improvements across the learning portfolio.

- **Run Post-Implementation Reviews**
  Conduct structured reviews after course deployment to evaluate what worked, what didn't, and what should change, creating actionable insights for future design efforts.

- **Maintain a Learning QA Backlog**
  Keep a prioritised list of quality assurance issues, enhancements, and improvement opportunities to ensure continuous, incremental refinements are tracked and addressed systematically.

- **Share Lessons Learned Across Teams**
  Document and communicate key findings, successful practices, and lessons learned to all stakeholders, promoting organisational learning and reducing repeated errors across teams.

Continuous Improvement Cycle
Evaluate model bias in feedback algorithms

Outcomes

The **Continuous Improvement Cycle** produces a learning program that is resilient, adaptable, and responsive to change. Key outcomes include:

- **Maintain Course Relevance and Effectiveness**
  Ensure the course continues to meet its learning objectives and reflect current industry practices and organisational priorities.

- **Collect and Analyse Feedback**
  Use structured methods, surveys, analytics, focus groups, to gather actionable feedback from all key audiences.

- **Incorporate Emerging Trends and Best Practice**
  Monitor the learning landscape and integrate innovations in instructional design, technology, and learner engagement.

- **Optimise Learner Experience and Engagement**
  Continuously refine the course to boost interactivity, personalisation, and overall learner satisfaction.

- **Balance Responsiveness with Stability**
  Use evidence-based methods to guide updates, avoiding unnecessary or reactive changes that may disrupt course cohesion.

Summary

The **Continuous Improvement Cycle** ensures that learning programs never stagnate. It transforms feedback into fuel for evolution, enabling instructional designers to adapt content, structure, and delivery in response to changing learner needs, business goals, and industry developments.

A disciplined approach to improvement, using tools like learning dashboards, structured review cadences, and stakeholder input, ensures updates are purposeful and aligned with strategic objectives. It also avoids the risk of overcorrection, where too many small changes erode the course's clarity or intent.

Ultimately, this step safeguards the long-term value of learning solutions. It maintains quality, enhances engagement, and ensures that courses remain current, effective, and capable of delivering meaningful results well into the future.

Regular Updates Based on Feedback

Why this is important

Regular updates based on feedback are essential to maintaining the quality, relevance, and effectiveness of learning programs.

As learner needs, technologies, and organisational goals evolve, training content must adapt to stay aligned. Feedback from learners, instructors, and stakeholders highlights areas for improvement, whether it's content clarity, instructional design, engagement levels, or technical functionality.

Acting on this feedback not only enhances the learner experience but also signals that the organisation values continuous improvement. Structured, timely updates help prevent obsolescence, support ongoing relevance, and build a culture of responsiveness and trust within the learning environment.

Tips

- **Establish Feedback Channels**
  Create multiple ways for learners and instructors to provide feedback, such as surveys, focus groups, or online forums.
- **Respond Quickly but Strategically**
  Address critical feedback swiftly, while planning more substantial changes as part of a structured update cycle.
- **Leverage Analytics**
  Use LMS analytics and performance metrics to identify areas needing improvement.
- **Engage SMEs**
  Collaborate with Subject Matter Experts to ensure updates maintain content accuracy and relevance.
- **Prioritise Updates**
  Rank feedback by urgency and impact to focus on changes that bring the most significant benefits.

Traps

- **Ignoring Feedback Trends**
  Dismissing recurring feedback can lead to unresolved issues and learner dissatisfaction.
- **Overloading with Updates**
  Making too many changes at once can confuse learners and disrupt course consistency.
- **Delaying Revisions**
  Procrastinating on updates can result in outdated content and loss of learner engagement.
- **Resource Constraints**
  Failing to allocate resources for regular updates can stall the continuous improvement process.
- **Neglecting Accessibility**
  Ignoring accessibility updates can exclude learners with disabilities from benefiting fully.

Techniques

- **Feedback Categorisation**
  Group feedback into categories (content, design, interactivity, etc.) to identify trends and prioritise updates.
- **Iterative Improvements**
  Use a phased approach to implement updates, starting with critical areas before addressing minor issues.
- **A/B Testing**
  Test updated content or features with small groups before a full rollout to ensure their effectiveness.
- **Gamification and Engagement Enhancements**
  Incorporate gamification elements, updated visuals, or interactive exercises based on feedback.
- **Trend Monitoring**
  Stay ahead of industry trends by regularly reviewing new tools, methodologies, and technologies for integration.

Continuous Improvement Cycle
Regular Updates Based on Feedback

Examples

- **Example 1**
  Feedback highlights confusion over a quiz question; the instructional designer rephrases the question for clarity.
- **Example 2**
  Learners request more real-world examples; additional case studies are added to relevant modules.
- **Example 3**
  Analytics show low engagement with a video; it is replaced with a shorter, interactive animation.
- **Example 4**
  Instructors report technical issues with a discussion forum; IT support resolves the problem, and a guide is added.
- **Example 5**
  Emerging industry standards require updated compliance content; the course is revised accordingly.
- **Example 6**
  Quarterly analysis reveals consistent learner confusion across multiple modules. The design team restructures the course sequence and navigation flow to reduce cognitive load.

How it's done

Regular Updates Based on Feedback in the Evaluate phase of the ADDIE model focuses on maintaining the relevance, quality, and effectiveness of instructional materials through iterative improvements.

1. **Collect Feedback**
   Gather input from learners and instructors using tools such as surveys, focus groups, and performance metrics.
2. **Analyse Trends**
   Review and categorise feedback to identify recurring issues, common themes, and specific requests for improvement.
3. **Prioritise Updates**
   Rank updates by their importance, urgency, and potential impact on learning outcomes to focus on changes that deliver the greatest value.
4. **Collaborate with SMEs**
   Work closely with Subject Matter Experts to validate updates, ensuring they are accurate, aligned with course objectives, and feasible to implement.
5. **Test Updates**
   Conduct pilot tests or A/B testing for new content, features, or changes to evaluate their effectiveness and functionality.
6. **Implement Changes**
   Roll out updates consistently across all delivery formats and platforms, ensuring a seamless learner experience.
7. **Communicate Changes**
   Notify learners and instructors about updates, providing clear instructions and guidance on using new or revised features.
8. **Evaluate Impact**
   Monitor post-update performance and engagement metrics to assess the effectiveness of the changes and refine further if necessary.

Continuous Improvement Cycle
Regular Updates Based on Feedback

Core Elements

- Feedback from learners and instructors has been collected and systematically reviewed.
- Trends, recurring issues, and improvement opportunities have been identified.
- Updates are prioritised based on their potential impact and urgency.
- Content updates have been validated by SMEs for accuracy and alignment with objectives.
- Pilot tests or A/B testing have been conducted to ensure updates are effective.
- Accessibility standards have been reviewed and maintained.
- Learners and instructors are informed about changes and provided with necessary guidance.
- Post-update metrics, such as performance and engagement, are being monitored to evaluate success.
- Update documentation is maintained and version controlled. Changes are logged to support audit readiness, historical review, and rollback if needed.

Checklist

1. Establish a structured feedback loop (e.g., post-course surveys, support queries, SME input)
2. Create and maintain a feedback and issue tracking system
3. Prioritise feedback based on learner impact, urgency, and feasibility
4. Assign ownership and timelines for content, technical, or assessment updates
5. Implement updates while maintaining instructional integrity and alignment with objectives
6. Validate all changes through SME review and quality assurance
7. Communicate updates to stakeholders, facilitators, and support teams
8. Version control and archive previous iterations for audit or rollback purposes

AI Considerations

- Use AI to aggregate and analyse learner feedback across cohorts and timeframes
- Auto-prioritise issues based on frequency, severity, and predicted learner impact
- Generate update recommendations based on feedback patterns and content analytics
- Track update history and automate version comparison (AI-driven diffing)
- Use AI to rephrase or rewrite sections flagged for improvement without altering intent
- Predict future update needs based on topic volatility and learner confusion signals
- Detect sudden spikes in dissatisfaction or drop-off to prioritise urgent updates.

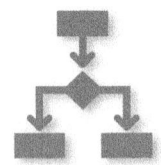

Key Takeaways

Regularly updating courses based on feedback ensures that instructional materials stay relevant, high-quality, and effective in meeting learner needs and organisational objectives.

By systematically collecting and analysing feedback, prioritising critical updates, and engaging SMEs in the validation process, instructional designers can create a structured approach to continuous improvement.

Monitoring the impact of updates through performance metrics and learner engagement helps refine courses iteratively, ensuring they remain dynamic and impactful in evolving learning environments.

This practice builds a sustainable learning ecosystem, one that evolves with its audience, absorbs feedback constructively, and keeps instructional design aligned with real-world impact.

Continuous Improvement Cycle
Identify Trends Across Projects

Identify Trends Across Projects

 **Why this is important**	Spotting patterns across multiple learning projects provides powerful insight into what's working, what isn't, and what's consistently emerging as a challenge or opportunity. While individual project feedback is valuable, aggregated trend analysis reveals deeper systemic issues, recurring learner needs, persistent design weaknesses, and transferable success factors. This sub-step enables instructional designers and L&D leaders to look beyond isolated courses and identify cross-program performance signals, such as consistent drop-off points, recurring requests for more interactivity, or repeatable success from particular formats or techniques. Recognising these trends allows organisations to refine their instructional standards, prioritise high-impact improvements, and reduce duplication of effort across teams. In essence, it shifts the focus from isolated optimisation to enterprise-wide learning evolution.
 **Tips**	• **Standardise Data Collection Across Projects** Use consistent evaluation frameworks and data structures to enable valid cross-program comparison. • **Review Both Quantitative and Qualitative Sources** Track not just scores or completion rates but also learner sentiment and open-ended feedback themes. • **Create Time-Based Comparison Windows** Analyse projects from similar timeframes (e.g. quarterly or annually) to detect patterns relevant to current strategies. • **Involve Multiple Stakeholders** Review findings with designers, SMEs, and delivery staff to capture multiple interpretations and validate emerging trends. • **Use Visualisation to Clarify Insights** Dashboards or trend heat maps make it easier to communicate complex patterns across large data sets.
Traps	• **Overgeneralising From Outliers** A highly visible success or failure in one program may not represent a trend, check for repetition and scale. • **Inconsistent Evaluation Methods** Without standardised metrics or feedback tools, cross-project analysis becomes unreliable. • **Lack of Contextual Awareness** Not all trends are universal, some issues may be linked to specific learner groups, regions, or content types. • **Ignoring Positive Trends** Don't just focus on what's broken, document what consistently works to replicate success. • **No Process for Acting on Trends** Spotting patterns is only useful if there's a follow-up mechanism to apply insights.

Continuous Improvement Cycle
Identify Trends Across Projects

Techniques

- **Meta-Analysis of Course Data**
  Aggregate and analyse completion rates, quiz scores, feedback themes, and engagement metrics across multiple projects.
- **Cross-Program Feedback Theme Coding**
  Use tagging or coding schemes to classify qualitative feedback by topic, then analyse frequency and sentiment across projects.
- **Comparative Visual Dashboards**
  Display course-by-course comparisons in performance, engagement, or satisfaction.
- **Lessons Learned Repository**
  Create a shared log of issues and insights from past projects that can be reviewed and filtered for trends.
- **Time Series Analysis**
  Track how specific metrics or feedback themes have shifted over time to identify emerging patterns.

Examples

- *Example 1*
  Across six onboarding programs, learners consistently rate interactivity low. Designers introduce simulations and branching scenarios in all future modules.
- *Example 2*
  A trend emerges showing that learner satisfaction is consistently higher for mobile-friendly courses. This leads to prioritisation of responsive design across the board.
- *Example 3*
  Post-course feedback in three departments highlights confusion around assessment instructions. A standardised assessment framework is introduced.
- *Example 4*
  Analysis reveals that shorter modules (under 10 minutes) lead to 20% higher completion rates, prompting a redesign of long-format programs.
- *Example 5*
  Cross-program sentiment analysis identifies a consistent call for more industry-specific case studies, this is flagged as a content strategy priority.

How it's done

1. **Collect Standardised Evaluation Data Across Projects**
   Ensure all learning initiatives use consistent tools and structures for feedback and performance tracking.
2. **Aggregate Data into a Central Repository**
   Combine survey results, LMS metrics, sentiment scores, and facilitator input from recent or related projects.
3. **Normalise and Clean the Data**
   Align naming conventions, remove outliers, and tag data for comparison.
4. **Apply Trend Analysis Tools or Frameworks**
   Use AI, dashboards, or manual review to identify recurring issues, themes, or outliers.
5. **Segment by Category**
   Group findings by content type, delivery mode, audience, or business unit for clearer interpretation.
6. **Validate Trends with Stakeholders**
   Share findings with SMEs, facilitators, or business leads to confirm meaning and priority.
7. **Document Actionable Insights**
   Convert trends into recommendations, linking them to future course updates, design standards, or instructional practices.

Continuous Improvement Cycle
Identify Trends Across Projects

Core Elements

- **Evaluation Data is Consistently Captured Across Projects**
  Common structures enable valid comparison of results and themes.
- **Data is Aggregated and Analysed**
  Course metrics and feedback are reviewed in combination to identify patterns.
- **Themes are Segmented and Prioritised**
  Trends are sorted by learner type, topic area, or course format to identify root causes.
- **Positive and Negative Patterns are Captured**
  High-performing practices are flagged for replication, not just issues.
- **Insights are Validated and Actioned**
  Trends are verified with stakeholders and converted into design improvements or strategic actions.
- **Knowledge is Archived for Reuse**
  Trends and insights are logged in a way that supports future project planning.

Checklist

1. Define what constitutes a "trend" in your learning context
2. Ensure evaluation tools are standardised across programs
3. Collect and clean feedback and performance data across projects
4. Apply AI or analysis tools to detect recurring themes and performance gaps
5. Segment trends by audience, format, or delivery model
6. Validate insights with project teams or business stakeholders
7. Document key findings in a central knowledge or design repository
8. Convert trends into specific improvement initiatives
9. Integrate lessons into design standards or briefing templates
10. Revisit trends periodically to monitor if they persist or evolve

AI Considerations

- **Cluster Feedback Themes Automatically**
  Use NLP to group qualitative feedback into consistent categories across courses.
- **Detect Patterns in Assessment Outcomes**
  Analyse test results across multiple programs to spot recurring weak points.
- **Visualise Trend Heat Maps**
  Generate dashboards that highlight where the same feedback or metric gaps appear repeatedly.
- **Predict Emerging Issues Based on Patterns**
  Identify where new projects are likely to encounter the same issues seen in prior ones.
- **Summarise Trend Reports for Stakeholders**
  Use AI to draft executive-ready summaries of key trends, risks, and recommendations.

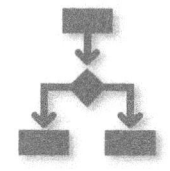

Key Takeaways

Identifying trends across projects transforms learning evaluation from a tactical process into a strategic advantage.

By analysing patterns over time and across teams, instructional designers can address root causes, reinforce best practices, and future-proof content.

This sub-step connects data to direction, ensuring that improvements are not just reactive, but informed by experience, insight, and scale.

Run Post-Implementation Reviews

Why this is important

Post-implementation reviews (PIRs) are critical for closing the loop on a learning initiative. They offer a structured opportunity to reflect on what worked, what didn't, and what can be improved for future rollouts. By engaging key stakeholders, project sponsors, facilitators, SMEs, and learners, PIRs provide a balanced perspective on both the process and the outcomes of the training intervention.

Unlike data-driven evaluations alone, PIRs capture experiential insights, team reflections, and contextual lessons that might otherwise be lost. They also serve as a catalyst for knowledge sharing and continuous improvement, helping instructional teams refine future project planning, execution, and evaluation strategies.

Tips

- **Schedule Reviews Early**
  Book PIRs before the project closes to avoid loss of knowledge or stakeholder disengagement.
- **Use a Structured Agenda**
  Frame discussions around objectives, challenges, outcomes, feedback, and lessons learned.
- **Invite a Cross-Functional Group**
  Include voices from design, delivery, business units, and learner groups for a holistic review.
- **Keep it Solution-Focused**
  Encourage constructive reflection and future-oriented thinking, not blame assignment.
- **Document Clearly and Share Widely**
  Summarise findings in a standard format that can be referenced for future projects.

Traps

- **Treating PIRs as a Tick-Box Exercise**
  Rushed or superficial reviews yield little value, set aside proper time and prepare attendees.
- **Focusing Only on Problems**
  Also document what worked well so it can be replicated or standardised.
- **Failing to Follow Through**
  Lessons learned are meaningless if they aren't logged, shared, and actioned.
- **Excluding Key Stakeholders**
  Omitting critical perspectives leads to incomplete insights and missed opportunities.
- **Poor Facilitation**
  Without skilled moderation, PIRs can spiral into complaints or lose focus.

Techniques

- **Plus/Delta Sessions**
  Use the simple "What went well / What could be improved" format to prompt discussion.
- **Timeline Reviews**
  Map project milestones and annotate what worked or stalled at each phase.
- **Thematic Analysis**
  Organise insights by topic (e.g. planning, content quality, technology, stakeholder engagement).
- **Anonymous Reflection Tools**
  Allow participants to submit input anonymously to surface honest feedback.
- **Facilitated Roundtables**
  Use experienced facilitators to keep discussions focused, neutral, and actionable.

Continuous Improvement Cycle
Run Post-Implementation Reviews

Examples

- **Example 1**
  A PIR after a leadership program rollout reveals confusion during onboarding. Future programs implement clearer facilitator handbooks.
- **Example 2**
  A digital skills course PIR highlights high satisfaction with content but poor LMS navigation. UX adjustments are prioritised for the next project.
- **Example 3**
  A cross-functional project team reflects on challenges with stakeholder alignment. Future initiatives begin with a formal stakeholder agreement phase.
- **Example 4**
  After a compliance module rollout, facilitators report low engagement. The team decides to integrate scenario-based learning in future versions.
- **Example 5**
  A PIR identifies that updates to materials during rollout were not version-controlled, leading to a revised content management protocol.

How it's done

1. **Schedule the PIR Shortly After Go-Live**
   Allow enough time for data and feedback collection, but act before momentum is lost.
2. **Gather Core Participants**
   Include SMEs, instructional designers, facilitators, project leads, and business stakeholders.
3. **Prepare the Review Framework**
   Use a template or agenda that covers objectives, outcomes, challenges, enablers, and lessons.
4. **Facilitate an Open and Constructive Discussion**
   Encourage transparency and focus on future improvement, not fault-finding.
5. **Record All Insights and Action Points**
   Document what worked, what didn't, why, and what should be done differently.
6. **Assign Owners for Follow-Up Actions**
   Ensure key takeaways are turned into improvement initiatives with clear accountability.
7. **Share Learnings with the Wider Team**
   Log results in a central repository and refer to them during planning for the next initiative.

Core Elements

- **A Scheduled, Structured Review Session Occurs**
  PIRs are not ad hoc, they're planned, timed, and methodically executed.
- **Multiple Perspectives Are Included**
  The review incorporates feedback from all major stakeholder groups.
- **Successes and Shortfalls Are Documented**
  Both achievements and areas for growth are explored and recorded.
- **Lessons Are Captured for Future Reference**
  Insights are added to shared knowledge bases or project close-out reports.
- **Accountability is Assigned for Actions**
  Follow-ups are tracked to ensure that lessons result in actual improvement.
- **Review Feeds Into Continuous Improvement Loops**
  PIRs directly inform future design, development, and implementation planning.

Continuous Improvement Cycle
Run Post-Implementation Reviews

Checklist

1. Schedule the PIR within 2–4 weeks of implementation
2. Define scope and objectives of the review session
3. Prepare agenda and supporting data (metrics, feedback, outcomes)
4. Invite a cross-functional group of stakeholders
5. Facilitate discussion using a consistent review framework
6. Document key findings, insights, and lessons learned
7. Identify what worked well and what requires change
8. Assign follow-up owners and deadlines for each action
9. Share the PIR summary with relevant teams
10. Store PIR documentation in a central knowledge repository

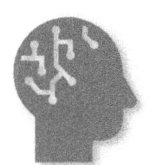
AI Considerations

- **Auto-Summarise Feedback into PIR Themes**
  Use AI to extract and group learner and facilitator feedback into key discussion areas.
- **Generate PIR Templates Based on Project Data**
  Pre-populate the PIR agenda with highlights from LMS analytics and sentiment analysis.
- **Detect Repeated Issues Across PIRs**
  Identify trends in feedback and process failures over time.
- **Visualise Timeline Deviations or Bottlenecks**
  Use AI-powered project analytics to show where schedule slippage or confusion occurred.
- **Draft PIR Summary Reports Automatically**
  Create a ready-to-share post-session report using meeting transcripts and action lists.

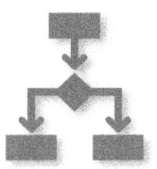
Key Takeaways

Post-implementation reviews aren't just a procedural formality; they're a learning intervention in their own right.

By reflecting on the full lifecycle of a learning initiative, teams gain clarity, build shared understanding, and plant the seeds for future success.

When properly facilitated, documented, and actioned, PIRs elevate the organisation's capacity for continuous improvement and establish a culture of reflective, data-informed practice.

Maintain a Learning QA Backlog

Why this is important

A Learning QA (Quality Assurance) backlog is a structured repository of known issues, improvement ideas, pending updates, and enhancement requests across learning programs. It ensures that all identified changes, whether flagged through feedback, testing, analytics, or audits, are captured, prioritised, and addressed over time.

Without a central backlog, course improvements often become ad hoc, reactive, or dependent on memory. Valuable insights get lost in inboxes or spreadsheets; while recurring issues remain unresolved across versions. A maintained QA backlog supports transparency, version control, accountability, and strategic improvement planning. It also enables teams to balance urgency against feasibility, ensuring that high-impact updates are implemented first.

This sub-step transforms scattered feedback into a continuous, trackable quality pipeline, making learning content more robust, consistent, and responsive to change.

Tips

- **Use a Dedicated Tool or Platform**
  Manage your backlog in a shared system like Trello, Jira, ClickUp, or a structured spreadsheet with clear columns.
- **Categorise by Issue Type**
  Tag entries as content, technical, design, engagement, or accessibility issues to aid sorting and prioritisation.
- **Include Source and Date**
  Record where each issue came from (e.g. learner feedback, SME review, analytics) and when it was logged.
- **Set Review Cadences**
  Regularly review and refine backlog items as part of sprint planning or evaluation cycles.
- **Link to Version Control**
  Reference which course version the issue relates to, and track when fixes are implemented.

Traps

- **Letting It Become a Graveyard**
  A backlog that is never reviewed or acted on quickly becomes a dumping ground.
- **Missing Context in Entries**
  Without details like screenshots, feedback quotes, or steps to replicate, issues are hard to triage or solve.
- **No Clear Prioritisation**
  Treating all issues equally leads to stagnation. Apply triage criteria to focus effort.
- **Lack of Ownership**
  Without assigned owners or timelines, issues linger indefinitely.
- **Overcomplicating the System**
  A backlog that's too complex or technical will discourage updates and participation.

Continuous Improvement Cycle
Maintain a Learning QA Backlog

Techniques

- **Kanban-Style Boards**
  Visualise backlog items as cards in columns like "To Review," "Approved," "In Progress," and "Released."
- **Issue Templates**
  Use a standard format for new entries: description, impact, priority, status, owner, and notes.
- **Backlog Grooming Sessions**
  Schedule regular meetings to review, clean up, and re-prioritise backlog entries.
- **Impact vs Effort Matrix**
  Use simple scoring to assess each item's value and difficulty, helping you prioritise effectively.
- **Status Tags and Colour Coding**
  Label items by urgency or area (e.g. "Critical: Assessment Error" or "Low: Image Alt-Text Update").

Examples

- *Example 1*
  Learners repeatedly report that a quiz question is unclear. The issue is logged in the backlog with screenshots and learner comments, assigned to the designer for the next update cycle.
- *Example 2*
  Analytics show a sharp drop in engagement halfway through a module. A backlog item is created to review and rework that section.
- *Example 3*
  An SME notices outdated terminology in a compliance course. The issue is added with a policy reference and scheduled for review post-audit.
- *Example 4*
  A technical issue affecting video playback on mobile is logged, triaged as high priority, and escalated to the multimedia team.
- *Example 5*
  A course revision note includes a suggestion to add a gamified recap. It's added as a "value-add" backlog item for future enhancement planning.

How it's done

1. **Establish a Backlog Repository**
   Choose a tool or format that supports collaboration, visibility, and filtering (e.g. Airtable, Notion, Jira).
2. **Define Logging Standards**
   Use a template to ensure entries include a clear description, source, priority, and owner.
3. **Create Categories and Tags**
   Standardise tags for content area, issue type, urgency, and update status.
4. **Log All Valid Issues and Ideas**
   Capture feedback from learners, instructors, analytics, audits, and SMEs.
5. **Assign Owners and Due Dates**
   Make sure every item has a responsible party and target timeframe for resolution or review.
6. **Prioritise and Groom Regularly**
   Sort the backlog periodically, archive resolved items and escalate high-impact ones.
7. **Link Backlog to Version Releases**
   Document when fixes are included in course updates and maintain change logs.
8. **Report on Backlog Status**
   Summarise open issues, resolved fixes, and update trends in team meetings or executive reports.

Continuous Improvement Cycle
Maintain a Learning QA Backlog

Core Elements

- **Backlog is Centralised and Shared**
  All course improvement items are captured in one visible, structured location.
- **Standard Logging is Applied**
  Issues include descriptions, dates, sources, and clear status labels.
- **Items Are Categorised and Prioritised**
  Content, design, technical, and accessibility issues are tagged and ranked for importance.
- **Ownership and Accountability is Defined**
  Each item has an owner responsible for resolution or escalation.
- **Review Cycles Are in Place**
  The backlog is updated and reviewed regularly to ensure relevance and progress.
- **Version Control and Fix Logs Are Maintained**
  Resolved items are archived with notes on when and how the fix was applied.

Checklist

1. Set up a shared backlog system (board, spreadsheet, or platform)
2. Use a consistent issue logging template
3. Tag each item by issue type, impact, and content area
4. Record the source and version reference of each entry
5. Assign owners and due dates to new entries
6. Prioritise using a triage matrix or visual labels
7. Link backlog fixes to scheduled version updates
8. Conduct regular backlog grooming sessions
9. Report on backlog trends in team retrospectives
10. Archive resolved items with notes and closure date

AI Considerations

- **Auto-Classify Feedback into Backlog Categories**
  Use NLP to convert learner comments into tagged backlog entries.
- **Predict Update Impact**
  Estimate the benefit of a fix based on frequency, learner sentiment, and performance trends.
- **Cluster Similar Issues**
  Detect and consolidate duplicate or related backlog items from across projects.
- **Suggest Priority Scoring**
  Use AI to recommend which items to address first based on historical urgency and impact.
- **Generate Fix Logs and Changelogs**
  Auto-summarise what was fixed and when, using AI-generated release notes.

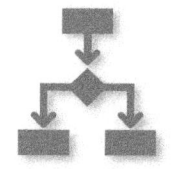
Key Takeaways

A learning QA backlog turns feedback into focus. By maintaining a structured log of issues and improvement opportunities, instructional teams gain visibility, accountability, and momentum in the refinement process.

This isn't just housekeeping, it's the operational backbone of continuous improvement, ensuring learning programs evolve systematically and sustainably.

Share Lessons Learned Across Teams

Why this is important

When learning teams operate in silos, valuable insights are lost. Sharing lessons learned across projects and teams ensures that success factors, pitfalls, and innovations are not only documented, but reused. This sub-step enables L&D functions to evolve collectively rather than repeating the same mistakes or reinventing the wheel on every project.

It fosters a culture of knowledge exchange, improves efficiency, and raises the overall quality of learning design and delivery. Whether it's through shared retrospectives, case studies, design templates, or internal showcases, circulating lessons learned amplifies the impact of each project beyond its immediate audience.

Ultimately, this practice turns isolated experiences into organisational capability.

Tips

- **Create Standardised Templates**
  Use a simple "What worked / What didn't / What we'd do differently" format to capture lessons consistently.

- **Use Internal Knowledge Repositories**
  Store lessons in a searchable platform like Confluence, SharePoint, or Notion for easy access.

- **Host Informal Sharing Sessions**
  Schedule monthly or quarterly "show and tell" meetings for project teams to present insights.

- **Make it Safe to Share Mistakes**
  Frame missteps as learning moments to encourage honesty and participation.

- **Align With Business Priorities**
  Emphasise lessons that relate to strategic initiatives, stakeholder relationships, or compliance risk.

Traps

- **Storing but Not Sharing**
  A repository no one reads isn't useful, surface lessons actively through meetings and workflows.

- **Overcomplicating the Process**
  Keep it light-touch; overly complex documentation discourages contribution.

- **Too Generic or Vague**
  Lessons like "start earlier" or "communicate more" don't help, get specific and contextual.

- **No Feedback Loops**
  If shared lessons don't inform future planning or design decisions, they get ignored.

- **Not Capturing Lessons in Real Time**
  Waiting until project close-out can result in forgotten insights, log them as you go.

Techniques

- **Lessons Learned Logs**
  Maintain a live list of issues, decisions, and successes during project delivery.

- **Post-Mortem Templates**
  Use structured forms to capture input from all project stakeholders post-implementation.

- **Learning Design Playbooks**
  Update internal best practice guides with validated patterns or warnings from recent projects.

- **Lunch-and-Learn Sessions**
  Informal presentations where teams showcase a recent project and key takeaways.

- **Internal Newsletters or Bulletins**
  Share highlights of lessons in monthly internal L&D updates.

Continuous Improvement Cycle
Share Lessons Learned Across Teams

Examples

- **Example 1**
  A project team learns that mid-course check-ins improve engagement. The insight is shared at a monthly design forum and becomes a standard practice across all programs.
- **Example 2**
  An accessibility misstep in a pilot module prompts a team to publish a checklist of inclusive design dos and don'ts for others to follow.
- **Example 3**
  A facilitator surfaces an innovative way to frame learning objectives. The team records it in the internal playbook for future adoption.
- **Example 4**
  After struggling with stakeholder engagement, a team documents a new communication strategy. It's later adopted by other project managers in the department.
- **Example 5**
  A post-project summary is uploaded to the L&D SharePoint site with a tag for "Onboarding" so other teams can search and apply it when developing similar content.

How it's done

1. **Capture Lessons Throughout the Project**
   Encourage teams to log insights, roadblocks, and innovations in real time using a shared document or tool.
2. **Standardise the Format**
   Use a consistent structure for documenting lessons (e.g. Context, What Worked, What Didn't, Recommendation).
3. **Review During Project Close-Out**
   Include a dedicated agenda item during post-implementation reviews to formalise lessons learned.
4. **Store in a Central Repository**
   Make the knowledge accessible to other teams via a digital platform with tags and filters.
5. **Share Through Multiple Channels**
   Use meetings, newsletters, team updates, and onboarding packs to communicate insights.
6. **Encourage Use and Attribution**
   Recognise when teams apply shared lessons and acknowledge contributors to promote knowledge-sharing culture.
7. **Review Lessons Periodically**
   Retire outdated advice, reinforce validated practices, and integrate insights into design templates and standards.

Core Elements

- **Lessons Are Captured in a Structured Format**
  Documentation is consistent, clear, and actionable.
- **Knowledge is Centralised and Accessible**
  Insights are stored in a shared platform, searchable by topic or project type.
- **Insights Are Communicated Actively**
  Lessons are surfaced through meetings, newsletters, or retrospectives, not just buried in files.
- **Lessons Are Linked to Decisions or Templates**
  Insights inform real improvements to planning, design, and evaluation.
- **Contribution is Recognised and Encouraged**
  Knowledge sharing is culturally valued, not seen as extra work.
- **Reviews Keep Lessons Fresh**
  The repository is maintained to reflect current tools, approaches, and contexts.

Continuous Improvement Cycle
Share Lessons Learned Across Teams

Checklist

1. Encourage teams to log lessons throughout project delivery
2. Use a consistent format for capturing what worked and what didn't
3. Include lessons learned in post-implementation reviews
4. Store lessons in a shared, searchable system
5. Tag lessons by project type, content format, or issue area
6. Communicate new lessons via meetings, bulletins, or forums
7. Reference past lessons during project planning
8. Recognise individuals or teams who contribute valuable insights
9. Integrate lessons into templates, playbooks, or QA standards
10. Schedule quarterly reviews to retire, update, or elevate key lessons

AI Considerations

- **Auto-Summarise Lessons from Project Logs**
  Use AI to extract recurring themes from project notes, feedback, or retrospectives.
- **Suggest Related Lessons When Starting a New Project**
  Use machine learning to match current project metadata with relevant past insights.
- **Tag and Categorise Lessons Automatically**
  Apply NLP to assign topics, regions, roles, or content types.
- **Detect Unused or Redundant Lessons**
  AI can flag lessons that are outdated or rarely referenced for cleanup.
- **Generate Digestible Lesson Recaps**
  Produce monthly summaries of lessons learned across the organisation using AI-generated briefs.

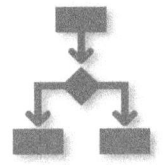

Key Takeaways

Sharing lessons learned across teams transforms isolated experiences into collective intelligence.

It accelerates improvement, prevents repeated mistakes, and lifts the quality of every future project.

When properly captured, stored, and shared, each lesson becomes a strategic asset; fuel for smarter decisions, faster execution, and stronger learning outcomes across the board.

www.ingramcontent.com/pod-product-compliance
Lightning Source LLC
Chambersburg PA
CBHW081532300426
44116CB00015B/2606